Anonymous

British and Irish public characters of 1798

Anonymous

British and Irish public characters of 1798

ISBN/EAN: 9783337126117

Printed in Europe, USA, Canada, Australia, Japan

Cover: Foto ©ninafisch / pixelio.de

More available books at **www.hansebooks.com**

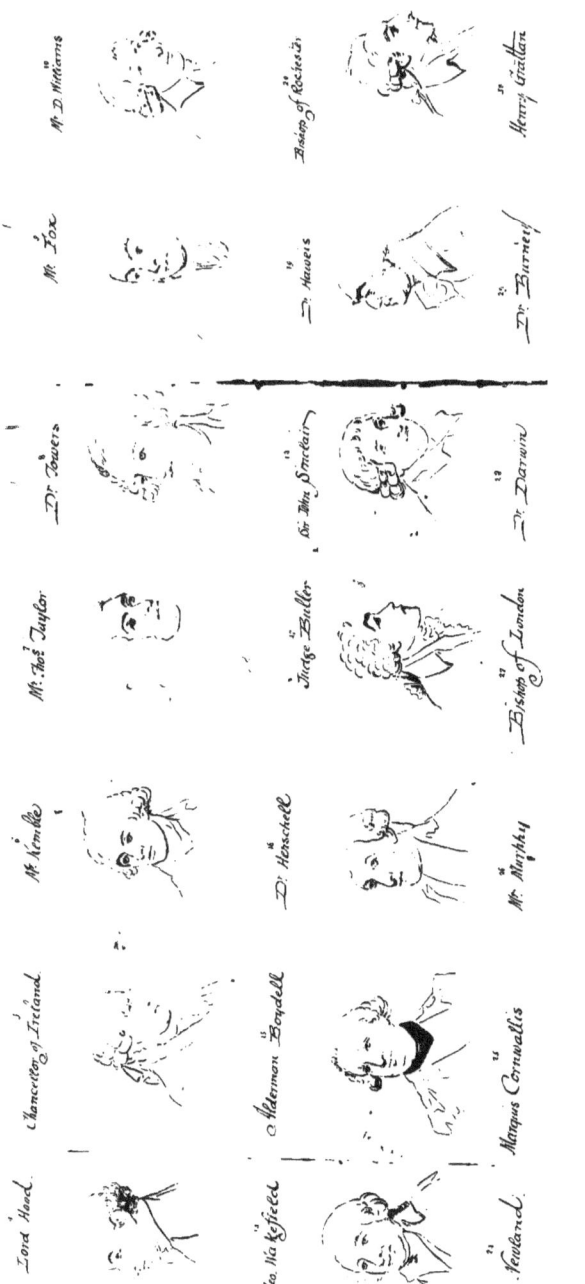

BRITISH and IRISH

PUBLIC

CHARACTERS

OF

1798.

MEMOIRS of the following Personages, are given in this Volume:

Earl of Moira,	Mr. Jackson, of Exeter,	Mr. J. Grose,
Sir John Sinclair,	Lord Malmesbury,	Mr. Kemble,
Mr. Roscoe,	Dr. J. White,	Miss Seward,
Earl of Liverpool,	Bp. of Worcester,	Lord Chancellor of Ireland,
Mr. A. Newland,	Earl of Buchan,	
Mr. Fox,	Mr. Northcote, R. A.	Mr. Cumberland,
Mr. Pitt,	Bp. of Llandaff,	Sir A. Macdonald,
Dr. Darwin,	Mr. H. Erskine,	Mrs Siddons,
Lord Hood,	Lord Charlemont,	Bp. of Salisbury,
Sir G. L. Staunton,	Mr. Grattan,	Sir John Scott,
Mr. T. Taylor,	Mr. W. S. Smith,	Duke of Norfolk,
General Melville,	Dr. T. Haweis,	Dr. Towers,
Bishop of London,	Mr. Dundas,	Lord Thurlow,
Dean Tucker,	Lord Kilwarden,	Marquis Cornwallis,
Lord Duncan,	Mr. Curran,	Dr. Priestley,
Bishop of Rochester,	Lord Monboddo,	Miss More,
Mr. Justice Buller,	Mr. D. Barrington,	Mr. Alderman Boydell,
Dr. Walcott,	Dr. O'Leary,	Mr. George Dyer,
Abp. of Canterbury,	Lord Yelverton,	Mr. D'Israel,
Mr. A. Murphy,	Mr. Isaac Corry,	Mr. D. Williams,
Earl of Dartmouth,	Mr. J. Beresford,	Mr. G. Wakefield,
Bishop of Durham,	Mr. J. Foster,	Mr. Opie, R. A.
Mr. King (the Comedian,)	Dr. Burney,	Lord Rokeby,
Bp. of Winchester,	Dr. Herschel,	Lord Nelson.

" ————I wish no other herald,
" No other speaker of my *living actions*,
" To keep mine honour from corruption,
" But such an honest chronicler————."

HEN. 8. Act 4. Sc. 2.

DUBLIN:

PRINTED FOR J. MILLIKEN, No. 32, AND JOHN RICE, 111 GRAFTON-STREET.

1799.

TO THE KING.

Sire,

AS the accuſtomed forms of ſociety do not permit Your Majesty to mix with your ſubjects at large, and to acquire, in perſon, a diſtinct and particular knowledge of their reſpective merits, actions, and characters, theſe Biographical Sketches are ſubmitted and addreſſed to you, with peculiar propriety, and with profound reſpect.

That Your Majesty may thus, in ſome meaſure, be enabled

bled to appreciate their diftinguifhed talents, to refpect their
illuftrious virtues, and to reward
their ufeful and meritorious actions, during the continuance of
a lengthened, happy, and prof-
perous reign, is the fervent wifh,
and devout prayer, of

 Your Majefty's
  moft humble ana
  moft obedient
   Subjects and Servants,

London, Nov. 1798.
     THE EDITORS.

THE object of the Work which is now submitted to the Public, is to exhibit, in the memoirs of the illustrious actors, the public and secret history of the present times. Respectable works of a similar description, have been published in various countries on the continent; none, however, have hitherto been attempted, upon the same plan, in this country.

BIOGRAPHY, in all its forms, is allowed to be the most fascinating and instructive species of literary composition. It not only possesses all the advantages of general history, the various excellencies of which may be judiciously interwoven with the lives of eminent personages, but it frequently discovers the minute and latent springs of great events, which, in the comprehensive range of History, would have escaped attention.

Many

Many of the attractions of Biography in general, and some additional advantages, are possessed by *contemporary Biography*. The memoirs of men, who are the present actors on the great theatre of life, who acquire and demand public confidence, and from whom further results of action or meditation are to be expected, necessarily excite a higher degree of curiosity, than the lives of those who have made their exit from the stage, by whom no future good or evil can be performed or perpetrated, and who, " dead, gone, and forgotten," are generally carried down the stream of oblivion, and swallowed up in the gulph of unregistered mortality.

It must be admitted, that the biographer of deceased persons is better enabled, by the independence of his situation, and a more extensive retrospect, to estimate the degree of virtue and vice, and to appreciate the sum total of merit and demerit with greater precision, than the contemporary biographer, who is restrained, by the extreme delicacy of his undertaking, from giving the finishing stroke to his delineations of character, whose incomplete materials prevent him from deducing general and important

portant conclufions in their proper latitude, and, in many cafes, from difcriminating between hypocrify and fincerity. Still, however, a writer of this defcription is better able to collect facts, and may in general, be more depended upon, as to the authenticity of his teftimony, than he who writes the lives of deceafed perfons. Many eminent men, refpecting whom pofterity have caufe to lament the deficiency of biographical information, have paffed their early days in obfcurity, and thofe who then knew them were either too ignorant, or too unobfervant, to be able to make any communications refpecting them. When Death has once fet his feal upon their labours, few or no opportunities offer of obtaining fatisfactory and circumftantial information; their early contemporaries are, probably, alfo gone off the ftage. From caufes like thefe, how little is known of fome of the moft diftinguifhed luminaries that have irradiated the political and literary hemifpheres! Of many we know only, that they filled elevated fituations, that they compofed fplendid works, made important difcoveries, died in a particular year, and were at length interred in fome venerable repofitory of the dead.

An annual publication like the prefent will beft provide againft a future deficiency of this kind, with regard to the diftinguifhed perfonages who now fill up the drama of public life in the Britifh empire. The Editors are not likely to commit themfelves, and the reputation of their work, by inferting direct falfehoods, or partial mifreprefentations: no character, of whom they now or may hereafter treat, can be thought infenfible to the love of contemporary or pofthumous fame; hence, fhould any undefigned error, or any inaccurate ftatement, inadvertently efcape them, it may be rationally prefumed, that the party affected, from a regard to his own reputation, will take the earlieft opportunity to correct fuch miftatements; or that fome friend, intimately acquainted with the fubject, in the candour and warmth of efteem, may be ftimulated to write a more particular and accurate account, for a fubfequent edition.

From thefe premifes * may it not be reafonably concluded, that this Work poffeffes

* Befide other arguments which may be urged in recommendation of this novel undertaking, the Editors might quote the example of fome of the moft illuftrious men in all ages and nations, who have judged it proper to write their own memoirs, and to publifh them during their life-time a legia legitimate claim to public patronage, as well from its promifed utility to future biographers and hiftorians, as from its being an highly entertaining and ufeful affemblage of interefting and important facts and anecdotes?

In refpect to the prefent volume, it is neceffary to remark, that the articles are written by a number of gentlemen, whofe adopted fignatures are affixed to their refpective communications. Such a multiplicity of facts in fo extenfive and various a group of characters could not have been fupplied by any one or two individuals. Although a delicate tafk, the mode generally adopted in the compofition of this Work, has been to apply to fome friend of the party, whofe intimate knowledge of the relative facts and circumftances qualified him to do ample juftice to the character. This indifpenfable arrangement, requifite to produce the faithful execution of the volume, has, however, occafioned a variety in the ftyle and manner of the feveral articles, which, at firft fight, may give it a fort of heterogeneous appearance, but will not detract from its real merit in the eftimation of the judicious reader.

It

It is possible that a fastidious observer, or other person more intimately connected with the subject of the several memoirs, may here and there detect some venial error, some trifling anachronism, or apparent misconstruction; for these the Editors can only atone, by expressing their earnest wish for more correct information, which will be thankfully received, and punctually attended to in a future edition. That some inaccuracies are unavoidable in a work of this nature, must naturally be expected by every person accustomed to habits of literary composition, or who possesses sufficient knowledge of the complicated occurrences which mark the career of public and private life.

The Editors are more seriously apprehensive left, in any instance whatever, they should unfortunately and unintentionally be a means of wounding the acute sensibility, the laudable ambition, or the generous pride of any individual;—no procedure could be more alien to their wishes and intentions. Any representation on the part of those who may think themselves, aggrieved, which may be transmitted to the Editors, shall be treated with marked deference and attention. The most scrupulous caution has been exercised,

to

to divest the *tout ensemble* of every appearance of national and political partialities. *No attachment to any particular set of men or opinions, no prejudices against men in place, no prepossessions in favour of men out of place, no bias towards any controverted points of theology, no personal antipathies, no malevolent exaggerations, no invidious disposition to detract from acknowledged virtue or merit, have influenced, in whole or in part, the conduct of the Projector and Conductors of the work.*

If the present volume should be honoured by a degree of approbation and patronage corresponding to the anxious wishes and expectations of the Editors, it is their design to present the Public with a similar volume in the course of the year 1799, and to continue the work in each succeeding year. That there will be abundant materials for such a continuation must be obvious, when it is considered, that the following illustrious and prominent characters are omitted in the present volume, only for want of room or competent materials: Lord Loughborough, the Marquis of Lansdowne, the Duke of Grafton, the Duke of Bedford, Lord Kenyon, Mr. Sheridan, Lord Grenville, the Duke of Portland, Earl Howe, Earl St. Vincent,

Vincent, Lord Bridport, Lord Auckland, Mr. Tierney, Mr. Wilberforce, Sir Joseph Banks, Mr. Weft, Earl Spencer, Earl Fitzwilliam, Mr. Haftings, Mr. Wyndham, the Earl of Lauderdale, the Duke of Leeds, Lord Somerville, and nearly three hundred other eminent and remarkable perfons, connected with the political and literary world.

For the fake of variety, no particular arrangement of the articles has been adopted; an attention to the fame object has alfo dictated the multifarious choice of characters. Each reader will probably judge of the requifite degree of publicity annexed to a perfonage, according to his own peculiar connexions and caft of thinking: it is believed, however, that no character is inferted, which is not juftly confidered as confpicuous in a very extended circle, and which does not poffefs a fufficient degree of merit, or original feature, to be properly entitled to public notice.

Communications for the fecond volume, or corrections of the prefent, are requefted to be addreffed to MR. PHILLIPS, No. 71, St. Paul's Church-yard.

November 10, 1798.

Portraits given in the Frontispiece, which will be found to be as striking Likenesses as any that have appeared, and all of them strongly characteristic.

1. LORD NELSON.
2. EARL MOIRA.
3. ARCH BISHOP OF CANTERBURY.
4. LORD HOOD.
5. CHANCELLOR OF IRELAND.
6. MR. KEMBLE.
7. MR. THOMAS TAYLOR.
8. Dr. TOWERS.
9. MR. FOX.
10. MR. DAVID WILLIAMS.
11. MR. D'ISRAELI.
12. MR. GEORGE DYER.
13. DR. PRIESTLEY.
14. MR. G. WAKEFIELD.
15. ALDERMAN BOYDELL.
16. DR. HERSCHELL.
17. JUDGE BULLER.
18. SIR JOHN SINCLAIR.
19. DR. HAWEIS.
20. BISHOP OF ROCHESTER.
21. MR. PITT.
22. MR. DUNDAS.
23. LORD DUNCAN.
24. MR. A. NEWLAND.
25. MARQUIS CORNWALLIS.
26. MR. MURPHY.
27. BISHOP OF LONDON.
28. DR. DARWIN.
29. DR. BURNEY.
30. MR. GRATTAN.

CONTENTS.

The Portraits are also given of those marked with the *.

		Page.
1.	THE EARL OF MOIRA*	1
2.	SIR JOHN SINCLAIR*	7
3.	MR. ROSCOE	17
4.	THE EARL OF LIVERPOOL	24
5.	MR. ABRAHAM NEWLAND*	29
6.	MR. FOX*	34
7.	MR. PITT*	52
8.	DR. DARWIN*	63
9.	LORD HOOD*	19
10.	SIR G. L. STAUNTON	69
11.	MR. THOMAS TAYLOR*	72
12.	GENERAL MELVILLE	90
13.	THE BISHOP OF LONDON	92
14.	DEAN TUCKER	98
15.	LORD DUNCAN*	109
16.	THE BISHOP OF ROCHESTER*	116
17.	MR. JUSTICE BULLER*	127
18.	DR. WALCOTT	130
19.	THE ARCHBISHOP OF CANTERBURY	136
20.	MR. ARTHUR MURPHY*	141
21.	THE EARL OF DARTMOUTH	147
22.	THE BISHOP OF DURHAM	149
23.	MR. KING (THE COMEDIAN)	152
24.	THE BISHOP OF WINCHESTER	156
25.	MR. JACKSON OF EXETER	158
26.	LORD MALMESBURY	162
27.	DR. JOSEPH WHITE	167
28.	THE BISHOP OF WORCESTER	173
29.	THE EARL OF BUCHAN	177
30.	MR. NORTHCOTE, R. A.	181
31.	THE BISHOP OF LLANDAFF	184
32.	MR. HENRY ERSKINE	191
33.	LORD CHARLEMONT	194
34.	MR. GRATTAN*	200
35.	SIR W. SYDNEY SMITH	215
36.	DR. THOMAS HAWEIS*	219
37.	MR. DUNDAS*	223
38.	LORD KILWARDEN	229
39.	MR. CURRAN	232

CONTENTS.

40. LORD MONBODDO 240
41. MR. DAINES BARRINGTON . . . 242
42. DR. O'LEARY 244
43. LORD YELVERTON 247
44. MR. ISAAC CORRY 251
45. MR. JOHN BERESFORD 254
46. MR. JOHN FOSTER 257
47. DR. BURNEY* 261
48. DR. HERSCHEL* 265
49. MR. JUSTICE GROSE 272
50. MR. KEMBLE* 273
51. MISS SEWARD 276
52. THE LORD CHANCELLOR OF IRELAND* 278
53. MR CUMBERLAND 285
54. SIR ARCHIBALD MACDONALD . . 288
55. MRS. SIDDONS 290
56. THE BISHOP OF SALISBURY . . 295
57. SIR JOHN SCOTT 296
58. THE DUKE OF NORFOLK . . . 299
59. DR. TOWERS* 303
60. LORD THURLOW 309
61. THE MARQUIS CORNWALLIS* . . 318
62. DR. PRIESTLEY* 328
63. MISS MORE 332
64. MR. ALDERMAN BOYDELL . . . 340
65. MR. GEORGE DYER* 347
66. MR. D'ISRAELI* 353
67. MR. DAVID WILLIAMS* . . . 357
68. MR. GILBERT WAKEFIELD* . . . 364
69. MR. OPIE, R. A. 378
70. LORD ROKEBY 383
71. LORD NELSON* 402

The Bookbinder is requested not to fold the Frontispiece across any of the Portraits.

PRINTED FOR

J. MILLIKEN,

32, GRAFTON-STREET.

1st. The Purſuits of Literature, a Satirical Poem in four Dialogues, with Notes; the eighth edition reviſed, price 6s. 6d. in boards.

2nd. A Tranſlation of the Paſſages, from Greek, Latin, Italian, and French Writers, quoted in the Prefaces and Notes to the Purſuits of Literature; to which is prefixed a prefatory Epiſtle, intended as a general vindication of the Purſuits of Literature, from various remarks which have been made on that work, by the Tranſlator:—price 3s. 3d.

3rd. The Imperial Epiſtle from Kien Long, Emperor of China, to George the Third, King of Great Britain, &c. &c. in the Year 1794; tranſmitted from the Emperor, and preſented to his Britannic Majeſty, by his Excellency George Earl Macartney, K. B. Ambaſſador Extraordinary to the Emperor of China:—price 1s. 7dh.

4th. The Shade of Alexander Pope on the Banks of the Thames, a Satirical Poem, with Notes; occaſioned chiefly, but not wholly, by the Reſidence of Henry Grattan, Eſq. Ex-Repreſentative in Parliament:—price 2s. 2d.
N. B. The three laſt Articles by the Author of the Purſuits of Literature.

5th. An Anſwer to the Addreſs of the Rt. Hon. Henry Grattan, Ex-Repreſentative of the City of Dublin in Parliament, to his Fellow-Citizens of Dublin, by Patrick Duigenan, L.L.D. the fifth Edition; to which is now added—The Addreſs of the Roman-Catholics of Dublin, aſſembled in Francis-ſtreet on the 27th of February 1795, with his Anſwer.—Mr. Grattan's Addreſs to the Citizens of Dublin.—A Letter ſuppoſed to be written by Mr Grattan to Dr. Duigenan.—price 4s. 4d.

6th. The Anti-Jacobin, or Weekly Examiner; a new Edition reviſed, corrected, and uniformly printed in two Large Volumes Octavo:—price one Guinea. This Work has been of ſignal ſervice to the Public by the union of Wit, Learning, Genius, Poetry, and ſound Politics.

7th. Copies of Original Letters from the Army of General Bonaparte in Egypt, intercepted by the Fleet under the command of Admiral Lord Nelſon.—French and Engliſh, with a Chart of Lower Egypt, illuſtrative of Bonaparte's intercepted correſpondence.—price 5s. 5d.

8th. The above Work in Engliſh only. 3s. 9dh.

PUBLIC CHARACTERS,

OF 1798.

THE EARL OF MOIRA.

FEW noblemen have made a more early, or a more meritorious figure in military and civil life, than the illustrious subject of this sketch. Francis, Lord Rawdon, Earl of Moira, was born December the 7th, 1754, and was created a baron of Great Britain in 1783.

Having completed his education about the commencement of the American war, his lordship entered into the army, and embarked with his regiment for that continent; where he took a very active part throughout the whole of the unfortunate contest with the estranged and alienated colonies.

Lord Rawdon's character, from the earliest period, has been uniformly marked by a cool and intrepid courage, governed by that calm serenity of soul which is the result of the most unblemished honour. He gave early proofs of the possession of this enviable qualification, when he was lieutenant of grenadiers at the memorable battle of Bunker's Hill. The late General Burgoyne, who, though not in the action, was familiarly acquainted with its detail, and indeed a spectator of the contest, in a letter written to England, makes use of this remarkable expression—" *Lord Rawdon*

Rawdon has this day stamped his fame for life." His lordship was afterwards at the storming of Fort Clinton.

In 1778, he was appointed adjutant-general to the British forces, under the command of Sir Henry Clinton, with the rank of lieutenant-colonel in the army. In this capacity he shewed himself not only brave, but active and judicious; and rendered essential service in the hazardous retreat of the British army through the Jerseys, from Philadelphia to New York, and also in the action at Monmouth. He afterwards embarked with the troops for Charlestown, and served at the siege of that place, where he acquitted himself with such singular judgment and distinguished valour, that, notwithstanding his want of years, and consequently presumed inexperience, he was appointed to the command of a separate corps in the province of South Carolina. In a short time after, he joined the army under Lord Cornwallis, and at the battle of Camden had the command of one of the divisions, with which he commenced the action, and which proved one of the most brilliant and decisive in favour of the British arms.

During Lord Rawdon's subsequent command in Charlestown, an affair happened in which (through a warm zeal for the service) he appeared to be much implicated; and which, although it has been, and still is, justified by his friends, was severely censured by the Americans, and afterwards condemned by many of the Opposition here. It became also an object of enquiry in the House of Lords. He stood, however, perfectly clear on the ground of honour and principle; and the worst insinuation never more than blamed a severe and warm disposition to enforce a rigorous military regulation. With regard to any possible imputation of inhumanity, his lordship's whole life has been of so opposite a complexion, and has been so uniformly marked by traits of the most refined philanthropy, that it

never

never was in the power even of party-obloquy to arraign him in that refpect.

Lord Rawdon on his return to England was created a peer of Great Britain, and nominated one of his Majefty's aids-de-camp.

About this time his lordfhip's conduct in the affair already alluded to (the execution of Colonel Hayne), was mentioned by the Duke of Richmond in fuch a manner as to give great umbrage; fufficient, indeed, to induce Lord Rawdon to call upon his grace for an explanation. After feveral meffages, through the interference of friends, the Duke of Richmond agreed to read fuch a recantation in the Houfe of Lords, as Lord Rawdon fhould think proper to dictate.

About the latter end of 1793, he was nominated to the command of a body of troops which was encamped in the neighbourhood of Southampton, and in conjunction with the emigrant corps, was to act offenfively againft France. The original object of their affembling being fhortly after altered for the purpofe of ftrengthening our little army upon the continent, the Earl of Moira embarked with them, and landed at Oftend. In his conduct on this occafion he difplayed much military knowledge, fharing every fatigue with the common foldier, and evincing an activity of mind which produced the moft beneficial effects. He managed the debarkation in fo fuperior a ftyle of military manœuvre, and continued his march up the country with fo much generalfhip, that the enemy, who lay in the neighbourhood, and were in confiderable force, fufpended a premeditated attack againft our line of pofts in Flanders, from a fuppofition, that Earl Moira's army was four times as numerous as it really was. Under the influence of this firft impreffion, his lordfhip proceeded on his march, without cannon, and with very little baggage, through an inclofed country, and with a moft formidable foe, commanded by one of the firſt generals in the republican ſervice, conſtantly hanging upon his flanks. By the rapidity of his motions, which were ſo well aided by the ſagacity of his original manœuvre at the debarkation, he ſucceeded in joining the Duke of York, whoſe advanced ſituation had become precarious in a high degree. On this occaſion his lordſhip had a moſt narrow eſcape: the vanguard of the French army, which by this time had been undeceived with regard to the real ſtrength of the expedition, entering a town at the ſame inſtant in which the Britiſh rear quitted it. Some partial ſkirmiſhes took place at Aloſt, halfway between Ghent and Bruſſels; which, although trifling, continued to add to his lordſhip's military character. Having thus accompliſhed the object of the expedition, he ſoon after returned to England, where he remained inactive, although ſtill inveſted with a ſort of command at Southampton.

Lord Rawdon in the Houſe of Peers has proved himſelf a clear, judicious, and able orator. His exertions to relieve the diſtreſſes of perſons impriſoned for ſmall debts, will remain a monument of philanthropy upon our parliamentary records; while his manly deportment throughout every debate in this and the ſiſter kingdom ſerves to prove, that his ſteadineſs as a ſtateſman is not inferior to his intrepidity as a ſoldier. We will venture to predict, in the face of much prejudice, that whenever the troubles of Ireland ſhall have ſubſided, Earl Moira's anticipation of them, and conſequent ſtruggles to prevent their exploſion, will more than counterbalance any poſſible miſapprehenſion of the real motives by which the leaders of that rebellion have been actuated. His unequivocal conduct at the late ſtate trials in Maidſtone, ſufficiently evinces, that the moſt inveterate foe cannot even inſinuate the fainteſt compromiſe with their inſidious views; whilſt the caution and judgment with which he has uniformly conducted himſelf, whenever the celebrity of his name has drawn him into any

ſpecies

species of political intercourse, will mark his character with no small degree of sagacity and penetration.

With regard to Earl Moira's private virtues, we shall not run the hazard of imputed adulation, when we say, that large as are his means, his equally extensive benevolence has made deeper inroads into his fortune, than perhaps that of any other character of the age. Uninfluenced by party-spirit, whenever individual merit has been brought within the circle of his observation, and viewing that merit through the impartial optics of general philanthropy, without suffering a prejudice to intervene from the want of high birth or family connexion, he has on more occasions than one, forerun the most sanguine expectations; and when it has no longer been in his power to assist the different objects of his patronage, he has softened the hardship of disappointment by the most friendly marks of sincerity and attention. It is, therefore, the less surprising, that in his retirement he should uniformly have escaped—what few good men do escape—the ingratitude of any one person who has ever been employed under, or been countenanced by his lordship.

With an acknowledged character of this high and honourable species, it is natural, that his access to the first branches of the royal family, should be easy, and that he should be always distinguished by the strongest marks of confidence and familiarity. The latter epithet is the more appropriate, because his reception at Carlton and York Houses is ever marked by the most unequivocal testimonies of friendship. His Royal Highness the Prince of Wales, whose cause he warmly espoused in the memorable discussion of the regency-bill, has on many occasions testified the strongest attachment to his lordship*; and it is well known,

---

* His lordship is a very active, we had almost said enthusiastic, freemason, and has always been the acting grand-master of that society, ever since

known, that the Duke of York made choice of Lord Rawdon to be his second in the affair of honour with Colonel, now Major-general, Lenox.

By the death of his uncle, the Earl of Huntingdon, Lord Rawdon acquired an ample fortune, and was permitted by the king to assume the arms and name of Hastings; and on his father's death he succeeded to the Irish title and patrimony of Earl of Moira. His mother possesses the ancient Barony of Hastings, and the other baronies in fee, belonging to the Earls of Huntingdon, which at her death will descend to him.

S.

since the Prince of Wales was elected to the office of Grand-master. His lordship drew up the elegant address to his Majesty, which was presented by the grand lodge of England, in 1793, and which may be considered as a complete refutation of the charges brought against the brotherhood by Abbé Barruel, and Professor Robison.

SIR

SIR JOHN SINCLAIR, BART. LL.D.

THE Sinclairs of Ulbſter in Caithneſs are an opulent branch of the family of the earls, who derive their titles from the name of the county. The late Mr. Sinclair enjoyed an extenſive eſtate in that northern ſhire; and his anceſtors, in a former period, muſt have undoubtedly poſſeſſed ſomewhat like a petty ſovereignty, claiming at leaſt the right of *pot* and *gallows*, or in other words, the power either of drowning or hanging their enemies. His rental is ſaid to have amounted to nearly fifteen hundred a-year; and when it is conſidered, that ſome of the lands are not at this day worth three halfpence an acre, and that it is a very favourable year indeed when the walnut will kernel, or the apricot reach maturity, it may be eaſily ſuppoſed, that a ſmall tract of territory will not produce that income.

John, born in 1754, is the ſon of the *laird of Ulbſter*, by Lady Jane Sutherland; being an only child, he received the firſt rudiments of his education under the paternal roof, from a private preceptor. While yet a boy, he gave frequent inſtances of his induſtry and application, and exhibited a taſte for books, and a turn for reſearch, which has invariably marked his character through life.

After the uſual preliminary ſtudies, the attractions of the high-ſchool at Edinburgh carried the *young laird* thither; he then removed to the univerſities of Glaſgow and Oxford; and paſſing through the various claſſes, with the approbation of all the profeſſors, who were loud in praiſe of his induſtry, he returned home.

Both in Scotland and Ireland there is but one profeſſion, excluſive of the military, to which the ſon of a man of fortune will ſtoop; this is the law. That which, in the

opinion

opinion of some, favours of the *quiddam mercenarium*, as much as any other employment, is the only one to which they will bend: every thing else, according to them, favours of trade; and it is to be feared, that agriculture, notwithstanding many illustrious examples to the contrary, is still considered somewhat in the same light as it was once by a Roman of equestrian rank *.

It was to the study of the law, then, that Sir John Sinclair first bent his mind. He accordingly repaired once more to the capital of Scotland, and became a member of the society of advocates. Here again his industry displayed itself, but took a new direction; for he was now constantly seen in their noble library, rummaging ancient titles, poring over moth-eaten records, and investigating the contents of musty parchments. In short, he then laid the foundation of a certain species of knowledge, which entitled him at one time to the praise of being more minutely acquainted with the *chartularies* of Scotland, than any of his contemporaries of the same standing. But it was not as an antiquary only that he acquired reputation, for he constantly frequented the *speculative society*, and first distinguished himself by his speeches there.

After revisiting England, where he must undoubtedly have acquired a taste for agriculture, he was returned member for his native county; and he soon distinguished himself from the rest of his countrymen, who, unless called upon *officially*, are generally very abstemious in the article of oratory; and now that *honest George Dempster* has retired, this circumstance alone would attract notice in the present age.

Sir John Sinclair first appeared in the character of an author in 1782, at which time he published "Observa-

* "Non fuit consilium socordia atque desidia bonum otium conterere: neque vero, *agrum colendo*, aut venando, *servilibus officiis* intentum, ætatem agere," &c.

SALL. BELL. CAT.

tions

tions on the Scottish Dialect;" on this occasion he candidly acknowledged, that he had been assisted by the late Sir John Henderson's papers.

But his principal work, and one indeed for which he was admirably fitted, both by nature and habit, was his " History of the Public Revenue of the British Empire;" of which Parts I. and II. were published in 1789, and Part III. in 1790. The period was peculiarly appropriate for a discussion of this nature, as Neckar had aroused the attention of all Europe, by his work on the finances of France, while the dispute between him and Calonne, tended not a little to develope the modern mysteries of finance; mysteries, which, like those of the BONA DEA in ancient times were till then doomed to be kept secret from all but the immediate votaries.

In every point of view, this must be allowed to be a most important work; and had the proper inductions been made, it would have saved us from many subsequent calamities. The progressive income of the public revenue, from 400,000l. in the time of William the Conqueror (1070), until 1788 in the reign of George III. when it amounted to only 15,572,971*l.*,* affords a very flattering proof of the revenues of the nation; yet when it is considered, on the other hand, that the war expences during the whole reign of William III. amounted to only 30,447,382*l*. and that the sum squandered in the project of subjugating America formed a total of 139,171,876*l*. it was easy to foresee the dangers inseparable from any other than a pacific system.

But Sir John does not content himself with dry details, for he enters on the ocean of financial speculation; and proposes, by economical arrangements, improvements in the existing revenues, new and additional taxes, and lucra-

* It is now estimated at about 27,000,000*l*. having experienced a rise of more than eleven millions and a half per ann. in the space of ten years.

tive

tive projects, to meliorate the national income, by the amazing fum of 13,796,874*l*. It muſt, however, be allowed, that ſome of his ſuggeſtions, if neceſſary, are at the ſame time humiliating; for he propoſes, amongſt other things, to ſell Gibraltar. One of his projects is perhaps immoral, as he recommends lotteries; another (a poll-tax) odious and infufferable; and a third, the reduction of the coinage, pregnant with miſchief. An exciſe on dreſs, to the amount of 100,000*l*. per ann. appears whimſical; but a tax on dogs, here firſt hinted, and computed at 62,500*l*. has been carried into execution, to the great diminution of the pleaſures of men of ſmall fortunes, attached to country ſports, and the *decimation* at leaſt of the whole canine race in Great Britain.

The following ſentiments are worthy of attention; would to heaven they had been followed up before it was perhaps too late! would to heaven that they were ſtill liſtened to by the governments of the nations to which they were then addreſſed!

" The more the people are loaded, the leſs they can
" bear in addition; the ſtruggle, therefore, between the
" rival nations, and the boaſt and glory of their ſtateſmen,
" ought to be, not who pays the moſt, but from whom
" the leaſt is exacted. May ſuch be the great ſource of
" competition between France and England: may the
" rulers of both kingdoms contend, for the future, whoſe
" adminiſtration ſhall prove the lighteſt, and leaſt burden-
" ſome: and may the rivalſhip never ceaſe, until both
" countries attain ſuch eaſe and abundance, that, in the
" memorable words of Henry IV. of France, 'le plus
" pauvre pût tous les Dimanches mettre une poule au
" pot;' or in the plain language of this country, until the
" pooreſt labourer can enjoy a comfortable dinner with his
" family on Sunday!"

Sir

Sir John foon after appeared before the public in the character of an author, or rather editor, of a work entitled, " The Statiftical Account of Scotland." In the year 1789-90, he had circulated among the clergy of that country a variety of queries for the purpofe of elucidating the national hiftory, and the moral, agricultural, and political ftate of North Britain. This admirable undertaking reflects great honour on the Caledonian priefthood, and obtained for the projector the appellation of the " patriotic fenator." The work in queftion has extended to thirteen volumes, of which the two firft were publifhed in 1791-2, and the others in 1793-4.

We had not been long engaged in the prefent conteft, to which however, we believe, he had at firft affented by his vote, before Sir John perceived the dreadful confequences likely to accrue to our finances from its progrefs, and even anticipated that ftoppage of money payments at the bank, which at one period was confidered as likely to give a death-blow to our credit. He accordingly addreffed a feries of letters to the governor and directors, as early as September, 1795, " on the pecuniary diftreffes, and the " means of preventing them," which do honour to his forefight. Thefe were publifhed in 1797.

Let us now confider Sir John Sinclair as a fenator. We believe, in the firft part of his political career, he was attached to Mr. Pitt; and it is but fair here to obferve, that the greater part of the nation were at one time, and perhaps ftill are, dragged by the chain of opinion after the triumphal car of that celebrated ftatefman. He foon, however, had occafion to change his mind; and we find him oppofing one of his favourite plans, known by the name of the commutation-act, which he qualified by the title of " a " wanton and unneceffary experiment."

During the important and critical period of the regency, when it was generally believed that new men and a new

fyftem

fyſtem would prevail *, Sir John appears to have joined the phalanx headed by Mr. Fox and Lord North; and, if not a rancorous, to have diſplayed an uniform hoſtility to the meaſures of Mr. Pitt; we accordingly find him, as member for Leſtwithiel †, ſupporting the previous queſtion, moved by Lord North, on Tueſday, December 16th, 1788, which, had it been carried, would have obliged Mr. Pitt to retire from the treaſury bench.

Three days after this (Friday, December 19th) he expreſſed his aſtoniſhment, that the Chancellor of the Exchequer " ſhould call the fyſtem of meaſures that he had " explained to the Houſe, a ſyſtem conſiſtent with the " principles of the conſtitution, when it was in *direct op-* " *poſition* to law." He aſſerted, on the contrary, that his project was equally hoſtile to the conſtitution and the laws, and forcibly deprecated the aſſumption of the power intended to be called forth during the ſuſpended exerciſe of royal authority. The proper and ſimple mode of procedure for the two Houſes to adopt, in his opinion, was for them to addreſs the only individual ‡, that all men's eyes were fixed upon, as the fit perſon to undertake the adminiſtration of government, in like manner as our anceſtors addreſſed the Prince of Orange a century ago; this, he conceived, would have been the direct conſtitutional line of proceeding; but what has been ſubſtituted, bore ſuch evi-

---

* In the " Appendix to the Hiſtory of the Public Revenue," printed in 1789, after mentioning his diſappointment at not receiving aſſiſtance from the records of the different offices, the author proceeds thus: " In the mean " while an event of a nature the moſt unforeſeen and diſtreſſing has taken " place, *from which* a change of government may be looked for, and as " his wiſhes for information may poſſibly be gratified by ſome future " miniſter, &c."

† He received this ſeat not as a favour from the crown, but as an equivalent for his intereſt in the diſtrict boroughs of Tain, Kirkwall, &c.

‡ The Prince of Wales.

dent

dent marks of ufurpation, and rendered it fo obnoxious to the welfare of the country, that he was determined to bring forward a plan of his own, to obtain a conftitutional eftablifhment of a regency, and when the right honourable member's fyftem came on again in that Houfe, he would fubject his propofal to their confideration.

When the grand queftion refpecting the flave trade was agitated, in 1792, Sir John afked certain queftions of Mr. Pitt, refpecting the horrid traffic of our own and foreign nations in their fellow men, but did not take any decided part on that fubject. It is difficult, indeed, precifely to define his opinions, but it is with pain we exprefs our belief, that they were averfe to the claims of outraged humanity.

During the fcarcity of corn that prevailed in 1795-6, we find him more honourably occupied. On Friday, December 11th, he made a motion for a felect committee, and recommended a *general inclofing bill*, the " intention" of which, " was to preclude calamity and diftrefs in future;
" to cut up famine by the roots; to prevent it again com-
" ing within the boundaries of this ifland; to render it
" unneceffary ever to grant bounties on the importation of
" foreign grain; all of which could be effected, by re-
" folving to cultivate the wafte, uninclofed, and unproduc-
" tive lands of the kingdom."

In March, 1796, he renewed the fame fubject; and after obferving that there was land enough in the country to feed its inhabitants, he ftated, that in 1795-6, it had been rendered neceffary to import one million of quarters of grain, at an expence of three millions fterling, great part of which was exported in coin, and had thereby contributed, in a great degree, to the then fcarcity of fpecie.

When the debate took place (February 28, 1796) refpecting the fituation of the bank, Sir John afforded a pregnant

nant inftance of his refearch, by quoting a precedent that occurred in 1696, when this fame great commercial company had ftruggled under fimilar difficulties; and it is not a little aftonifhing, that the Chancellor of the Exchequer appeared to be totally unacquainted with the proceedings of the period alluded to, although they were ftrictly in point.

When Mr. Pitt introduced his bill for the redemption of the land-tax, it was ftrenuoufly oppofed by " the patriotic " fenator," who objected to it on a variety of grounds.

Sir John Sinclair has been twice married; firft to a relation of the Earl of Lauderdale, and fecondly to a daughter of the late Lord Macdonald; by the latter he has a fon, and by the former two daughters.

Previoufly to his nomination to be prefident of the Board of Agriculture, he eftablifhed a fociety at Edinburgh, for the improvement of Britifh wool; and he has exhibited fpecimens of Orkney fheep, whofe fleeces are far fuperior in point of finenefs, although we believe not in *length,* to thofe of Spain.

In the courfe of the prefent war, he has raifed two battalions, called the " Rothfay and Caithnefs fencible infantry," of both of which he is colonel; his commiffions are dated March 7th, and December 19th, 1794. The fecond is now ferving in Ireland.

It may not be amifs here to remark, that his regiment is dreffed after the ufual manner of the highlanders, with a very becoming and indeed decent alteration in refpect to the covering of the *lower extremities*; the men wearing *trews,* or clofe tartan trowfers, inftead of the *kilt,* or fhort petticoat, which permits the knees to remain naked, and in fome of the military movements, even expofes the pofteriors! In a differtation lately written by him on that fubject, he endeavours to prove this to be the ancient Celtic drefs,

drefs, and quotes Gibbon, Henry, &c. befides fome traditional authorities on this fubject. He has alfo brought forward the evidence of ancient Scotch ballads, particularly that of " Tak' your Auld Cloak about ye;" fuppofed to be written in the time of Robert Bruce:

" In days when our King Robert rang,
" His *trews* they coft but ha'f a crown,
" He faid they were a groat ou'r dear,
" And ca'd the taylor thief and loun."

It will appear from what has been mentioned, that Sir John Sinclair is a man of great perfeverance and induftry. He has attained a very confiderable degree of knowledge, in refpect to the finances and refources of this country, and has of late years, experienced a marked oppofition from Mr. Pitt, who by means, perhaps, not very liberal, is faid to have tumbled him down in the twinkling of an eye from the chair of the Board of Agriculture.

He has been impeached of recommending camps in the neighbourhood of the metropolis, in time of peace; a fyftem perhaps but too familiar with the prejudices of his early life. The friends of the premier alfo accufe him of having written a letter to a great perfonage, at the diffolution of the laft parliament, foliciting a *feat* in either of two great houfes, and obferving, that an hereditary one would be moft confonant to his dignity as prefident of the Board of Agriculture. It is to his pretended difappointment on this occafion, that they trace the origin of a kind of *armed neutrality*, and a derelection of the premier, to whom he was once fo greatly attached.

It is impoffible to decide with any degree of accuracy refpecting charges fo vague and fecret in their very nature; we can only obferve, that he is one of the ableft and moft opulent, and we are inclined alfo to confider him as one of the moft independent of our modern legiflators.

Sir John Sinclair was created a baronet, February 4th, 1786; but whether his claims originated from the title of his original anceftor, Sir George Sinclair of Clythe, who fat in the Scottifh Parliament, at the beginning of the prefent century, or in his own merits, the author of this fketch is unable to determine.

Previoufly to his receiving patent honours, he had become entitled to academical ones, having obtained the degree of Doctor of Laws fome years before.

A.

MR. ROSCOE.

THE hiſtory of the celebrated author of the Life of Lorenzo de Medicis, evinces the wonderful effects which reſult from aſſiduous induſtry, ſuperadded to the intuitive rapidity of genius. Favoured by no advantages of education, foſtered by no patronage, raiſed by the native energies of his mind alone, Mr. Roſcoe has reached a pitch of literary eminence, which is rarely attained even by thoſe who have made the beſt uſe of the privileges of academic inſtruction.

His parents moved in the humbler ſphere of life; they were of courſe precluded by their circumſtances from giving their ſon a very extenſive education; and, with a ſtrange perverſeneſs of temper, he obſtinately refuſed to attend at the day-ſchool where his father wiſhed him to be taught writing and arithmetic. In conſequence, he had not even the common opportunities of acquiring knowledge uſually enjoyed by thoſe of the ſame ſtation in life as himſelf. He was thus fated to be the architect of his own fame.

But though he threw off the trammels of the ſchool, he was not idle:—he read much, and thought more.

At an early age he was articled as clerk in the office of Mr. Eyes, an attorney, in Liverpool. Soon after this period he was ſtimulated to undertake the ſtudy of the Latin language, by one of his companions boaſting that he had read Cicero de Amicitia, and ſpeaking in high terms of the elegance of the ſtyle, and the ſentiments of that compoſition. Mr. R. immediately procured the treatiſe in queſtion; and ſmoothing the difficulties by perpetual reference to his grammar as well as to his dictionary, he drudged through the task which emulation had incited him to undertake. The success which he experienced in his first effort prompted him to proceed; and he did not stop in his career till he had read the most distinguished of the Latin classics. In this pursuit he was encouraged by the friendly intercourse of Mr. Francis Holden, an eccentric genius and excellent scholar.

Having made considerable progress in the Latin language, Mr. R. still without the assistance of a master, proceeded to the study of the French and Italian. The best authors in each of these tongues soon became familiar to him; and it is supposed that few natives of the country have so general and recondite a knowledge of Italian literature, as the subject of the present memoir.

During the whole of this period, Mr. R. regularly attended at the office; and his seasons of study were the intervals of business.

His attachment to the muse was of a very early date. While yet a boy he read with avidity the works of the best English poets. Of their beauties he had an exquisite sense; and it may easily be imagined that the earliest of his compositions were of the poetical class. " Mount Pleasant," a descriptive poem, which he wrote in his 16th year, is a record not only of the fertility of his genius, but of the correctness of his taste.

Soon after the expiration of his clerkship, Mr. R. was taken into partnership by Mr. Aspinwall, a very respectable attorney of the town of Liverpool; and the entire management of an office, extensive in practice, and high in reputation, devolved upon him alone. In this situation he conducted himself in such a manner as to gain universal respect. For notwithstanding his various pursuits, he had paid strict attention to his profession, and had acquired a liberal and minute knowledge of law. And in clearness of
comprehension,

comprehenfion, and rapidity of difpatch in bufinefs he had few equals.

About this time he commenced an acquaintance with the late * Dr. Enfield, and the prefent Dr. Aiken, then refident at Warrington, the former being tutor in the belles lettres, in the Warrington academy, and the latter eftablifhed as a furgeon in that town. Thefe gentlemen had the honour of being early fenfible of his furprizing talents, and they contracted with him a friendfhip which was fure to be lafting, as it was built on the folid bafis of mutual efteem.

Mr. R. feems to have been almoft intuitively gifted with a correct tafte in the arts of painting and ftatuary. On the 17th December, 1773, he read to the members of a fociety, formed in Liverpool, for the encouragement of defigning, drawing, painting, &c. an ode on the inftitution of the aforefaid fociety, which was afterwards publifhed, together with his poem entitled Mount Pleafant. Of this fociety he was a very active affociate, and occafionally gave public lectures on fubjects appropriate to the object of the inftitution.

When the voice of humanity was raifed againft the flave trade, Mr. R. fearlefs of the inconvenience to which the circumftances of his local fituation might expofe him, ftood forth a zealous and enlightened advocate for the abolition of that inhuman traffic. In his boyifh days, indeed, he had expreffed his feelings on this fubject in the following beautiful lines, which are extracted from the above-mentioned poem, Mount Pleafant, p. 13 :

> There Afric's fwarthy fons their toils repeat,
> Beneath the fervors of the noon-tide heat;
> Torn from each joy that crown'd their native foil,
> No fweet reflections mitigate their toil;

From

---

* When Dr. E. publifhed the 2d vol. of the Speaker, Mr. R. furnifhed him with an Elegy to Pity, and an Ode to Education.

From morn to eve, by rigorous hands oppreſt,
Dull fly their hours, of every hope unbleſt :
Till broke with labour, helpleſs, and .forlorn,
From their weak graſp the ling'ring morſel torn ;
The reed-built hovel's friendly ſhade deny'd ;
The jeſt of folly, and the ſcorn of pride ;
Drooping beneath meridian ſuns they lie,
Lift the faint head, and bend the imploring eye ;
Till death, in kindneſs, from the tortured breaſt
Calls the free ſpirit to the realms of reſt.
  Shame to mankind! but ſhame to Britons moſt,
Who all the ſweets of liberty can boaſt ;
Yet, deaf to every human claim, deny
That bliſs to others which themſelves enjoy :
Life's bitter draught with harſher bitter fill,
Blaſt every joy, and add to every ill ;
The trembling limbs with galling iron bind,
Nor looſe the heavier bondage of the mind.

Thus, by his own reflections, Mr. R. was prepared to enter with ardor into the views of the friends of ſuffering humanity. He had frequent converſations with Mr. Clarkſon, who firſt drew the attention of the kingdom at large to this national diſgrace. A ſpecious pamphlet was publiſhed in defence of the trade, intituled, *Scriptural Reſearches into the Licitneſs of the Slave Trade*, and written by a Spaniſh Jeſuit of the name of Harris. Mr. R. anſwered it with great ſpirit and acuteneſs, in a counter-pamphlet intituled, *A Scriptural Refutation of a Pamphlet lately publiſhed by the Rev. Raymund Harris.*

But this copious and intereſting ſubject awakened all his ſympathies, and the public were gratified by a moſt affecting poem, intituled, *The Wrongs of Africa*. This poem Mr. R. intended to complete in three parts. The two firſt appeared in 1787 and 1788, but the lovers of genuine poetry have to lament that he has not yet fulfilled his promiſe of favouring them with the publication of the third.

A mind

A mind fo active and generous as Mr. R's could not be uninterested in that stupendous event, the French Revolution. He caught the enthusiastic glow which warmed the breasts of the friends of freedom, while they beheld a mighty nation throwing off the fetters of despotism; and fondly hoped that the consequences of their exertion would be lasting peace, good order, and equal laws. He tuned the lyre on this bewitching theme, and proclaimed the praises of Freedom in a translation of an ode of Petrarch, which found its way into the *Mercurio Italico*; a song intuled, *Millions be Free*, and the famous poem, *The Vine-covered Hills*, which may be classed among the most finished compositions in the English language.

During the season of tumult and discord, which succeeded the attempt of the combined powers to reinstate, in the plenitude of its authority, the despotism of France (an attempt in which this country, fatally to itself, too cordially united), Mr. R. was busily employed in writing the History of Lorenzo de Medicis. This work was begun about the year 1790. It may be presumed that it has now passed through the ordeal of criticism: more than two years have elapsed since its publication. The literary world have had time to recover from the dazzle of surprize—and the buz of ignorant applause, raised by the leaders of literary fashion, is still. The sentence of sober judgment confirms the verdict which was passed according to the dictates of first impressions. The liberal acumen of Parr has assayed the life of Lorenzo, and has found it sterling gold. Its dignity and grace have shielded its author from the mercilefs tomahawk of the writer * of the *Pursuits of Literature*; and we may fairly presume that its rank is fixed among the most splendid ornaments of English literature.

* Mr. Mathias.

The admiration with which the public have been affected by the perusal of this work will, no doubt, be encreased by a knowledge of the circumstances in which it was compofed. At the time when it was projected, Mr. R. lived at the diftance of two miles from Liverpool, whither he was obliged daily to repair to attend the bufinefs of his office. The dry and tedious details of law occupied his attention during the whole of the morning and afternoon; his evenings alone he was able to dedicate to ftudy; and it will be eafily conceived, that a gentleman, furrounded by a numerous family, and whofe company was courted by his friends, muft have experienced, even at thefe hours, a variety of interruptions. No public library provided him with materials. The rare books which he had occafion to confult, he was obliged to procure in London at a confiderable expence. But in the midft of all thefe difficulties the work grew under his hands. In order that it might be printed under his own infpection, he eftablifhed an excellent prefs at Liverpool, and fubmitted to the difgufting toil of correcting the proofs. The Hiftory of Lorenzo de Medicis was at length publifhed early in the year 1796.

Soon after the publication of his hiftory, Mr. R. relinquifhed the profeffion of an attorney, and entered himfelf at Gray's Inn, with a view of acting as a barrifter.

He took advantage of the leifure which the relinquifhment of bufinefs afforded him, to enter upon the ftudy of the Greek language; to which, according to the report of his intimate friends, he has made confiderable progrefs.

The public have, with concordant voice, called upon Mr. R. for the life of Leo X.; and Lord Holland, and Lord Briftol have, with great liberality, promifed their affiftance in procuring from Italy, and other parts of the continent, whatever documents he might think it neceffary to confult in the execution of fo grand a defign. The

lovers

lovers of polite literature will be glad to hear that Mr. R. has actually begun this expected work; but such is the troubled state of Europe, that he is debarred, at present, from the use of materials which might be collected abroad.

In the course of his conduct, Mr. R. has uniformly maintained a character of simplicity, sincerity, and benevolence. He acts uprightly without effort. Ill-fated genius cannot plead his history as a precedent for irregularity of life; nor will his example sanction the herd of men of abilities, who deem their talents a licence to live in idleness, and prey upon the public. His resources are in his own exertions. He is, in every sense of the word, an independent man. Long may he enjoy the blessings which are the meed of virtue!

M.N,

THE EARL OF LIVERPOOL.

THE rife of this nobleman muft be allowed to have been rapid; and if we are to believe his enemies, it is unexampled in our annals, fince the time of the Spenfers. This, however, is not ftrictly true, for it might be eafy to point out many others who have been fully as fortunate in the courfe of the prefent reign, and attained equal honours with perhaps inferior pretenfions.

On his being ennobled, it was obferved, with more rancour than truth, that his family difgraced the peerage; whereas the truth is, that on the fcore of birth, his pretenfions are fuperior to many of thofe with whom he affociates, either in the fenate, or at the council board. His anceftors have been fettled more than a century at Walcot, near Charlbury, in Oxfordfhire. His grandfather, Sir Robert Jenkinfon, married a wealthy heirefs at Bromley, in Kent; and his father, who was a colonel in the army, refided at South Lawn Lodge, in Whichwood Foreft.

Charles Jenkinfon received the firft rudiments of his education at the grammar-fchool of Burford, two miles diftant from his father's houfe; and many perfons are ftill living in that neighbourhood, who addrefs him as their old fchool-fellow. He was afterwards placed on the foundation in the Charter Houfe, and feems to have been fo well fatisfied with the inftitution, that he educated his eldeft fon, the prefent Lord Hawkefbury, there. From this eminent feminary he was removed to Oxford, where he firft imbibed, perhaps, his political fentiments, and was entered a member of the Univerfity College. There he took two degrees, that of B.A. and A.M. and feems to have made
himfelf

himself first known by some verses on the much-lamented death of the Prince of Wales, the father to his present Majesty.

In 1753, he removed from Oxford, without obtaining, and perhaps without soliciting, a fellowship; and in 1753, published his first prose tract, entitled, "A Discourse on the Conduct of the Government of Great Britain, with respect to Neutral Nations during the present War." He afterwards wrote several other pamphlets; and one in particular, on the benefit resulting from a militia, or armed national force, independent of a standing army. This abounds with many manly and patriotic sentiments, and has been lately quoted against himself in the House of Peers: on that occasion his lordship did not deny that he was the author, but contented himself with apologizing for his errors, on account of his extreme youth.

To the former of these productions, his rise in life has been falsely attributed; it was allowed by every one to be an able performance; but like many others of the same kind, it might have lain in the warehouse of his bookseller, and he himself remained for ever in obscurity, had it not been for the intervention of a gentleman of the same county, with whom he luckily became acquainted.

Sir Edward Turner of Ambroseden in Oxfordshire, being of an ancient family, and possessing a large fortune, ambitioned to represent his native county in parliament. Having attained considerable influence by means of a large estate, a hospitable and noble mansion, which as well as the family house at Blackheath has been since taken down, and the materials sold by his eldest son Sir Gregory Page Turner, Baronet, he accordingly stood candidate as knight of the shire. He was, however, strenuously but unsuccessfully opposed; for in addition to his own, he possessed the court interest. The struggle, notwithstanding this, was long and violent, and it still forms a momorable epoch in the

history

history of contested elections. But for nothing is it more remarkable, than for its being the fortunate occurrence in Mr. Jenkinson's life, which produced all his present greatness; for the contending parties, having as usual, called in the aid of ballads, lampoons, verses, and satires, this gentleman distinguished himself by a song in favour of Sir Edward and his party, which so captivated either the taste or the gratitude of the baronet, that he introduced him to the Earl of Bute, then flourishing in all the plenitude of power.

It is known but to few, perhaps, that his lordship, who placed Mr. J. at first in an inferior office, was not atall captivated with him, for it was entirely owing to the repeated solicitations of the member for Oxfordshire, that he extended his further protection. After a longer trial, he became the Premier's private secretary, and in some respect a member of his family, participating in his friendship and favour, and living with him in an unrestrained and confidential intercourse.

Such a connexion as this could not fail to prove advantageous; and accordingly, in March, 1761, we find him appointed to be one of the Under-secretaries of State, a situation which presupposes an intimate acquaintance with the situation of foreign affairs, and a pretty accurate knowledge with respect to the *arcana imperii* in general.

He, however, did not remain long in this station, for after the lapse of about fourteen months, he received the lucrative appointment of Treasurer of the Ordnance; this he relinquished in 1763, for the more confidential office of joint Secretary of the Treasury; a situation for which he was admirably qualified, by his knowledge of the state of parties, and the management of a House of Commons, of which he himself had been some time a member, having obtained a seat for Cockermouth.

To

To the Rockingham administration, which succeeded in 1765, he was both personally and politically odious, and he accordingly lost all his appointments; but in the course of the same year, he had one conferred on him by the king's mother, the late Princess Dowager of Wales, which no minister could bereave him of; this was the auditorship of her Royal Highness's accounts.

This circumstance added to his close intimacy with the discarded minister, awakened the jealousy of the patriots; and if we are to credit their suspicions, he became, in the technical language of that day, the " go-between" to the favourite, the princess-mother, and the throne.

When Lord Bute retired into the country in disgust, promising to relinquish public affairs, a great personage is said to have construed this into an *abandonment*, and to have looked out for advice elsewhere; from that moment Mr. Jenkinson was ranked as one of the leaders of the party called the " king's friends," and his Majesty has always since distinguished him by a marked partiality to his merits.

Honours and employments now fell thick upon him. In 1766, he became a Lord of the Admiralty, and in 1777, a Lord of the Treasury. Soon after this he obtained the * clerkship of the pells in Ireland, and was nominated a Lord of Trade; in 1786, he was created Lord Hawkesbury, Baron of Hawkesbury in the county of Gloucester, and on May 28th, 1796, was advanced to the dignity of Earl of Liverpool; at which period he was authorized by his Majesty to quarter the arms of that commercial city with those of his own family. These are great honours, but the well chosen motto which he has adopted for his escutcheon, proves that he considers himself as not undeserving of them †.

* It is proper here to remark, that this was purchased from Mr. Fox, having constituted part of his patrimony.

† PALMA NON SINE PULVERE.

While in the House of Commons, Mr. Jenkinson spoke frequently, but since his recent elevation, speaks but seldom; whatever he says, however, is listened to with the utmost attention, and the throbbings of expectation are never more feelingly experienced by the servants of the crown, than when he utters his wishes either at the council-board, or in parliament.

His lordship formerly experienced much odium, which indeed is always attached to the charge of favouritism, for, when the Earl of Bute made his *apotheosis*, his political mouth was supposed to drop on the shoulders of Mr. Jenkinson. He is now, however, a peer, and a privy counsellor, and in one of those situations the temporary, and in the other the constitutional adviser of the crown; he is therefore empowered both by office and by law to deliver his opinion to his sovereign.

It would be unjust to omit that the earl of Liverpool has always paid great attention to the trade of his country. It was he who drew up the treaty of commercial intercourse with America; and he is also said to have not only pointed out, but to have *created* the whale fishery in the South Seas.

Respecting the part he took during the American war, no one ever spoke more decisively, or perhaps more intemperately than his present associate the Chancellor of the Exchequer, and of the share they both have in the management of this country, and the government of Ireland, and the present contest with France, posterity will be able to judge more coolly, and more fairly than their own contemporaries.

MR.

MR. ABRAHAM NEWLAND.

THE signature of this gentleman is pretty familiar throughout every part of Great Britain, and seems to give the same currency to a *bank-note* that the names of the notorious John Doe and Richard Roe confer on a *capias*. Abraham, however, has this in his favour, that he is no fictitious person, made up of shreds of parchment, but a man, a real living man, constituted of flesh, blood, bones, sinews, marrow, and muscles; and while the place of abode of the former gentlemen are so little known, even in Chancery-lane, Lincoln's-inn, Gray's-inn, Serjeant's-inn, or the Temple, that none of their inhabitants, from the judge to the ticket-porter, know where they lodge, and the Sheriffs of Middlesex, if ordered to take one of the rogues into custody, must be under the necessity of returning *non est inventus* on the back of the writ, there is not a boy about the Royal Exchange who cannot point out the *great house*, where honest Abraham is to be seen strutting about, with a pen behind his ear, for several hours every day!

The trade of Europe, during the middle ages, was confined almost exclusively to the provinces that skirt the Mediterranean and the Baltic. The oppressions every where experienced by the Jews from the Christians, taught them, from cruel necessity, the art of transferring their riches from one nation to another; and the mysteries of banking and of bills of exchange, are supposed to have originated in Italy.

A colony of Lombards, by means of the arms of the duchy *, and the name of their nation, have given sign-

* The three balls are the arms of Lombardy.

posts to our pawn-brokers, and an appellation to the residence of our principal bankers *.

It was not, however, until nearly two centuries after this epoch, notwithstanding the growing increase of our commerce, that a national bank was established, and notwithstanding David Hume, towards the latter period of his life, affected to consider public credit as a *hardier plant* than he had at first imagined, yet it is a long time before mankind becomes so metaphysical as to suppose that a horse, a ship, an estate, or even a province, may be represented by a slip of flimsy paper, that would not be able to contain half the legal jargon sufficient to constitute the conveyance of a house or a homested!

Indeed, this mode of reasoning is supported by facts, for it was found impossible to create a great national bank, either under the house of Tudor, or the house of Stuart. Such a tyranny as that exerted by Henry VIII. would have driven the proprietors into beggary in the course of a fortnight. Charles II. who cheated the *goldsmiths*, or bankers of his day, by plundering the exchequer of the money lodged there, and whom the *Gothamites* of later times have placed in the centre of the exchange, dressed in a Roman habit, as if he had been the protector of trade, might have proved nearly as fatal to a banking company, by his own distresses, joined to the perpetual cravings of his courtiers and mistresses, as the indiscriminate ferocity of Henry. Nel Gwyn alone, would have put a *German subsidy* in requisition!

In fine, we all know, that an establishment of this kind failed in monarchical France, and that it has been several times ineffectually attempted under the republic. It was not until five years subsequent to our own revolution, that the bank of England was established (in 1693), under the

* Lombard-street.

auspices

auſpices of a prince emphatically termed " the DELIVERER;" thus proving to demonſtration, that liberty and public credit are inſeparable from each other. At Berlin, Vienna, and Madrid, we hear of *court bankers*, but a national bank is ſtill unknown.

This eſtabliſhment has combated and overcome a multitude of difficulties; for its notes at one time, in conſequence of the arts practiſed by adherents to the Houſe of Stuart, experienced a diſcount; and it is but a ſhort time ſince, that the precious metals contained within its vaults have been kept from circulation, and all money-payments ſuſpended by act of parliament. Even this, however, it has ſurvived; for the known wealth of the eſtabliſhment, the punctuality of its offices. and the admirable economy of their arrangements, have attracted and moſt deſervedly retained the confidence of the nation.

Of theſe officers, the moſt eminent, moſt noted, and perhaps alſo the moſt reſpectable, is the ſubject of theſe memoirs. Mr. Newland, born in 1729, or 1730, at the houſe of his father, a baker, in King-ſtreet, Southwark, was appointed a clerk in the bank of England, a little more than half a century ago, being nominated on the 27th February, 1748. Diſtinguiſhing himſelf by that regularity and order ſo neceſſary in money concerns, he roſe through the various gradations of ſervice, until January 19, 1775, when he attained the reſpectable and confidential office of chief caſhier to the firſt commercial company in Europe.

He is now in the 68th or 69th year of his age, and has ſomething commanding and reſpectable in his perſon. His deportment is alſo genteel, his manners are affable, and his activity and attention ſtill exhibit a pattern for the imitation of the junior clerks. His manner of tranſacting buſineſs is eminently methodical; and he is known to have undeſignedly given offence to a few of the ſubſcribers to

the

the voluntary contributions, by a rigid and minute attention to the provisos of the act of parliament, and the instructions of the directors. On this occasion, the zeal of some of the newspapers got the better of their discretion, and they made many equally ridiculous and impotent reflections on the character of a person, who generously contributed 200*l.* towards the very measure of which they supposed him to be the enemy.

The wealth of this gentleman has been the subject of much conjecture. He is certainly rich, but no suspicion can attach to this circumstance, when his opportunities, his emoluments, and his economy are considered. He is, however, no churl; for a sum of money being wanted for rebuilding the church of St. *Peter-le Poor* in Broad-street, it was instantly advanced by him to the parish, at the usual interest, although he could have easily turned it to better account.

At a certain period of life, men both attain and retain habits either of regularity or dissipation. At fifteen minutes past nine o'clock in the morning, he is seen constantly at his desk, and is never absent from his duty until three in the afternoon. He resides in a *suite* of apartments in the bank, annexed to his office, as chief cashier; and being a bachelor, his establishment is not large. During a period of thirty or forty years, he has not been once absent, except during a few weeks illness; and therefore trips to Margate, Brighton, and the other fashionable watering places, have neither impeded his duties, nor added to his expences.

The only relaxation he has allowed himself for many summers past, is a daily ride in the Islington stage-coach, to a cottage at Highbury, where he drinks tea; and after contemplating *the beauties of the country*, returns regularly in the evening to the bank.

As a private character, this gentleman ranks very high; and in his social hours he is a good companion, enjoying
the

the pleasures of the table in moderation, and laughing heartily at *a good story*, of which he is paffionately fond.

It is almoft impoffible to contemplate the immenfe fums of *paper-money* which literally pafs through his hands, both as chief cafhier to the bank, and fecretary and agent to the commiffioners appointed by act of parliament for the reduction of the national debt, without thinking of the lines of Pope:

> " Blefs'd paper credit! laft and beft fupply!
> " That lends Corruption higher wings to fly!
> " Gold imp'd by thee can compafs hardeft things,
> " Can pocket ftates, can fetch or carry kings.
> " A fingle leaf fhall waft an army o'er,
> " Or fhip off fenates to fome diftant fhore:
> " A leaf like Sibyl's, fcatter to and fro
> " Our fates and fortunes as the winds fhall blow;
> " Pregnant with thoufands flits the fcrap unfeen,
> " And filent fells a king or buys a queen."

A.D.

THE HONOURABLE (lately RIGHT HONOURABLE)
CHARLES JAMES FOX.

ALL the great men of the prefent day, are either the offspring of, or immediately defcended from new families. The ancient nobility repofe under the laurels of their anceftors, not deigning to apply to any of the learned profeffions, and deeming commerce and agriculture unworthy of their purfuits, (a few illuftrious characters excepted), they delegate their domeftic concerns, to the care of their upper fervants, and not unfrequently the bufinefs of the nation is entrufted to their proxies. This, perhaps, will be the beft apology for the multitude of plebeian fcions, recently ingrafted on the ftock of ancient ariftocracy; and although it may puzzle Norrey and Clarencieux, to find them either arms or anceftors, certain it is, that the *life blood* of nobility has been infufed into the peerage through the conduit of democracy.

It may be alfo neceffary to preface this article with another obfervation, of which fome of the moft confpicuous characters of the prefent political drama, afford more than one pregnant inftance; that the younger fons of our nobility are more fuccefsful in their political efforts than the elder *. This may be eafily accounted for; the heir to a great fortune, and an illuftrious title, knows not how foon both may devolve upon him, and when that event takes place, to what further object can his ex-

* The following remarks are made by the late Lord Orford, better known by the name of Horace Walpole.
" William Pitt, Lord Chatham, was a fecond fon, and became prime mi-
" nifter of England. His rival and antagonift was Henry Fox, Lord Holland,
" a fecond fon likewife. Lord Holland's fecond fon, Charles Fox, and Lord
" Chatham's fecond fon, William Pitt, are now rivals and antagonifts.

pectations

pectations point? He finds that he has been born a legiflator, and that a large fortune is entailed upon his perfon; here then are wealth and honours not only within his grafp, but actually within his power. It is otherwife with the junior branches, for they have in general but little in poffeffion, and every thing to look for; they inherit all the exquifite relifh for pleafure that their feniors enjoy to fatiety, and are only deficient in the means of gratification. Like the dove of Noah, they fcarcely find a refting place for their feet on the earth; and they are exactly in the fituation of an invading general who has burnt his fhips, for they muft advance on, or perifh!

Charles James Fox, is the younger fon of Henry, who was himfelf a younger fon of Sir Stephen Fox, celebrated lefs for his own birth, than the circumftance of being a father at the age of eighty, an event not incredible however, and rendered in the prefent inftance unfufpicious, by the decorous conduct, and acknowledged virtue of the partner of his bed. Henry entered early into public life, and fuch was his addrefs in parliament, during the reign of George II. that he foon attained not only fome of the moft arduous and honourable, but alfo the moft lucrative fituations in the gift of the crown, for in the year 1754, he was appointed fecretary at war; then fecretary of ftate for the Southern department, and after being *oufted* by the great Mr. Pitt, afterwards Earl of Chatham, we find him filling the immenfely beneficial office of pay-mafter general of the forces, accumulating great wealth, and incurring the animadverfions of the firft city of the empire. Such indeed was his confequence, that at a time when patents of peerage were not very common, he was ennobled by his prefent Majefty, in 1763, by the title of Baron Holland of Foxley.

His fon, Charles James, was born January 13th, 1749, and if by his father's fide, he claffed among the *novi homines,*

D 2   by by his mother's, his defcent muft be allowed to be fplendid, for Lady Georgiana Carolina Lennox, was the daughter of the late Duke of Richmond; and as fuch, in addition to that of the King of Sardinia, fhe was allied to the two rival, but related families, which had fo long contefted for the throne of Great Britain—thofe of Brunfwic and Stuart.

But it is not to fuch vulgar claims as thefe, that the future hiftorian will have recourfe; he will dwell with ardour on the early promife of genius, the precocious talents of the boy, the matured wifdom of the philofopher and the ftatefman, and while the abilities and virtues that adorn the character of this hero, bring him forward on the canvas, thefe inefficient and involuntary pretenfions will be caft into the fhade, and fcarcely be diftinguifhed in the back ground.

The fecond fon proved Lord Holland's favourite child, and at length became the darling of his old age. Perceiving in him the feeds of all the qualities that conftitute greatnefs, he was at infinite pains to give fcope to his intellectual vigour, to expand the fhoots, and difclofe the bloffoms of fo promifing a plant. From his earlieft infancy he intended him for parliamentary bufinefs, and by converfing with him always as if he had been a man, he actually made him one before the ufual time. He is even faid to have fubmitted his difpatches to his perufal, while in office, and to have complied with his corrections.

This country much about the fame time, beheld in the perfons of two rival orators, two wonderful inftances of ftatefmen, retiring from the field of contention, and devoting the remainder of their lives to the education of their two younger fons, with whom they were accuftomed to talk about public affairs, and fometimes to place on a table in order to hear them declaim. Occupied the better part of their days in hoftilities againft each other, the enmity of the families feems to have become hereditary, for it is kept up by their children, who ſtill maintain a rivalſhip, even after they had abjured the principles of their refpective fires.

In compliance with the future deſtination of his fon, Lord Holland preferred a public to a private education, and accordingly fent Charles to Weſtminſter fchool. After diſtinguiſhing himfelf here, he removed to Eton, where Dr. Barnard, the late provoſt, found him not only uncommonly eager after amufements, but eminent fuccefsful in claffical attainments. His private tutor, while a member of this celebrated inſtitution, was Dr. Newcome, afterwards Biſhop of Waterford, who, while he was frequently vexed at the diffipation of his pupil, had occafion at the fame time to be highly gratified with his progrefs. Here he formed his early friendſhip with the Earl of Fitzwilliam, Lord Carliſle, his own relation the Duke of Leinſter, and fome of the firſt men of the age. It was here alfo, that * one of them anticipated his future reputation in the following lines:

> " How will my Fox, alone by ſtrength of parts,
> " Shake the loud fenate, animate the hearts
> " Of fearful ſtatefmen, while, around you ſtand
> " Both Peers and Commons lift'ning your command;
> " While TULLY's fenfe its weight to you affords,
> " His nervous fweetnefs ſhall adorn your words.
> " What praife to PITT to TOWNSHEND e'er was due,
> " In future times my Fox, fhall wait on you."

His father being, in the uncourtly language of thofe days, " a rank Tory," Charles was fent to finiſh his education at Oxford, where he is reported, in imitation of Penelope, to have regained by his daily toils, the labours loſt by his nocturnal aberrations.

* Lord Carliſle.

At

At length he began to pant after a more unreſtrained intercourſe with ſociety, and conſequently to be difguſted with reſtraints, and tired with the uniformity of a collegiate life. The moſt eaſy, as well as moſt likely way to rid himſelf of this, was to evince an ardent deſire to ſee the world; and as his ſtudies were now completed, his father, as uſual, indulged the wiſhes of his darling ſon. Thoſe who have been accuſtomed to ſee Mr. Fox of late years, without being acquainted with the minute particulars of his early life, will ſcarcely believe, that at this period he was one of the greateſt *beaus* in England; that he indulged in all the faſhionable elegance of attire, and vied, in point of *red-heels*, and *Paris-cut-velvet*, with the moſt ſhewy men of the times. Theſe and ſimilar qualifications were diſplayed in moſt of the courts of Europe, in the courſe of the grand tour; and if he did not return like his maternal anceſtor*, with all the vices of the continent, he at leaſt brought a wardrobe replete with all its faſhions. Nor will a ſtrict regard to hiſtorical truth permit the omiſſion of more culpable tranſgreſſions, for he is ſaid, amidſt the ardour and impetuoſity of youth, to have expended, or rather laviſhed, vaſt ſums of money in † play, and to have contracted immenſe debts. Let it be recollected, however, that he was at this very time between two and three years ſhort of that period, when the law declared him to be no longer a minor.

His enemies have carefully reminded us, that the firſt political act of his life was a violation of the conſtitution of his native country; for at the general election in 1768, he took his ſeat for Midhurſt, in Suſſex, a borough under

---

* Charles II.
† Dr. Biſſet, in his life of Burke, aſſerts, that his father, Lord Holland, who accompanied him to Spa, firſt excited an itch for play in his youthful mind, by allowing him five guineas a night to be ſpent in games of hazard. But as this reſts on the mere aſſertion of that gentleman, it will be difficult to give credit to the report,

the

the influence of his family, when he was only nineteen years of age, and confequently ineligible. It is with pain too, it is here reluctantly recorded, that the firſt effort of his eloquence was hoſtile to liberty*; but, befides his extreme youth, the bent of his education, the prejudices of his family, and the wifhes of a fond father, ought all to be taken into confideration; and if a complete vindication does not enfue, an ingenuous mind will not be at a lofs for an apology.

During all the proceedings of the Houfe relative to the Middlefex election, Mr. F. ſtood forward as the champion of the miniſtry, and exhibited no common addrefs and activity on the occafion. From the firſt moment of his entering the fenate, he, indeed, difplayed all the qualities of the orator; and Lord North, then chancellor of the exchequer, deemed his merits fo confiderable, that in the beginning of 1772 he nominated him to a feat at the admiralty board, and in the latter part of the fame year made him, in fome meafure, a partner with himfelf in the management of the empire, by appointing him a lord of the treafury.

Amidſt this feeming devotion to the court, there were not wanting opportunities when he fhook off the trammels of dependence, and allowed his manly mind to take its full fcope. Not the leaſt memorable of thefe was during the debate on the bill brought into the Houfe of Commons by Sir William Meredith, to give relief from fubfcription to the xxxix articles of the church of England; and in the liberal fentiments delivered on that occafion, he has firmly and uniformly perfevered, until the prefent moment.

But the time had now arrived, when a new direction was to be given to his purfuits. The real caufe of this event,

---

* His firſt fpeech was in oppofition to Mr. Wilkes, then confined in the King's Bench; and whatever the *motives* of that gentleman might be, difpaffionate men will now be ready to avow, that on this occafion, his caufe was not only popular but juſt.

which

which involved fo many important confequences, can only be guefled at. The fons of the Lords Guilford and Holland, were both poffeffed of talents; the one, perhaps, afpired to, the other enjoyed, the fupreme command; and like two great men of antiquity, the firft, perhaps, could not brook a fuperior, nor the fecond a rival. The enmity was firft developed in the refufal of a petty appointment; it encreafed on the memorable examination of the Rev. Mr. Horne, now John H. Tooke, at the bar of the Houfe of Commons; and finally became public, in confequence of the following billet, couched with all the energy of Spartan brevity:

" His Majefty has thought proper to order a new com-
" miffion of the treafury to be made out, in which I don't
" perceive your name.

"NORTH."

" The Hon. Mr. Fox."

Confidering this not merely as an injury, but an infult, the enmity of Mr. Fox from that moment became public, and he at length raifed fuch a conftitutional oppofition to the adminiftration of the noble lord who had thus treated him in a manner bordering on contempt, that he, in the end, fubverted his power, and dragged his antagonift to the very edge of the fcaffold.

In the mean time, Lord Holland died, leaving a large fum of money, and confiderable eftates in the neighbourhood of Kingfgate, with the houfe there, built in imitation of Tully's Formian villa, on the coaft of Baiæ, to his fon Charles. He was thus in poffeffion of a plentiful fortune, and had he retained it, would have ftood upon high ground in point of confequence: for thefe bequefts, in addition to the clerkfhip of the pells in Ireland, foon after fold to Mr. Jenkinfon, now Lord Liverpool, muft have pro-

duced

duced a nett annual income of more than 4000*l. per annum.*

After the diffipation of this large property, a common mind would have, perhaps, bent under the calamity; his, on the contrary, feems to have rebounded from the fall; and inftead of finking into defpair, to have actually foared into celebrity, and even independence.

A new and a noble field now opened to his ambition; and he commenced his career as a patriot, on principles which Locke has upheld, and Sydney would not have blufhed to fupport. The members of that adminiftration, fuppofed by fome to be only the puppets of a northern peer, had rendered themfelves detefted by the oppreffion of Mr. Wilkes, the profecution of the printers, the countenance given to the riots at Brentford, and the military execution in St. George's-fields.

Another event of infinitely greater magnitude now filled up the bitter draught of popular odium; and the previous oppreffion, and threatened fubjugation of America, aroufed a general fpirit of refiftance within the mother country, and pointed the finger of public vengeance at the devoted head of the premier. Fortunately for Mr. Fox's confiftency, his conduct refpecting the tranfatlantic conteft, was ever ftrictly uniform; and on this, as on a fubfequent occafion, he faw afar off, anticipated the impending calamities, and predicted the accumulation of misfortunes, which afterwards overwhelmed the nation.

Accordingly, in 1774, he oppofed the introduction of the Bofton Port bill, and apologifed for the conduct of the colonies. In his fpeech on this occafion, he arraigned the conduct of the minifter in bold and energetic language, and explained the principles of the violated conftitution, with an eloquence worthy of the caufe. The treafury-bench began, for the firft time, to calculate the lofs it had fuftained, the oppofition to eftimate the ftrength it had acquired,

while

while the people rejoiced to behold, in the person of a youthful senator, whom they had been taught to consider as an enemy, a firm, an intrepid, and an eloquent advocate, such as would not have disgraced Rome in her best days.

On this occasion, he sat on the same seat as a Saville, a Barré, a Dunning, and a Burke, with the last of whom he had frequently broken a lance, in the war of argument, from the opposite side of the house; and he has since candidly avowed, that from this celebrated man he first imbibed those enlightened maxims of government, professed and acted upon by the pupil, alas! when the master himself seemed to have abandoned them.

On the discussion of Mr. Burke's conciliatory propositions, in 1775, he strenuously supported the liberal schemes of policy pointed out by that gentleman, and spoke and voted during the whole contest in direct opposition to that criminal system, which it had been fondly and fallaciously prognosticated was to produce the unconditional submission of the colonies, and lay them prostrate at the feet of the mother country!

At length all the evils that had been foreseen were realised. America, driven to despair, declared herself free and independent; monarchical France exerted her protecting arm across the Atlantic; the capture of Burgoyne and Cornwallis proclaimed the triumphs of liberty; and a new conflagration lighted up in Europe, by the firebrands that had been scattered in another hemisphere, wasted the strength, and exhausted the resources of England.

At the general election in 1780, the family-borough of Midhurst falling into other hands, and Mr. F. blushing, perhaps, at the idea of violating the very spirit and essence of a constitution, which he now began, for the first time, to understand and venerate, determined to become a candidate for the city of Westminster; and he at length succeeded,

after

after a violent contest, in which he baffled not only all the interest of the Newcastle family, but also all the influence of the crown, both of which were powerfully, but unsuccefsfully, exerted against him. Being now the representative, not of a petty venal borough, but of a great city, and that too without any expence to himself, he appeared in parliament in a more dignified capacity, and acquired a confiderable increafe of weight and confequence.

Soon after this, the ministry began to totter, and the political *rats* were in motion, in order to defert the finking fabric. A minority, at firft contemptible in point of numbers, but always formidable in refpect to integrity and abilities, and which then claimed the prefent premier amongft the moft zealous of its partifans, had increafed in power and popularity. The ministers were affailed within by the thunders of eloquence; without, they were overwhelmed by the clamours of an indignant people: to proceed in the war was ruin; and to recede, betrayed them into perfonal danger. At length the " noble lord in the blue ribbon" was hunted into the toils, and it was hoped by many, that public juftice awaited his mifdeeds; for in a conteft, in which oceans of blood had unjuftly flowed, fome one muft have been criminal: and who more proper for an expiatory facrifice, than the oftenfible author of fo many calamities? Alas! had punifhment been but inflicted on one fingle folitary individual, all our fubfequent calamities might have been averted, and the world taught to believe, that even in refpect to *great offenders,* fome connexion ftill exifted between guilt and punifhment!

But the Rockingham party contented themfelves with the defeat of their opponents; and Mr. Fox, of courfe, was nominated to a feat in the cabinet, and appointed one of the fecretaries of ftate. The merit of this fhort-lived administration was confpicuous. Notwithftanding they had fucceeded to an empty exchequer, and a general war, they

yet

yet determined to free the people from some of their numerous grievances; and had they remained a little longer in power, infinitely more would have been effected. Contractors were excluded by act of parliament from the House of Commons; custom and excise officers were disqualified from voting at elections; the proceedings in regard to Middlesex were rescinded; while a reform-bill, rather specious, however, in name, than in reality, abolished a number of useless offices. A more generous policy was also adopted in respect to Ireland; a general peace was already meditated; an ancient ally was attempted to be soothed by an offer of negociation*; and America, which could not be restored, was at least intended to be conciliated.

In the midst of these promising appearances, the nobleman, who was the key-stone that supported the discordant materials of the political arch, died suddenly, and the council board was instantly divided by political schisms.

The Marquis of Lansdowne, who appears at this period to have had the ear of the king, and a majority in the cabinet, was immediately entrusted with the reins of administration, and Mr. Fox determining, (to make use of his own language,) " never to connive at plans in private, " which he could not publicly and consistently avow," retired from office with a numerous and respectable body of his friends.

In the mean time, the party left in possession of all the great offices, concluded a peace with America, France and Holland; but their administration proved of short duration, for a grand political confederacy had now been formed against them. This, under the name of " the coalition," soon subverted their power, and supplanted them in office. No event, in our time, has produced more obloquy than

---

* Mr. Fox, wishing to detach the Dutch from the coalition with the house of Bourbon, wrote a letter to M. Simolin, the Russian Minister, in which he offered to form a new treaty on the basis of that of 1674.

the

the alliance between Mr. Fox and Lord North; and it is not to be concealed, that it was even then pregnant with inauspicious results, and has since been productive of the most sinister consequences, as it enabled an ambitious young man to give the first stab to the constitution, by setting a vote of the House of Commons, hitherto deemed inviolable, at defiance. The "India Bill," of which Mr. Burke is said to have been the penman, proved the rock, on which the vessel of the ill-paired colleagues foundered; and it is not a little memorable, that their more fortunate rivals revived this very measure, and carried it triumphantly through Parliament!

We now behold Mr. Fox once more, divested of power, reduced to shelter himself against accidents in the representation of the * Orkney Isles; and to contend with an unexampled perseverance for a seat as member for Westminster; which, after a memorable scrutiny, and an immense expenditure, he at length obtained.

He has since been re-elected to the same honourable post, and has steadily combated, as a representative of the people, the influence of the crown; which, in his opinion, alone constitutes, and produces all their grievances. His subsequent conduct has been such as to restore the current of popularity, and raise his name higher than before. His grand maxim, and surely it is immediately connected with the prosperity, and, perhaps, the existence, of a manufacturing and commercial country, is the maintenance of peace. With this object in view he opposed a contest with Russia, about the fortress of Oczakow, and a conflict with Spain concerning the peltry of Nootka Sound.

---

* This is rather incorrect, Mr. Fox being returned for the district of boroughs, called Tain, Dingwall, &c. &c. Even here, however, he was opposed by Sir John Sinclair, but the interest of the present Lord, then Sir Thomas Dundas, finally prevailed.

During

During the first stages of that melancholy event which led to the regency bill, Mr. Fox was wandering through the delightful regions of modern Italy, and seemed enchanted once more to tread on classic land. From this charming spot, he was called to witness and to participate in far different scenes, and finally to behold the party he opposed more firmly seated in power than before.

He has been blamed for his conduct during the impeachment of Mr. Hastings, but he was supported by a majority of the House of Commons on that occasion, and by nearly all his political enemies. This measure was absolutely necessary, in order to clear the honour of the nation, and prove to the oppressed inhabitants of India, that in England they would still find avengers. It is not to be denied, however, that the trial was spun out to a most oppressive length, and that the supposed culprit at last ceased to be odious in the eyes of the people. The forms of the House of Peers, as a court of justice, are indeed unfavourable to the dispatch of business, but the managers ought, perhaps, either to have accelerated these, or to have withdrawn from a struggle, when they perceived that the first step towards punishment consisted in the oppression of even a guilty individual!

No sooner did the French nation evince a sincere desire to shake off the dominion of absolute power, than he hailed the auspicious dawn of rising liberty, and deprecated the interference of this country, in a quarrel hostile to the principles on which she had founded her proud pre-eminence. On this occasion, he experienced the dereliction of many of his associates, and among others of that man of whose lips he had first imbibed the principles of freedom. Finding, however, that he and his friends were reduced to a scanty minority, he has since retired, in a great measure, from public business, and left the minister to triumph by means of the majorities in his interest. Nor is this all, for his

his name has been lately struck out from the list of privy counsellors; an event unexampled in the present reign, and only once exercised during the last, in respect to a nobleman * accused of cowardice and disaffection.

As an orator, Mr. Fox is assuredly the first man of his age. He simplifies the most abstruse details, he analyzes the most complex arguments, and he reduces the most subtile positions to the test of first principles. Animated himself, he animates others. Unambitious of melodious words and studied phrases, that dwell only on the ear, the correctness of his reasoning assails the judgment, while the irresistible thunders of his eloquence at once influence and captivate the senses. Struggling continually against the stream of power, he yet appears inferior to no man, and he wants only to stand on the " 'vantage ground" of success, to be viewed as the greatest man of his time.

As an author, he has produced several specimens of poetical composition, which with a due culture might have attained excellence. His verses to Mrs. Crewe, beginning with the following lines, have often been praised:

" Where the loveliest expression to features is join'd,
" By nature's most delicate pencil design'd;
" Where blushes unbidden, and smiles without art,
" Speak the softness and feeling that dwell in the heart," &c.

His invocation " to Poverty" must, however, be allowed to be superior, and it contains a national reflection that may offend some; it ought, however, to be recollected, that the English, *at that period*, were much disgusted with the temporising conduct of their northern neighbours:

" O Poverty! of pale consumptive hue,
" If thou delight'st to haunt me still in view,
" If still thy presence must my steps attend,
" At least continue, as thou art, my friend.

* Lord George Germaine.

" When

"When Scotch example bids me be unjuſt,
"Falſe to my word, unfaithful to my truſt,
"Bid me the baneful error quickly ſee,
"And ſhun the world to find repoſe with thee.
"When vice to wealth would turn my partial eye,
"Or int'reſt ſhutting ear to ſorrow's cry;
"Or courtiers' cuſtom would my reaſon bend,
"My foe to flatter, or deſert my friend;
"Oppoſe, kind Poverty, thy temper'd ſhield,
"And bear me off unvanquiſh'd from the field.
"If giddy Fortune e'er return again,
"With all her idle, reſtleſs, wanton train,
"Her magic glaſs ſhould falſe Ambition hold,
"Or Ay'rice bid me put my truſt in gold;
"To my relief, then, virtuous goddeſs, haſte,
"And with thee bring thy daughters ever chaſte,
"Health! Liberty! and Wiſdom! ſiſters bright,
"Whoſe charms can make the worſt condition light,
"Beneath the hardeſt fate the mind can cheer,
"Can heal affliction and diſarm deſpair;
"In chains, in torments, pleaſure can bequeath,
"And dreſs in ſmiles the tyrant hour of death!"

His letter * " To the worthy and independent Electors of the City and Liberty of Weſtminſter," is his only avowed proſe publication, and this has experienced a nearly unexampled ſale, having run through twelve or thirteen large editions. On this occaſion, he makes a manly appeal to his conſtituents; and in a clear and perſpicuous ſtyle deprecates the idea of foreign alliances, and inſiſts on the neceſſity of acknowledging the French Republic as an independent ſtate. While alluding to the ridiculous project of ſubjugating that power, by external force, he expreſſes himſelf thus:

" The conqueſt of France!!! O! calumniated cruſa-
" ders, how rational and moderate were your projects!
" O! much-injured Lewis XIV, upon what ſlight grounds
" have you been accuſed of reſtleſs and inordinate ambi-
" tion! O! tame and feeble Cervantes, with what a

* Publiſhed in 1793.

" timid

"timid pencil and faint colours have you painted the portrait of a difordered imagination!"

Of the *private* life of this great orator, the public may be anxious to have a few authentic particulars. Mr. Fox no longer refides any part of the year in town, having difpofed of his houfe in South-ftreet; when he vifits London, which is but feldom, he ftays fometimes at the houfe of his old friend General Fitzpatrick, and fometimes at a hotel in the neighbourhood of New Bond-ftreet. Except during the fhooting feafon, when he vifits Mr. Coke, &c. in Norfolk, he lives chiefly at St. Ann's-hill, near Chertfey. There he fuperintends the cultivation of his grounds, enjoys the pleafure of horticulture, and amufes himfelf in forming his fhrubberies. To " the rofe," the theme of the Perfian poets, he feems particularly attached; for he has a parterre near his houfe, in which there are no lefs than thirty different fpecies. He alfo poffeffes a great tafte for botany; and has been at infinite pains to render himfelf mafter of the Linnæan fyftem.

In general, he rifes about feven o'clock, mounts his horfe inftantly, rides to the river, and plunges into the Thames. He then returns to breakfaft, which is over before ten. The forenoon is, for the moft part, dedicated to his books; and is accordingly fpent in his ftudy. Before dinner, he takes a walk or ride, around the neighbouring village, fits down to table a little after three o'clock, and lives well, and like a gentleman, without any appearance, however, of luxury or oftentation. After indulging in a few glaffes of port or fherry, he retires with his guefts about fix, to the tea-room, which prefents a moft delightful profpect in the fummer feafon; and after a couple of difhes of coffee, a glafs of *liqueur de Martinique* is handed round to the company.

The evenings are generally dedicated to domeftic entertainments. Sometimes he reads, and then generally aloud; at other times he plays at fome manly game on the lawn, or liftens to the mufic of a favourite lady while fingering the *piano-forte*, or the pedal harp. The evening is not unfrequently spent at the HOLLAND, a charming octagon building, dedicated to his nephew, Henry, Lord Holland, and inscribed to him. From this building is to be seen a most luxuriant view of the surrounding country; but the eye is unwilling to roam abroad, as it is ornamented with beautiful paintings by the hand of Mrs. Armstead.

While the hirelings of ministry are representing him as plotting against the state, he is, most probably, perusing Homer in the original language; and the immortal bard, or the " conspirator," is, perhaps, dandling a child in his arms, or, peradventure, if it be in the summer season, playing at trap-ball on the grass!

In person Mr. Fox is somewhat above the middle size, and, of late years, is rather inclined to be fat. His features which are strongly marked, exhibit an appearance of shrewdness and ability; and his eye in the midst of debate, or the animation of converse, flashes with fire.

No portrait has been oftener painted, and he must be a very inaccurate artist, indeed, who cannot hit off the saturnine complexion, the piercing look, and the arch and bushy eye-brow of the great commoner. The chissel, as well as the pencil, has been employed in giving durability to his resemblance, for a great number of busts have been executed, of late years, in marble, by * Nollekens; and one in *terra cotta* has still more recently been finished by Merchant, as a model for a gem.

The following dedication to Mr. Fox, is by one of the greatest scholars of the age:

CAROLO JACOBO FOX.

Quòd veram illam & absolutam eloquentiam
non modò colueris, sed cultam, qua potuit,

---

* No less than thirty-two have been finished by this sculptor, at sixty guineas each, for the Empress of Russia, the Dukes of Devonshire and Portland, Lord Albemarle, &c. &c. &c.

ad

ad Salutem Patriæ Dignitatemque tuendam contulerit;
Quòd in fufcipiendis five amicitiis, five inimicitiis,
has femper voluerit Mortales
habere, illas Sempirernas;
Quòd Mente folida invictaque permanferit in propofito,
atque improborum fpreverit minas;
Quòd in Caufa, quæ maxime popularis effe debuiffet,
Non populariter ille quidem,
ut alii ficte et fallaciter populares,
fed ftrenue ac fortiter verfatus fit;
Quòd denique, in fœdiffimo illo
Optimi prudentiffimique Senatus naufragio,
Id demum, imò id folum,
quod turpe effet,
Miferum exiftimârit, atque adeò cum bonis
Libere πολιτευτίον ftatuerit,
potius quam periculofe & fimulate & cupide
inter malos,
Librum huncce ea, qua par eft, Obfervantia.
D. D. D.
A. E. A. O.

THE RIGHT HONOURABLE WILLIAM PITT,

CHANCELLOR OF THE EXCHEQUER, &c. &c.

IT is, at all times, a difficult, delicate, and sometimes a dangerous task, to attempt the delineation of the life and character of a minister of state. The passions of the generality of men are too much agitated to attend to cool discussion while they contemplate the immediate political situation of their country, more especially in a period like the present, so replete with important and singular events.

The subject of this article is, in many points of view, the most conspicuous prime minister which modern Europe has ever beheld, whether he be considered in respect to his very splendid talents, his wonderful success in life, or the singular events which have occurred during his administration. His history will include the annals of the most remarkable epoch in modern times; and he will be justly deemed, by future ages, the lever which gave motion to the proceedings of all the cabinets of Europe. A large share of the good or evil which may result, will be solely ascribed to his councils. In short, he may be considered as uniting the striking qualities of the Cecils, the Walsinghams, the Richlieus, the Mazarines, the Straffords, the Louvois, the Alberonies, and the Walpoles; to none of these is he inferior in abilities, in eloquence, or in the various arts and consummate policy of the courtier and the statesman.

This country never had a minister of whom such different opinions have been entertained, as of the present, and indeed no former one was ever placed in such critical circumſtances. The hiſtory of this illuſtrious ſtateſman, compriſing, as it neceſſarily muſt, a review of his politica life, will be reſorted to, at ſome future period, as one of the moſt intereſting and inſtructive performances that can occupy the attention of mankind.

William Pitt, the illuſtrious Earl of Chatham, had two ſons, one of whom, the preſent able miniſter, is the youngeſt. He was born May 8, 1759, at a time when his father's glory was at its zenith; and when, in conſequence of the wiſdom and integrity of his councils, and the vigour and promptitude of his meaſures, Britiſh valour reigned triumphant in every part of the globe.

On the acceſſion of his preſent majeſty, that great ſtateſman, in conſequence of new arrangements, chiefly occaſioned by the riſing influence of the Earl of Bute, retired from the ſtation which he had ſo honourably filled; and conſigned his elder ſon to the inſtructions of able tutors, he devoted his own time to the education of WILLIAM, on a ſtrong and well-founded perſuaſion (as he was in the habit of ſaying) that "he would one day encreaſe " the glory of the name of PITT."

His claſſical knowledge Mr. Pitt acquired under the care of a private tutor at Burton Pynſent, the ſeat of his father; and the Earl took great pleaſure in teaching him, while ſtill a youth, to argue with logical preciſion, and ſpeak with elegance and force. He judiciouſly accuſtomed him to the practice of mahing accurate enquiries reſpecting every ſubject that caught his attention, and taught him not to remain ſatiſfied with a ſuperficial obſervation of appearances.

This leſſon brought him into an early practice of cool and patient inveſtigation, rarely, if ever acquired, by thoſe who prefer the trappings of eloquence, and the ſhowy ornaments of language, to plain ſober diction, and pertinent matter of fact.

Under

Under such an able paternal tutor, an acute mind could not fail to imbibe a store of sound practical knowledge. The earl, with his usual perspicuity, fancied he saw in his son a future statesman, and in all probability, a future minister of his country also. It was a laudable ambition in a father, and to gratify it he spared no exertions; directing his whole attention to the great object of rendering his son accomplished in all things requisite to form a public character, and to preserve the lustre already attached to the name of WILLIAM PITT.

He, himself, frequently entered into forced disputations with him, and encouraged him to argue with others, upon subjects far above what could be expected from his years. In the management of these arguments, his father would never cease to press him with difficulties; nor would he permit him to stop, till the subject of contention was completely exhausted. By being inured to this method, the son acquired that quality which is of the first consequence in public life—a sufficient degree of firmness, and presence of mind, as well as a ready delivery, in which he was wonderfully aided by nature.

That he might have all the benefits of education which this country could give him, and, at the some time, by a rapid progress through the necessary studies, qualify himself early for the senate, he was taken at between fourteen and fifteen years of age from his father's roof, and from the care of a very enlightened and worthy clergyman, Mr. (now Dr.) Wilson, and sent to Pembroke college, Cambridge, where he was admitted under the tuition of Messrs. Turner and Prettyman, both very able and well qualified tutors, and willing to second, to the utmost of their power, the intentions of his father. Mr. Prettyman was also his private tutor, and a better choice could not have been made, as far as classical and mathematical knowledge were concerned. For eloquence he could not look

up

up to either of his tutors; but his father's example and precepts required no farther affistance. In Cambridge he was a model to the young nobility and fellow-commoners; and it was not doubted that if the privileges of his rank had not exempted him from the ufual exercifes for the bachelor's degree, he would have been found among the firft competitors for academical honours. On his admiffion, according to cuftom, to his mafter's degree, the public orator found it needlefs to fearch into his genealogy, or even to dwell much on the virtues of his father, the eyes of the univerfity were fixed on the youth; the enraptured audience affented to every encomium, and each breaft was filled with the livelieft prefentiments of future greatnefs. To the honour of Mr. Pitt it muft be fpoken, that he has been duly fenfible of the care taken of his rifing years. His inftructors have received repeated marks of his acknowledgment. Dr. Wilfon, his firft inftructor, is now canon of Windfor; and one of his fons has a lucrative finecure in Jamaica. The worthy Dr. Turner is dean of Norwich; Dr. Prettyman has received the Bifhopric of Lincoln, and the Deanery of St. Paul's, and will, doubtlefs, not be overlooked in future promotions.

He was afterwards entered a ftudent at Lincoln's Inn; and made fo rapid a progrefs in his legal ftudies, as to be foon called to the bar, with every profpect of great fuccefs.

We are informed, that he once or twice went upon the Weftern circuit, and appeared as junior counfel in feveral caufes. He was, however, deftined to fill a more important ftation in the government of his country, than is ufually to be obtained through the channel of the law.

At the general election, 1780, we find him nominated by fome of the moft refpectable perfons in Cambridge as a candidate to reprefent that univerfity; but notwithftanding his high character in the univerfity, he found very few to second his pretensions. In the following year, however, he was returned for the borough of Appleby, by the interest of Sir James Lowther. On taking his seat in the House of Commons, he enlisted himself on the side of the party which had constantly opposed the minister, Lord North, and the American war, and which regarded him with a degree of veneration; recognising in his person the genius of his illustrious father revived and acting, as it were, in him.

One of his first acts, as a member of the House of Commons, was extremely well calculated to increase his popularity; this was his motion for a committee of the House, to consult upon the most effectual means to accomplish a more equal representation of the people in parliament. His propositions were, indeed, rejected; but he continued to repeat and renew them from time to time; and thus kept up the public attention to this great object, and made it more generally canvassed than it ever had been before.

On the death of the great Marquis of Rockingham, the old Whig party fell into a state of disunion, nearly bordering upon dissolution. A new arrangement took place soon after, and Lord Shelburne became the able first Lord of the Treasury, carrying along with him Mr. Pitt, who astonished the country, and, indeed, all Europe, by the phenomenon of a chancellor of the Exchequer at the age of *twenty-three!*

His popularity at this period effectually screened him from every charge which his youth and inexperience might justly have warranted, and which were strongly urged against him by the adverse faction. The situation of the country was extremely critical. The American war had become generally odious; and all hearts panted for a cessation of hostilities. This desirable object was, therefore, the first consideration with the new ministry.

The

The combined powers had recently experienced great humiliations, and consequently the opportunity was not to be lost. A general peace accordingly took place; but the terms of it were reprobated by a considerable part of the nation. On this occasion, Mr. Pitt delivered in his place a most masterly defence of himself and his colleagues, which produced a corresponding, though not successful effect. The administration, of which he was the most distinguished member, was therefore short lived. On its dissolution, the young statesman withdrew into retirement, and afterwards went abroad for some time, visiting Italy, and several of the German courts.

On the coalition's taking place, Mr. Mansfield's seat for the university became vacant, by accepting the office of solicitor-general, and Mr. Pitt determined to oppose him: with this view he went down to Cambridge; but was treated with contempt, by the heads and senior members. One threw the door almost in his face, and wondered at the impudence of the young man, thus to come down and disturb the peace of the university! From such a scene he retired in a few days, in disgust; though the assurances of support from several independent masters of arts, kept alive the few hopes remaining in his breast, of future success. A few months, however, changed the scene; the coalition ministry was thrown out, he came down in triumph to the university, was received with open arms, carried his election with a considerable majority, and was able, also, by his influence, to make Lord Euston his colleague. For a time the tergiversation of the senate was a theme of conversation;—the most notorious of the gown who changed their sides, were marked by the contempt of the unsuccessful, but laughed at their own disgrace, under the rewards of the successful candidates; mitres and stalls, and livings, became the portion of the Cambridge men. But few of the independent masters who would

have

have supported him when out of power, and did support him on his accession to the ministry, were to be found among his supporters at the next election; they considered him to have given up those principles of liberty, and that zeal for the reform of parliament, which had, with his great talents, entitled him to their notice.

An occasion, suddenly offered, in 1784, for bringing Mr. Pitt forward once more on the great theatre of politics, as a candidate for fame and power. The British dominions in India had long been in an alarming situation, and it was generally admitted that an immediate remedy was indispensably necessary to preserve them. With this view, Mr. Fox, then Secretary of State, formed, digested, and brought forward his India bill, which he carried through its several stages with a high hand.

The coalition ministry, as composed of such an heterogeneous mixture, notwithstanding their majority in the House of Commons, were generally obnoxious to the nation, and this bill was particularly offensive to the great body whom it immediately affected. Lord North and his new allies were accordingly dismissed, and Mr. Pitt became Premier, assisted by the advice of Lord Thurlow, as keeper of the great seal—arrangements which, at that time, were however, only considered as temporary.

He then astonished the commercial and political world, by his own India bill! He had, however, the mortification to find the majority of the House of Commons against him; and he was placed in the peculiar situation of a minister acting with a small minority, and that too in opposition to the strongest confluence of talents ever combined against any administration. He, however, remained firm in his seat amidst a general confusion; and though the House had petitioned his majesty to dismiss his ministers, our young premier ventured to inform the representatives of the nation that their petition could not be complied with!

This

This struggle between the commons and the crown was of the greatest importance; but the people at large were of opinion that the former encroached upon the regal prerogatives; and on the question being in a manner thrown into their hands by a dissolution of parliament, a new one was returned, which changed the majority, and preserved the minister in a post which he has maintained ever since!

Various public measures have, of course, during a period of fourteen years, been brought forward by this active minister; to notice which, would far exceed the bounds of a memoir so limited in its object as the present. They are incorporated into the history of his country, and familiarly recollected by his contemporaries.

The commercial treaty with France was a bold scheme, and evinced deep political and mercantile knowledge. But the most critical circumstance in the annals of Mr. Pitt's administration, and that on which his biographer should dwell the most, is the period when the regal powers were, in a manner, unhappily suspended, and all the wisdom of the legislature was required to form a regency. It was a crisis not only novel, but of extreme magnitude, as likely to become the precedent for future times; no such incident having till then occurred in the annals of our history.

Some statesmen would have worshipped the rising sun. Mr. Pitt and his colleagues, however, pursued a different course, and thereby added greatly to their popularity, and effectually secured themselves in power.

If, on some occasions, he has courted the favour of the people, he certainly has not always sacrificed at their shrine. He appears, indeed, to have a proper conception of the value in which popular esteem is to be held, but to be sensible that it ought not to influence the conduct of a legislator, when it is evidently repugnant to the true interests of the country.

When

When the revolution took place in France, the situation of the prime minister of this kingdom became once more extremely critical. Perhaps it was fortunate for the country, that the administration at that time enjoyed the good opinion of both king and people; as violent contentions of party-spirit, at such a juncture, might have led to consequences very injurious to the happy constitutional government of Great Britain.

The situation of Europe has assumed a new face, since the monarchy of France was shaken from its ancient basis. A war has ensued totally different from all former wars. In judging, therefore, of the merits of those who are concerned in managing the affairs of the nation, it is impossible to have recourse either to precedents, or to old political principles. A new mode of action, a new scheme of politics was to be devised, and adapted to the existing circumstances.

If any merit be due to boldness of invention, to vigour of execution, to wide extension of plans, and to firmness and perseverance of conduct, certainly the present administration has an undoubted claim to public gratitude.

An attention to commerce has greatly distinguished Mr. Pitt's administration, particularly during the present contest. Perhaps there is no man in the kingdom better acquainted with the principles of trade than he is. The oldest and most experienced merchants have been astonished at his readiness in conversing with them upon subjects which they thought themselves exclusively masters of. Many who have waited upon him in full confidence that they should communicate some new and important information upon matters of trade, have, to their great surprize, found him minutely and intimately acquainted with all those points to which they conceived he was a stranger. By the close attention which he has uniformly paid to the mercantile interests, he has certainly secured to himself an exclusive basis of support,

which

which has enabled him not only to resist a most vigorous opposition, but to carry into effect financial measures that, till his time, were deemed impracticable.

Some men have charged him with political apostacy, on the ground of his having abandoned, if not opposed, the project of a parliamentary reform. If he really considers such a reform as no longer necessary, it will be difficult to exonerate him from this heavy accusation. But there certainly is a great difference between absolute apostacy, and an occasional cessation from a particular system of opinions or line of conduct. It does not follow that Mr. Pitt is an enemy to necessary reform, because he considers the existing circumstances of the country as too critical to admit the trial of the experiment.

As a public speaker, Mr. Pitt is not to be characterised by overstrained parallels drawn from the orators of antiquity. He possesses more of the elegance and grace of Cicero, than of the fire of Demosthenes. He is, however, more of the acute logician, than of the persuasive rhetorician. His voice, though clear and powerful, possesses not the modulations that charm the ear, and steal upon the heart; moreover, he seems incapable of producing any grand effect upon the passions of his auditors, and he is at times extremely careless in his choice of expressions. His language is generally good, but he sometimes descends into vulgarity and incorrectness. All his deficiencies, however, are more than counterbalanced by a conclusive and forcible method of reasoning, by a facility of stating his arguments, which makes them not only conceivable to the meanest understanding, but gives them frequently a precision and vigour which may be pronounced irresistible.

The Premier also possesses an advantage of inestimable value, in a minister of state, namely, a great command over his temper, added to much coolness, during the ardour of debate.

This

This enables him to reply clearly and particularly to the arguments of his opponents, and to defend his own cause by often turning their own weapons upon themselves. Though he is confident, and frequently, it must be confessed, even arrogant in his speeches, which sometimes provokes the opposition orators to use harsh language, yet he seldom loses his own temper, or retorts in anger.

His action is not strictly graceful, which is in some measure owing to the disadvantage of an exterior, which however dignified, is yet not amiably winning, for he is very tall, and deficient in *en bon point*. His countenance is also severe and forbidding, expressive indeed (in the language of physiognomists) of a capacious mind, and inflexible resolution; but also of a too lofty and perhaps unbending spirit.

Mr. Pitt forms in all points a direct contrast to his great political opponent: and it is certainly a curious circumstance, that two such extraordinary men should be as opposite in their private characters as in their public career. In debate Mr. Fox is vehement, Mr. Pitt cool. The one is frank and open, the other close and reserved. The urbanity of the ex-minister gains him friends among all parties, the *hauteur* and *sang froid* of the premier does not conciliate even his associates. Mr. Pitt is the same guarded and unbending politician in his social hours that he is in the House of Commons.

In private life, his sole pleasure are of an official and convivial nature.

Ambition is the ruling and master-passion of his soul, before which every other sinks into insignificance: at the shrine of this goddess, and at that of Bacchus, he is supposed alone to pay his devotions. That his health and talents may not suffer by the latter, and that his country may prosper under the influence of the former, is the earnest wish of the writer of this article.

J. W.

ERASMUS

ERASMUS DARWIN, M.D. F.R.S.

IS the fon of a gentleman of landed property, near Newark-upon-Trent. From a country fchool he was transferred to the univerfity, and entered at St. John's, Cambridge, where, being intended for the practice of medicine, he took the degree of M.B. in 1755; and in his thefis defended the opinion that the motion of the heart and arteries are produced by the immediate *ftimulus* of the blood.

On the death of the prefent king's father, when all the men of talents in the nation bewailed the lofs of a prince whom they had fondly confidered as a fecond Mæcenas, he contributed to the Cambridge collection of odes and elegies: but his verfes on that occafion do not feem to have argued any great chance for celebrity, as they were undiftinguifhed from the exertions of far inferior men, and afforded no great promife of future excellence.

After an education admirably adapted to his intended profeffion, and a previous degree of M.D. Dr. Darwin determined to practife, and finding the bufinefs of the capital, entirely monopolized by a few men of celebrity, brought into notice by the zeal of friends, family connexion, and the recommendation and intereft of the great, he determined to fettle in the country. Luckily for the city of Litchfield, that place was pitched upon for the fcene of his labours, and he refided there for a great number of years. If he ftill retained a tafte for poetry, it was either carefully fuppreffed, or the favours of the mufe concealed; he, however, diftinguifhed himfelf as a philofopher and phyfician, for as far back as 1758, he publifhed in vol. 50 of the

Philofophical

Philosophical Transactions, " An Attempt to confute the Opinion of Henry Earle, concerning the Ascent of Vapour; and " An Account of the Cure of a periodical Hæmopte, by keeping the patient awake." This was followed by " Experiments on Animal fluids in the exhausted receiver."

In the mean time, he had bred his son Charles, a promising young man, to his own profession, and sent him to Edinburgh, at that time, as now, the great European school of physic. There he was unfortunately carried off by a fever, at the very time he was enquiring into the nature and cure of diseases, before he had attained the 20th year of his age! To the sorrowing father was left the mournful task of being the editor of his posthumous work; and he accordingly published in 1780, " Experiments establishing a Criterion between Mucilaginous and Purulent Matter: And an Account of the Retrograde Motions of the Absorbent Vessels of Animal Bodies in some diseases."

In 1782, the Botanical society of Lichfield published Linnæus's " System of Vegetables," which is thought to have been chiefly the production of Dr. Darwin, one of its two principal members.

Early in 1789, Dr. Darwin, enlisted again by science in the train of the Muses, burst forth like a comet in the hemisphere of poetry, by the publication of the " Botanical Garden;" Part II.* of which, containing " the Loves of the Plants," then made its first appearance. The idea of the sexual system had long before been elucidated by the great Swedish naturalist; and it indeed seems to have been coeval with, and most probably, long anterior to, Claudian:

---

* Four editions of this volume, and three of the second have been already published.

" Vivunt

" Vivunt in Venerem frondes; nemus omne per altum,
" Felix arbor amat ; nutant ad mutua Palmæ
" Fædera, populeo fufpiret Populus ictu,
" Et Platani Platanis, Alnoque affibelat Alnus."

The poem confifts of four cantos; the three firft of which are followed by a dialogue, and the preface contains a fummary of the Linnæan arrangement. The intention of this part of the work is to render an attachment to Botanical ftudies at once more common and more delightful.

" BOTANIC MUSE ! who, in his latter age,
" Led by your airy hand the Swedifh fage,
" Bade his keen eye your fecret haunts explore,
" On dewy dell, high wood, and founding fhore ;
" Say on each leaf, how tiny Graces dwell ;
" How laugh the Pleafures in a bloffom's bell ;
" How infect loves arife on cobweb wings,
" Aim their light fhafts, and point their little ftings."

The fcientific turn of the notes, and the agreeable medium of the poetry,* excited an uncommon degree of curiofity for the publication of Part I. containing " the Economy of Vegetation," which, on account of fome experiments, was delayed until 1791. On this occafion he recurs to Lucretius:

" It Ver, et Venus; et Veneris prænuncius ante
" Pennatus Graditur Zephyrus Veftigia propter,
" Flora quibus mater, præfpergens ante Viai
" Cuncta coloribus egregiis et odoribus opplet."

* Some of tie lines are peculiarly expreffive, fuch as
" On her fair bofom fits the Demon ape
" Erect, and balances his bloated fhape ;
" *Rolls in their marble orbs his gorgon-eyes,*
" *And drinks with leathern ears her tender cries.*"
The " vampire-wings" of the Ague, " the young wonder," with which the cherubs, while riding on their little reeds,
" ————————touch the fliding fnail
" *Admire his eye-tipped horns, and painted mail,*" &c.
are expreffions peculiarly felicitous.

At the beginning of Canto I. the genius of the place, the scenery of which is borrowed from a garden, about a mile from Lichfield, where a cold bath was erected by Sir John Floyer, solicits the appearance of the goddess who presides over botany, who, on her descent, is received by Spring and the Elements. Then follows the explosion of chaos, the revolution of the stars, the appearance of lightning, the rain-bow, luminous flowers, the glow-worm, fire-fly, electric-eel, medusa, steam-engine, &c.

The following lines deserve great praise; and not the least merit is, that posterior discoveries seem to be fast realizing the predictions of the poet:

" Soon shall thy arm, UNCONQUER'D STEAM! afar
" Drag the slow barge, or drive the rapid car;
" Or on wide-waving wings, expanded bear
" Thy flying chariot through the fields of air.
" ———Fair crews triumphant leaning from above,
" Shall wave their flutt'ring 'kerchiefs as they move;
" Or warrior-bands alarm the gaping crowd,
" And armies shrink beneath the shadowy cloud.
" So mighty Hercules o'er many a clime
" Wav'd his huge mace in Virtue's cause sublime,
" Unmeasur'd strength with early art combin'd,
" Aw'd, serv'd, protected, and amaz'd mankind.——
" First," &c.

The second Canto commences with an address to the Gnomes. We then find the earth thrown from a volcano of the sun; its atmosphere, ocean, and journey through the zodiac are described. We then hear of primeval islands, paradise, or the golden age; the first great earthquakes, continents raised from the sea, &c.

The third, and last Canto, commences with an address to the Nymphs; next follows the theory of rain, and of tides; an account of marine animals, rivers, boiling fountains in Iceland, and warm medicinal springs, such as Buxton, &c. &c.

It is easy to perceive, in this very interesting performance, that Dr. Darwin has had recourse to the Rosicrucian machinery, in his "Botanic Garden," for the same reason that Pope adopted it, in his celebrated poem of "the Rape of the Lock." In the formation of the planets, he employs the doctrines of Buffon; in his natural history, he bends at the shrine of the Swede, while he follows the new doctrines respecting air, from the Priestleian and Lavoiserian systems.

A deep attention to botany, and a thorough conviction of the advantages arising from system, induced Dr. Darwin to turn his mind towards the improvement of his own profession, and to become, as it were, the Linnæus of Medicine. Impressed with this novel idea, in the beginning of 1794 he published the first volume of his "Zoonomia, or the Laws of Organic Life," in which, leaving his former work in possession of the vegetable world, he proposes " to reduce the facts belonging to animal life into classes, " orders, genera, and species; and by comparing them " with each other, to unravel the theory of diseases."

Much preliminary matter is given in separate sections, respecting the immediate organs of sense; and an able theory of ideas follows. We next meet with the laws of animal *causation*, and an exemplification of the transitions of irritative into sensative, and of sensative into voluntary motions; on this occasion, we find a dissertation on *unperceived ideas*, and learn, " that all our perceptions are ideas " excited by irritation, and succeeded by sensation." Respecting the doctrines of *stimulus* and *exertion*, the author is a great advocate for the system of the late unfortunate Dr. Brown, which he ably and amply elucidates and explains.

Proceeding in an ascending ratio, he considers sleep and revery, giddiness and drunkenness; with an account of the diseases arising from the last of these, &c. &c.

In 1796, vol. II. made its appearance; and as the former may be confidered as ftrictly theoretical, this contains a practical application of the principles, and is divided into two grand fections: containing, firft, the nature and cure of particular difeafes; and, fecondly, the operation of medicines.

Of this work, it has been faid by a celebrated profeffor of the medical art, that the " Zoonomia bids fair to do " for phyfic, what the Principia of Sir Ifaac Newton has " done for natural philofophy:" after this, it would be folly to add our mite of praife.

Dr. Darwin now refides at Derby, where he enjoys an extenfive practice, and univerfal efteem. While his ample and capacious mind grafps the grandeft operations of nature, he can yet condefcend to comparatively infinite fubjects, provided they be connected with human happinefs. A proof of this exifts in the attention lately paid by him to a fubject in which the deareft interefts of fociety are involved—the education of females—or the beft means of making affectionate daughters, good wives, and tender mothers!

SIR GEORGE LEONARD STAUNTON, Bart.

IS the fon of a gentleman, of fmall fortune, in the kingdom of Ireland, and was fent by his parents, early in life, to ftudy medicine at Montpelier, where he took the degree of M.D. After he had finifhed his ftudies, he repaired to London, where he employed himfelf in tranflating fome medical effays, written by Dr. Storck of Vienna; and, with wonderful facility in the knowledge of different languages, he at the fame time drew up in French, for the *Journal Etranger*, a comparifon between the literature of England and France.

About the year 1762, Dr. Staunton embarked for the Weft Indies, as we find from a farewel letter written to him by the late Dr. Johnfon, given by Mr. Bofwell, in his life of that great man. This letter is replete with excellent advice, and does equal credit to the writer and the perfon to whom it is addreffed.

Dr. S. refided for fome years in the Weft Indies, where he acquired a genteel addition to his fortune by the practice of phyfic; purchafed an eftate in Grenada, which he cultivated; and had the good fortune to obtain the friendfhip of the prefent Lord Macartney, governor of that ifland, to whom he acted as fecretary, and continued in that capacity until the capture of it by the French, when they both embarked for Europe. Having ftudied the law, Sir George, while at Grenada, ferved the office of Attorney General of the ifland.

Soon after Lord Macartney's arrival in England, he was appointed governor of Madrafs, and took Mr. S. with him (for he feems now to have loft the appellation of *Doctor*) as his fecretary. In this capacity, Mr. S. had feveral opportunities

portunities of difplaying his abilities and intrepidity, particularly as one of the commiffioners fent to treat of peace with Tippoo Sultaun, and in the feizure of General Stuart, who feemed to have been preparing to act by Lord Macartney as had been before done by the unfortunate Lord Pigot. Mr. S. was fent with a fmall party of feapoys to arreft the general, which he effected with great fpirit and prudence, and without bloodfhed.

On his return to England, the India Company fettled on him a penfion of 500*l. per annum*, the king created him a baronet of Ireland, and the Univerfity of Oxford conferred on him the degree of L.L.D.

It having been refolved to fend an embaffy to China, Lord Macartney was felected for that purpofe, and he took his old friend and countryman along with him, who was not only appointed fecretary to the embaffy, but had alfo the title of envoy-extraordinary and minifter-plenipotentiary beftowed on him, in order to be able to fupply the place of the ambaffador, in cafe of any unfortunate accident.

The events of this embaffy, which on the whole proved rather unpropitious, are well known, and are given to the public in two quarto volumes, written by Sir George[*]. When we confider the fhort time he took to compile them, and the fevere illnefs he actually laboured under at the time, and with which he was attacked foon after his return, we cannot withhold our praife and approbation.

As a further proof of the efteem in which the India Company held Sir George Staunton, they appointed his fon, who accompanied him in the voyage, a writer to China; and had the father's health permitted, he would again have attended Lord Macartney in fome honourable

---

[*] The Dutch Eaft India Company have fince undertaken a fimilar embaffy, and we underftand the very interefting narrative of it by VAN BRAAM, will fhortly make its appearance in the Englifh language.

and confidential ſtation to his government at the Cape of Good Hope.

The memoirs of Sir George Staunton, if drawn up at full length, would exhibit a ſtrong and ardent mind, labouring occaſionally under difficulties, and ſurmounting dangers by patience, talents, and intrepidity. His conduct in the ſeizure of General Stuart, demonſtrates his reſolution and preſence of mind; and when treating with TIPPOO, he had the addreſs to induce M. Suffrein to ſuſpend hoſtilities, even before he had received advice from his court of the treaty of peace being ſigned between Great Britain and France.

MR. TAYLOR, THE PLATONIST.

THE subject of this article from his enthusiastick and undiverted attachment to the religion and philosophy of Plato, has been called by different writers, "the modern Pletho *," "the apostle of Paganism †," and "the gentile priest of England ‡."

This very singular man was born in London, in the year 1758, of obscure but worthy parents; and though in his literary career he has accomplished Herculean labours, yet we are informed that his body has been from his childhood weak and diseased; for at the early period of six years of age, alarming symptoms of a consumption induced his family to remove him for three years to Staffordshire. On returning thence, in his ninth year, he was sent to St. Paul's school, to be educated for a dissenting minister. Here, it seems, he soon gave indications of that contemplative turn of mind, and that aversion to merely verbal disquisitions, which have since become such predominant features in his character. In proof of this, Mr. Ryder, one of the masters of the school, whenever a sentence occurred remarkably moral or grave, in any classick which young Taylor was translating to him, would always preface it by saying to the youthful Platonist: "Come, here is something worthy the attention of a philosopher §."

* In the second edition of the Curiosities of Literature.

† See Analytical Review of his Sallust.

‡ See Pursuits of Literature.

§ Thus too, at an early period, one of the first scholars of the age, discovered the *critical* turn of his mind: for when, on reading the Latin Testament, *at Jesus* was printed instead of *ait Jesus*, he shrewdly conjectured that *at* must be a verb, and be derived from *ao*.

The

The boy, indeed, was so disgusted with the arbitrary manner in which the dead languages are taught in that, as well as in all other public schols, that he entreated, and at length prevailed on his father to take him home, and abandon his design of educating him for the ministry. The parent complied, indeed, but with great reluctance, as he considered the office of a dissenting minister, the most desirable and the most enviable employment upon earth!

About this time Mr. T. happened to become acquainted with a Miss Morton, the eldest daughter of a respectable coal merchant in Doctor's Commons, for whom, although he was but twelve years of age, he conceived such an attachment, as neither time nor distance could dissolve nor impair. This young lady (his present wife) had received an elegant education, and united with an agreeable person, uncommon modesty, liberality, and artless manners. Mr. T. has often declared that he was then as deeply in love as the most famous hero of romance, and that to see and converse with his adored fair one, formed the very summit of his wishes.

During Mr. T.'s residence at home, while his father was yet undetermined as to his future situation in life, he happened to meet with Ward's Young Mathematician's Guide, and was so struck, in looking over the book, with the singularity of *negative quantities*, when multiplied together producing *positive* ones, that he immediately conceived a strong desire to become acquainted with mathematics. His father, however, who was deeply skilled in modern theology, but utterly unacquainted with this sublime and most useful species of learning, was, it seems, averse to his son's engaging in such a course of study; but Mr. T.'s ardour soon enabled him to triumph over all opposition, by devoting the hours of rest to mathematical lucubrations, though to accomplish this he was obliged to conceal a *tinder-box* under his pillow.

To

To this early acquaintance with those leading branches of mathematical sciences, arithmetic, algebra, and geometry, Mr. T. ascribes his present unrivalled attachment to the philosophy of Plato, and all the substantial felicity of his life.

About this time, viz. at the age of fifteen, Mr. T. was placed under an uncle-in-law at Sheerness, who happened to be one of the officers of that dock yard. Here at his leisure hours, which were but few, he still pursued the study of the speculative part of mathematics; for he was of opinion that those sciences were degraded when applied to practical affairs, without then knowing that the same sentiment had been adopted by Pythagoras, Plato, and Archimedes. Here, likewise, he read Bolingbroke and Hume, and by studying their works became a convert to the *sceptical philosophy*.

The behaviour, however, of his uncle-in-law was so very tyrannical, and his opportunities for the acquisition were so very inadequate to his thirst for knowledge, that after having been in what he considered a state of slavery during three years, he determined to break his fetters, and, as he could find no other refuge from oppression, cast himself once more into the arms of the church.

For this purpose he left Sheerness, and became, during the space of two years, a pupil of one of the most celebrated dissenting preachers. Under this gentleman he recovered his knowledge of the rudiments of the Latin and Greek tongues, but made no great advances in the attainment of those languages, as his mind, naturally propense to the study of things, required an uncommon stimulus, to make it stoop to an attention to words. This stimulus, the philosophy of Plato and Aristotle could alone inspire.

Mr. T. it seems, during this course of ministerial study renewed with redoubled ardour his acquaintance with Miss M.; and what indeed is singular in the extreme, was able

able to unite in amicable league, courtship and study. Hence he applied himself to Greek and Latin in the day, paid his addresses to his fair one in the evening, and had the courage to begin and read through the Latin quarto of Simpson's Conic Sections at night.

About this time Mr. T. entered on the study of the modern philosophy, and thinking himself qualified by his knowledge of the more abstruse parts of mathematics, to understand the system of the universe as delivered in the *Principia* of Newton, he began to read that difficult work. We are informed, however, that he soon closed the book with disgust, exclaiming " Newton is indeed a great ma-" thematician, but no philosopher!" He was principally induced, it seems, to form this conclusion, by Sir Isaac's assertion * " that every the least possible particle of matter " or body, attracts all bodies at all distances; that the " being, whatever it is, that attracts or impels bodies to-" wards each other, proceeds from those bodies to which " it belongs, and penetrates the whole substance of the " bodies on which it acts." It appeared to him, that from this assertion it must inevitably follow, that bodies act immediately or by themselves, without the intervention of any other being, in a place where they are not, since attraction is the *immediate* action of attracting bodies ; that they thus act in many places at the same time; that they penetrate each other; and that the least particle of matter is extended as far as the limits of the universe: all which consequences he considered as glaringly absurd.

Thus far the stream of Mr. T.'s life may be said to have run with an equal tenour, limpid and unruffled, compared with its course in the succeeding period, in which it resembled some dark river rolling with impetuous rage to the main.

The time now drew nigh, in which Mr. T. was to leave his fair one for the university. But as her father, in his

* Prop. 6, 7, & 8, L. 3.

absence,

abſence, intended to marry her to a man of large fortune, who had made her the offer of his hand, Miſs M. to ſecure herſelf from the *tyrannical* exertion of parental authority, generouſly conſented to unite herſelf to our philoſopher on condition that nothing further than the marriage ceremony took place, till he had finiſhed his ſtudies at Aberdeen. This he immediately aſſented to, and the indiſſoluble knot was tied.

But when the fates are adverſe, how vain are the moſt prudent projects! how unfortunate the moſt generous intentions! The low cunning of Mr. T.'s mother-in-law diſcovered the ſecret, ſoon after the union of the platonic pair; who, from a combination of eccleſiaſtical indignation with parental rage, were for a time expoſed to the inſult of undeſerved reproach, and the bitterneſs of real diſtreſs.

We are happy to find, however, that Mr. and Mrs. T. exculpate their parents on this occaſion: Mr. T. entirely aſcribing his father's conduct to the malicious miſrepreſentation of his mother in-law, and the anger of the church, and Mrs. T. to the unnatural and ſelfiſh conduct of ſome of her very near relations.

Whether Mr. T.'s great averſion to preſbyterians and preſbyterian miniſters, originated in this or ſome other circumſtance, we are unable to determine. Certain, however, it is, that he has ever ſince conſidered the clergy of this deſcription, as men implacable in their reſentments, whom neither pity can ſoften, nor penitence appeaſe; and has often been heard to ſay, that of all the chriſtian ſects, the members of the church of England are the beſt, and the preſbyterians the worſt.

Such indeed was the diſtreſſed ſituation of this young couple at this period, that we are informed they had no more than ſeven ſhillings a week to ſubſiſt on, for nearly a twelvemonth! This was owing to the baſe artifice of
one

one of Mrs. T.'s relatives, who was left executor, and who prevailed on her father, at this time in a dying state, to let him pay her what he had left her as he pleased. Mr. T. endeavoured indeed to obtain employment as an usher to a boarding-school; but it was some time before he was able to effect this, as he was abandoned both by friends and relatives, and could not even borrow ten shillings and sixpence, which it seems is the usual fee of those who procure such situations.

At length he was separated from his partner in affliction, and settled as usher to a boarding-school at Paddington. As his embarrassments were such, that he was unable to remove Mrs. T. from Camberwell, where she then resided, and the only time he was permitted to see her was on Saturday afternoon, he could enjoy but little of her company. This little, however, was doubtless dear in proportion to its brevity, and the remembrance of past pain would, it may be presumed, be lost in the overflowings of reciprocal love.

Mrs. T.'s affection was, indeed, as we are informed, so great for her unfortunate husband, that though then in a state of pregnancy, she almost deprived herself of the necessaries of life, that she might purchase out of her weekly pittance of seven shillings a comfortable dinner for Mr. T. on Saturday; and letters, it seems, during this painful separation passed between them, replete with sentiments which express the most tender and disinterested regard.

Mr. T. however, finding the situation of an usher in itself extremely disagreeable, and when attended with such a separation from his partner in calamity, intolerable, determined if possible to obtain a less irksome employment; and at length, by the exertion of his few friends, he obtained a clerk's place in a respectable banking-house in the city. In this situation, however, he at first suffered greatly; for as his income was but fifty pounds a year, and this

paid

paid quarterly, and as he had not any money to spare for himself, and could not from his embarrassments quit his lodging at Camberwell, he was unable to procure nutriment in the course of the day, adequate to the great labours he endured. Hence, he was so exhausted by the time he had reached home in the evening, that he frequently fell senseless on the floor.

We are informed that Mr. T. soon after he was settled in this employment, took a house at Walworth, by the assistance of a friend, who had been his schoolfellow; finding a residence at some small distance from town, necessary for his own health, and that of Mrs. T. and much more favourable to the cultivation of his mind, of which he never seems to have lost sight, even amidst the lassitude of bodily weakness, the pain incident to uncommon fatigue, and the immediate pressure of want.

About this time Mr. T's studies, it seems, were chiefly confined to chemistry. Of all the authors in this branch of natural philosophy, he was most attached to Becher, whose *Physica Subterranea*, he read with great avidity, and became a complete convert to the doctrines of that illustrious chemist. He did not, however, neglect mathematics; but, in consequence of having thought much on the quadrature of the circle, and believing he had discovered a method by which the rectification of it might be geometrically, though not arithmetically, obtained, he found means to publish a quarto pamphlet on that subject, which he entitled " A new Method of reasoning in Geometry." The substance of this pamphlet, as it did not attract the attention of the public, he has since given to the world in a note, in the first volume of his translation of Proclus on Euclid.

Hitherto Mr. Taylor's studies may be considered as merely preparatory to those speculations, which were to distinguish him in the literary world; at least, they are

considered

considered in this light by the followers of Plato. It appears too, that, without knowing it, he was led to the myſtick diſcipline of that ſublime philoſopher, in the exact order preſcribed by his diſciples; for he began with ſtudying the works of Ariſtotle. He was induced, it ſeems, to engage in this courſe of ſtudy, by a paſſage in Sir Kenelm Digby's treatiſe " on Bodies and Man's Soul," in which he ſays, " that the name of Ariſtotle ought never " to be mentioned by ſcholars but with reverence, on ac- " count of his incomparable worth." This eulogium from a man who was very far from being a Peripatetic, determined Mr. T. to enter on the ſtudy of Ariſtotle, as ſoon as he could procure any of his works, and had ſufficiently recovered his knowledge of Greek.

By a fortunate circumſtance, he ſoon met with a copy of that philoſopher's Phyſics, and before he had read a page, was ſo enamoured with his pregnant brevity, accuracy, and depth, that he reſolved to make the ſtudy of Ariſtotle's philoſophy the great buſineſs of his life. Such, indeed, was his avidity to accompliſh this deſign, that he was ſoon able to read that great maſter in the original; and has often been heard to ſay, that he learned Greek rather through the Greek philoſophy, than the Greek philoſophy through Greek.

However, as he was engaged every day in the banking-houſe till at leaſt ſeven in the evening, and ſometimes till nine or ten, he was obliged to devote part of the night to ſtudy. Hence we are informed, that for ſeveral years, while he was at the banker's, he ſeldom went to bed before two or three o'clock in the morning; and having, by contemplative habits, learned to diveſt himſelf during the time which he ſet apart for ſtudy of all concern about the common affairs of life, his attention was not diverted from Ariſtotle, either by the inconveniencies ariſing from his ſlender income, or ſolicitude about the buſineſs of the day.

By

By the assistance of Aristotle's Greek Interpreters, therefore, Mr. T. read the Physics, books *de Anima, de Cœlo,* Logick, Morals, and Metaphysicks, of that philosopher: for, in the opinion of Mr. T. a man might as reasonably expect to understand Archimedes, who had never read Euclid, as to comprehend either Aristotle or Plato, *who wrote obscurely from design,* without the assistance of their Greek commentators. Hence he has often been heard to say, that the folly of neglecting the invaluable commentaries of the ancients, on those philosophers, is only to be equalled by the arrogance of such as affect to despise them; since these interpreters possessed a traditional knowledge of the Greek philosophy, had books to consult on that subject which are now lost, spent their whole lives in the study of it, were men of the deepest erudition, and must be infinitely better qualified to explain the meaning of the text of Plato and Aristotle, than any modern can pretend to be, because the Greek was their native tongue. Mr. T. even carries his attachment to these interpreters so far as to assert, that from the oblivion in which they have been so long concealed, the philosophy of Plato and Aristotle has not been accurately understood for upwards of a thousand years.

Mr. T. therefore, who, by divesting himself at night of those habits of business which he had been contracting in the day, may be said in this respect to have resembled Penelope, made it a constant rule to digest what he had learned from Aristotle, while he was walking about with bills. This, when he was once master of his employment, he accomplished with great facility, without either committing mistakes, or retarding his business. We are, indeed, informed from good authority, that while in that department, he was always distinguished for accuracy and dispatch.

Mr. T. having in this manner applied himself to the study of Aristotle, and presuming that he was sufficiently instructed in his philosophy, betook himself to the more sublime speculations of Plato; considering the Peripatetick discipline, when compared with that of Plato, as bearing the relation of the less to the greater mysteries: and in this light it seems, the two philosophies were always considered by the best of the Platonists.

Mr. T. had not long entered on the study of Plato, before he met with the works of Plotinus, which he read, we are told, with an infatiable avidity, and the most rapturous delight, notwithstanding the obscurity of his diction, and the profundity of his conceptions. After having been well imbued in the doctrines of Plotinus, he betook himself to the six books of Proclus, on the Theology of Plato, a work which he found to be so uncommonly abstruse, that he has been heard to say, he did not thoroughly understand it, till he had read it thrice over.

While he was engaged in the study of Proclus, who appears upon the whole to be of all the Platonists Mr. T's greatest favourite, the celebrated Mrs. Woolstoncraft, and her friend Miss Blood, resided with our Philosopher for nearly three months. Mr. T. has been known to observe of Mrs. W. that during her stay with him, he thought her a very modest, sensible, and agreeable young lady; that she often heard him explain the doctrines of Plato, and was always pleased with his conversation on that subject; but confessed herself more inclined to an active than a contemplative life. She often too complimented him on the tranquillity of his manners, and used to call the little room which he made his study, "the abode of peace."

Mr. T. observed, that he afterwards called on her when she lived in George street, and that he has there drunk wine with her out of a *tea cup*; Mrs. W. remarking at the time, that she did not give herself the trouble to think

whether

whether a wine-glafs was not a neceffary utenfil in a houfe. He added, he has heard her fay, "that one of the condi-
"tions fhe fhould make previous to marriage, with the
"man fhe intended for her hufband, would be this—that
"he would never prefume to enter the room in which fhe
"was fitting, till he had firft knocked at the door."

But to return from thefe eccentricities, which would not have been worthy of remark in a woman of lefs merit, to our Platonift. When Mr. T. had been nearly fix years at the banking-houfe, he became fo difgufted with the fervility of the employment, and found his health fo much impaired from the combination of fevere bodily and mental efforts, added to an incurable diforder in the bladder, which he had laboured under for a long time, that he determined to emancipate himfelf, if poffible, from flavery, and live by the exertion of his talents.

In order to effect this, he turned his attention to a fubject, which he had often thought on in the days of his youth, viz. the poffibility of making a *perpetual lamp*; as he was convinced from Licetus and Bifhop Wilkins, that fuch lamps had been conftructed by the ancients. He began, therefore, to make fome experiments with phofphorus, determining for a while to defcend from mind to matter, and ftoop in order to conquer. In the courfe of thefe experiments, he found that oil and falt boiled together, in a certain proportion, formed a fluid, which when phofphorus was immerfed in it, both preferved and increafed its fplendor.

In confequence of this difcovery, he exhibited at the Free Mafons' tavern a fpecimen of phofphoric light, fufficient to read by at the diftance of a yard; but the room in which this was fhewn being fmall, and very warm from the weather, and the number of perfons that came to fee it, the phofphorus caught fire, and thus raifed a prejudice againft the invention, which could never afterwards be be removed. This exhibition, however, procured Mr. T. fuch friends * as at length enabled him to emancipate himfelf from the banker's, and procure fubfiftence for himfelf and his family by literary toil.

His firft effort after this, to emerge from obfcurity, was by compofing twelve Lectures on the Platonic philofophy, at the requeft of Mr. Flaxman, the ftatuary, who had been one of the auditors of Mr. T's Lecture on Light, and who very benevolently permitted him to read his Lectures in the largeft room of his houfe. He likewife procured for him fome very refpectable auditors, fuch as Sir William Fordyce, the Hon. Mrs Damer, Mrs. Cofway, Mr. Romney, &c. &c. and was the means of his becoming acquainted with Mr. Bennet Langton, well known for his great intimacy with the late Dr. Johnfon.

To this gentleman he read his Platonic Lectures, with which Mr. L. was fo much pleafed, as likewife with the converfation and uncommon application which our Platonift had given to ftudy, that he at length mentioned him to the king, under the appellation of *a gigantic reader*, in hopes that the rays of royal attention might be fo ftrongly collected upon him, as to diffipate the obfcurity in which he was then involved, and give additional vigour and ardour to his purfuits. Mr. L. it feems, mentioned him thrice to his Majefty, who was pleafed to enquire after his family, and to exprefs his admiration of Mr. T's. ardour and perfeverance in the purfuit of knowledge, in a fituation fo unfavourable to its acquifition as that of a banker's clerk; but we do not find that this well-meant effort on the part of Mr. L. procured our Platonift any patronage from the throne.

---

* This, we are informed, was principally through the means of Mr. Geo. Cumberland, the author of feveral ingenious works.

About this time, Mr. T. became acquainted with Mr. William Meredith of Harley-place, a circumstance which he justly considers as forming, by far, one of the most important and fortunate events of his life. This gentleman, as we are informed, in addition to an ample fortune, possesses a most elegant and liberal mind; and though concerned in a very extensive trade, has found leisure for the study of the best English writers, and the best English translations of the works of the ancients. He became deeply enamoured with the doctrines of Plato, from Mr. Sydenham's translation of some of that philosopher's dialogues; and this fondness for Plato, at length occasioned his attachment to Mr. Taylor.

We are happy in being able to assure the public on good authority, that under the very noble and singular patronage of this gentleman and his brother Mr. George Meredith, he was enabled to give the world his translation of " the Hymns of Orpheus," the " Commentaries of Proclus on Euclid," and the " ballad of Cupid and Psyche." The abilities of the latter of these gentlemen, and his knowledge of the science of architecture, which he has displayed in many beautiful drawings, have seldom been equalled, or will rarely be excelled. We likewise do not in the least doubt but that Mr. T. in the course of his stormy life, has experienced the liberality of these gentlemen upon occasions with which we are entirely unacquainted.

While Mr. T. was engaged, under the patronage of Messrs. W. and G. M. in translating and illustrating at his leisure hours the Commentaries of Proclus (for the principal part of his time was employed in teaching the Classics), the Marquis de Valady took up his residence for three or four months at Mr. T's house. As the public have already been much gratified with anecdotes* of this singular cha-

* See " Biographical Anecdotes of the Founders of the French Republick." Vol. I.

racter,

racter, and particularly with his adventures with Mr. T. we shall insert in addition to those, the following particulars, which our Platonist has been heard to mention respecting him.

The Marquis, who professed himself a rigid Pythagorean, under the notion that a community of possessions in *every thing* was perfectly Pythagoric; often conversed with Mr. T. on this subject, and once asked him, if he did not think it true Pythagorean friendship, for the wife of the married to be shared by the unmarried friend. The *hint was broad.* But Mr. T. thought proper not to take it; on the contrary he severely reprobated the idea, as entirely foreign from that purity of conduct which forms the basis of the Pythagoric and Platonic philosophy.

He likewise once told Mr. T. that if he had a son, he should make him, as soon as he had the proper use of his limbs, climb a high tree every morning for his breakfast, and afterwards fling him into a river, in order to learn him to swim.

Dining once at Mr. Bennet Langton's, with Mr. T. Mr. (now Dr.) Burney, and many other eminent scholars, he exclaimed to his friend, as soon as he left the house, " God keep me from Critics!" This was occasioned by a dispute which arose at that time respecting the propriety of the epithet *ocean stream*, which Mr. T. had made use of in his translation of one of the Orphic hymns. Mr. T. urged in his defence, that this epithet was employed by Homer, Hesiod and Plato. To this Dr. B. replied, that Homer indeed had the expression ωκεανον ποταμον, *the ocean-river*, but that a *river* was not a *stream.* Mr. T. then observed that these words were considered as synonimous by no less poets than Milton and Sir John Denham. By Milton, when speaking of the leviathan (Paradise Lost, book I.), he says,

" —— ar

" ———————— or that sea beast
" Leviathan, whom God of all his works
" Created hugest, that swim th' *ocean stream.*"

And by Denham, in the first of those famous lines on the Thames:

" O could I flow like thee, and make thy *stream*
" My great exemplar, as it is my theme."

The genius of the Marquis seemed naturally inclined to war. Whenever he went to bed, he was heard to repeat as he was going up stairs, those animated lines of Neptune to the Greeks, from the Iliad by Pope:

——————" On dastards dead to fame,
" I waste no anger, for they feel no shame !"

And if ever any one attempted to prove that modern warriors were equally heroic with the ancient ones, he would indignantly exclaim, in the words of Minerva to Tydides:

" Such Tydeus was, and such his martial fire;
" Gods! how the son degenerates from the sire !"

We find that Mr. T. soon after the Marquis left him, came into the possession of six or seven hundred pounds, in consequence of the death of a relation of his wife. A considerable part of this, it seems, Mr. T. spent in relieving the necessities of his own relations; but was not sufficiently a man of the world to know how to dispose of the remaining part of it to his own advantage. About five or six years after this, he again seems to have laboured under the pressure of want; to relieve which, with incredible diligence, he translated, and illustrated with copious introductions and some notes, five of the most abstruse of Plato's Dialogues, in the short space of about seven months; the copy of which he sold for no more than forty pounds!

After

After this, he wrote his "Differtation on the Eleufi-"nian and Bacchic Myfteries," in confequence of fome confiderable information on that fubject which he had obtained from the perufal of three Greek manufcripts in the Britifh Mufeum. One of thefe, it feems, is the Commentary of Proclus on the Parmenides of Plato, and is a folio volume confifting of four hundred pages. This with the other two, which are likewife folio volumes of no inconfiderable fize, Mr. T. had the courage to copy for his own private ufe.

Shortly after this, he tranflated the Platonic Salluft " On the Gods and the World;" the " Pythagoric Sentences of Demophilus;" and Five Hymns of Proclus: likewife Two Orations of the Emperor Julian; and Five books of Plotinus: all which, we are informed, he fold for no more than twenty pounds!

But the moft laborious of all his undertakings, and for which he feems to have received lefs in proportion than for any of his other publications, was his tranflation of Paufanias. When this tafk was firft propofed to Mr. T. by the bookfeller, Mr. Samuel Patterfon, well known to the literary world by feveral very ingenious publications, happening to be prefent, obferved, " that it was enough to break a man's heart." " O (replied the bookfeller) nothing will break the heart of Mr. T.!" This Herculean labour our Platonift accomplifhed in the fpace of ten months, though the notes are of fuch an extent, and fo full of uncommonly abftrufe learning, that the compofition of them might be fuppofed to have taken up a much longer time. For that arduous work, we almoft blufh to fay, Mr. T. received no more than fixty pounds; and we are grieved to add, that his health was greatly injured by his exceffive application on that occafion. We are indeed informed, that the debility of his body became fo extreme after this, that at times he was incapable of any exertion; and what is fin-

gular,

gular, he has ever since been deprived of the use of his forefinger in writing.

Our Platonist, however, in a short time exhibited an indubitable proof that he possesses an ardour which neither toil can abate, embarrassments impede, nor even debility extinguish; and which, like gunpowder set on fire, seems to rise with renewed vigour, in proportion as it has been compressed. Notwithstanding the extreme lassitude of his whole bodily frame, and the difficulty with which he was able to write, he engaged, under the patronage of an anonymous gentleman of fortune, to translate all those dialogues of Plato which have not been clothed in our native dress by Sydenham and others, together with his epistles, in order that by revising what has been already done, he might give the whole of Plato to the world in an English garb. This great undertaking we understand he accomplished in the space of about two years; and the work now only waits for a liberal patronage to be made public.

Under the patronage too of the same gentleman, he has translated the greater part of Aristotle's Nichomachean Ethics, and at present we hear Messrs. W. and G. Meredith have engaged him to translate Aristotle's Metaphysics, of which he has already nearly accomplished the first three books.

We are likewise happy to inform the public, from good authority, that Thomas Brand Hollis, esq. has been for many years much attached to our Platonist; that he frequently invites him to his table; and that he has always shewn himself active in promoting his welfare, though we are uncertain as to the time when Mr. T's intimacy with Mr. Hollis commenced.

We shall only add, that Mr. T. is at present assistant secretary to the Society for the Encouragement of Arts, Manufactures, and Commerce; a situation which he obtained by a very considerable majority of votes, through

the

the uncommon exertion of his friends; and that prior to this, some of them had procured him a situation in one of the public offices, to the fatigues of which finding his strength by no means adequate, and the employment appearing to him extremely servile, he relinquished it almost immediately after his nomination, and composed the following lines on the occasion:

To ev'ry power that reigns on high,
Swifter than light my thanks shall fly,
That from the B***k's dark dungeons free,
I once more hail sweet liberty:
For sure, I ween, fate ne'er me doom'd
To be 'midst sordid cares entomb'd,
And vilely waste in groveling toil
The mid-day blaze and midnight oil,
To some poor darkling desk confin'd;
While the wing'd energies of mind
Oppress'd and crush'd, and vanquish'd lie,
And lose at length the pow'r to fly.
 A doom like this be his alone,
To whom truth's charms were never known;
Who many sleepless night has spent,
In schemes full fraught with *cent per cent*.
The slave of av'rice, child of care,
And lost to all that's good and fair.

GENERAL MELVILLE,

A Man of amiable manners, and extensive information, is the son of a Scotch gentleman of small fortune. Entering early into the army, at the beginning of the war of 1756, he had risen to the rank of major, in the 38th, or Durour's, regiment of foot; with which regiment he embarked for the West-Indies, and served under General Hopson when that officer made his unsuccessful attack on Martinico.

The army having after this proceeded to Guadaloupe, the major served under General Barrington in the reduction of that place; and when Fort-Royal was taken, he was appointed to command it. No sooner was he invested with this post, than he was immediately attacked by the enemy; but by a judicious sally he forced their entrenchments, and spiked their cannon. On this occasion the *commandant* was wounded, but not so as to preclude him from the exercise of his talents, for he was entrusted by the conqueror with the office of lieutenant-governor of the island.

Soon after this, he was made lieutenant-colonel of the 38th regiment, which, we believe, is the last *regimental* promotion he obtained in the army.

On the establishment of the governments of the ceded islands upon the peace, Colonel Melville was appointed governor of Grenada, in which capacity he resided on the spot for several years, and acquired a handsome estate there. While in this situation, he was honoured with the local rank of major-general in the West-Indies, and has since risen to the full rank of general in the army, to which station he was promoted in 1780.

This gentleman's ample fortune, and the unfortunate * accident which deprived him of his sight, have rendered

---

* This melancholy event occurred in consequence of the explosion of some gun-powder, while in actual service.

any profitable poſt in the army on the one hand unneceſſary, and on the other impracticable.

Since his return from the Weſt-Indies, the general has aſſociated much with the literary world, and to his honour be it ſpoken, has been very active in promoting public charities of all kinds, of which the preſent flouriſhing ſtate of the Scots' corporation is a ſtrong evidence. He has alſo written two or three much eſteemed papers for the Royal Society, of which he is a member; theſe are to be met with in the Philoſophical Tranſactions.

When Tobago was relinquiſhed at the peace of 1783, General Melville and Sir William Younge were ſent to France by the proprietors of lands in that iſland, to ſolicit ſome terms in their favour, as it had been ceded without the neceſſary ſtipulations for their property. Their miſſion, although not completely ſucceſsful, was on the whole proſperous.

While General Melville governed Grenada, a party was formed, and ſome complaints were tranſmitted home againſt him : it is but candid, however, to ſuppoſe, what every one perſonally acquainted with that gentleman will be moſt readily diſpoſed to believe, that on this, as on every other occaſion, he conducted himſelf, with a due regard to propriety.

The General is a man of very liberal principles, both in reſpect to politics and religion, having voted at the Weſtminſter election for John Horne Tooke, eſq. and been one of the ſubſcribers to Mr. David Williams's chapel, in Mortimer-ſtreet.

We have only to add, that he is uncommonly ſkilled in military affairs, and that his converſation is rarely to be equalled for its fluency and propriety.

BEILBY

BEILBY PORTEUS, D.D.
LORD BISHOP OF LONDON.

RELIGION, in looking round among her moſt brilliant ornaments, and moſt powerful advocates of the preſent age, can hardly fix upon a more favourite object, than the very amiable and truly primitive prelate, who now claims our notice. Far be it from us to depreciate the merits of any divine, much leſs to exalt the character of one member of the epiſcopacy at the expence of another. Still we are confident, that all ranks and parties will agree with us in ſaying, that a more beautiful picture of genuine chriſtian ſimplicity, united with epiſcopal dignity, was never exhibited to public obſervation, than in the ſubject of this biographical ſketch.

Dr. Beilby Porteus is a native of Yorkſhire, and was born about 1731. His father was a reputable tradeſman, who, after giving his ſon a good education, at the grammar ſchool of Rippon, under the Rev. Mr. Hyde, ſent him to Cambridge, where he was entered of Chriſt's College. In this reſpectable ſociety he diſtinguiſhed himſelf by an aſſiduous application to his ſtudies, directing them in an eſpecial manner to that ſacred function for which he had an early predilection, and in which he has ſince ſo eminently ſhone.

He took his degree of B.A. in 1752, and in the courſe of the ſame year gained one of the medals given for the beſt claſſical eſſay by the Duke of Newcaſtle, then Chancellor of the Univerſity.

March 14, 1754, he was appointed one of the Eſquire Beadles of the Univerſity, which office he reſigned July 3, 1755, and in the ſame year, took his degree of Maſter

of

of Arts. Nearly about this time he was elected Fellow of his College, and was made one of the preachers at Whitehall chapel. In 1759, he obtained the Seatonian prize, for the beſt compoſition on DEATH. This poem evinces great poetical powers, and as it is the only piece of his, in this line, that has ever appeared in public, except a few verſes on the death of the late king, we truſt that the reader will be pleaſed with an extract from it in this place. The part we ſelect is the poet's concluding prayer:

"At thy good time,
"Let death approach; I reck not—let him but come
"In genuine form, not with thy vengeance arm'd;
"Too much for man to bear. O rather lend
"Thy kindly aid to mitigate his ſtroke.
 "And at that hour, when all aghaſt I ſtand
"(A trembling candidate for thy compaſſion)
"On this world's brink, and look into the next;
"When my ſoul, ſtarting from the dark unknown,
"Caſts back a wiſhful look, and fondly clings
"To her frail prop, unwilling to be wrench'd
"From this fair ſcene, from all her 'cuſtom'd joys,
"And all the lovely relatives of life,
"Then ſhed thy comforts o'er me; then put on
"The gentleſt of thy looks.—Let no dark crimes,
"In all their hideous forms then ſtarting up,
"Plant themſelves round my couch in dread array,
"And ſtab my bleeding heart with two-edg'd torture —
"Senſe of paſt guilt, and dread of future woe.
 "Far be the ghaſtly crew! And in their ſtead
"Let cheerful memory, from her pureſt cells,
"Lead forth a goodly train of virtues fair,
"Cheriſh'd in earlieſt youth, now paying back,
"With tenfold uſury, the pious care,
"And pouring o'er my wounds the heav'nly balm
"Of conſcious innocence. But chiefly Thou,
"Whom ſoft-ey'd Pity once led down from heav'n
"To bleed for man, to teach him how to live,
"And oh! ſtill harder leſſon! how to die;
"Diſdain not Thou to ſmooth the reſtleſs bed
"Of ſickneſs and of pain. Forgive the tear
"That feeble nature drops, calm all her fears,
"Wake all her hopes, and animate her faith,

"Till

" Till my rapt foul, anticipating heaven,
" Burfts from the thraldom of incumb'ring clay,
" And, on the wings of ecftacy upborne,
" Springs into liberty, and light, and life!"

In 1760, appeared a fingular piece of infidelity, under the title of " The Hiftory of the Man after God's own Heart," written by Peter Annet, with a view of expofing the facred hiftory to contempt, on account of the defects in the character of David. Though this performance was exceedingly deficient in point of argument, it was calculated to do confiderable mifchief from its fophiftry, boldnefs, and vivacity. On this account, feveral able writers undertook to vindicate the fcriptures, and among the reft our ingenious divine publifhed a fermon, preached Nov. 29, 1761, before the Univerfity of Cambridge, which he entitled, " The Character of David, King of Ifrael, impartially ftated."

This difcourfe, it is fuppofed, recommended him to the patronage of Dr. Secker, then Archbifhop of Canterbury, who appointed him about this time one of his domeftic chaplains, and in 1762 prefented him to the rectory of Witterfham in Kent.

In 1764, that excellent prelate gave him the rectory of Bucking, in the fame county, and alfo a prebendal ftall in the cathedral church of Peterborough.

May 13, 1765, Mr. Porteus was married by the Archbifhop to Mifs Hodgfon, of Parliament-ftreet, and in the fame year he obtained the valuable living of Hunton. He was created doctor of divinity, July 7, 1767, and in the month following the Archbifhop gave him the rectory of Lambeth, vacant by the death of Dr. Denne, with which he was allowed to hold the rectory of Hunton.

In 1768 Archbifhop Secker died, and by his will intrufted to his chaplains, Drs. Porteus and Stinton, the revifion and publication of his Lectures on the Church Catechifm,

Sermons,

Sermons, &c. This trust was most faithfully executed; and to the sermons, which were published in 1770, was prefixed an elegant memoir, respecting the venerable author, solely written by Dr. Porteus; this was reprinted in a separate form in 1798, with additions, and it is surely sufficient praise to observe, that this piece of biography obtained the approbation of Dr. Johnson.

In 1776, our divine became master of St. Crofs, an option of Archbishop Secker; and in January following he was deservedly raised to the episcopal bench, by the translation of Dr. Markham from the see of Chester to the Archbishoprick of York. This promotion, it is generally understood, was owing to the immediate solicitation of the Queen, to whom Dr. Porteus had been particularly acceptable as a private chaplain, when she was indisposed. In this station he conducted himself with primitive zeal, and blended with true episcopal dignity all the simplicity and earnestness of a christian minister.

In 1776, observing the negligence with which that awful day appropriated by the church, in early ages, to the commemoration of the sufferings and death of the Redeemer was treated, especially in the metropolis, his lordship printed " An earnest exhortation to the religious Ob- " servance of Good Friday, in a Letter to the Inhabitants " of Lambeth." This address excited considerable notice, and the ingenious Mr. Robert Robinson, of Cambridge, published a pamphlet in reply to it, under the title of the " History and Mystery of Good Friday."

The Bishop, however, had the satisfaction to see that his exhortation was attended with the desired effects. The Society for promoting Christian Knowledge seconded his laudable endeavours, by causing his pamphlet to be printed in a cheap form, and circulated in great abundance, by which means, numbers were induced to see the necessity of paying a proper respect to this solemn anniversary; so that

that from that time it has ufually been kept in the metropolis and its vicinity with great ſtrictneſs.

In 1783, the Biſhop of Cheſter preached before the Society for Propagating the Goſpel in Foreign Parts, on which occaſion he pleaded in a forcible and pathetic manner the cauſe of the African ſlaves, in our Weſt Indian ſettlements. This ſermon attracted conſiderable notice; and led the way to great exertions on behalf of thoſe unfortunate victims of avarice and oppreſſion.

In 1787, on the death of Biſhop Lowth, Dr. Porteus was tranſlated to the ſee of London, a circumſtance which gave univerſal ſatisfaction to every friend of religion, whether in or out of the eſtabliſhment.

In 1792, his Lordſhip was the means of founding a ſociety for the converſion of negro ſlaves in the Weſt Indies, which we have the ſatisfaction to find has been very ſuccefsful. His exertions in the cauſe of chriſtianity have been unremitted, and conducted upon the moſt liberal principles. The breath of cenſure has not ventured to aſſail his name, even with the ſuſpicion of reproach. Men of all parties have concurred in praiſing his candour, faithfulneſs, moderation, and liberality of mind.

In order to counteract the ſpirit of infidelity, his Lordſhip commenced during laſt Lent a ſeries of Lectures on the Truth of the Goſpel Hiſtory, and the Divinity of Chriſt's Miſſion, which he preached in St. James's church, Weſtminſter; and which will be reſumed at the ſame ſeaſon next year. Theſe were delivered every Friday, before crowded and admiring audiences, compoſed of perſons of all perſuaſions. His warm and impreſſive manner, plain but forcible language, clear and convincing arguments, aided by a moſt captivating eloquence, not only drew from the multitudes who heard him the unanimous voice of applauſe, but, it is to be hoped, produced a more ſubſtantial good, in bringing conviction home to many minds.

The

The Bishop is, we believe, a more frequent preacher than the rest of his brethren; for he is not only ready to assist public charities by his elocution, but during his summer residence in the country, he often ascends the pulpit to explain the principles, and enforce the precepts, of our sublime religion.

We cannot close this imperfect sketch of so brilliant a character, without mentioning one part of his conduct, which entitles him to additional praise. The point we allude to, is the moderate spirit he has manifested in the agitation of political questions. Though he has uniformly voted with his Majesty's ministers; he has not made himself an active partizan, by throwing fuel upon the unhappy fire which distracts the public mind. On the contrary, he has steered that pacific course, which becomes an ambassador of the Prince of Peace; the apostle of him who emphatically said, that " he was not the king of this world."

Bishop Porteus is not only eminent for his piety, but also for his literary accomplishments, which rank him amongst the most elegant scholars of the age. His style is pure and classically correct, at the same time that it is remarkably plain and free from ornament.

Besides the pieces already mentioned, he is the author of two volumes of most excellent sermons; and several Charges and small tracts, on religious subjects.

W.

H   JOSIAH

JOSIAH TUCKER, D.D.

DEAN OF GLOUCESTER.

THIS venerable divine, so long, and so justly celebrated for his commercial sagacity, was born at Laugharn, in Caermarthenshire, in the year 1712. His father was a farmer, and having a small estate left him at or near Aberystwith, in Cardiganshire, he removed thither; and perceiving that his son had a turn for learning, he sent him to Ruthin school in Denbighshire, where he made so respectable a progress in the classics, that he obtained an exhibition at Jesus College, Oxford.

The journey from his native place to the university was long, and at that time very tedious, on account of the badness of the roads. Our young student for some time travelled on foot. At last, old Mr. Tucker feeling for his son's reputation, as well as for his ease, gave him his own horse, that he might visit Oxford more reputably.

Upon his return, young Josiah, with true filial affection, considered that it was better for him to walk to Oxford, than for his father to repair on foot to repair to the neighbouring markets and fairs, which had been, in fact, the case, owing to this new regulation. The horse was accordingly returned; and our student for the remainder of the time he continued at the university, actually trudged backwards and forwards with his baggage on his back!

At the age of twenty-three he entered into holy orders, and served a curacy some time in Gloucestershire.

About 1737, he became curate of St. Stephen's church in Bristol, and was appointed minor canon in the cathedral of that city. Here he attracted the notice of that profound divine, Dr. Joseph Butler, then bishop of Bristol, and afterwards of Durham. In consequence of this, the bishop appointed Mr. Tucker his domestic chaplain; and the latter has told the writer of this article, that they frequently walked in the palace-gardens in the dark, generally conversing upon metaphysical and theological subjects.

Oftentimes the good bishop would be sunk in a profound reverie, in which he would continue for a considerable period, and then all at once break out with some singular remark. After one of these absences of mind, he suddenly asked Mr. Tucker, " whether he did not think " it possible that whole communities of men might be seiz- " ed with a fit of madness?"

The question was so odd, that the chaplain was silent, and thought the bishop's intellects a little disordered for the time. A greater share of experience and closer observation of mankind, especially during great political epochs, have, perhaps, given our divine reason to think there is more justness in the observation than he was at first inclined to suppose!

By the interest of this amiable and learned prelate, Mr. Tucker obtained a prebendal stall in the cathedral of Bristol; and on the death of the pious and ingenious Mr. Catcott, well known by his treatise on the Deluge, and a volume of excellent sermons, he became rector of St. Stephen. The inhabitants of that parish consist chiefly of merchants and tradesmen, a circumstance which greatly aided his natural inclination for commercial and political studies.

In 1745, he preached an excellent sermon before the governors of a very laudable institution, then first erected in the city of Bristol. In this discourse, the preacher took a course which has rarely been pursued: instead of dwelling, as most have done, upon the benevolent tendency of

these establishments, he considered them " as so many re-
" formatories, or schools, erected for the revival and pro-
" pagation of morality and religion, and as means which
" may conduce towards a national reformation in the com-
" mon people."

After mentioning, briefly indeed, but pointedly, the general depravity of the lower ranks, he says, " Nay, and
" when their extravagancies have run to that height as to
" call for *corporal punishment*, and the censure of the ma-
" gistrate, there are no hopes or prospect of *reclaiming*
" them by that means. For they have made it a sort of
" point of honour to outbrave the punishment; as for the
" shame and infamy attending it, these things make *now*
" but little impression on them: so that we have nothing
" left of discipline in our places of chastisement and con-
" finement, but their names. For our *houses* of correcti-
" on, as they are called, are so far from answering the
" original ends of their institution, that they *corrupt* more
" than *correct*, and *harden* rather than *reform*; so as to
" make the *young* offender, if sent there, to be threefold
" more the child of hell than he was before."

This strong censure, perhaps, is full as applicable to the objects upon which it was originally made now, as it was above half a century back.

When the famous bill was brought into the house of commons for the naturalization of the Jews, Mr. Tucker, considering the subject with an enlarged mind, took a decided part in favour of the measure, and was indeed its most able advocate.

The opponents of the bill, transported with an extraordinary zeal for the Christian religion, which they affected to think was in danger by this step, treated our divine with great rudeness and virulence on the occasion. He was not only severely attacked in pamphlets, newspapers, and magazines; but the pious people of Bristol, who
had,

had, perhaps, hardened their hearts into intolerance by a traffic in human flesh, burnt his effigy dressed in canonicals, together with his letters on behalf of naturalization!

In 1753, he published an able pamphlet on the "Turkey Trade," in which he demonstrates the evils that result to trade in general from chartered companies.

At this period, Lord Clare (afterward Earl Nugent) was returned to parliament for Bristol, which honour he obtained chiefly through the strenuous exertions of Mr. Tucker, whose influence in his large and wealthy parish was almost decisive on such an occasion. In return for this favour the Earl procured for him the Deanery of Gloucester, in 1758, at which time he took his degree of doctor in divinity.

So great was his reputation for commercial knowledge, which to a nation situated like our's is of the first importance, that Dr. Thomas Hayter, afterwards Bishop of London, who was then tutor to his present majesty, applied to Dr. Tucker to draw up a dissertation on this subject for the perusal of his royal pupil. It was accordingly done, and gave great satisfaction. This work, under the title of "The Elements of Commerce," was printed in quarto, but never published.

Dr. Warburton, however, who after having been member of the same chapter with the Dean, at Bristol, became Bishop of Gloucester, thought very differently from the rest of mankind, in respect to his talents, and favourite pursuits; and said once, in his coarse manner, that "his "Dean's trade was religion, and religion his trade."

But in refutation of this charge, we might produce the Dean's various publications on moral and religious subjects, which shew him to be not only deeply versed in theology, but also, what is far better, a man of genuine philanthropy.

In the year 1771, when a strong attempt was made to procure an abolition of subscription to the thirty-nine articles, Dr. Tucker came forwards as an able and moderate advocate of the church of England. Though he resisted with strong and clear arguments the claims of the petitioners on that occasion, he yet candidly admitted that some reformation of the liturgy was wanted, and instanced particularly the Athanasian Creed, which he considered as too scholastic and refined, for a popular confession of faith, and as the Nicene Creed is admitted, he further deemed the other to be superfluous.

About this time he published "Directions for Travellers," in which he lays down excellent rules, by which gentlemen who visit foreign countries may not only improve their own minds, but turn their observations to the benefit of their native country.

That excellent prelate, Archbishop Secker, was highly pleased with this useful performance, and sent the author some observations which he had made in the course of his perusal of it. The public would be much gratified by a new edition of these "Directions," with the Archbishop's observations annexed.

In 1772, the Dean printed a small volume of sermons, in which he explains the doctrines of *election* and *justification*, upon scriptural grounds, in opposition to what has been called the *evangelical system of faith*. At that time a very violent dispute was carried on between the Calvinistick and the Arminian Methodists, the former headed by Messrs. Toplady and Hill, and the latter by the Messrs. Wesleys and Fletcher.

The year following he published "Letters to the Rev. Dr. Kippis, wherein the claim of the church of England to an authority in matters of faith, and to a power of decreeing rites and ceremonies, is discussed and ascertained," &c. 8vo.

The

The difpute between Great Britain and her colonies in North America, began now to affume a very ferious and portentous afpect, and nothing lefs than an open rupture was expected, in confequence of the obftinacy of the one, and the firmnefs of the other.

The Dean was an attentive obferver of this conteft. He examined the affair with a very different eye from that of a party-man, or an interefted merchant, and he difcovered, as he conceived, that both fides would be better off by an abfolute feparation. The more he thought on this fubject, the more he was perfuaded that extenfive colonies were an evil, rather than a benefit to any commercial nation.

On this principle, therefore, he publifhed his " Thoughts upon the Difpute between the Mother Country and America." He demonftrated that the latter could not be conquered, and that if it could, the purchafe would be dearly bought. He warned this country againft commencing a war with the colonies, and advifed that they fhould be left to themfelves, an event which would be productive of infinite good to Great Britain.

This pofition and advice ftartled all parties, as well thofe who were advocates for American freedom, as thofe who were zealots for coercive meafures and taxation. By both the Dean was confidered as a fort of madman, who had rambled out of the proper line of his profeffion to commence political quack; and it is remarkable that thofe two great men, Dr. Johnfon and Edmund Burke, treated the Doctor's hypothefis with great contempt, though the one was the champion of, and the other an enemy to, taxation.

Mr. Burke's language in the Houfe of Commons refpecting the Dean's propofal was, indeed, exceeding harfh and illiberal. In his famous fpeech on American taxation, April 13th, 1774, this famous orator, called him

" the

"the advocate of the court faction, and I suppose," he adds, " that his earnest labours in this vineyard will raise " him to a bishopric." The Dean was actually roused into resentment on this occasion, and he accordingly published a letter to Mr. Burke, in which he not only vindicates the purity of his own principles, but retorts upon his adversary in very forcible and manly terms.

The ground of Mr. Burke's enmity to the Dean, was the latter's strenuous opposition to his being elected to represent Bristol in parliament. Dr. Tucker had a high opinion of Lord Nugent's parliamentary conduct and abilities, added to which, he owed him much on the score of gratitude. He therefore considered himself as bound to support his interest in Bristol, with all the power he possessed. This excited Mr. Burke's dislike to the Dean of Gloucester, and sharpened his wit on the subject of his political opinions.

Our author, however, went on vindicating and enforcing his favourite system, in spite of all the obloquy with which it was treated both in the senate and from the press. As the war proceeded, many intelligent persons began to see more truth and reason in his sentiments, and time has at last demonstrated that he was completely in the right. Towards the close of that unhappy contest, the Dean assumed the appellation of CASSANDRA, alluding to the ill success with which his warnings had been attended. This signature is found at the end of those hints and short essays which he frequently printed in the newspapers, and which it were to be wished some person would collect and preserve, left they should sink into unmerited oblivion.

When the terrors of an invasion were very prevalent, in 1779, the Dean circulated, in a variety of periodical publications, some of the most sensible observations that were ever made on the subject, in order to quiet the fears of the people. He states at length, and with great accuracy,
the

the numerous difficulties that muft attend the attempt to invade this country, and the ftill greater ones that muft be encountered by the invaders after their landing. Thofe obfervations have been reprinted, with good effect, in the courfe of the prefent war.

In 1781, the Dean publifhed, what he had printed long before, " A Treatife on Civil Government," in which his principal defign is to counteract the doctrines of the celebrated Mr. Locke and his followers. The book made a confiderable noife, and was very fharply attacked by feveral able writers on the democratic fide of the queftion, particularly by Dr. Towers.

The year following he clofed his political career with a pamphlet entitled " *Cui Bono ?*" in which he balances the profit and lofs of each of the belligerent powers, and recapitulates all his former pofitions on the fubject of war and colonial poffeffions.

His publications fince that period have confifted of fome tracts on the commercial regulations of Ireland, on the exportation of woollens, and on the iron trade.

In 1777, he publifhed feventeen practical fermons, in one volume, octavo. In the year 1778, one of his parifhioners, Mifs Pelloquin, a maiden lady of large fortune and moft exemplary piety, bequeathed to the Dean her dwelling-houfe in Queen-Square, Briftol, with a very handfome legacy, as a teftimony of her great efteem for his worth and talents.

It fhould be recorded to his praife, that though enjoying but very moderate preferment (for to a man of no paternal eftate, or other ecclefiaftical dignity, the Deanery of Gloucefter is no very advantageous fituation), he has, notwithftanding, been a liberal benefactor to feveral public inftitutions, and a diftinguifhed patron of merit.

The celebrated John Henderfon, of Pembroke college, Oxford, was fent to the univerfity and fupported there at the Dean's expence, when he had no means whatever of gratifying his ardent defire for ftudy.

We fhall mention another inftance of generofity in this place, which refle&ts the greateft honour upon the Dean. About the year 1790, he thought of refigning his re&tory in Briftol, and without communicating his defign to any other perfon, he applied to the Chancellor, in whofe gift it is, for leave to quit it in favour of his curate, a moft deferving man, with a large family.

His Lordfhip was willing enough that he fhould give up the living, but he refufed him the liberty of nominating his fucceffor. On this the Dean refolved to hold the living himfelf, till he could find a fit opportunity to fucceed in his obje&t. After weighing the matter more deliberately, he communicated his wifh to his parifhioners, and advifed them to draw up a petition to the Chancellor in favour of the curate. This was accordingly done, and figned by all of them, without any exception, either on the part of the diffenters or others.

The Chancellor being touched with this teftimony of love between a clergyman and his people, yielded at laft to the application; in confequence of which the Dean cheerfully refigned the living to a fucceffor well qualified to tread in his fteps.

Since that time he has refided chiefly at Gloucefter*, viewing his approaching diffolution, which in the courfe of nature cannot be far diftant, with the placid mind of a Chriftian, confcious of having done his duty both to GOD and MAN.

* He married a Mrs. Crowe, of that City, in 1781.

Here follows a tolerably correct list of the Dean's works:

THEOLOGICAL AND CONTROVERSIAL.

1. A Sermon, preached before the governors of the infirmary of Bristol, 1745.
2. Letters in Behalf of the Naturalization of the Jews.
3. Apology for the Church of England, 1772.
4. Six Sermons, 12mo. 1773.
5. Letter to Dr. Kippis, on his Vindication of the Protestant dissenting Ministers.
6. Two Sermons and Four Tracts.
7. View of the Difficulties of the Trinitarian, Arian, and Socinian Systems, and Seventeen Sermons, 1777.

POLITICAL AND COMMERCIAL.

8. A Pamphlet on the Turkey Trade.
9. A brief View of the Advantages and Disadvantages which attend a Trade with France.
10. Reflections on the Expediency of naturalizing foreign Protestants, and a Letter to a Friend on the same Subject.
11. The Pleas and Arguments of the Mother Country and the Colonies stated.
12. A Letter to Mr. Burke.
13. Quere, whether a Connection with, or Separation from, America, would be for national Advantage?
14. Answers to Objections against the Separation from America.
15. A Treatise on Civil Government.
16. *Cui Bono.*
17. Four Letters on National Subjects.
18. Sequel to Sir William Jones on Government.
19. On the Dispute between Great Britain and Ireland.
20. Several Papers under the signature of Cassandra, &c. on the difficulties attendant on an invasion.
21. A Treatise on Commerce. (Mr. Coxe, in his Life of Sir Robert Walpole, says that this was printed, but never published.)

MISCEL-

MISCELLANEOUS.

22. Directions for Travellers.
23. Cautions against the Use of Spirituous Liquors.
24. A Tract against the Diversions of Cock-fighting, &c.

W.

ADMIRAL LORD VISCOUNT DUNCAN.

WHATEVER may be thought of the origin of the prefent war, or the principles upon which it has been conducted; whatever humiliating ideas may, on fome grounds, prevail in the minds of Englifhmen while they are reviewing the hiftory of this extraordinary and eventful conteft;—there can ftill be but one opinion refpecting the conduct of our naval commanders, in general: and every Britifh heart muft glow with rapture at the confideration, that the honour of the national flag, fo far from being tarnifhed in a fingle inftance, has received greater luftre than ever diftinguifhed it at any former period.

Among the eminent names whom the pen of the hiftorian will have to dwell upon with peculiar fatisfaction, when engaged in recording the naval events of the prefent war, that of Adam Lord DUNCAN will be proudly confpicuous.

This diftinguifhed veteran was born at Dundee, in Scotland, July 1ft, 1731, and was the younger fon of a very ancient and reputable family, which has for a long feries of years held the lordfhip of Lundie in the fhire of Perth. The family eftate, the rental of which is about 500*l*. a year, came to Lord Duncan about two years ago, in confequence of the death of his elder brother, Colonel Duncan.

The younger branches, even of a refpectable family, have generally to force their way in life by their own merits and exertions. Lord Duncan accordingly owed but little to his relations. He was very early fent to fea, a profeffion which cofts but a trifle in the outfet, and is generally attended with but fmall expence after the young adventurer is thus difpofed of. Much is not known of the admiral's early fervices; but we are warranted in conjecturing that they muft have been meritorious, by his attaining to the rank of

poft-post-captain, February 25th, 1761, at which time he was appointed to the command of the Valiant. About this period, he was honoured with the friendship of that gallant officer of the old school, Lord Keppel, and was with him at the taking of the Havannah; and when Keppel was appointed to a flag, he chose Duncan to be his captain.

He was also a member of the court-martial which sat upon the trial of that distinguished veteran; and continued attached to him by the strongest ties of intimacy and friendship, till his death.

On September 24th, 1787, he was made a rear-admiral; in 1793, he was promoted to the rank of vice-admiral; and in 1795, he became admiral of the blue.

Hitherto he had moved on in his profession regularly, but with little notice, for it had not been his lot to get employed on any service that was likely to bring him forward to the public view.

His appointment, at last, to that station, in which he has all at once obtained laurels equal to those which adorn the brows of men who have been more extensively employed, seems to have been owing to his relationship to Mr. Secretary Dundas, whose niece he married, and by whom he has several children.

This alliance procured for him an appointment which it was understood he was best fitted for, the North Sea station. Nor does it at all reflect upon his Lordship to say, that his circumstances stood in need of being thus employed. With hardly any other fortune than half-pay as an Admiral, it was natural enough for him to be anxious to get engaged in active service, for the benefit of a wife and children whom he loved. The scene of action which he chose was an arduous one. The severity of the winter season, in that sea, must also have been very trying to a man of his Lordship's time of life. Moreover he had to

encounter

encounter with difficulties still more troublesome and painful to a British officer: we allude to the mutinous spirit which prevailed in his fleet, in common with the other naval squadrons in the Channel.

In the midst of all these unpleasant circumstances, his Lordship manifested a cool and steady mind. He kept his station with such persevering ardour, in the most boisterous season of the year, that the enemy could not by any means effect their design of escaping from their ports. The indefatigable Admiral continued blockading them, either with the whole, or part of his squadron, till the summer of 1797, when the mutiny raged in his fleet in a most alarming manner. Even when he was left with only three ships, he still remained firm in his station off the Texel, and succeeded in keeping the Dutch ships from proceeding to sea; a circumstance, in all probability, of as high consequence to the nation as his subsequent victory.

His behaviour at the time of the mutiny, will best be seen from the speech which he made to the crew of his own ship, on June 3d, 1797, and which, as a piece of artless and affecting oratory, cannot but be admired by the most fastidious taste. His men being assembled, the Admiral thus addressed them from the quarter deck:

" My lads—I once more call you together, with a sorrowful heart, from what I have lately seen—the disaffection of the fleets; I call it *disaffection,* for the crews have *no grievances.* To be deserted by my fleet, in the face of an enemy, is a disgrace which I believe never before happened to a British Admiral: nor could I have supposed it possible. My greatest comfort under God is, that I have been supported by the officers, seamen, and marines of *this ship*; for which, with a heart overflowing with gratitude, I request you to accept my sincere thanks.

" I flatter

"I flatter myself much good may result from your example, by bringing those deluded people to a sense of the duty which they owe, not only to their King and Country, but to themselves. The British Navy has ever been the support of that Liberty which has been handed down for us by our ancestors, and which, I trust, we shall maintain to the latest posterity; and that can only be done by unanimity and obedience.

"This ship's company, and others who have distinguished themselves by their loyalty and good order, deserve to be, and doubtless *will be*, the favourites of a grateful country; they will also have from their inward feelings a comfort which must be lasting, and not like the fleeting and false confidence of those who have swerved from their duty!

"It has often been my pride with you to look into the Texel, and see a foe which dreaded coming out to meet us.—My pride is *now* humbled indeed!—My feelings are not easily to be expressed!—Our cup has overflowed, and made us wanton. The all-wise PROVIDENCE has given us this check as a warning, and I hope we shall improve by it. On Him, then, let us trust, where our *only* security can be found.

"I find there are many good men among us; for my own part, I have had full confidence of all in this ship; and once more beg to express my approbation of your conduct.

"May GOD, who thus far conducted you, continue to do so; and may the British Navy, the glory and support of our country, be restored to its wonted splendour, and be not only the bulwark of Britain, but the terror of the world. But this can only be effected by a strict adherence to our duty and obedience; and let us pray that the Almighty GOD may keep us in the right way of thinking. GOD bless you all!"

The

The crew of the Venerable were so affected by this impressive address, that on retiring there was not a dry eye among them.

On the suppression of the mutiny, the Admiral resumed his station with his whole fleet off the coast of Holland, either to keep the Dutch squadron in the Texel, or to attack them if they should attempt to come out. It has since been discovered, that the object of the Batavian Republic, in conjunction with France, was to invade Ireland, where doubtless they would have been cordially welcomed by numerous bodies of the disaffected. Hence it will be seen, that the object of watching and checking the motions of the Dutch Admiral was of the utmost consequence.

After a long and very vigilant attention to the important trust reposed in him, the English Admiral was necessitated to repair to Yarmouth-roads to refit. The Batavian commander seized this favourable interval, and proceeded to sea. That active officer, Capt. Trollope, however was upon the look-out, and having discovered the enemy, immediately dispatched a vessel with the glad intelligence to Admiral Duncan, who lost not an instant of time, but pushed out at once, and in the morning of the 11th of October, fell in with Capt. Trollope's squadron of observations, with the signal flying for an enemy to the leeward.

By a masterly manœuvre, the Admiral placed himself between them and the Texel, so as to prevent them from re-entering without risking an engagement. An action accordingly took place between Camperdown and Egmont, in nine fathoms water, and within five miles of the coast. The Admiral's own ship, in pursuance of a plan of naval evolution which he had long before determined to carry into effect, broke the enemy's line, and closely engaged the Dutch Admiral de Winter, who, after a most gallant defence, was obliged to strike. Eight ships were taken, two of which carried flags!

I All

All circumstances considered—the time of the year, the force of the enemy, and the nearness to a dangerous shore—this action will be pronounced by every judge of nautical affairs, to be one of the most brilliant that graces our annals.

The nation was fully sensible of the merit and consequence of this glorious victory: politicians beheld in it the annihilation of the designs of our combined enemies; naval men admired the address and skill which were displayed by the English commander in his approaches to the attack; and the people at large were transported with admiration, joy, and gratitude.

The honours which were instantly conferred upon the VENERABLE Admiral, received the approbation of men of all parties. October 21st, 1797, he was created Lord Viscount Duncan of Camperdown, and Baron Duncan of Lundie in the shire of Perth. On his being introduced into the House of Peers, on November the 8th, the Lord Chancellor communicated to him the thanks of the House, and in his speech said: " He congratulated his Lordship
" upon his accession to the honour of a distinguished seat
" in that place, to which his very meritorious and *unpa-*
" *ralleled* professional conduct had deservedly raised him;
" that conduct (the Chancellor added) was such as not
" only merited the thanks of their Lordships' House,
" but the gratitude and applause of the Country at large:
" it had been instrumental, under the auspices of Provi-
" dence, in establishing the security of his Majesty's domi-
" nions, and frustrating the ambitious and destructive de-
" signs of the enemy."

In the last session of Parliament, a pension of 2000*l. per annum* was granted to his Lordship, for himself and the two next heirs to the peerage.

In person, Lord Duncan is of a manly, athletic form, six feet three inches high, erect and graceful, with a countenance that indicates great intelligence and benevolence.

His

His private character is that of a most affectionate relative, a steady friend, and, what crowns the whole with a lustre superior to all other qualities or distinctions, he is a man of great and unaffected piety.

The latter virtue may excite in some persons a smile of contempt; but the liberal-minded will be pleased to read that Lord Duncan feels it an honour to be a Christian.

He encourages religion by his own practice; and the public observance of it has been always kept up where he has held the command.

When the victory was decided, which has immortalized his name, his Lordship ordered the crew of his ship to be called together, and at their head, upon his bended knees, in the presence of the Dutch Admiral, who was greatly affected with the scene, he solemnly and pathetically offered up praise to the GOD OF BATTLES!

Let it be added here, that his demeanour, when all eyes were upon him, in the cathedral of St. Paul's, on the day of general thanksgiving, was so humble, modest, and devout, as greatly to increase that admiration which his services had procured him.

In short, Lord Duncan is one more instance of the truth of the assertion, that piety and courage are inseparably allied; and that the latter quality, without the former, loses its principal virtue.

ΧΛΣ

DR. SAMUEL HORSLEY,

LORD BISHOP OF ROCHESTER.

OF all the right reverend members of the epifcopal bench, no one has obtained more celebrity than this learned prelate.

We are well aware, that a Bifhop who has fo greatly diftinguifhed himfelf in political, as well as theological, controverfy, will be regarded by different men with very oppofite fentiments. Our aim, however, has no exclufive reference to either of thefe objects; and therefore we fhall ftudy to give a faithful delineation of the character before us, without the flighteft attention to the fpirit of party, whether that party be of a religious or political complexion.

Dr. Samuel Horfley is the eldeft of the three fons of the Rev. Mr. Horfley, formerly minifter of St. Martin's in the Fields. The grandfather of the Bifhop was bred a diffenting divine, but he afterwards thought proper to conform to the eftablifhment.

His Lordfhip was born about the year 1737, and received the ground-work of his education at Weftminfter fchool, whence he was removed to the Univerfity of Cambridge.

He applied himfelf, while there, chiefly to the ftudy of mathematics; and not content with carefully reading the writings of the acuteft of the moderns of that line, he went back to the profoundeft of the ancients, and made himfelf thoroughly mafter of their moft intricate reafonings.

Having taken his degree of Mafter of Arts, he accepted an invitation to go to Oxford, as private tutor to the prefent

sent Earl of Aylesford. From that University he received a degree of Doctor of Laws, and in 1769 printed at the Clarendon press, his edition of the Inclinations of Apollonius, a geometrical work of considerable value, though exceedingly abstruse. Previous to his time, mathematical learning had been in little repute at Oxford; but since that period it has grown into fashion there, so that this University can hardly be said to fall short of her sister, in that great branch of human knowledge.

Here our author first conceived the design of publishing a complete edition of the works of Sir Isaac Newton; to which end he began to collect the necessary materials.

On leaving the University, Dr. Horsley came to London, where he was elected fellow of the Royal Society, of which he was also chosen secretary in 1773. He continued to serve that office, with the greatest credit to himself, as well as benefit to the scientific world, till the resignation of the late president, Sir John Pringle, when finding that the *connoisseurs* and *virtuosi* were gaining ground, he retired.

Soon after his settling in the metropolis, Dr. Horsley was noticed by that observing and excellent prelate, Bishop Lowth, who invited him to become his domestic chaplain. It is somewhat remarkable, that at this time he was suspected of not being quite orthodox in his theological sentiments, and those who pretended to smell heresy in him, wondered at Bishop Lowth's taking him under his patronage. The only grounds for this suspicion, were his being a profound mathematician, and his close intimacy with Dr. Maty and other men of science, who were avowed Socinians.

In 1774, Bishop Lowth presented him to the rectories of St. Mary Newington and Albury, both in the county of Surrey; and in the course of the same year he married a Miss Botnam.

In

In 1776, he published proposals for a complete and elegant edition of the works of the immortal Newton, which appeared in 1779, in five volumes quarto, with an excellent dedication to the king in Latin.

It was expected that a large memoir respecting the Prince of Philosophers would have been prefixed to this edition; and considerable disappointment was of course experienced by the public, when nothing of this kind appeared. Certain it is, that the learned editor gave room for this expectation, and had actually made some progress in the life. He moreover had conversed with Dr. Johnson upon the subject, who advised him to write it in Latin, as best suited to the dignity of the character. This biographical *desideratum*, however, has not yet made its appearance; and we are apprehensive that it never will.

In 1778, when the controversy was on foot between Drs. Priestley, Price, and others, respecting materialism, and philosophical necessity, Dr. Horsley preached a sermon on Good Friday at St. Paul's Cathedral, which he afterwards published. In this ingenious discourse he reconciles, with much force of argument, the doctrine of divine Providence with the free agency of man, and combats the necessarian hypothesis with great, and, in the opinion of his friends, complete success.

About this time he was appointed Archdeacon of St. Albans, by Bishop Lowth, who also presented him to the valuable living of South Weald in Essex.

In 1783 Dr. Priestley published his celebrated work the "History of the Corruptions of Christianity." It need hardly be mentioned, that the principal design of this work was to overthrow the catholic doctrine respecting Christ's divinity.

Great was the triumph manifested by the unitarian party on the publication of this elaborate history. The outcry made by them on the occasion, naturally roused the attention

tion of those who adhered to the Orthodox confession, and Dr. Horsley seized this opportunity of shewing, not only the soundness of his faith, but his abilities for the most intricate branches of theological controversy.

In the summer of this year, he delivered to the clergy of the Archdeaconry of St. Albans a charge, in which he expressly controverted the Socinian position—that the doctrine of the Trinity was not maintained by the Christian church in the first three centuries; and he not only gave a flat contradiction to Dr. Priestley's assertion on this point, but charged him with having taken, without acknowledgement, the whole of his argument from Zwicker and other eminent Socinians of the last century.

This discourse, at the request of his reverend auditory, was printed, with an appendix, explaining and confirming the positions which it contained.

Dr. Priestley, whose pen is that of a ready writer, was not to be daunted at meeting with so formidable an antagonist; on the contrary, he rushed at once into the battle, with the impetuosity of a man who seemed to place all his reputation, as a combatant, upon the event of this contest. He, of course, instantly replied to the Archdeacon, in a series of letters, which contained all his former assertions, expressed in a more confident tone than before. Dr. Horsley was aware of the advantage which the precipitancy of his opponent had given him, and, therefore, in his answer, which was also in the epistolary form, he noticed the frequent slips in Greek quotation, and reference, which the Doctor had made; and with great adroitness, left it to the reader to judge, whether so hasty and incautious an historian was to be depended upon in a matter of such importance.

But he did not merely expose the Doctor's mistakes. He followed up the attack by numerous proofs in behalf of the common belief, drawn from the early fathers of the church and the purest ecclesiastical historians. The display of reading

ing and acute refearch in thefe letters is wonderful. The ftyle alfo is admirable; and though at times it affumes a lofty manner, yet the reader of tafte finds himfelf charmed with the elegance of the language, and the clofenefs of the reafoning.

Dr. Prieftley continued the combat, by another feries of letters, to which the Archdeacon again replied. The controverfy here clofed on the part of the latter, who fignified that it was an endlefs tafk to contend upon an exhaufted topic, with one who was never difpofed to ceafe difputing till he had obtained the laft word. In 1789, Dr. Horfley collected thefe tracts, and printed them in one volume octavo, with fome additions, particularly a fermon on the incarnation, preached at Newington, on Chriftmas-day, 1785, and which having a material relation to the controverfy in queftion, he thought proper to infert in this collection.

While this difpute was going on, our learned divine was engaged in another, which made nearly as much noife as the firft, at leaft in the fcientific world. When Sir Jofeph Banks came in as prefident of the Royal Society, on the refignation of Sir John Pringle, the mathematical and philofophical members of the Newtonian fchool were difgufted at the extraordinary preference which was fhewn to fubjects, as they conceived, of an inferior nature, to thofe which ought in their opinion to engage the firft learned fociety in the world. It has been faid, that cabals were formed by thofe members of the old ftamp againft the prefident and his friends; but of this no proof was ever brought forward.

In 1784 the latter ventured upon a ftep which could not fail to fan the fmothering flame into a blaze. The council thought proper to difmifs the learned Doctor Hutton from the office of Latin fecretary for foreign correfpondence, upon the very frivolous pretence, that it was improper fuch

a poft

a post should be filled by a person who did not reside in the metropolis. The scientific members took fire at this treatment of one of the ablest and most respectable of their body. Accordingly, in several meetings of the society, attempts were made to lessen the influence of the president *, and to reinstate Dr. Hutton in his place, but without success. In this contest between philosophy and the *virtuosi*, Dr. Horsley made the most conspicuous figure. Finding, however, that his labours and those of his learned associates were in vain, he forsook (to express it in his own forcible language) " that temple, where Philosophy once reigned, " and where NEWTON presided as her officiating minister."

In 1786 Dr. Horsley obtained, without either solicitation or even expectancy, a prebend in the cathedral church of Gloucester. His friend on this occasion was Lord Thurlow, then Chancellor; who, without being personally known to Dr. H. or receiving any application on his behalf, resisted every request that was made for this valuable preferment, and bestowed it upon the man whom he justly considered as having merited it the most of any divine in this age.

During the year following, the Doctor preached an ordination sermon in the cathedral of Gloucester, in which he maintained with great strength this position—that on the cessation of miraculous gifts, human learning is substituted by divine appointment, as an essential qualification for the christian ministry. At the command of the venerable prelate before whom it was delivered (Doctor Samuel Halifax) this ingenious discourse was soon after printed; and excited considerable notice, and some controversy.

Next year Dr. Horsley was elevated to the episcopal bench, on the translation of Dr. Smallwell from the see of St. David to that of Oxford. Lord Thurlow, on this occasion, was again his steady and unsolicited patron; and it is

* Sir Joseph was accused, in an able pamphlet of that day, of taking very improper means to obtain the admission or rejection of candidates.

well

well known that he made it a point to bring in his friend, in opposition to candidates who were backed by all the force of ministerial influence.

Soon after his admission to the House of Lords, Dr. Horsley had an opportunity of displaying his eloquence and learning, which he did to great advantage, on Earl Stanhope's motion for a revision and reform of the canons of the church. His speech on this occasion afforded uncommon pleasure to the house; and what was rather remarkable, drew from the noble Earl just mentioned a very liberal encomium.

On the great struggle made by the protestant dissenters in 1790, to obtain a repeal of the Corporation and Test acts, a pamphlet appeared, entitled " a Review of the Case of the Protestant Dissenters," which was written with such boldness and elegance on the High Church side, that, though anonymous, all parties concurred in attributing it to the Bishop of St. David's; nor in fact were they wrong in their conjecture.

The year following, he made a conspicuous figure in consequence of his primary charge to the clergy of his diocese; in this he maintained the old-fashioned doctrine of *justification by faith alone*, and pressed it home upon his hearers, that the too common practice of preaching mere *morality* was destructive of vital religion.

This charge, of a complexion so very different from what had been usually delivered in cathedral churches, attracted considerable notice. Those who were attached to the Calvinistic principles, or, as they are commonly called, Evangelical Christians, were enraptured with the sentiments conveyed in this discourse. Others, on the contrary, conceived that the Bishop had mistaken the doctrine of the gospel, on the subject of justification; while the Unitarians were extremely irritated at the harsh terms in which his Lordship had mentioned their sect and creed

in

in his charge. Several replies were accordingly publifhed to it; but the learned prelate feemed to confider himfelf fuperior to the adverfaries who wifhed to provoke him again into controverfy.

His conduct in the fee of St. David's is highly praifeworthy. Of all the bifhoprics, no one exhibited more poverty, or more ignorance, on the part of the clergy, than this. Many of the curacies, when his lordfhip entered upon the government of this extenfive diocefe, did not exceed ten pounds *per annum*, and fome of the churches were actually ferved for five! It may eafily be concluded what fort of divines a great part of thefe poor minifters were, under fuch circumftances. What was ftill worfe, the multitude of candidates for orders increafed yearly, fo that Wales poured her fuperfluous clergy into England, to the difgrace of the cloth, and the real injury of fuch as were regularly bred. The writer of this has no inclination to fport himfelf at the expence of any body of men; but he could entertain the reader with many whimfical anecdotes refpecting the learning and ingenuity of the Welch clergy. A reform was, therefore, neceffary, but to accomplifh it required a ftrong and perfevering mind.

Our indefatigable prelate was not to be daunted by any obftacles. He obtained, with the greateft poffible difpatch, an accurate and minute ftate of his diocefe. He then gave notice to the beneficed clergy, who did not refide, that they would be compelled to refidence, or to allow their curates a more liberal falary. By this means, he remedied that fhameful abufe, of one man's ferving feveral churches on the fame day; limiting a curate to two only, and thofe within a moderate diftance from each other.

Having regulated the condition of the clergy, he proceeded to a ftricter courfe, with refpect to candidates for holy orders, admitting none without perfonally examining

them

them himself, and looking very narrowly into the titles which they produced.

With all this vigilance, his Lordship acted to them as a tender father, encouraging them to visit him during his stay in the country, which was usually for several months in the year, assisting them with advice, and administering to their temporal necessities with a liberal and paternal hand.

In his progress through the diocese he frequently preached in the parish churches, especially on the days when the sacrament was administered, and bestowed considerable largesses upon the poor.

He kept a most hospitable table at his episcopal palace, at Aberguilly, near Caermarthen, to which the neighbouring gentry and clergy were always welcome. In short, he was a blessing to that poor people; and they followed him with grateful hearts, and parted from him with infinite reluctance. This is not an ideal picture: it is a true but imperfect sketch of actual life; and such as the feeble painter had opportunities of seeing more than once.

On January 30th, 1793, the bishop of St. David's was appointed to preach before the House of Lords, and as the recent murder of the king of France was the general topic of conversation and pity, the abbey was greatly crowded. That discourse is in print; and whatever may be thought of the notions on government, which distinguish it, there can be but one opinion concerning its very beautiful and pathetic peroration. When published, the bishop appended to his sermon a long vindication of the character of Calvin, from the charge of being a friend to rebellion and regicide.

The following year he was translated, on the death of Bishop Pearce, from St. David's to Rochester, on which occasion he resigned all his other church preferments.

When

When he entered upon his office as Dean of Westminster, he found many things in the condition of that church which stood in great need of reformation; and with his usual activity, he instantly set about the work. In particular, the salaries of the minor-canons and officers were extremely low, and by no means proportionate. With a most commendable spirit of liberality, therefore, he obtained an instant advance, and then began to regulate the conduct and duty of the persons whom he had so materially assisted. Had he, on the contrary, set about a more exact discipline, without attending to the necessities of these men, they would, perhaps, have justly considered him as a severe taskmaster, and murmured at his regulations. By this mode of conduct, he gained their esteem and gratitude; and it may safely be said, that no man ever filled that station with such popularity as the present dean.

In the career of politics, his popularity, perhaps, is not quite so great. The zeal which he displays in the agitation of public measures, and the promptness with which he expresses his sentiments on the side of the established order of things, civil and religious, have procured him many enemies. Without endeavouring to extenuate any thing in his conduct that is reprehensible, let it be permitted for us to say, that his language has been often greatly misrepresented, and been made by his adversaries to express a meaning which the right reverend prelate holds in abhorrence. He has been too apt to express his sentiments in abstract propositions, which may be made, by artful men, to signify what never entered into his lordship's mind. Were we to act so generously, as to put the best construction upon his observations, and that certainly ought to be done, unless his own explanation proved decisive, in all probability, we should find here less occasion for censure, and more for commendation.

But

But to leave his political reputation to its fate. In 1796, he printed, without his name, a moſt profound and elegant diſſertation on "the Latin and Greek Proſodies," dedicated to Lord Thurlow. In this learned performance he ſhews an uncommon depth of penetration into, and acquaintance with, the nature and conſtruction of the ancient languages; and approves himſelf a moſt powerful, though perhaps not an invincible advocate for the uſe of the Greek accents.

We underſtand that this zealous and active prelate is now deeply engaged in a work upon the prophecies of the Old and New Teſtament; and from his known powers, as a profound thinker and calculator, there can be no doubt entertained of the value of his performance, ſhould he, as it is to be hoped he will, favour the world with the fruits of his reſearches.

Beſides the works already mentioned, biſhop Horſley is the author of ſome ingenious papers on mathematical ſubjects, various ſermons on public occaſions, and ſeveral epiſcopal charges.

He has been twice married. By his firſt lady he had two children; one only of whom is living, who is at preſent at Chriſt-church college, Oxford.

JUDGE

JUDGE BULLER.

SIR FRANCIS BULLER is the eldest son of the late John Buller, Esq. of Morval, in the county of Cornwall. The extensive parliamentary interest of his family is well known; this, joined to his own abilities, could not fail to raise him, early in life, to an eminent rank in his profession.

After being educated at Winchester school, he was called to the bar in the year 1763, and brought into parliament soon after. This with a lawyer is generally a prelude to a silk gown, but it was not immediately obtained. His professional *debut* did not promise much eminence, for he commenced his career as a special pleader, having studied the practical part of this dull but necessary branch of legal science under the present Judge Ashurst, and like his precursor he was always ranked among the most eminent in that particular line. This character, accordingly, soon brought him into great repute as a common-law draughtsman; and Erskine, after having laid by his sword, first brandished a pen at his desk.

His practice at the bar was, at the same time, very considerable.

In 1772, Mr. Buller published " An Introduction to the Law of NISI PRIUS," which is a *noli me tangere* of its kind, and will long continue to enjoy a high degree of estimation; indeed, in every thing that did not require an appeal to the passions, he shewed himself a master: then only he failed! His eloquence, as a counsel, was neither pleasing nor powerful, but on the other hand, few judges deliver themselves with more propriety than him; his language being dignified, and his manner, perhaps, somewhat too authoritative. This affords a proof that the oratory suited for the bar, is essentially different from that adapted for the bench.

The *borough* interest of his family, added to a matrimonial alliance with that of the late Earl Bathurst, at length procured

cured him a filk gown, the place of a Welch judge, and even elevated him to the coif, while yet a very young man. He was accordingly called to the degree of fergeant at law, on being appointed one of the juftices of the court of King's Bench.

In this capacity his abilities had full play, as he poffeffes great quicknefs of perception, readily forefees the confequences of facts, and anticipates the drift of an argument at the firft glance; but, like the great lawyer whom he has been ambitious of copying, he is fometimes rather too hafty in drawing his conclufions.

As foon as he affumed the ermine, he inftantly attracted the particular attention of Lord Mansfield, and although the youngeft judge that ever was promoted to the bench, yet his opinion had always more influence with the Chief Juftice than that of any of his colleagues.

Our Judge has alfo at times been accufed of fomewhat bordering on petulance of difpofition, which has led him into rather unpleafant altercations. An inftance of this occurred at the famous trial of the Dean of St. Afaph, when, after pufhing his oppofition to his quondam pupil, Mr. Erfkine, to threats and defiance, he at length fuffered him to fet his authority at nought, and even allowed him to proceed in the interrogatories the Judge had fo ftrenuoufly oppofed.

When Lord Mansfield was about to retire, he exerted the remains of his once-powerful intereft to procure the nomination of Buller to fucceed him, and is even faid to have retained his poft, on that very account, fome time after he had been difabled by his infirmities from performing its duties.

Some time fince Sir Francis exhibited a wifh to retire from the King's Bench, and propofed an exchange for a feat in the Common Pleas, but difficulties then occurred, which deferred the accomplifhment of his wifhes. He was then fecond on the Bench, and had he removed during

the

the life of Judge Gould, he must have sat as third only in the Common Pleas; but on the death of that truly venerable and honest man, he had his wish gratified, by a removal from the supposed object of his displeasure.

He was lately placed at the head of the Special Commission for trying the state prisoners at Maidstone, and he must be allowed by all candid men to have conducted himself with great impartiality. A circumstance happened on this occasion which gave the judge an opportunity to shew his impartiality to great advantage; we mean the discovery of the letter written by the Rev. Mr. Younge, son of the Secretary of the Board of Agriculture; of which we shall not say a single word, as he is now under prosecution by the Attorney General.

The compliments paid by the judge to Mr. Fox, the Duke of Norfolk, Lord Suffolk, and other noblemen and gentlemen in Opposition, have drawn down upon his head the abuse of some of the Ministerial papers; and by a strange fatality, the great lawyer, formerly suspected of leaning towards despotism, is considered by them as at present too little attached to prerogative.

Sir Francis resides at his country-seat in a manner worthy the imitation of his brethren of the long robe. Unbending from the restraint of the coif, he lives without ostentation; but his table is a hospitable one, and he pays every attention to his guests. Gay, facetious, liberal in his conversation and opinions, he despises the petty prejudices of the day, and proves that he has considered mankind, rather in the character of a philosopher than a lawyer.

Much to his honour he has improved great portions of the waste land in his neighbourhood, and when these are brought into a state of cultivation, he builds cottages, and portions them out into little farms, at easy rents.

Thus, while he is benefiting the present age, he is also creating a noble fortune for his posterity!

K   JOHN

JOHN WOLCOTT, M.D.

THIS gentleman, better known by his poetical appellation of *Peter Pindar*, is a native of that part of Devonshire which has been called the Garden of England. He was educated, we believe, at Kingsbridge, near which he was born. The schoolmaster of that town, an exceeding good scholar, and a man of most amiable manners, was a quaker.

The uncle of our bard being a single man, and established at Fowey, in Cornwall, as an Apothecary, took his nephew when young, with a view to his succeeding him in his business. Here he acquired a tolerable share of medical knowledge: and was in great esteem with his kinsman, and the neighbourhood. At his leisure hours he cultivated his mind by the perusal of the best modern writers; and improved himself considerably in the art of drawing, to which he shewed an early propensity.

On the appointment of Sir William Trelawney to be Governor of Jamaica, about the year 1769, Mr. Wolcott felt a strong inclination to accompany him, especially as that gentleman was a distant relation of his own, and a great friend to the family. He accordingly pressed his uncle not only to give his assent to the project, but also to solicit the favour from Sir William.

The old gentleman was at first extremely concerned at this turn in his nephew's mind. It was a complete overthrow of his favourite scheme respecting him, and it was moreover depriving himself of a most useful assistant. Remonstrances however were vain; and therefore, with the greatest good nature, he waited upon the governor, and obtained the favour that the young adventurer should make one in his suite.

In the voyage the ship touched at Madeira, where Peter, enchanted with the beauties which Nature so luxuriantly exhibits in that island, wrote some exquisite sonnets. On his arrival at Jamaica, he commenced surgeon, with which he blended the practice of his physic, and was actually nominated Physician General to the island. A circumstance however occurred that diverted him for some time from his medical career, and threw him into the arms of a profession for which few men were less qualified.

The incumbent of the most valuable living in Jamaica happened to pay the last tribute to nature long after the Doctor settled there. Whether his practice had not been sufficiently lucrative, or what other motive possessed him, we know not, but certain it is, he looked upon the vacant rectory with a wishful eye. As there was no clergyman at hand to supply the place of the deceased, the physician of the body commenced physician of the soul, and actually officiated for a considerable time in this capacity, reading the prayers of the church of England, and preaching occasionally.

Fearing, at length, that he should be superseded, by a regular minister properly instituted to the living, the Doctor set out for England, carrying with him strong letters of recommendation to the Bishop of London, that he might not only be ordained but also be appointed to the church which he had served.

But though his application was backed pretty strongly by some very considerable friends in England, the Bishop refused to admit him, on the ground, we believe, of his having presumed to perform the ministerial duties without being properly licensed thereto.

In consequence of this disappointment, the Doctor declined revisiting his patients and parishioners in the West Indies; but having previously obtained the degree of M.D.

from one of the Scotch univerfities, he went down to the place of his former refidence, and after living there fome time, removed to Truro, where he practifed for feveral years as a phyfician, with great credit and fuccefs. About this time his uncle died, and left him nearly 2000*l.*

The doctor's fatirical vein fhewed itfelf on various occafions in Cornwall; particularly in fome humorous jokes, which he played off upon the late Mr. Rofewarne, of Truro, and other gentlemen of the neighbourhood. He was alfo engaged in fome troublefome and expenfive lawfuits; one of which was with the corporation of Truro, relative to their right of putting upon him a parifh apprentice. In confequence of thefe difputes, he found that part of the world difagreeable, and therefore refolved to quit it for a fphere more congenial to his talents and difpofition.

During his refidence in this county, the Doctor had an opportunity of bringing forward to the world an eminent natural genius, who otherwife might have been buried in total oblivion, or at the moft have been a fign-painter in his native country. The perfon we allude to was JOHN OPIE, whofe rude drawings in common chalk, efpecially likeneffes, our Doctor viewed with fome curiofity and admiration in his rides through the village of St. Anne, where Opie was a parifh apprentice to one Wheeler, a houfe carpenter.

Thefe drawings were fo fuperior to what could be expected in fuch a place, and from fuch a perfon, that the phyfician was induced to become his inftructor and his patron. He accordingly furnifhed him with materials, and gave him leffons, by which he profited in a manner that furprifed and delighted the benevolent tutor. Having made a rapid progrefs, Opie went to Exeter, where he acquired fome knowledge of oil painting. From that city he removed to London, and under Sir Jofhua Reynolds became one of the moft eminent artifts of the age.

We are forry to remark, however, that a violent mifunderftanding took place during fome years between the

doctor

doctor and his pupil, and from what we can learn, the cause originated in the forgetfulness with which the latter affected to treat his obligations to the former.

Of the Doctor's poetical productions while he was engaged in the practice of physic, we have seen only one specimen; but that is an excellent one, and we trust our readers will be pleased with us for inserting it in this place.

In the year 1776, when Mr. Polwhele, well known by his various publications, was at Truro-school, he had given to him for an evening exercise, to be translated into English, the following beautiful Latin Epigram on sleep:

> Somne levis, quamquem certissima mortis imago,
> Consortem cupio te, tamen esse tori :
> Alma quies, optata veni ; nam, sic, sine vitâ
> Vivere, quam suave est ; sic, sine morte, mori.

Of this epigram the doctor was requested to give a translation, which he produced in a few minutes as follows:

> Come, gentle sleep, attend thy vot'ry's prayer,
> And tho' death's image to my couch repair,
> How sweet, thus lifeless, yet with life to lie,
> Thus, without dying, O how sweet to die !

Our author's first literary production was an "*Epistle to the Reviewers*," 4to. 1782, a truly laughable piece of satire, and certainly discharged against fair game. His next performance was "*Lyric Odes to the Royal Academicians*," 1785, in which is a happy mixture of wit, taste, and elegance, but at the same time it must be allowed, that a want of candour distinguishes the criticisms, and particularly with respect to the paintings of Mr. West.

In the year following, he published another set of odes to the members of the Royal Academy, bearing the same characteristics. About the same time he produced a performance of more originality and boldness. This was the *Lousiad*, a mock heroic poem, abounding in wit, humour, and strength.

The foundation on which our Satirist erected this lively piece, was this:—His Majesty one evening at supper observed ferved a human hair upon his plate, among fome green peas. This offenfive object occafioned a decree to be iffued forth, that all the cooks, fcullions, &c. in the royal kitchen, fhould have their heads fhaved. Great murmurings were excited by this mandate; but the law, like that of the Medes and Perfians, was irrevocable.

On this incident, Peter formed his exquifite production; only changing the hair, by virtue of the *licentia poetica*, to a living animal.

His next production was an epiftle to JAMES BOSWELL, Efq. the felf-fufficient attendant upon Dr. Johnfon to the Hebrides. This was followed by " BOZZI and PIOZZI," in which the folly of tittle tattle biographers is expofed in the happieft manner.

The greateft fuccefs attended our author's publications. Never did any fatirift difplay fuch various excellence. Thofe who difapproved his fentiments, and were offended at his freedom and want of refpect for authority, could not read his poems with unmoved mufcles. To give a catalogue of his numerous writings would be needlefs. There can be no occafion to fpecify at length what is univerfally known, and as univerfally admired. Though our author has fhone moft confpicuoufly as a fatirift, and here indeed his fplendour has been of an extraordinary brilliancy, yet the reader of his fonnets will fometimes be difpofed to regret his having devoted fo much of his time and genius to temporary and perfonal fubjects.

The admirers of poetical elegance may laugh at our bard's pleafant tales and whimfical defcriptions; but they will feel a more exquifite fenfation on reading the tender and fentimental effufions of his pen.

The Doctor, we underftand, lately fuperintended a new edition of Pilkington's Dictionary of Painters, to which he made fome additions. Before we conclude, it may not be amifs to remark, that in his converfation our fatirift

does

does not exhibit either that facetiousness or acerbity which are so eminently displayed in his works.

Neither ought we to finish this article without observing, that Messrs. Robinsons, Golding, and Walker, agreed, in 1795, to pay Dr. W. an annuity of 240l. per annum, for the copy-right of his works. Unfortunately, owing to some obscurity in drawing up the agreement, it has been contended by one party, that it implies only those of the poet *already* published, while the others wish to include all that may hereafter be given to the world, by the facetious Peter.

We are sorry to add, that an action at common law, has been succeeded by a chancery suit; and without entering into the merits of a question, on which some future Chancellor may decide, in the course of the *nineteenth century*, we most cordially recommend an amicable adjustment, and immediate compromise to all parties. What a pity, that the rapacious harpies of the law should be permitted to swallow up the patrimony of the Muses!

Our poet, we believe, once more practises as a physician. Lately recovered from an *asthma*, he has acquired an intimate acquaintance with the theory of that disease, and is himself a living instance, that with skilful management it is not fatal, even in its last and worst stages. He has also minutely investigated the structure of that delicate organ, the human ear.

This is a species of knowledge neither to be obtained on the summit of Parnassus, nor drawn from the fountain Hippocrene; but there is a certain universality in genius, which, indeed, constitutes one of its chief characteristics.

W.

JOHN

JOHN MOORE, D.D.

LORD ARCHBISHOP OF CANTERBURY.

Primate of all England.

SOME of the ablest and best prelates of whom the Church of England has to boast, originally arose from very humble situations in society. The catalogue of her primates, in particular, almost entirely consists of persons of lowly extraction. Cranmer, Parker, Grindal, and Whitgift, the great pillars of the church establishment, after the separation from the papal yoke, were all of a mean descent, if, as in the vulgar phraseology of common life, poverty and meanness be synonimous.

Archbishop Abbot was educated and maintained by public charity.

Laud's father was a weaver; so was Tillotson's; and none of them appear to have been in circumstances to provide for his son.

Potter was a servitor in his college; and both Herring and Secker were more indebted to good fortune, and lucky hits in life, than to family connections, for their elevation to the episcopal bench.

Nor has this been the case only with the Church of England. The most eminent of the Roman pontiffs sprung from obscurity; and the poor people in Italy, until of late, have been accustomed to excite in their children an application to study, by relating to them the story of Pope Sixtus the Fifth. That great man was the son of a cottager; and on his elevation to the *tiara*, he used to say in contempt of the pasquinades that were made upon his birth, that he was *(domus natus illustri*)* " born of an illustrious house,

* This is a play upon words, and unfortunately loses much of its point by translation.

" because

"because the sun-beams passing through the broken walls
"and ragged roof, *illustrated* every corner of his father's
"hut!"

Dr. Moore, the present Archbishop of Canterbury, is a native of Gloucester, where his father was a butcher, in such low circumstances that he could not afford the expences necessary to give his son that liberal education which he both desired and deserved.

He was therefore brought up at the free school of his native city, and on account of his docility of behaviour and promising talents, some friends procured for him an humble situation in Pembroke College, Oxford, whence he afterwards removed to Christ-Church.

While at college, he applied himself to his studies with considerable assiduity, and acquired great respect by his modest demeanour, the regularity of his conduct, and his classical attainments.

He had, however, with all these qualification, no higher prospect before him than that of a country curacy, till one of those lucky circumstances happened, which sometimes occur in the great game of human life, and bring the obscurest individual to the most unlikely of all situations.

The late Duke of Marlborough affected to love the study of mathematics; and in consequence of that propensity, Mr. Blifs, Savilian professor of geometry and astronomer royal, was frequently at Blenheim. In one of his visits there, the Duke asked the Professor to recommend him a young man qualified to act as private tutor to the Marquis of Blandford. Blifs, whose ideas never went beyond the present circumstance, had no thoughts of his own son, but was puzzling his brains to pitch upon some person that might answer the Duke's purpose. At the time he was thus ruminating, young Moore happened to be strolling in the park, and as he was of the same college with the Professor, who respected his character, he at once mentioned him

him to his Grace, as one well qualified to undertake the charge.

In confequence of this recommendation, Mr. Moore was fent for, who very readily accepted the offer which was made him. But the pride of the Duchefs would not permit her to allow her fon's tutor to dine in her prefence; and therefore Mr. Moore was obliged to put up with a place at the fecond table. The mortification arifing from this circumftance, perhaps, was not then very great: but it is remarkable, that this haughty dame when fhe became a widow, actually courted the very fame tutor to receive her hand!

Few men in Mr. Moore's circumftances would have fcrupled how to act on fuch an occafion. His prudence, however, made him forefee that no real good could well refult to him from an acceptance of the propofal; and he accordingly declined it. This generous conduct endearing him to his pupil and the whole family, every exertion was made to promote his advancement in the church.

As a firft ftep, the young Duke fettled an annuity of 400l. upon Dr. Moore, and obtained for him, in 1769, a golden prebend in the cathedral of Durham, to which a valuable living was annexed. In 1771, his Grace perfonally folicited for him, of the King, the Deanery of Canterbury, and obtained it; in 1775, he was made Bifhop of Bangor.

On the death of Dr. Frederick Cornwallis, in 1783, the fee of Canterbury was offered to the two greateft prelates that then ornamented the Englifh Church, Lowth and Hurd. The former declined the tranflation, from his great age, and the latter from his attachment to his own diocefe of Worcefter. It is reported, but upon what ground we will not venture to fay, that his Majefty, on this, defired each of thofe great men to recommend one of the bifhops to him, as the fitteft in their judgment to fill the metropolitical

litical chair; and that they both, without having any knowledge of each other's opinion, mentioned Dr. Moore.

To have suppressed this anecdote in this place would have been wrong, because the story has been very generally reported, and it *may* be true. As for our part, we are inclined to believe that the real fact is otherwise, and that his advancement to the primacy was the effect of the same patronage which first raised him in the church. Most undoubtedly he had not evinced any of those strong powers which could have produced so remarkable a predilection in his favour among his learned brethren; besides, we might say, that it is very unlikely a preferment of such consequence should, in a manner, be suffered to go *a-begging*.

Let the matter be as it may, Dr. Moore obtained the *ne plus ultra* of ecclesiastical dignity, and his conduct in it has been so decorous, as to reflect great honour upon himself and his patrons. The see of Canterbury requires a very temperate person; and his grace has exactly steered that course, which his illustrious predecessors, Tillotson and Secker, pursued with credit to themselves and benefit to the church.

He has wisely avoided taking any active part in political disputes, neither has he adopted any steps to inflame the minds of dissenters on the one hand, nor to alarm the friends of orthodoxy on the other.

When any measure has been before the House of Peers, in which the interests of the church were at all concerned, his Grace has generally been an able, but moderate, speaker. During his primacy, the extension of toleration, and episcopacy have taken place; for the Catholics have been greatly relieved, and Bishops have been appointed in America. Both these circumstances had his Grace's countenance and support. He has, moreover, been the constant friend of merit; and numerous acts of generous patronage might be recorded in his praise.

It

It too frequently happens, that men of obscure origin affect to forget the lowly stock from whence they sprang. An elevation for which they were no way prepared by family connections, generally turns their heads dizzy with false pride; and then a view of their humble descent becomes offensive. Former friendships and situations are consequently wiped out of their remembrance, and poor relations are carefully shunned, or cast into shade, to subsist on a pittance privately bestowed, that they may not tarnish the dignity of the great personage to whom they have the fortune to be allied. He who rises superior to this common failing, is a true philosopher, and worthy of our esteem.

Dr. Moore no sooner began to taste the sweets of prosperity, than he eagerly hastened to communicate a portion of them to his family; and as he advanced in preferment, his attention to them was proportionably encreased. This is an eulogy far more honourable than that derived from the most illustrious talents, or the most splendid actions.

The Archbishop has only printed two sermons; the one preached on the 13th of January, 1777, before the Lords, and the other on the fast-day in 1781.

His Grace married a sister of Lord Auckland, by whom he has several children.

ARTHUR

ARTHUR MURPHY, ESQ.

THAT eminent conftellation, which once illuminated the literary hemifphere with fuch fplendour, and in which JOHNSON fhone with the moft diftinguifhed luftre, has, for fome time, been reduced to a very fmall number of luminaries.

The veteran who now calls for our confideration, long moved in this illuftrious circle with confiderable reputation, and enjoyed a degree of applaufe, on account of his productions, which has been the lot of but few. He has, however, feen the greateft ornaments of literature cut off, and hardly any others worthy notice arifing in their place. He has beheld the new philofophy fpreading its glare wide around, and obtaining admiration; and he has lived to witnefs a new theatrical tafte, ufurping the province of the genuine drama, and threatening complete deftruction to one of the fineft branches of poefy.

He has alfo exifted long enough to witnefs a revolution, not only in matters of a political nature, but in manners, fentiment, and amufements. Surely fuch a man, ftill retaining all his faculties in their priftine vigour, cannot contemplate the furrounding fcene, in which he is nearly ifolated, without feeling all his fenfibilities wounded! But let us wave reflection, and proceed to narrative.

Mr. MURPHY was born in Cork, about the year 1727, and received in that city the rudiments of his education. From Ireland he was fent to the Jefuit's College at St. Omer's, and attained in that learned feminary a very extenfive knowledge of the Latin language.

His uncle, who refided in the Weft-Indies, defigning him for trade, he was placed in a banking-houfe in Lombard-ftreet. But the Mufes foon attracted him from the bill-book and the ledger; and inftead of applying himfelf to

commercial

commercial studies, all his attention was devoted to the writings of the most elegant authors, ancient and modern.

The counting-house was of course soon entirely abandoned; and, with a very scanty pittance of this world's store, he entered himself, in 1750, a member of the Society of Gray's Inn, and became an adventurer in literature, partly from necessity, and partly from choice.

At first, indeed, he formed the design of adopting the stage as a profession, but after two or three essays, one of which was in the character of Othello, he found himself better qualified to *write* plays than to *act* them *.

His first literary undertaking that we know of was the Gray's Inn Journal, which he commenced in 1752, and

---

* Charles Churchill, the celebrated satirist, was perhaps too severe on this attempt on the part of Mr. Murphy, whom he always persecuted with a rancour that seemed, from its violence, to have arisen in personal dislike:

"In person tall, a figure form'd to please,
"If symmetry could charm, depriv'd of ease;
"When motionless he stands we all approve:
"What pity 'tis the THING was made to move!

"His voice in one dull, deep, unvary'd sound,
"Seems to break forth from caverns under ground;
"From hollow chest, the low sepulchral note
"Unwilling heaves, and struggles in his throat.

"Could authors butcher'd give an actor grace,
"All must to him resign the foremost place;
"When he attempts, in some fav'rite part,
"To ape the feelings of a manly heart,
"His honest features the disguise defy,
"And his face loudly gives his tongue the lie.

"Still in extreme, he knows no happy mean,
"Or raving mad or stupidly serene:
"In cold-wrought scenes the lifeless actor flags,
"In passion, tears the passion into rags.

"Can none remember?—yes—I know all must—
"When in the MOOR he ground his teeth to dust;
"When o'er the stage he Folly's standard bore,
"Whilst Common Sense stood trembling at the door."

ROSCIAD, l. 363.

continued

continued for two years. This work was not without its merit, or even celebrity, though when compared with the other periodical papers of the same time, particularly the formidable Rambler, it sinks into insignificance. This publication, however, was the means of introducing the author to the acquaintance of Dr. Samuel Johnson, and as the anecdote is curious, it is worth relating in this place.

Mr. Murphy was on a visit at the country-house of Foote, when a paper was wanted for his journal. Being ill-disposed for composition, the English Aristophanes produced a new French miscellany, in which was an Eastern apologue remarkably ingenious. This pleased our author so well, that he translated it at once, and sent it to his printer. On his return to town, he found that this tale had been taken by the French writer from Johnson's Rambler without acknowledgment. Hurt at this unintentional plagiarism, Murphy waited upon Johnson, and made his apology. The moralist was easily pacified; and an acquaintance commenced, which continued till Johnson's death.

At the beginning of the present reign, Murphy enlisted as a party-writer, in vindication of Lord Bute's administration; and though his labours were but feeble, in comparison with the keen attacks of Opposition, he was handsomely rewarded by those whose cause he espoused.

At this time he was in habits of intimacy with Mr. Wilkes; and though they were engaged in a paper war, the former in the *Auditor*, and the latter in the *North Briton*, yet they knew not, for some time, that they were fighting with each other. On the discovery of the secret, Wilkes's partizans entered into a resolution to oppose any new piece which Mr. Murphy might bring forward on the stage. Accordingly, when our Author's farce of " What we must all come to," was performed, a violent party-spirit manifested itself; and the piece, though free from any political allusions, was *damned!* Some years afterwards it was again produced,

duced, under the title of "Three Weeks after Marriage," when it received unmixed applause, and has continued a favourite entertainment ever since.

Murphy expostulated with Wilkes on the conduct of his friends, and the patriot not only disavowed any share in their proceedings, but promised, that should any future occasion offer, he would himself come forward with his party in the offended bard's support.

As a political writer, Mr. Murphy never rose to any distinguished eminence, otherwise we suppose he would have obtained either preferment or a pension. The only thing with which he was favoured, as far as we know, was the post of Commissioner of Bankrupts, which he held till the appointment of Lord Thurlow to the great seal; and when the present Chancellor came into office, he replaced his old friend upon the list.

Though regularly called to the bar by the society of Lincoln's Inn, after a long struggle, he never obtained any extensive practice, nor any share of credit on account of legal abilities. He, however, went the Norfolk circuit for a considerable time.

As a writer, he has shone most in dramatic poetry; and it may be said of him, what few who have written for the stage can boast, that he has been equally successful in comedy and tragedy. His pieces in the former line evince great knowledge of the world, and a minute acquaintance with the human character, combined with that liveliness of fancy which is essentially necessary to produce the sensations of mirth.

In his tragedies, one remarks a happy delineation of character, joined to a due mixture of the pathetic and heroic, clothed with language at once appropriate, easy, and elegant. So great has been the success of his plays, that though the receipts of the *former* Drury-lane theatre never amounted to three hundred pounds a night, he gained eight hundred

hundred pounds by his "Grecian Daughter;" and very near the same sum by "His Way to keep him."

Mr. Murphy's intimacy with the first geniuses of the age tended greatly to improve his taste, and consequently to render his productions elegant. Such an association is of wonderful benefit to a rising and emulous writer. In the company of such as Johnson and Burke, a man possessed of any portion of genius could not fail to have improved his mind. To have been in habits of close friendship with these persons required no small portion of literary and moral merit.

Mr. Murphy had the credit of introducing Johnson to the acquaintance of Mr. Thrale. He was also a member of the club which Johnson instituted in Essex street.

In 1762 he wrote an Essay on the Life and Genius of Henry Fielding, prefixed to the complete edition of that writer's works, for which he received a considerable sum. On this occasion he behaved in a manner which few biographers will, perhaps, be disposed to imitate. A considerable quantity of letters and anecdotes were put into his hands, by Sir John Fielding and others, to elucidate the memoir. On examining these communications, he found that many of them were well adapted to amuse the public, but that at the same time they tended to tarnish the memory of the deceased. He, therefore, suppressed them; and gave to his production the qualified title of an essay. He followed a similar line of conduct with respect to the life of his friend Johnson, which was published in 1791, and for which he was handsomely rewarded.

About the same time appeared his translation of Tacitus, in four quarto volumes. In this work he had been engaged for many years; and there is a circumstance respecting it which does Mr. Murphy infinite honour. Not long before the publication of this work, a nobleman of high rank and consequence in the political world signified to the translator his wish to have it dedicated to him. Murphy, however,

L   had

had previously determined to inscribe his labours to the man whom he most esteemed, the immortal BURKE, and he accordingly made a noble sacrifice of interest to friendship!

His last literary production was a tragedy never performed, entitled "Arminius;" and he has been lately engaged in writing the life of the modern Aristophanes, Samuel Foote.

Mr. Murphy's classical knowledge and taste appear to great advantage in his Latin poems, particularly in a version of Gray's Elegy; and we remember to have seen an elegant translation of Addison's Letter from Italy, written by him, but never printed.

Mr. Murphy usually resides at Hammersmith, enjoying an easy independence. He is a very entertaining companion, abounding in anecdotes, of which he is engagingly communicative in company. His character is highly respectable; and he enjoys the intimacy of some of the first personages in the kingdom.

We are sorry, however, to observe, that his health is on the decline, and that he has been obliged to go to Bristol, for the benefit of the waters.

W.

EARL OF DARTMOUTH.

WILLIAM, Earl of Dartmouth, succeeded his father in the year 1743, being then only twenty-five years of age. In 1755 he espoused a rich heiress of the name of Nichols, by whom he got a very considerable addition to his fortune, and in 1757 was chosen Recorder of Litchfield.

His Lordship being of a pious turn of mind, his conduct has been chiefly marked by an attention to religious duties, for which, as well as correctness of manners, he has been more distinguished than most men of the same rank. Notwithstanding this, he has not entirely abstracted himself from public affairs, for we find him at times filling some of the most considerable offices in the state.

His Lordship connected himself early in life with the Rockingham party, and when they came into power in 1765, he was made First Lord of Trade, and sworn of the privy-council.

He, however, does not seem to have continued staunch to his old friends, for although he went out with them, yet about the year 1772 he was induced to accept of the post of Secretary of State, and soon after removed to the head of the board of trade. In this situation he took a warm and decided part against the Americans, which recommended him so much to his Majesty, that in 1775 he had the custody of the Privy Seal confided to him, which office he retained during the whole remaining term of Lord North's administration.

The noble Lord, who, along with the late Baron Smythe, was the chief supporter of the *evangelical preaching* at the Lock chapel, is by many considered a methodist. It is somewhat remarkable that a man of his retired and serious turn of mind should engage in the busy career of politics.

Soon after his dismission, he joined the coalition, and by them was appointed Lord Steward of the Houshold, which place he retained about nine months, and when his friends were driven out of power, he retired with them, and has continued ever since in the walks of private life.

During the struggle about the regency he took the side of the prince, for which his Highness shewed his gratitude, by appointing his son, Lord Lewisham, Warden of the Stannaries of Cornwall.

Lord Dartmouth is esteemed a man of sense, and was considered as a tolerable speaker in the House of Lords. In private life, he bears the character of a good husband, a good parent, and a kind master; and is, on the whole, one of the most inoffensive among the nobility.

So early as the year 1755, we find the late Mr. James Hervey, author of the " Meditations," &c. one of his Lordship's intimates, speaking highly of his pious disposition.

He was also the close friend of the late Countess of Huntingdon, Mr. George Whitfield, and all the eminent supporters of Calvinistical Methodism. It must be allowed, that as a *private* man he has borne himself with an uniform character through life; and with the *profession* of piety, has invariably connected the *practice* of it.

THE

THE HON. AND REV. DR. SHUTE BARRINGTON,

LORD BISHOP OF DURHAM.

John Shute Barrington, who was created an English Viscount in the year 1720, was the intimate friend of the immortal Locke, and, like him, a firm assertor of the liberties of mankind, an acute metaphysician, and an able expositor and defender of the sacred scriptures. His Lordship died the latter end of 1734, and left behind him six sons, five of whom have arrived at great eminence in the professions of the army, navy, the law, and the church.

The subject of our present notice was the youngest of these, and was born about the year 1732. He received his education at Eton school, whence he was removed to the university of Oxford, where he was entered of Merton College; but he afterwards went to Christ-church, of which he became a student.

He entered into holy orders in 1756, and the year following took his degree of Master of Arts. June 10th, 1762, the degree of Doctor of Laws was conferred upon him; and in 1766, on the death of Dr. Taylor, he was presented to a canon residentiaryship in the cathedral of St. Paul.

In the year 1769 he was made Bishop of Landaff; and while in that station he brought a bill into the House of Lords, the object of which went to check the encreasing evil of matrimonial infidelity, by preventing persons divorced by parliament from marrying those with whom they had been criminal. His Lordship observed, that many acts of adultery had been committed solely with the intention to obtain separation, in order to form new alliances; and therefore, he was desirous of putting a legal barrier against that licentious practice. In this attempt he

was

was supported by the opinion of the ablest lawyers and divines in the kingdom. His laudable design, however, fell to the ground; though had it taken place much good would have been effected by it, and the long catalogue of divorces must have been drawn within a very narrow compass.

In the year 1782, his Lordship was translated to the see of Salisbury, where he distinguished himself greatly by his liberality in repairing and beautifying the noble cathedral of that diocese; and on the death of Bishop Egerton, in 1791, he was translated to Durham, with the approbation of every well-wisher of the church and state.

In his episcopal capacity, his Lordship has conducted himself with great dignity of manners, and with the most exemplary attention to the duties of his office.

He has been very watchful over the behaviour of his clergy; and has shewn a most commendable circumspection with respect to the character and qualifications of candidates for holy orders.

With a laudable zeal to promote the study of sacred literature, he bestows premiums upon such candidates as excel in the Hebrew and Greek languages. This, we believe, is quite a novel practice; and doubtless, were it generally followed, it would only create a spirit of emulation in young persons preparing for the church, but would, moreover, render most of them ashamed of appearing before the Bishop or Archdeacon without a tolerable share of sacred learning.

One anecdote of his Lordship does high honour to his liberality and his piety. A relation of Mrs. Barrington having experienced some embarrassments and disappointments in life, wished to mend his situation (being a military officer), by entering into the church, thinking that the Bishop would provide handsomely for him. On making the necessary application to his kinsman, he was asked

what

what preferment would satisfy him. To this home question he readily answered, that about 500*l* a year would make him a happy man. "You shall have it," said his Lordship, "but not out of the patrimony of the church. "I will not deprive a worthy and r gular divine to provide for a necessitous relation. You shall have the sum you mention yearly out of my own pocket."

The Bishop has published several single sermons, and some episcopal charges, which have been greatly esteemed. He also contributed some valuable notes to Mr. Bowyer's "Conjectures on the New Testament," and he has given the world an edition of his father's "Miscellanea Sacra," in three volumes, 8vo. with many additions and corrections.

Though a supporter of administration, he has conducted himself in parliament with great moderation.

W.

MR. KING.

THE character of an actor, in private life, has been usually beheld, throughout all Europe, with a certain degree of coolness, bordering on contempt. In Spain, we believe comedians are not admitted to *confession*, at this very day; and it is well known, that in France, previously to the abolition, or at least the *limitation* of the Monarchy, they did not enjoy the rites of sepulture, or, in other words, were not permitted to participate of " a Christian burial." In this country, illiberal prejudices are happily of less avail, and the names of Shakspeare and of Garrick have contributed not a little to shield the whole profession from indiscriminate contumely.

The object of this memoir, known to all lovers of the drama, by the familiar name of " Tom King," seems to have received a better education than the bulk of the fraternity. His family, which was respectable, sent him to a good grammar school in the country, whence, at a proper period, he was removed to London, and articled to an attorney.

He soon, however, became captivated with the stage; and quitting his profession, accompanied Shuter, and joined a strolling company, about thirty miles from London. This of course, irritated his parents, who, instead of endeavouring to reclaim, abandoned and sent him to shift for himself. If Tate Wilkinson is correct in his dates, Mr. King must now have been on the stage full half a century, for he tells us that he played under Mr. Garrick in 1748.

Those who have seen this excellent actor of late, will scarcely be induced to believe, that for many years after his first appearance he almost exclusively acted in tragedy.

In

In 1748, he performed George Barnwell; and next year appeared in Dublin in the character of the Roman Father!

He at length obtained an engagement at Bath, where he contracted a friendship with Miss Baker, at that time a celebrated dancer, and who is at present his wife.

His success at Bath recommended him to the managers of Drury-lane, who employed him at a small salary, and entrusted him only with inferior parts; nor could he, for some time, obtain any character in the least suitable to his talents. He therefore quitted that theatre, repaired again to Ireland, and acted in a considerable number of comic characters, with great applause. He had, by this time, contrived to form in Dublin a very reputable set of acquaintance, and would probably have remained in that country, had he not foreseen the divisions which were likely to take place in its theatrical concerns. He accordingly applied to Mr. Garrick, and the fame of his merit having reached England before his offer, he was engaged at a genteel salary.

Garrick immediately brought him out in the character of *Tom*, in the " Conscious Lovers;" in which, and many other comic situations, he obtained uncommon applause. But what raised his fame to the standard at which it afterwards stood was his inimitable performance of *Lord Ogleby*, in the " Clandestine Marriage," which he executed in so masterly a style, as to obtain the most flattering attention, and greatly assist the run of that excellent comedy.

It is said, that Garrick intended to play the part himself, but could not fix on a mode of doing it to his mind. On this he desired King to try it, and was so pleased with the first specimen he gave at the rehearsal, that he declared, if he could support the same style of acting throughout, it would be one of the first comic characters on the stage.

On the death of Mr. Powell, in 1765, Mr. King purchased his share of the Bristol theatre, which turned out

profitable

profitable to him; and with his winter engagement at Drury Lane, produced a very handfome income. He fold it, however, a few years after, to Mr. Palmer, of the theatre at Bath (late of the poft-office), and purchafed the property of Sadler's Wells; but this not being fo productive as he wifhed, he difpofed of it to Mr. Wroughton.

When Mr. Sheridan and the other partners purchafed Drury-lane houfe, that gentleman's inimitable comedy of " The School for Scandal" was brought out. This afforded Mr. King a new opportunity of difplaying his talents for comedy, in the character of *Sir Peter Teazle*; and when Sheridan embarked fo deeply in politics, as to prevent his attending the duty of the theatre, he delegated his power to King, and appointed him acting manager.

A little before this, Mr. K. had abfented himfelf during a whole feafon from the ftage; on his return, he wrote an interlude for his introduction, called " A dramatic Olio," which was well received. He has alfo written " Love at firft Sight," a ballad farce, acted at Drury-lane in 1765; and " Wit's laft Stake," another farce, played at the fame houfe in 1769.

But in the midft of this profperity, and when he had realized a handfome fortune, a paffion, which he had long fuppreffed, is reported to have broke out, and deftroyed his pleafing profpects. While under Mr. Garrick's dominion, and a candidate for public favour, he difcovered an infurmountable propenfity to play; and although cautioned againft it, yet he could not refift, but loft all his earnings at the gaming-table. One night, however, Fortune fmiled, and he gained fo large a fum as 2000l. On this he is faid to have immediately made a moft folemn declaration, both to Garrick and his wife, " that he would never touch a dice-box again!" It has even been faid, that he executed a bond for a fum of money to the former, under penalty of forfeiture in cafe he ever gamed. King kept his refolution for many years, until by the death of his friend
" Davy,"

"Davy," he perhaps deemed himself absolved from his engagement: having then an extensive circle of genteel acquaintance, he was induced to enter himself, about the year 1784 or 1785, a member of the club at Miles's, merely from the love of society, and fully secure, as he thought, against the allurements of play. He was, however, at last tempted; and losing, at first, some small sums, became vexed, and ventured deeper, until that fortune he had been so long accumulating by his exertions was almost totally exhausted. In consequence of this, he parted with his pretty little villa at Hampton, and exchanged his house in Gerrard-street for a small one in Store-street, Bedford-square.

Nor was the loss of fortune the only disappointment that ensued. He was at that time in treaty with Dr. Ford for a share of Drury-lane theatre, but this unlucky transfer of his property rendered him incapable of making good the payment. Some trifling dispute having occurred, in consequence of this, Mr. King, in anger, resigned his two situations, as actor and manager at Drury-lane theatre.

He was, however, under the necessity of relying once more on the stage for a maintenance; and accordingly, in 1788, he repaired to Dublin, the scene of his juvenile triumphs, where he was again received with all that warmth and enthusiasm so delectable to an old favourite.

On his return, he performed a stipulated number of nights at Covent-garden theatre, both to the advantage of himself and the manager; and next season he resumed his situation at Drury-lane.

Last year, actuated by motives of sincere friendship, Mr. Smith, who had long quitted the stage, came to town, expressly on purpose to play *Charles*, in the "School for Scandal," for his benefit; and the house, as might be expected, was, in the language of the theatre, "a bumper!"

Mr. King is undoubtedly the first comic actor the stage has possessed for many years, and also stands unrivalled in the happy art of delivering a lively prologue.

THE

THE HON. BROWNLOW NORTH,
LORD BISHOP OF WINCHESTER.

THIS refpectable prelate is half-brother of the late Frederick, Earl of Guildford, the amiable but unfortunate minifter of this country, in perhaps one of the moft eventful period of its hiftory.

His Lordfhip was educated at Eton fchool, whence he removed to Trinity college, Oxford, which he afterwards left for a fellowfhip of All-Souls.

Here he took his degree of LL.D. and on entering into holy orders, was preferred to a canonry of Chrift-Church; in 1770 he was advanced to the Deanery of Canterbury, and appointed one of the king's chaplains; the year following, he was confecrated Bifhop of Litchfield and Coventry.*

In 1774, he was tranflated and confirmed in the fee of Worcefter; and in 1781, he was removed to Winchefter.

In all the fituations he has filled his Lordfhip has obtained diftinguifhed reputation; and every church over which he has prefided ranks his name in the catalogue of its moft munificent prelates.

When he was Bifhop of Worcefter, he promoted that excellent inftitution for the benefit of the widows and orphans of poor clergymen belonging to his diocefe, in aid of the charity derived to them from the mufic meeting, and alfo for the relief of the aged infirm incumbents of fmall livings, and of poor curates with large families.

His Lordfhip's manner is highly dignified, yet condefcending; he blends authority and watchfulnefs with tendernefs and benevolence. He is juftly regarded as the

* Dr. North was Dean of Canterbury before he was twenty-nine years old, and Bifhop of Litchfield and Coventry at the age of thirty-three.

father

father of his diocese; and his charities, which are very extensive, are judiciously administered.

His Lordship has invariably preserved through life the esteem of men of all parties and persuasions. During a long residence in Italy, whither he went on account of his health, he attracted the universal regard of the dignified clergy of the Roman communion. In short, the suavity of his manners and his elegant deportment excited in many a high degree of respect for the English HIERARCHY.

Dr. North at one time took an active part in the great political questions of the day. In 1784 he supported Mr. Fox's celebrated India bill in the House of Lords; and during another important period, we find his name in every division of the peers in favour of the Prince of Wales's uncontrouled right to the Regency.

As Bishop of the see of Winchester, he is prelate of the Garter, the *insignia* of which order are constantly worn by his Lordship.

He is now a widower, and has four daughters and two sons.

MR. WILLIAM JACKSON, of EXETER.

THIS elegant compofer, and ingenious writer, was born at Exeter in May, 1730. His father was an eminent grocer in that place, and afterwards mafter of the city workhoufe.

He gave his fon a very liberal education; and perceiving that the bent of his genius lay towards mufic, he complied with his inclinations, and put him under the tuition of Mr. Sylvefter, then organift of the cathedral church of St. Peter, in Exeter, with whom he continued two years. After leaving Mr. Sylvefter, Mr. Jackfon went to London, about the year 1748, where he became a pupil of Mr. Travers, organift of the King's chapel, and of St. Paul's, Covent-garden, with whom he alfo remained two years, and then returned to his native city, where he taught mufic for many years with great reputation. He alfo publifhed feveral beautiful compofitions, marked by the moft chafte conceptions, the moft elegant tafte, and the moft correct knowledge of the principles of harmony. In fhort, all his pieces were received with applaufe, and ftill rank very high in the mufical world.

Notwithftanding his great and univerfally acknowledged merit in his profeffion, he obtained no fituation as an organift till Michaelmas, 1777, when he fucceeded Mr. Richard Langdon as Sub-chanter, Organift, Lay-vicar, and Mafter of the Chorifters, in the cathedral of Exeter.

Mr. Jackfon, early in life, married Mifs Bartlett, a milliner at Exeter, who is ftill alive, and by whom he has had feveral children, three of whom only are now living, two fons and a daughter. One of the former (the elder) went to China, and returned thence with a competent fortune,

which

which he intended to enjoy in his native city, in the bosom of his family: but the appointment of an Embassy to the court of Pekin, called him from his retirement into service, and he accordingly accompanied Lord Macartney on that mission, and now resides once more at Exeter. The youngest son living is employed at present at Turin, as Secretary to our Ambassador at that court.

After amusing the circle of his friends with several ingenious pieces of his writing in prose and verse, Mr. Jackson appeared as an author in the year 1782, at which time he published in two small volumes, 12mo. "Thirty letters on various Subjects." These formed a miscellaneous collection on literature and science, and evinced extensive knowledge, united with an elegant taste. On poetry, music, and painting, his opinions are allowed to be very ingenious, and have obtained general approbation. But in some respects he manifested a paradoxical spirit, particularly in the instance of *spontaneous generation*, a notion which he attempted to illustrate, and revive, from the oblivion in which it had so long and deservedly sunk. These letters, however, on the whole raised our author's credit very high. It was not, however, till 1795, that he thought proper to publish a new edition of them, although they had been out of print for several years before. To that edition, which is in one volume octavo, there are several additions and corrections.

During the present year Mr. Jackson has added a second volume, under the title of "The Four Ages; with Essays on various Subjects." In this ingenious work he considers the four mythological ages as characteristic of so many distinct periods of the world, but in a different order from that in which the poets have placed them. Among the essays there is a most curious and entertaining one, on the character of Gainsborough the painter, of whom some whimsical anecdotes are given.

In

In the year 1792, a literary fociety was inftituted at the Globe Inn, Fore-ftreet, Exeter, of which the firft members were Dr. Downman, prefident; Mr. Polwhele, author of " The Hiftory of Devonfhire;" Mr. Jackfon; the Rev. Mr. Swete, of Oxton; Mr. Hole, author of an " Effay on the Arabian Nights Entertainments;" Mr. Sheldon, the Anatomift; and other ingenious gentlemen refident in Exeter, or its environs. Each produced in his turn an effay in profe or verfe, which was read at the regular meeting of the fociety. An octavo volume of thefe was printed in 1796, which reflects great honour upon this inftitution. The papers, however, appear without the names of the authors, which in our opinion is a piece of delicacy not to be commended: and as we are not bound by any rules of fecrefy, we fhall not fcruple to mention thofe which belong to the gentleman of whom we are now fpeaking.

Mr. Jackfon has no lefs than three in this volume, all of them connected with each other in point of fubject. Thefe are, effay the eleventh, " On Literary Fame, and the Hiftorical Characters of Shakfpeare;" effay xviii. " An Apology for the Character and Conduct of Iago;" and effay xviii. " An Apology for the Character and Conduct of Shylock." The firft is certainly the beft, and will be read by thofe who admire our immortal bard with great pleafure, and even with improvement. Mr. Jackfon is peculiarly happy in throwing new light upon the point which he undertakes to illuftrate, and he brings his various reading to bear with great force upon the fubject. He is ingenious in his apology for Iago, and fays many things to " extenuate" his conduct; but that in behalf of Shylock is far more convincing and fatisfactory. Thefe effays are lively, pleafant, and exceedingly well written.

Mr. Jackfon poffeffes the advantage of a chafte, correct, and even elegant ftyle. The reader will not flumber over
his

his pages, nor when he has perused either of his volumes will he wish to lay it by in peace: he will recur to it often with new avidity, and receive from it fresh pleasure. The same may be said of his literary as of his musical compositions, that they will always charm with the force of novelty and delight, though repeated a thousand and a thousand times.

In temper and conversation he is what he appears in his writings, pleasant, social, communicative, and abounding in judicious remarks and entertaining anecdotes.

LORD MALMESBURY.

THIS diſtinguiſhed nobleman, whoſe name will frequently occur in the hiſtory of George the Third, would have inherited philoſophy as well as fortune from his anceſtors, could the one have been as eaſily tranſmitted as the other.

His father, James Harris, Eſq. the celebrated author of HERMES, was the ſon of Elizabeth, ſiſter to Anthony, Earl of Shafeſbury, the immortal author of the CHARACTERISTICS. Mr. Harris was born at Saliſbury, in 1708, and after receiving a claſſical education in that city, was removed to Wadham college, Oxford, which he left without taking a degree.

He repreſented the borough of Chriſt-church, in Hampſhire, in ſeveral parliaments; but did not obtain any public office till the year 1763, when he was preferred to a ſeat at the Admiralty-board, which he reſigned ſoon after, on being appointed to another on the Treaſury-bench. In July, 1765, he was deprived of his place, and continued out of office until 1774, when he became Secretary and Comptroller to the Queen, which poſt he held till his death, December 21ſt, 1780.

His only ſon, JAMES HARRIS, now Lord Malmeſbury, was born April 20th, 1746, and being early deſigned for a public life, received an education accordingly.

Under ſo profound and elegant a ſcholar as Mr. Harris, the ſon could not but derive every aſſiſtance calculated to render him an ornament to his family. His education, prior to his removal to Oxford, was conducted chiefly under the eye of his father. He alſo left college without taking a degree, and was very early employed as Secretary to an embaſſy at one of the Northern courts.

In

In 1772, he appeared in the character of Envoy-extraordinary at Berlin; and in the following year both he and his father were returned members of parliament for the borough of Chrift-church. His diplomatic conduct gave fo much fatisfaction to the government which he reprefented, that in 1775 he was made Knight of the Bath, and about the fame time was appointed Envoy-extraordinary to the court of Ruffia.

After refiding a confiderable time at Peterfburgh, he was employed as ambaffador at the Hague; which important ftation was occupied by him in the year 1787, when Holland was threatened with a revolution, which was averted for fome time, by an humiliating recourfe to the affiftance of Pruffian bayonets. The conduct of Sir James Harris on that occafion was peculiarly offenfive to the patriots; but it was fo highly fatisfactory to the Prince of Orange and the King of Pruffia, that they beftowed upon him the privilege of bearing the Pruffian eagle in his arms, with the motto appertaining to the Houfe of Naffau, in confideration of the fignal fervices which he had rendered them.

Thefe diftinctions were confirmed by his own fovereign in 1789, and Sir James was created a peer, September 15th, 1788, by the title of Lord Malmefbury, Baron of Malmefbury, in the county of Wilts.

His Lordfhip remained out of employment from that time till the government found it expedient, at the end of 1796, to comply with the wifh of the people in endeavouring to obtain the reftoration of peace. No man at that time appeared more fit to be entrufted with fuch an important charge than Lord Malmefbury; and we believe that his *firft* appointment to this ftation was with the entire approbation of all parties. His Lordfhip's negociation, however failed; and he was enjoined to quit Paris, by a peremptory

peremptory order of the French Directory, in forty-eight hours, December 17, 1796.*

Whatever opinions may be entertained respecting the conduct of the two powers, in this negociation, or the views with which they were actuated, it must be allowed that his Lordship evinced on that occasion the most consummate knowledge of diplomatic business.

A second attempt to put an end to this long and sanguinary contest was thought proper to be made by our ministers in June, 1797, and Lord Malmesbury was again appointed to the office of negociator. The necessary preliminaries having been accordingly settled with the Directory, his Lordship and suite set out on the 30th of that month for Lisle, the place fixed upon as the seat of business, and the French government immediately extended a chain of telegraphs between that city and Paris.

It would be foreign to our purpose to enter into the merits of the political manœuvres practised in this diplomatic game. The French Commissioners shewed themselves adroit enough for his Lordship, though an old practitioner, versed in all the arts of modern intrigue. Their demands, as far as they avowed them, were abundantly extravagant; and the care with which they concealed their objects, was dexterous indeed. After playing with each other until the patience of all Europe was exhausted, and suspicions began to take place on the score of sincerity, the Commissioners had recourse to their old method of putting an end to the negociation, and actually dismissed his Lordship, upon the plea that he was not vested with full powers to resign the whole of the conquests made by this country from France and her allies during the war.

* The Directory conceived that he had been tampering as a partisan, rather than treating like a diplomatic agent.

The

The English minister accordingly quitted Lisle, and arrived in London on the 20th of September, without having effected a single step favourable to the great object on which he was employed. It has been indeed said, in the senate of a neighbouring country, that the "Irish Directory" impeded his operations, by means of their agent!

Without throwing the slightest reflection upon his Lordship's talents, or inclinations, we yet cannot but acquiesce with the opinion of many very respectable politicians, and those too of the most moderate cast of sentiment, that after the ill success which attended his former mission, it was bad policy in the ministry to employ the same person in a similar negociation.

Some have even ventured to say, that the line of practice in which his Lordship has usually been engaged, rendered him an unfit person to be charged with this business. Different times, people, and occasions, certainly call for different kinds of treatment. New modes, and even a new language, should be adopted, in negociating with a people who have thrown aside old political ceremonies and considerations; and therefore another kind of ambassador should have been sent to treat with them, than one whose whole life had been occupied in the knowledge and practice of the ancient diplomatic forms.

Whether this sort of reasoning be right or wrong, we shall not take upon us to determine. But we cannot help regretting, that when his Lordship's first attempt failed, his Majesty's ministers had not put it out of the power of their adversaries to accuse them of insincerity, by employing another minister, when they thought it expedient to treat once more for the restoration of peace.

This nobleman possesses the confidence of the present administration, and is intimately acquainted with its views relative to continental politics. It is not difficult, therefore, to prognosticate, that his diplomatic talents will not be suffered to rust in obscurity.

Lord

Lord Malmesbury married, July 28th, 1777, the daughter of Sir George Amyand, Bart. by a sister of Sir George Cornwall, Bart. and has by his lady several children.

He has two sisters living; one married, the other single, and residing at his Lordship's seat, the manor-house of Great Durnford, about four miles from Salisbury, only remarkable for its neat and embellished pleasure-grounds. In the same village still stands the cottage to which the great author of Hermes retired from the busy world, and in which he wrote the chief part of his works. It is unoccupied, but its furniture, &c. is in all respects carefully and religiously preserved by Lord Malmesbury, in the exact state in which it was left by his father. This very interesting cottage is entirely secluded from the public eye, being surrounded on three sides by walls, and only open on the west side, which adjoins the Avon. His Lordship generally spends a few weeks in every year at the manor-house in great retirement.

W. J.

JOSEPH

JOSEPH WHITE, D.D.
LAUDIAN PROFESSOR OF ARABIC,
In the Univerſity of Oxford.

THE lives of ſuch men as have riſen from very low ſituations in life to diſtinguiſhed eminence, by the ſtrength of their talents alone, are among the moſt uſeful articles of biography, becauſe they hold out encouragement to young perſons of a like deſcription to exert their abilities with perſeverance; and, at the ſame time, afford a leſſon to thoſe who have it in their power to aſſiſt genius. Had CHATTERTON met with a friend, generous enough to put him in a line where he might have turned his talents to an honourable and beneficial account, he would not, probably have ſought an early grave as a refuge from his miſeries.

The very ingenious and worthy ſubjeƈt of the preſent article was born of parents in indigent circumſtances in Glouceſterſhire. His father was, we are informed, a journeyman weaver, and brought his ſon up to the ſame profeſſion. Being, however, a ſenſible man, and for one in his ſituation, tolerably educated, he gave him what little learning was in his power. This excited a thirſt for greater acquiſitions.

Young White inherited a ſerious caſt of temper from his parents; and he employed all the time he could ſpare in the ſtudy of ſuch books as fell in his way. His attainments at length were ſo very reſpeƈtable, that he began to be talked of as a prodigy of learning in his native village. A neighbouring gentleman of fortune luckily chanced to hear of this celebrated ſcholar; and curioſity inclined him to ſee and converſe with him. The modeſty of the ſelf-inſtruƈted youth recommended him to favour, while the reſpeƈtability respectability of his knowledge rendered him an object of admiration. The gentleman felt that it was a pity such a flower should

> ———— "blush unseen
> "And waste its sweetness in the desert air:"

He accordingly encouraged his scholastic ambition. He assisted him also considerably in his studies: and so rapidly did the young plant flourish under his fostering care, that the generous patron sent him to the University of Oxford, where he was entered of Wadham College. There he applied himself with such assiduity to his studies, and conducted himself with so much regularity, as to gain the general esteem of the members of that society.

On the 19th of February, 1773, he took the degree of Master of Arts, and about that time engaged in the study of the oriental languages, to which he was induced by the particular recommendation of Dr. Moore, now Archbishop of Canterbury. That discerning man observed a dint of application in Mr. White, united with a peculiar turn for philological enquiries, which he thought might turn to his account, if devoted to one object. Fortunately he hit upon the one which was best suited for Mr. White, and which has been of the most essential service to him. He had before acquired a tolerable share of Hebrew learning; and, consequently, his progress in the Oriental languages was greatly facilitated thereby.

In 1775, he was appointed Archbishop Laud's Professor of Arabic; on entering upon which office he pronounced a masterly oration, which was soon afterwards printed with the title of "De Utilitate Ling. Arab. in Studiis Theologicis Oratio habita Oxoniis in Schola Linguarum, vii. id. Aprilis, 1775." 4to.

In this discourse the Professor endeavours to prove the vast importance and utility of the Arabic language, particularly

cularly in elucidating the sacred writings. He therefore dwelt upon the necessity of this branch of literature, and enforced the study of it with an ardour which was natural for one in his situation. The oration had its effect; and many were actually led to study the Arabic, who had before treated it as barren and unprofitable.

He was at this time Fellow of his College, being elected in 1774. In 1778, Mr. White printed the Syriac Philoxenian Version of the four gospels, the MS. of which Dr. Gloucester Ridley had given to New College. This version was entitled, Sacrorum Evangeliorum Versio Syriaca Philoxeniana Ex. Codd. MSS. Ridleianis in Bibl. Coll. Nov. Oxon. repositis, nunc primum edite, cum Interpretatione et Annotationibus Josephi White, &c." 2 vols. 4to.

November 15, 1778, he preached a very ingenious and elegant sermon before the University, which, according to custom, was soon afterwards printed, under the title of " A Revisal of the English Translation of the Old Testament recommended. To which is added, some Account of an ancient Syriac Translation of great Part of Origen's Hexaplar Edition of the LXX. lately discovered in the Ambrosian Library at Milan." 4to. About this time he was appointed one of the preachers at Whitehall chapel.

In 1780, Mr. White published " A Specimen of the Civil and Military Institutes of Timour or Tamerlane: a Work written originally by that celebrated Conqueror in the Moful Language, and since translated into Persian. Now first rendered from the Persian into English, from a MS. in the Possession of William Hunter, M.D. with other Pieces." 4to.

The whole of this work appeared in 1783, translated into English by Major Davy, with Preface, Indexes, Geographical Notes, &c. by Mr. White, in one volume, 4to.

In Easter term, 1783, being then Bachelor of Divinity, he was appointed to preach the Bampton lecture the next year. As soon as he was nominated he sketched out the plan; and finding assistance necessary to the perfection of it in such a manner as he wished, he went down to Devonshire, on a visit to Mr. Samuel Badcock, then settled as a dissenting minister at South Molton. Doubtless in this interview the scheme was well digested, and Mr. Badcock undertook his share of the task with that promptitude for which he was remarkable. This visit released the Professor's mind from a considerable burthen which had oppressed it. Where, indeed, could he have found such an auxiliary? The pen of Badcock, was not only that of " a ready" but of an elegant writer. His style was chaste, flowing, and nervous. He had, moreover, an universal knowledge of theological learning. In controversy, he was quite at home. No wonder, therefore, that the Bampton lectures were admirable in point of language, and forcible in respect to argument.

Let us not, however, detract from the lecturer's merit. Great was the genius which formed the plan, and gave a body to the work. Mr. White acted with prudence in calling to his aid such men as Badcock and Parr. Yet his own share of these labours was sufficient to entitle him to the celebrity which they have procured him, and he is only to be blamed for not having acknowledged his obligations to those elegant scholars, in a preface to the volume, when it was published.

As soon as the lectures were delivered, the applause with which they were received was general throughout the University. They were printed the same year, and met with universal approbation. A second edition appeared in 1785, to which the author added a sermon, which he had some time before preached before the University, on the necessity of propagating christianity in the East-Indies.

Mr.

Mr. White's reputation was now established, and he was considered as one of the ablest vindicators of the Christian doctrines modern times had witnessed. Lord Thurlow, without any solicitation, gave him a prebend in the cathedral of Gloucester, which at once placed him in easy and independent circumstances. Soon after this he took his degree of Doctor of Divinity, and was looked up to with the greatest respect in the University, as one of its chief ornaments, until the year 1788, when the death of Mr. Badcock disclosed his share in the admired lectures. At first, Dr. White was astonished; but the letters that had passed between Badcock and him, on this very subject, were not only in existence, but in the hands of one who felt himself gratified in being the possessor of so important a secret. In addition to this, there was found among the papers of the deceased, a promissory note for 500*l.* from the Doctor; the payment of which was demanded, but refused by him on the ground that it was illegal in the first instance, as not having the words " value received," and secondly that it was for service to be rendered in the history of Egypt, which the Doctor and Mr. Badcock had projected. The friends of the deceased, however, were of a different opinion; and the Doctor very properly consented to liquidate the debt.

Notwithstanding this concession, Dr. Gabriel, who possessed the letters, printed them in 1789, in order, as he said, to vindicate the character of the deceased, as well as his own, both of which had been assailed on this occasion. In consequence of this publication, Dr. White printed " A Statement of his literary obligations to the Rev. Mr. Samuel Badcock, and the Rev. Samuel Parr, LL.D." By this it appeared, that though Mr. Badcock's share in the lectures was considerable and important, yet that it was not in that proportion which had been represented. As to Dr. Parr's, it consisted simply of verbal corrections.

Thus

Thus ended this curious difpute, which at that time threw the whole Univerfity into confufion and even contention. The Doctor's apology, however (for fuch in fact his ftatement is to be confidered), gave fufficient fatisfaction, not only to his fellow academics, but to the literary world at large.

Since that period the Profeffor has vacated his fellowfhip, by taking to himfelf a wife, and accepting a college living, in Norfolk, where he refides during a confiderable part of the year. In his parfonage-houfe, he has a printing prefs, with a large quantity of oriental types, and there he is at prefent bufily engaged in printing the Syriac Old Teftament, defcribed in the appendix to his fermon on the neceffity of a revifal of the Englifh tranflation of the Bible. His man and maid fervant labour at the prefs, and Mrs. White affifts her hufband in compofing.

Among Mr. Badcock's papers was found an analyfis of the projected hiftory of Egypt, in Dr. White's hand-writing. It is a very mafterly fketch; and we hope the learned Profeffor will find time to complete a defign, for the execution of which he has in a manner pledged himfelf to the public; and which, in confequence of recent and important events, we think will bring him more credit and profit than the publication of the Syriac Bible.

Dr. White is the reviewer of publications in Hebrew and fubjects of oriental literature in " the Britifh Critic."

RICHARD

RICHARD HURD, D.D.

LORD BISHOP OF WORCESTER.

THIS learned and truly venerable prelate was born at Congreve, a village in Staffordshire, where his father was a respectable farmer, who intending his son for the church, placed him under the tuition of that eminent scholar Anthony Blackwall.

Having attained a sound classical knowledge, he was sent to Cambridge, where he was admitted of Emanuel College, of which he afterwards became fellow; and was presented by his society to the living of Thurcaston in Lincolnshire.

In this retirement he devoted himself to the duties of his situation, and the cultivation of letters. Here he prepared his edition of Horace, which he judiciously dedicated to Bishop Warburton, then considered as the colossus of literature, and the first critic of his day. Few persons had a keener eye to discern the merits of men than Warburton; and though no one, perhaps, had a more haughty mind, or ever treated his adversaries with such coarse severity, yet certain it is, that he was entirely destitute of envy, and dreaded not the depreciation of his own fame, in consequence of the rising reputation of others.

He allured Mr. Hurd from his beloved state of seclusion, and brought him forward to the world, almost against his own inclination. He made him Archdeacon of Gloucester, and by way of acquiring popularity for him in the metropolis, associated him with himself in the situation of preacher at the chapel in Lincoln's-Inn.

The object of the Bishop was soon obtained. His discourses procured general admiration; and the preacher attracted the notice and friendship of the *great* Earl of Mansfield,

field, through whose interest he obtained the distinguished office of Preceptor to the Prince of Wales, a situation for which no man in the kingdom was better calculated, and the duties of which he performed with great honour to himself, and, it is to be hoped, benefit to his royal pupil.

Preferment was now certain; nor was it long withheld. In 1775 he was made Bishop of Litchfield and Coventry; in 1781 he was appointed clerk of the closet to the king; and on the 30th of June, of the same year, he was confirmed in the see of Worcester.

On the death of Dr. Cornwallis, Archbishop of Canterbury, in 1783, that dignity was offered to Bishop Hurd; but he had obtained a situation more congenial to his wishes, and therefore he declined it.

Since his translation to Worcester, his Lordship has almost wholly secluded himself from the busy world, residing chiefly at Hartlebury-castle, the episcopal palace of his diocese. This ancient and noble pile he has enriched by a large and inestimable library, containing the greater part of the books that had belonged to Mr. Pope and Bishop Warburton, which he has bequeathed for the use of his successors.

Here he exhibits a faithful and beautiful picture of primitive episcopacy; beloved and venerated by all ranks, as well of the laity as the clergy.

It remains to say something of his Lordship's literary character; and it would not be exaggerated praise, to assert that he stands at the head of the present generation of English scholars, eminently superior to those of his own age and standing, and unrivalled by such as are younger than himself.

He has shewn his critical powers and taste to the greatest advantage in his edition of Horace's " Epistolæ ad Pisones," &c. with an English commentary and notes; and also in his edition of Cowley's works. The first appeared in 1759, and the latter in 1772.

But

But the work which procured him the greatest reputation, was his " Moral and Political Dialogues, with Letters on Chivalry and Romance," 3 vols. 8vo. 1765. Some of the pieces had appeared before, without a name, and their success probably led the ingenious author to publish a complete and enlarged edition. These dialogues evince a profound knowledge of the English history and constitution, and breathe a warm attachment to the cause of liberty.

As a theological writer, his principal productions are two volumes of excellent sermons, preached before the Society of Lincoln's-Inn; and another of Discourses on the Prophecies, at the lecture founded by Bishop Warburton at the same place. In these compositions we observe deep thinking, close logical reasoning, fervent piety, and chaste and elegant language.

As a disputant, Dr. Hurd appeared to great advantage in a pamphlet, entitled " Remarks on Mr. Hume's Essay on the Natural History of Religion." This anonymous performance irritated the philosopher considerably, and he expressed his resentment in terms that shewed how much he had been hurt by the castigation.

The attachment manifested by Dr. Hurd to Bishop Warburton has often brought upon him very illiberal censures. About the time of his first connection with that great prelate, he printed an " Essay on the delicacy of Friendship," in which Dr. Jortin and Dr. Leland of Dublin were treated rather roughly for their want of due respect to the author's patron. When we recollect the motives which produced this essay, we see no reason to blame Dr. Hurd; his zeal for his friend was commendable, though it perhaps carried him rather beyond the line of prudence. When reflection operated on his mind, he accordingly saw reason to disapprove of his hastiness; and much to his honour, took great pains to suppress the obnoxious pamphlet. It would have been perhaps better if it had been suffered to sink into

that

that oblivion which the author wiſhed; as unfortunately, on his Lordſhip's publiſhing a large and magnificent edition of his friend's works in 1788, one of the greateſt ſcholars of this age, too officiouſly perhaps, and too much in that very ſpirit which he wanted to expoſe, reprinted the Eſſay, with ſome other " Tracts by Warburton and a Warburtonian."

When Biſhop Hurd's edition of Warburton's works appeared, the world was greatly diſappointed at not finding the long-expected life of that celebrated character. This afforded freſh ground for cenſure, and it was by no means ſpared. In conſequence of this complaint, he printed a prefatory diſcourſe, by way of introduction to the work, containing a brief but elegant memoir of the author. It is ſuppoſed that on his Lordſhip's deceaſe a more copious biography of his ancient friend and patron will be left for publication: this, of courſe, will exhibit a hiſtory of Engliſh literature, for half a century.

We had nearly forgotten to mention, that the earlieſt production of his Lordſhip's pen, which has appeared in print, was an Ode on the Peace of Aix-la-Chapelle.

W.

DAVID

DAVID STEWART ERSKINE,
EARL OF BUCHAN.

IF the love of freedom, and the love of literature; if eminent proficiency in the fine arts, and an eager fondness to patronife the fame proficiency in others; if claffical and patriotic enthufiafm, affociated with not a few of the moft amiable and refpectable moral virtues;—are calculated to recommend any man to the efteem and praife of his contemporaries, David, Earl of Buchan, cannot eafily fail of obtaining their higheft approbation.

This nobleman is the reprefentative of a younger branch of the illuftrious family of the Erfkines, Earls of Marr, whofe virtues and wifdom recommended them for a feries of generations to the very honourable and confidential office of tutors to the ancient Kings of Scotland. At the univerfity of Glafgow, in early youth, he applied with ardent and fuccefsful diligence to every ingenious and liberal ftudy. His hours of relaxation from fcience and literature were frequently paffed in endeavours to acquire the arts of defign, etching, engraving, and drawing, in the academy which the excellent, but ill requited, ROBERT FOULIS for fome time laboured to fupport in that weftern metropolis of Scotland.

Succeeding to the hereditary eftates and honours of his family, he from that moment evinced a generous ambition to maintain and exalt, by his perfonal exertions, the true dignity of the Scottifh peerage, and the name of ERSKINE.

The king's minifters had been long accuftomed, at each new election, to tranfmit to every peer a lift of the names of fixteen of his fellow-peers, for whom he was required to give his vote, in the choice of the members who fhould reprefent the nobles of Scotland in the Britifh parliament; and to this humiliating ufurpation, the defcendants of the most illustrious names had accustomed themselves tamely to submit! The Earl of Buchan, with the spirit of an ancient Baron, took an early opportunity of declaring, that he would oblige the Secretary of State who should insult him with such an application to wash away the affront with his blood. The practice from that time ceased; and ministers were obliged to adopt some other less offensive mode of exercising their electioneering influence over the Caledonian peerage.

The Earl had two very promising brothers, both younger than himself; and on their education he earnestly bestowed that care which was to be expected from the kindness and vigilance, not merely of a near relation, but of a prudent and affectionate parent. The fortunes of his family had been, from different causes, not dishonoured indeed, but impaired so considerably, that they could no longer afford an annual income sufficiently ample to support its dignities with due splendour, and enable him to gratify all the generous wishes of a munificent spirit. Struck with this, he resolutely adopted a plan of economy, admirably fitted to retrieve and re-establish those falling fortunes; and his endeavours (perhaps the most honourable and difficult which a young and liberal-minded nobleman could resolve upon), without subjecting him to the imputation of parsimony, have been crowned and rewarded with opulence.

He perceived, with concern, that since the days of Sibbald, and Gordon of Straloch, the study of the antiquities of the Scottish history had been shamefully and unhappily neglected; and it is chiefly owing to his patriotic exertions, that the Royal Antiquarian Society of Scotland is indebted for its existence.

The High School of Edinburgh is confessedly one of the best seminaries in the kingdom, for the initiation of youth in the first principles of the Latin language. By frequent visits to this seminary, the Earl of Buchan has sought every opportunity

opportunity of recommending to public notice the skill and attention of the teachers, as well as the happy proficiency of their pupils; and a premium, his gift, is annually bestowed at the university of Aberdeen, upon the successful competitor in a trial of excellence among the students.

On reviewing the memorials of the Scottish nobility, Lord Buchan felt his enthusiastic veneration in a particular manner excited, by the science and virtues of the illustrious Napier, the inventor of logarithms, and the most eminent discoverer in philosophy of which Scotland can as yet boast. With a generous hand he aspired to crown the memory of his illustrious countryman with due honours; and in a well-written biographical memoir, displayed his life and character to the reverence and imitation of the present age. The enthusiasm of Lord Buchan has also instituted an annual festive commemoration of Thomson, at Ednam, the scene of that poet's birth. Mr. Pinkerton, the historian and antiquary; Burns, who was prematurely snatched away from the admiration of the present age; Tytler, the translator of Callimachus; and a long list of other men of genius, have been so fortunate as to attract the patronage and friendship of Lord Buchan.

The life of Andrew Fletcher has been by his care happily illustrated; and we owe to him some precious fragments of speeches and essays, by that incomparable patriot, which had not been before printed.

The Earl of Buchan's exertions have been as invariably faithful to the cause of Liberty as of Literature. He has been always understood to be among the most zealous votaries of the principles upon which the revolution of 1688 was accomplished. His voice, his writings, his exertions in every manly and honourable mode, have ever been ready to resist any threatened infringement of those principles, in the British legislature or government. When the new dawn of a revolution favourable to genuine liberty broke forth in France, he was not among the moſt tardy to hail its riſe, and to bleſs its progreſs. When the kings of Europe aroſe in arms for the purpoſe of once more binding the genius of that nation in the fetters of deſpotiſm, the Earl could not view the ill-omened enterpriſe without devoutly wiſhing that its force might be ſhattered againſt the ſacred armour of that virtue, and new-born freedom, which it boaſted to deſtroy.

On beholding thoſe exceſſes into which the French have been hurried in the progreſs of their revolutionary career, he lamented that the errors of humanity are ever too cloſely aſſociated with its moſt ſplendid and heroic exertions, yet without abandoning thoſe generous wiſhes for the immortal eſtabliſhment of Gallic freedom, which he had before accuſtomed himſelf to entertain.

Long may he ſurvive to do honour to the age by his virtues; to ſuſtain by his voice and his exertions the cauſe of genuine Britiſh freedom; and to patroniſe that literature and thoſe fine arts, in which he himſelf excels!

T. N.

JAMES NORTHCOTE, ESQ. R.A.

THIS ingenious artist is descended from the ancient and respectable family of the NORTHCOTES, which has been settled in Devonshire at least ever since the conquest, has given several high-sheriffs to the county, many representatives for it in parliament, and on which a baronetage was conferred in the reign of James the First.

The subject of the present article was born at Plymouth in the year 1746. His father was an eminent tradesman in that town, and brought up his son to his own business. His propensity to the elegant arts, however, prevailed over the drudgery of a mechanical employment; and at length he determined to abandon the occupation in which he had been engaged, and devote himself entirely to his favourite object. With this view he came to London, and placed himself under the care and tuition of his countryman and friend Sir Joshua Reynolds, then in the zenith of his glory. That great man was ever ready to lend his helping hand to aspiring merit; and he gave Mr. Northcote his utmost assistance towards perfecting himself in the art of painting. Our artist continued with Sir Joshua five years, living with him in all the familiarity of friendship, and introduced by him to the most eminent characters of the age.

In the summer of 1777, Mr. Northcote set out for Italy, following in this the example and advice of his great master. He visited every part of that delightful country, which at that time was the unrivalled seat of the fine arts. At Rome he continued near three years, which he found short enough for the wonders and the beauties which abounded in it to engage the consideration of a man of taste, who was desirous of treasuring up in his mind the most extensive knowledge of the sciences connected with his profession.

During

During his refidence in Italy, he profited fo well by the opportunities he met with, and obtained fo extenfive an acquaintance with the firft artifts of the age and country in which he was, that he became greatly refpected. His talents and deportment procured him the honour of being elected a member of the ancient Etrufcan Academy at Cortona, of the Imperial Academy at Florence, and of the Academy Del Forti, at Rome.

While at Florence, he painted a portrait of himfelf, for the academy, which is a compliment always expected from every new member.

He returned to England in 1780, and came by the way of Flanders, not only becaufe it was during the time of war, but that he might have the advantage of obferving all that could be feen of the eminent mafters of the FLEMISH SCHOOL.

Thus amply furnifhed with every requifite that could conftitute him a mafter in his profeffion, he entered upon it in the metropolis of his native country, fhortly after his arrival, and foon obtained the moft diftinguifhed reputation. In 1786 he was chofen a member of the Royal Academy, and in every fubfequent exhibition at Somerfet-houfe his productions have borne a confpicuous part.

Perhaps the moft perfect picture from his pencil was exhibited the year he was admitted of the academy. The fubject is—the two young princes murdered in the tower. The ftory is ftrikingly and affectingly told; the drawing is perfectly correct, and the affaffins are particularly well delineated. This picture was purchafed by Alderman Boydell, and an engraving from it graces his fplendid edition of Shakfpeare. Our artift has alfo painted fome other pieces for the fame work; all of which have great merit, but none in an equal degree with that juft mentioned.

In the exhibition of 1796, Mr. Northcote produced a feries of moral pictures, defigned to fhew the oppofite effects

of

of seriousness and levity in two young women in menial situations of life. He clearly had HOGARTH in view; but though his pictures are good, they tell not what they are meant to express with the force which characterizes that inimitable artist's productions. These have since been engraved.

It redounds greatly to his praise, that his pencil has never in the slightest instance deviated from morality and decency. The reputation which Mr. Northcote has acquired as a painter is doubtless well merited. His colouring is chaste, forcible, and distinct; his pictures have that breadth of light and shade which is one of the most agreeable properties of a good painting, and which is yet so seldom observed, even in the works of masters. His historical pieces shew a great and an accurate acquaintance with the subject, much study, and that vigour of conception which is the true characteristic of native genius.

In private life, Mr. Northcote is greatly esteemed, as a modest, unassuming, virtuous, well-informed, and communicative man.

W.

RICHARD WATSON, D.D.
LORD BISHOP OF LANDAFF.

THIS liberal-minded prelate was born in the village of Everſham, about five miles from Kendal, in the county of Weſtmoreland, in the year 1737. His father was a clergyman, and maſter of the free grammar-ſchool in Kendal, where our divine received the whole of his ſchool education, prior to his going to the univerſity of Cambridge, to which he brought with him a good ſtock of claſſical learning, a ſpirit of perſevering induſtry, and a very bad provincial accent, which he retained for a long time. He was admitted of Trinity College, and diſtinguiſhed, while there, by a cloſe application to his ſtudies, and conſtantly wearing a coarſe mottled Weſtmoreland coat and blue yarn ſtockings.

In taking his degrees he ſtood high among the wranglers, and the ſuavity of his manners, the regularity of his conduct, and the reſpectability of his talents, procured him a fellowſhip and a college tutorſhip. On the former occaſion he was oppoſed by Mr. Poſtlethwayte, who was deeply verſed in mathematics, but knew nothing of the world. Poor Poſtlethwayte, with all his ſkill, could *demonſtrate* himſelf fit only for a ſmall country living, while Watſon made his way to a profeſſorſhip and a mitre. He, indeed, ſoon obtained the eſteem of his own ſociety, and of the univerſity at large, to which a ſpirited oppoſition made by him to an improper recommendation of a candidate by the Duke of Grafton greatly contributed. This circumſtance redounds to the honour both of Dr. Watſon and the Duke, for the latter was ſo ſenſible of the propriety of the other's conduct, that he cultivated his acquaintance, and from that time they have been cordial friends.

It was not long after this, that he was elected public profeſſor of Chymiſtry, though he was then actually ignorant of the firſt principles of that ſcience. His electors, however, had no reaſon to repent of their choice, for he ſoon

soon made up by diligence the want of preparatory acquirements. He passed whole days, and sometimes nights, in the laboratory, assisted by a good practical chymist whose name was Hoffman. In their first experiments, they destroyed numerous retorts, injured their health, endangered their lives, actually blew themselves up, and at length did the same by their workshop. But our professor was not to be intimidated by all these discouraging circumstances. He possessed an indefatigable spirit, which was destined to overcome difficulties.

His chymical character was at last completely established; and his lectures, which were crowded with auditors, acquired him a high reputation. He was next advanced to the *Regius* Professorship of Divinity, on the death of the learned Dr. Rutherforth, and about the same time he married.

Dr. Watson very early distinguished himself in the career of politics, by his attachment to those Whig principles which have, until of late, uniformly distinguished Cambridge from her sister university. He chose a critical time to display these principles, and to gain himself popularity : this was the year 1776, when the subjects of government and civil liberty were generally discussed. His sermon preached before the University on the anniversary of the Restoration, was printed under the title of " The Princi-" ples of the Revolution vindicated ;" and attracted a degree of attention exceeded only by Bishop Hoadley's famous sermon on the kingdom of Christ. In the course of the same year, he also published another discourse preached before the University on the anniversary of the King's accession. The publication of these brought on a controversy; but the only piece worth noticing on this occasion, was " An Heroic Epistle to Dr. Watson," by the facetious author of " An Epistle to Sir William Chambers," under the appellation of " Macgregor."

He soon after gave more satisfaction to the religious world, and gained a higher portion of applause from the public

public at large, by an "Apology for Chriſtianity, in a Series of Letters addreſſed to Edward Gibbon, Eſq." This work, though perhaps it is not ſufficiently copious, raiſed the author's reputation very high, both as a controverſialiſt, and a polite writer. The manner in which the divine has treated the deiſtical hiſtorian has been greatly admired by all but incorrigible bigots, and held up as an excellent example for imitation. Mr. Gibbon declined entering into a diſcuſſion of the diſputed points with the profeſſor; but he wrote him a very polite letter, to which he received as polite an anſwer. The correſpondence has been printed by Lord Sheffield, and it does honour to both parties.

Dr. Watſon printed another political ſermon, preached before the univerſity of Cambridge, February 4th, 1780, being the day appointed for a general faſt, which diſcourſe is of the ſame complexion as thoſe above-mentioned.

In 1781 he publiſhed a volume of Chymical Eſſays, addreſſed to his pupil the Duke of Rutland. This work was received by the public with ſuch great and deſerved approbation, as to encourage the author to give the world, at different times, four additional volumes, all of equal merit with the firſt.

In the preface to the laſt volume, he has theſe remarkable obſervations: " When I was elected profeſſor of divi-
" nity in 1771, I determined to abandon for ever the ſtudy
" of Chymiſtry, and I did abandon it for ſeveral years;
" but the *veteris veſtigia flammæ* ſtill continued to delight
" me, and at length ſeduced me from my purpoſe.

" When I was made a Biſhop in 1782, I again deter-
" mined to quit my favourite purſuit: the volume which
" I now offer to the public is a ſad proof of the imbeci-
" lity of my reſolution. I have on this day, however,
" offered a ſacrifice to other people's notions, I confeſs,
" rather than to my own opinion of *epiſcopal decorum*—I
" have deſtroyed all my chymical manuſcripts.—A proſpect
" of returning health might have perſuaded me to purſue
" this

" this delightful science; but I have now certainly done
" with it for ever; at least, I have taken the most effec-
" tual step I could to wean myself from an attachment to
" it; for with the holy zeal of the idolaters of old, who
" had been addicted to curious arts—*I have burned my books.*"

At length, Dr. Watson's merits, and the recommendation of the Duke of Rutland, procured him a seat on the episcopal bench, on the translation of Bishop Barrington from the see of Landaff to Salisbury. This bishopric being poor, he was permitted to hold with it the Archdeaconry of Ely, a Rectory in Leicestershire, and the divinity professorship, to which is annexed the valuable living of Samesham.

The gratitude of another pupil of Dr. Watson's is still more memorable. The late Mr. Luther, of Ongar, in Essex, at his decease, in 1786, bequeathed to his tutor the sum of 20,000*l*.

The Bishop was hardly warm in his seat, before he brought himself into pretty general notice, as the advocate of ecclesiastical reform, in " A Letter addressed to the Archbishop of Canterbury." In this letter his Lordship stated, with no small force, and with considerable pathos, the hardships of the inferior clergy, and the necessity of an equalization of church preferments. Though his arguments were conclusive, and though the facts which he stated were incontrovertible, yet many friends to his scheme thought him rather too precipitate and irregular in bringing forward his sentiments on this subject. An address to the metropolitan, through the medium of the press, from the junior prelate on the bench, was considered as a mode of proceeding not quite in the strict line of ecclesiastical propriety, nor the best calculated to attain the object in view.

This letter, accordingly drew down on his Lordship some very severe strictures from the pen of Mr. Cumberland, a writer of great powers, but who on this occasion was far from manifesting a commendable temper.

The

The public curiosity was greatly excited when it was understood that he was appointed to preach before the Lords, January 30th, 1783. His discourses at Cambridge were still fresh in every person's remembrance, and therefore somewhat unusual was expected on this occasion. The abbey was uncommonly crowded; but the Bishop conducted himself with extreme caution, and delivered a sermon admirable in its composition, and very temperate in its sentiments.

In 1786, his Lordship published at Cambridge, "A Collection of Theological Tracts," in six volumes octavo, designed entirely for the use of students in divinity. This collection consists of pieces on the most interesting subjects in sacred literature, by different writers, many of which were become exceeding scarce. Little else is wanting to form such a compilation, but great reading, candour, and judgment. These are sufficiently displayed in this edition; and it cannot but prove an inestimable library of divinity to every candidate for holy orders.

At the time of the King's illness, the Bishop voted with those Lords who considered the Prince of Wales as having an absolute right to an unqualified assumption of the Regency. As the see of St. Asaph was then vacant by the death of the worthy Dr. Shipley, some persons were disposed to think that Bishop W. had his eye upon a translation thither. The King, however, recovered, the Regency of course dropt to the ground, and the bishopric of St. Asaph was filled by Dr. Halifax.

In June, 1791, the Bishop delivered a charge to his clergy, in which he took occasion to touch upon the great revolution which had recently taken place in France, and to advert to the state of things at home, chiefly with respect to the condition of the church, and the pretensions of dissenters. Some of his hearers took notes of his Lordship's discourse, copies of which were not only circulated with great industry throughout the diocese, but spread over all parts of
the

the principality, and even reached Lambeth. Alarmed at the intention evidently manifested by this mode of circulation, the Bishop lost no time in publishing a faithful copy of his charge, which completely did away the evil designs of his enemies.

In the course of the present eventful contest, his Lordship has exhibited himself, in general, the steady advocate of pacific measures; and he has made some admirable and very impressive speeches in his place in the house, on the necessity of adopting a conciliatory spirit.

But one of the best services which he ever rendered to the public, was in counteracting the poisonous principles of " The Age of Reason," by an " Apology for the Bible, in a series of Letters addressed to the author of that work." 1796. This has doubtless been of infinite service in maintaining the cause of truth; as it is written in a popular manner, and with a dignity of expression and power of argument most admirably adapted to impress the mind with that respectful seriousness which is so necessary to produce a rational conviction.

It is to be lamented, however, that the Bishop has given some advantages to the infidels, by passing over in silence certain parts of the Bible objected to by them. From that silence much has been inferred; and it certainly would have been more noble, and in fact more prudent, to have expressed his free opinion concerning those passages.

At the beginning of the present year, his Lordship printed a very seasonable and animated " Address to the People of Great Britain." In this performance the Bishop waves discussing the merits or demerits of the war, as to its origin. He considers the nation as reduced to the alternative either of an absolute submission to the enemy, or a vigorous prosecution of the contest. Preferring the latter to the former, he pleads for great sacrifices, and calls upon his countrymen to make very strenuous exertions.

Every body allowed this address to possess great merit as
a composition;

a composition; but many who have made financial politics their study, conceived that the Bishop had gone out of his depth, while others think, and doubtless with reason, that he has departed from all his former principles.

That such a tract, coming from such a man, should produce replies, is not to be wondered at. The weight of his Lordship's character was well known. His popularity was very great; and those who were adverse to the sentiments which he now expressed, were sensible that they would have a very extensive influence upon the public mind. The prosecution of two of his Lordship's antagonists, has inflicted a deadly wound on the liberty of the press, and thus rendered controversy safe only on one side of the question!

The Bishop is a good public speaker; his action is graceful, his voice full and harmonious, and his delivery chaste and correct.

As a writer he is distinguished by a style plain and neat, but strictly pure, nervous, and argumentative.

As a bishop his character is most excellent; and as far as his influence extends, he hath been uniformly the patron of merit. His family consists of six children; and his chief residence is Colgarth Park, delightfully situated near the lakes in his native country.

Besides the pieces already mentioned, he hath written: "Richardi Watson, A. M. Coll. Sacr. Sanctæ Trin. Soc. et Chemiæ Professoris in Academia Cantabrigensi Institutionum Chemicarum in prelectionibus Academicis explicatum Pars Metallurgica." 8vo. 1766. "An Essay on the Subjects of Chymistry, and their general Divisions." 8vo. 1771. "A Defence of revealed Religion, in two Sermons preached in the cathedral church of Landaff. "A Charge to the Clergy of that Diocese, in June, 1795." Sermons and Tracts," one volume, 8vo.; and a "Charge to his Clergy, in 1798." A. T.

THE HONOURABLE HENRY ERSKINE.

HENRY ERSKINE, the brother of David Earl of Buchan, is supposed to possess even a double portion of his genius. He received, in early youth, the advantage of that liberal and literary education which in Scotland is rarely denied even to the meanest yeoman; and has, till of late, been most solicitously bestowed on the children of nobility. The fortune which he inherited was not sufficient to enable him to bury his talents in frivolous idleness, and he chose the practice of the law for his professional pursuit. He was accordingly admitted, when very young, a member of the Scottish *Faculty of Advocates*, and distinguished himself alike at the bar, in the societies of his companions, and those elegant and fashionable assemblies unto which his high birth and personal accomplishments introduced him, by an unrivalled sprightliness of fancy, and quickness of apprehension. When all contended in wit, and sportive humour, the supreme praise scarcely ever failed to be bestowed on Henry Erskine.

The elocution of the Scottish bar, even then, favoured not a little of the unction of Donald Cargill, or George Whitefield. Young Erskine, in his first pleadings, displayed with an inimitable felicity a certain grace, liveliness, and ease, which needed but to be heard, in order to put to shame those vile compositions which had been before admired. Every thing concurred to promise him a most brilliant career. But it was feared, that parts so lively, and success so splendid, might prove fatal, by seducing him into that negligence, and that self-conceit, which, alas! too often blight the richest buds of opening genius. The anxiety of his friends, the invidious rivalry of his competitors, were alike ready to suggest that dissipation, frivolity, or petulant self-applause, must soon expose him to be outstripped in his professional career, by the most sober spirited of his brother-advocates, in the same manner as the hare in the fable is said to have been left behind by the snail. The event, however, proved far otherwise.

He had the good sense to perceive that, in order to excel, he ought to dedicate himself with inflexible ardour and perseverance to the attainment of professional excellence, and acquire by unremitting practice that honourable independence of fortune which was necessary to give due lustre to his talents. In a short time he became an Elder, and a Speaker in the general assembly of the church of Scotland, the best theatre for deliberative eloquence which his native country affords. He vigilantly seized every occasion for the exercise of his abilities, as a lawyer and a pleader; and soon convinced the world that he was determined to become a steady practitioner.

Having obtained in marriage the only daughter of Mr. Fullerton, a lady of a respectable family, and who brought him a very handsome fortune, that event tended happily to confirm him in those habits of assiduity, for which he had begun before to be distinguished.

Every successive year now encreased his employment at the bar, and he was soon accounted, if not the very first, at least in the foremost rank. Eminent as a wit, and an advocate, his political sentiments could not long be a matter of indifference to the circle in which he moved. Like his brother, the Earl of Buchan, he avowed himself a staunch and ardent Whig, and naturally gained the notice and the friendship of the most illustrious votaries of Whiggism, as well in England as in Scotland.

After the conclusion of the American war, when Charles Fox, along with that great political party of which he was the informing and guiding genius, were, for a short time, masters of the energies of the British government, Henry Erskine was the man whom they chose as the confidential lawyer of their administration in Scotland. They accordingly hastened to appoint him *Lord Advocate*; and so splendid was his reputation as a lawyer, and so liberal his character as a man of integrity and honour, that the voice even of his political enemies, could scarcely refrain from applauding the nomination.

But

But Fox and his party were quickly driven from the helm; and Erſkine was difmiſſed from his official ſituation, to make room for one who was, indeed, a very worthy young man, but deſtitute alike of powerful talents, and juridical experience. This loſs, however, could neither degrade the character of Erſkine, nor leſſen his practice at the bar. He had before been, and he ſtill continued to be, the lawyer, whom, on every great occaſion, both parties were anxious to retain as their firſt counſel.

Upon a vacancy in the office of Dean of the Faculty of Advocates, of which he has ſince been ſo ſhamefully bereft, that refpectable body, perhaps the moſt illuſtrious juridical corporation in Europe, beſtowed the office on Henry Erſkine; with an eagerneſs which ſeemed to demonſtrate, that they conferred equal honour on him and themſelves by the choice.

Although a man of wit and talents, he has not been ſo imprudent as to laviſh his honourable gains in a careleſs profuſion of expence, inſtead of accumulating them for a patrimony to his children. Neither did the fatal ſchiſm in the Whig party, in confequence of the diverſity of ſentiments with which the events of the French revolution were beheld in Britain, betray him into any political inconſiſtency. On the contrary, he ſtill firmly adhered to thoſe principles of freedom, which Fox and himſelf had been accuſtomed to conſider as the genuine grounds of the Britiſh revolution in 1688.

Since the commencement of the preſent war, a period, during which the colliſions of party-ſpirit are become more fierce and violent than before, various practices, too mean and diſhonourable to be worthy of aught but contemptuous oblivion, have been recurred to, in order to hurt the character and diminiſh the practice of Henry Erſkine, by men who could not win his virtue to their ſide, and who were deſirous to diminiſh that afceadancy to which they could not aſpire in the career of generous emulation. But talents, fortune, and character, ſuch as his, may defpiſe calumny, and ſmile at the impotence of malice.

O LORD

LORD CHARLEMONT.

WHEN high rank is united with great virtues, and both are embellished by learning, taste, and talents, we then see man in his proudest form; we overlook or forget all that is weak, frail, and mortal, in human nature, and look up to him as a being of a superior order. Such a character is the Earl of Charlemont; a nobleman, on whom, even in times of the most imminent danger, neither turbulence, faction, nor slander, has dared to cast an aspersion.

Of his Lordship's early life, a great part was spent abroad; charmed with the arts, the climate, and the language of Italy, it was for many years his favourite residence. With the rest of the world, however, he was intimately acquainted; as at every court which a young nobleman generally visits, he spent more than the usual time. In all, he was respected and beloved; and he has been heard to say, that when he returned home, there was not a country in Europe in which he was not more known, and had not more of those connections which sweeten life, than in his native Ireland!

Home, however, his Lordship did at length return to, at about the age of thirty, and it is said to have been hastened by a disorder contracted, as is supposed, from poison, administered by the jealousy of a woman with whom he had an amorous intercourse. Of this disorder, the malignity had baffled the efficacy of all the medical skill which his Lordship found abroad, and it remained for the honour of an Irish physician, if not radically to remove the disease, at least to alleviate its force, and preserve a life which was to be the ornament and pride of his country. The physician in question was the celebrated Dr. Lucas, a man distinguished, not more by the success of his medical exertions in his Lordship's case, than by the zeal and energy which he displayed as a political writer, and a popular representative.

Having thus recovered a moderate share of health by the skill of the Irish patriot, and prescribed for himself a degree

of

of temperance and strictness of regimen which few men would have had the steadiness to observe, his Lordship began to think of an heir. Although accustomed to view beauty in its most fascinating forms amidst the brilliancy of courts, the splendour of wealth, and the attractions of polished manners, he did not seek these qualities in a wife. He married a young lady, the daughter of a provincial clergyman, possessed of good sense, and a most amiable disposition; therefore, better chosen than if recommended by high birth, riches, or beauty; in consequence of this marriage, his Lordship has several children, the eldest of whom (Francis-William) is Lord Caulfield, a young nobleman of whom it is reasonable to hope, that he will emulate the virtues of his father.

Lord Charlemont having felt, from his early residence abroad, the mortification of being a stranger in his native country, resolved that his son should have a domestic education. Lord Caulfield was therefore educated at the college of Dublin, where he distinguishes himself, not more for the possession of a sound and masculine understanding, than for precocious industry, and mild, though somewhat gloomy, manners.

From the moment in which Lord Charlemont first embarked in public life, he has invariably promoted the best interests of the country. He affected not, however, in any instance, that popularity which follows rather the shewy and insincere professions of the demagogue, than the wise and well-judged measures of him who serves his country more from a motive of duty than a thirst of fame. With him, patriotism was a virtue which he practised for its own sake, and without attention to any consequences, except the approbation of his own mind, and a strict attention to the public welfare.

That his political conduct has uniformly resulted from the purest motives, nothing, perhaps, could more strongly prove, than the manner in which his Borough of Charlemont has been represented. Though his Lordship does not possess wealth sufficient to render the septennial receipt of 4000*l*.

(the

(the usual price for two mis-representatives!) an object of no importance, yet, in no one instance, has he yielded to the impulse of venality; for he has never sold, to the highest bidder, the office of legislator to his country! In the representatives of his borough, his Lordship required only talents, and virtue; and it has been his peculiar good fortune to have always selected men eminently possessed of both.

Among those who have represented Charlemont since it fell into his Lordship's hands, Mr. Grattan is the most conspicuous. And it was the member for this Borough, who wrought the independence of Ireland. In the House of Peers, his Lordship contributed to that great event, if not by his eloquence, for he is not a public speaker, at least by his vote, his influence, and his example.

These virtues and services of Lord Charlemont were neither unobserved nor unrewarded by the public. He was accordingly raised by the unanimous voice of the people, more fully and faithfully expressed than it had been on any other occasion, to the most honourable situation which it was in their power to bestow, that of commander-in-chief of an army self-appointed, and self-paid, consisting of 80,000 freemen, including all the gentry and the nobility of the kingdom. To this command of the Old Volunteer army of Ireland, he was for several years successively elected; nor did this relation between that extraordinary body of men and his Lordship cease, until a difference of political opinion had arisen, which induced him to resign. That difference arose on the question of admitting the Catholics to participate in the power of the state. The idea was first broached in an address from the volunteers of Ulster to his Lordship, at a time when they had been reviewed by him in the neighbourhood of Belfast. He in very plain, but very polite and respectful terms, expressed, in his answer, his difference of opinion on that question. A discordance of sentiment, on a point of such moment, must have been fatal to that cordiality of affection which had alone reconciled him to the troublesome, though

highly

highly honourable, fituation to which he had been raifed: he therefore fhortly afterwards refigned his command; and government having for fome time before withdrawn its countenance from the volunteer army, it gradually dwindled into infignificance.

Of a reform in the reprefentation his lordfhip has been long a friend, and was among the firft of thofe noblemen and gentlemen, who, when the queftion was agitated, and the great difficulty appeared to be, how individuals fhould be fatisfied for the annihilation of their property, made an offer of a voluntary furrender of their boroughs to the public.

On the queftion of the regency, too, he adopted that fide which alone was thought compatible with the independence of Ireland. He was one of thofe, who, in oppofition to the partizans of Mr. Pitt, afferted the right of that kingdom to appoint its own regent; and, as they conftituted a majority in the two houfes, they accordingly offered the regency to the heir apparent. For this, and fome other political offences, he was fhortly afterwards removed from the government of the county of Armagh, an office to which he might be almoft faid to have an hereditary right.

In a mind like that of his lordfhip, cultivated, vigorous, and pure, error is feldom a plant of perennial growth. The opinion which he fo honeftly entertained, and fo boldly avowed to the volunteer army of 1784, he feems to have fince changed for thofe of a more liberal complexion, as he has fince fupported the Catholic claim to the elective franchife, which parliament acceded to in 1796, and is at prefent an advocate for what is called *catholic emancipation*.

Of that fyftem of coercion which preceded the late infurrection in Ireland, of the burning of villages, hanging their inhabitants, tranfporting perfons fufpected without trial, ftrangling and whipping to extort confeffion, and billeting the military at free quarters in diftricts in which individuals had been diforderly, his lordfhip has been uniformly the declared enemy. He, therefore, was one of the very few who

who supported Lord Moira in his parliamentary reprobation of these measures, and in recommending those of peace and conciliation. Nothing, however, can be more remote from his character, than that of a factious man, or a systematic oppositionist. He has supported Great Britain in the war, merely because Great Britain was engaged in it, without any relation to the abstract merit of the contest ; and he has acceded chearfully to every law, and every measure, which the government thought necessary, against the assault of foreign force or domestic disaffection.

Unexceptionable, however, as Lord Charlemont's political conduct has been, it is not as a politician that he is exclusively entitled to our regard. He is more highly estimable, perhaps, as a man of taste and literature. As a general scholar, he has not his equal in the Irish Peerage. Possessing a respectable knowledge of the learned languages, he is also intimately acquainted with those of modern Europe, particularly the Italian, in which he is an adept. To his love of letters, Ireland owes, in a great measure, the establishment of the only literary society (except the university) which she possesses, namely, the Royal Irish Academy, which was incorporated by royal charter in 1786, and of which his lordship has, since its foundation, been annually elected president. Of this office, he discharges the duties, *con amore*, constantly attending its meetings, unless when ill health prevents, presiding with a father's care over its concerns, and occasionally contributing to fill the pages of its transactions. In these volumes, his lordship has published three essays, which are highly respectable ; one on a contested passage in Herodotus ; another on an ancient custom at Meteline, with considerations on its origin; and a third on the antiquity of the Woollen manufacture in Ireland, which he has proved from some passages in the Italian poets.

These, however, constitute but a small part of what his lordship has written. To some of his friends he has shewn, at various times, materials for larger works. With them, it is to be feared, the public will not be favoured during his life; and they will, probably, be left to the mercy of a posthumous editor.

Among the lovers and the judges of the fine arts, he holds a very conspicuous rank. At his house in Rutland-square, Dublin, is to be seen a most respectable collection of the great masters in painting and sculpture, both ancient and modern; and of his taste in architecture, his temple of Marino, within a couple of miles of the metropolis, is a beautiful specimen.

In parliament he has never been a speaker, he seems to want nerves for an orator, and to be solicitous rather of the pleasures of study, than of those raptures which result from the involuntary bursts of an applauding auditory. In conversation he is communicative, affable, and cheerful, in an extraordinary degree; equally apt to catch as to impart satisfaction: nor is it the frippery of fancy which escapes him; the effusions of his full mind flow like the waters of a deep river, at once placid and majestic, uniform and profound.

Of his time he is remarkably economical; every hour has its allotted occupation, nor is this arrangement varied but on occasions of considerable moment. So regular is he even in his rides, that you might ascertain the time of the day to a minute by the spot on which you find him. His figure is exceedingly venerable, and striking. Upwards of sixty, his long grey hairs, and bending form, give him the appearance of much greater age, while the placidity of his countenance irresistibly impresses the idea, that wisdom and virtue have been the companions of his life. It is a remarkable circumstance, that the precarious state of his health, since his partial recovery from the disaster of his youth, has made it necessary for him to use the cold bath throughout the year; and, even in the depth of the severest winter, he has not dared to intermit the practice.

HENRY

HENRY GRATTAN.

Henry Grattan was born in the capital of Ireland, about the year 1751. His father, an eminent barrister, though possessing considerable talents, and deriving a competent share of practice, from the good opinion entertained of his skill and integrity by the citizens of Dublin, yet never rose to any high legal situation. The Recordership of the city, a place at that time worth about 600*l. per annum,* and to which the corporation elect, was the only office he ever filled. To wealth accumulated by the industry or the success of his ancestors, Henry, therefore, could not look; he was taught early to depend for his future fame and fortune on his own exertions.

At the usual time he was entered a student of Trinity College, Dublin, where he was soon distinguished as the powerful competitor of two class-fellows, whose good fortune and talents have since raised them to the highest situations in the state, the Earl of Clare, Lord Chancellor of Ireland, and Mr. Foster, the Speaker of the House of Commons.

Of some of the most shining characters which the Dublin University has given to the world, it has been observed, that during their residence in that seminary their talents were not exercised, nor their powers known: Mr. Edmund Burke exhibits one memorable instance in behalf of this assertion: but in respect to Mr. G. and his celebrated contemporaries, that collision which results from a rivalry of acquirements and talents, called forth a full exertion of the mental faculties, and they were therefore distinguished as men possessing first-rate parts, before they were called to exhibit them on the theatre of life. After taking a degree, Mr. G. was, in 1772, called to the Irish bar, and for a few years attended the four courts with an empty bag, and a mind too elastic to be confined to the forms of pleading, and too liberal to be occupied by the pursuits of a mere lawyer,

Disgusting

Difgufted at laft with a profeffion, in which he perceived he could never rife but by habits to which he could not crouch, he retired, not wealthy, but poffeffing from his father, who was now dead, a patrimony, which, with economy, might have fecured him independence. It was not long before he was made known to Lord Charlemont, who had for fome time been returned to Ireland. By his Lordfhip, who has always fhewn equal fagacity in difcovering and zeal in promoting genius, he was returned to parliament for his borough of Charlemont. Entering into legiflature under fuch aufpices, it was natural to expect that Mr. G. would become the advocate of his then fuffering and dependent country. Ireland, indeed, at that time, was in a ftate of perfect humiliation, being confidered merely as a province to the fifter country. Her legiflature was a petty council, incapable of originating laws; and her courts of juftice were fubordinate to thofe of England, and incompetent to a final decifion: deftitute of foreign commerce, from which fhe had been excluded by Britifh monopoly, her manufactures were crufhed by the weight of Britifh competition, and the induftry of her people checked from want of encouragement to excite it; in fhort, difcontent, bankruptcy, and wretchednefs covered the face of the country.

To evils of fuch magnitude, and which the calamities brought on by the unfortunate conteft with America, greatly aggravated, the narrow policy of the times was applying petty palliatives. Subfcriptions were collected, to keep the artificers from famifhing; affociations were formed to wear only domeftic manufactures; and parliament itfelf looked, for fome time, no further than to alleviate the preffure of the immediate evil. Mr. G. however, whofe mind was formed to embrace fomething beyond prefent objects; who was accuftomed to trace effects to their caufes; perceived that the root of thofe calamities was not a temporary ftagnation of trade from the American war, but rather to be found in the unjuft reftraints impofed by Great Britain on

the

the exertions of the country; and that to attempt their cure by temporary expedients, would be to roll up the stone of Sysiphus.

He was the first, therefore, who had the boldness and the wisdom to urge the legislature to complain of those restraints; his efforts were seconded by the unanimous voice of the country; and such was the efficacy of a political truth, thus urged, and thus supported, that even the whole force of British influence was found unequal to resist it. The Irish legislature adopted, and decreed the sentiment; and after some hesitation on the part of the British legislature, the commerce of Ireland was in part opened to her children. A temporary gleam of satisfaction was shed over the country by this *concession*, as it was called, of the British parliament: for so accustomed had the people been to exclusion, to penalties, and restriction, that a relaxation or suspension of any of these was looked on as the conferring of a positive benefit, rather than the cessation of an actual injury.

Mr. G.'s name was now become an object of adoration to the people, and by the volunteer associations, which the dangers of the war had called forth, he was looked up to with peculiar respect. In this state of affairs, the re-action of popularity upon patriotism seemed to impart new energy to his mind.

Mr. G. continued to exert himself with indefatigable assiduity in the senate, and by leading the mind of the public, and even of the legislature itself, to the consideration of national rights, and the actual political situation of their common country, with respect to England, he was clearing the way for that measure which they meditated—a declaration of the legislature in favour of national independence.

By obtaining freedom of commerce for the country, he had already, indeed, done much toward the attainment of the great object; for he had removed the key-stone of the arch, and thus weakened the cohesion of the whole fabric—he had introduced a spirit of innovation upon the old

system

system of British domination, and the vigour with which innovations on such systems are opposed, proves their malign efficacy. Mr, G. therefore, who observed with pleasure, no doubt, the operation of those causes on the public mind, endeavoured by an industrious exertion of oratorical powers in the senate, to increase their force, and second their effect. His eloquence, of a cast more warm and animated than either parliament or the people had usually felt, and exerted upon subjects respecting which the human mind is susceptible of the greatest degree of enthusiastic fervor, was gratified by complete success. Directed by a sagacious understanding, which could catch the moment propitious to exertion, and proportion its zeal to its object, his parliamentary speeches taught a subjugated nation to pant for independence; while public voice, highly animated on this subject, and seconded by the loud assent of 80,000 men in arms (for to so many did the volunteer associations amount!), kindled, even in the cold bosom of parliament itself, a desire to assert their dignity, and rescue its authority from the gripe of British usurpation.

Of this sentiment, so novel in an Irish legislature, that had long forgotten the pride of independence—of this energy, which arising from extrinsic circumstances, rather than a native and internal principle of virtue, was therefore likely soon to vanish, when those circumstances should cease to exist—Mr. G. availed himself; he caught, as he inspired, the generous flame; and by one of those extraordinary displays of impassioned eloquence, to which even the eloquent cannot rise, but when a momentous object seems to furnish adequate powers, he gave rise to the celebrated declaration, that the King, Lords, and Commons of Ireland only, could make laws to bind Ireland in any case whatsoever.

Mr. Grattan's popularity was now at its *acmé*. The achievement of a nation's independence by an individual, unaided by any force or any influence but that which genius
and

and which truth afford, was considered as the result of talents and of virtue almost above the lot of humanity. The legislature itself seemed for once to participate in the feelings of the people, for in the fervor of admiration, it was proposed that £.100,000 should be voted to him, as a mark of approbation.

In its full extent, this proposition was not adopted, for on a subsequent sitting, when the vote was before the Committee, they reduced it to £50,000; to that amount, however, the grant was confirmed, and Mr. G. actually received the money.

The declaration of rights of the Irish legislature, however unwelcome it must have been to the minister and parliament of England, was received there with that kind of acquiescence with which we assent to what is inevitable. A negociation was immediately instituted between the two nations, which terminated in the repeal of the 6th of Geo. I. the act by which the British Parliament declared its right to bind Ireland by British statutes.

On the subject of this repeal, a question arose, which suspended, for a considerable time, Mr. Grattan's popularity. It was contended by Mr. Flood, a gentleman, who, though he did not originate the measure of declaring the legislative independence of the country, yet co-operated to promote it, that as the 6th of Geo. I. was an act only declaratory of a right, asserted by the British Parliament to have been vested in it prior to the enaction of that statute, the " simple repeal" of the statute did not involve a renunciation of the right ; and he insisted, that notwithstanding that repeal, Great Britain might, and from her former conduct towards Ireland probably would, resume the exercise of it. He therefore advised the legislature to demand of the British parliament, a full and explicit renunciation of all right in future to bind Ireland. This opinion was adopted by the people ; and carrying with it all the force which reason or experience

can

can give to a propofition in politics, met very powerful fupport even in both houfes of parliament. Mr. G. whofe fagacity this objection to a fimple repeal had eluded, and who, from a principle of vanity, perhaps, which has its ftrong hold even in minds of the firft clafs, affected the exclufive honour of originating and conducting the emancipation of his country, applied all his power of reafon, of fophiftry, and of eloquence, to combat this doctrine of Mr. Flood.

He contended, that the repeal of a declaratory law, accompanied by fuch circumftances as attended that of this, muft be confidered, as implying a renunciation of the right; but that, even if it were not fo, and that Great Britain fhould be fo unjuft and impolitic as to refume the right, when fhe fhould recover means to fupport it by power, an explicit renunciation would be but a flender defence againft injuftice, fupported by force; that in fuch circumftances, the true fecurity of the people would confift, not in an act of parliament, but in that patriotic energy which would enable them to defend, as it had already enabled them to affert, their independence; and that to force Great Britain, in this her hour of diftrefs, to confefs herfelf an ufurper, by an exprefs renunciation of a right which fhe had exercifed, would be as ungenerous to her, as it would be ufelefs to Ireland.

With the people thefe arguments had no weight, and in the fenate they were borne down by the irrefiftible force of truth and experience, feconded by the powerful and logical eloquence of Mr. Flood. In popular eftimation, indeed, Mr. G's character had been falling for fome time; it was certain he had received the money which parliament had voted him; and it was infinuated, that for the prompt payment of it, and other confiderations, he had engaged with adminiftration to counteract the independence which his former exertions had obtained. But in fuch infinuations there is the beft reafon to believe there was no truth. It is, however, certain, that in the conteft with Mr. Flood, on the efficiency of a fimple repeal, Mr. G. not only reafoned weakly, but that in many inftances, connected with that difpute, he acted intemperately. On one occafion particularly, he pronounced a philippic againft Mr. Flood, which was lefs diftinguifhed by genius and point, than by acerbity and virulence. His antagonift replied, perhaps in a ftyle too much like that of his opponent. Both parties immediately left the Houfe of Commons, but were prevented from terminating the conteft in a duel, by being inftantly put under arreft, and bound in a large fum to keep the peace. Mr. Flood, in the courfe of the next evening, pronounced one of his beft fpeeches, containing a hiftory and defence of his former political life, which had been on the preceding night violently arraigned by Mr. Grattan. Mr. G. endeavoured to reply, but was prevented by the clamours of the Houfe.

Fruftrated in the hope of carrying on exclufively to its completion, a revolution (for fuch it may be called) which he had fo fuccefsfully and honourably commenced, and finding the tide of popularity now running ftrong againft him, Mr. G. feems for fome time to have completely fecluded himfelf from politics. During this interval, he married a lady of the name of Fitzgerald, not, however, as the name would indicate, of the Leinfter family, but one who poffeffed qualities much more valuable than thofe of high birth or great connections, for fhe is a woman of the moft angelic difpofition, and of whom Mr. G. remains, after a lapfe of fo many years, what he had been in a very high degree before his marriage, an enamoured lover.

Though Mr. G. during this period, did not take an active part in political affairs, he remained ftill in parliament, and voted as his confcience bade, fometimes with and fometimes againft the minifter. It is towards the clofe of the year 1785, when under cover of a commercial arrangement, it was fuppofed a defign had been formed by the Britifh miniftry to fubvert the newly-acquired independence of the Irifh

parlia-

parliament, that we find Mr. G. again alert and vigilant at his poft. Of the celebrated propofals which were then offered to the Houfe of Commons in Ireland, by an agent of the crown, and which are ftill remembered and execrated in that country by the name of " Orde's Propofitions," one was, " that the Parliament of Ireland, in confideration of " being admitted to participate equally with Great Britain " in all commercial advantages, fhould, from time to time, " *adopt* and *enact* all fuch acts of the Britifh Parliament as " fhould relate to the regulaton or management of her com- " merce, &c." This, it was contended, would fink the Parliament of Ireland into a mere regifter to the Britifh Legiflature. Whether or no this would really be the cafe, or whether there was any thing unreafonable in ftipulating that the country, which was admitted to fhare in the commerce of another, fhould adopt the fame commercial regulations as this latter; it is certain, that this opinion was entertained not only by the public in general, but by fome of the ableft men in both houfes, and among them by Mr. G. who gave to the whole fyftem the moft unqualified and ftrenuous oppofition. This oppofition proved fuccefsful, the meafure was relinquifhed, and Mr. G. thenceforward continued to refift, with the moft zealous and preferving firmnefs, what he called the principles of the " Old Court; principles which he looked on as tending to degrade Ireland, by corruption and influence, to the fame defpicable and miferable ftate in which fhe had been reduced previoufly to the year 1783.

From this period, we find Mr. G. an active leader of the country party in the Houfe of Commons; loved by the people, and dreaded by the cabinet. His popularity, which had fo fuddenly funk, on his acceptance of the parliamentary boon, and his fupport of the fimple repeal, had now rifen to its former level; and the nation found, that notwithftanding one unfortunate deviation, he was ftill an upright and independent fenator. Among the various meafures which now occupied his attention, was the eftablifhment

ment of a provision for the clergy, independent of tythes. For many years the peasantry of the south of Ireland, who were exclusively catholics, had been discontented, not so much with the payment of tythes to protestant pastors, as with the rigid and oppressive manner in which they had been collected by proctors and tythe-farmers. That portion of the country had been kept by this cause for almost half a century in disturbance; and in some instances it had affected the province of Ulster. Mr. G. proposed a measure which would have removed every discontent, and at the same time have secured a provsion for the clergy equal to that which they then possessed, easy and certain to them, and to the peasantry neither oppressive nor unpleasant. This plan was, however, opposed by the collective influence of the established church, and of course rejected by the legislature. Another measure wich he proposed to Parliament about the same time, viz.—a bill to promote the improvement of barren land, by exmpting reclaimed ground from the payment of tythe, for seven years—was but little calculated to restore the favour of the priesthood; they accordingly resisted and defeated te project, and continued thenceforward to hate, if not to clumniate, its author.

The Whig-club had for some tme become a political body of considerable consideration. Mr. G. was one of the first, if not the very first member of it, in point of talent and popularity. At his instance it was that the members of the club, who had been since its institution the advocates of a liberal system, which they consided necessary to the security of the constitution and independence of the country, came now to a resolution, by whih they publicly pledged themselves never to accept office under any administration, which should not conced certain measures to the people:—these consisted princally of a pension-bill, a bill to make the great officers of the crown responsible for their advice and measur, another to prevent revenue officers from voting at elections, a place-bill, &c.

This explicit declaration of a sincere and fixed purpose respecting those essential subjects, gave the society much weight with the public, and enabled them, after a long opposition on the part of administration, to effect their purpose; a pension bill, a plea bill, a responsibility-bill, were at last yielded by the court, as concessions of the first importance, though they had for so many years resisted them as unnecessary and unwise.

The celebrity which Mr. G. had attained by his opposition to Mr. Orde's system, and his subsequent exertions in the popular cause, procured for him, in the year 1790, an honourable and easy election, as representative for the metropolis.

During the existence of the parliament which then commenced, there occurred, however, a question, on which Mr. G. and a very considerable proportion of his constituents materially differed; this was, the claim of the catholics to the elective franchise. From his first entrance into parliament, with a mind as liberal as it was enlightened, he had always been the decided friend of every measure which tended to abolish those political distinctions, which were founded only on a difference of religious tenets; for he conceived that such distinctions had retarded the progress of the country towards civilization and industry.

The corporation of the city of Dublin, on the contrary, prone, by situation, and habit, to religious bigotry, looked on the catholics at once with suspicion and contempt. Enjoying a monopoly of municipal honour and emoluments, by the exclusion of all who professed a different faith from the franchises of the capital, they considered every attempt to restore them to those franchises as an attack on their property, or a violation of their rights. Besides these causes the administration had, by some recent institutions, obtained a paramount influence in the corporation; and to perpetuate religious distinctions, which had hitherto kept Ireland weak, was still the court policy. This influence, therefore, operating in conjunction with other causes, rendered the municipal officers of Dublin incapable of participating in that increased liberality of sentiment which had now every where begun to dissipate prejudice and dispel bigotry. On the question of admitting the catholics to the privileges of the constitution, the corporation and Mr. G. accordingly differed; and had not circumstances occurred, which prevented him from becoming again a candidate for the capital, there can be no doubt that he would not have been a second time elected its representative.

The war with France had taken place; Mr Grattan approved of it, or rather he considered Ireland as bound with all its might to assist Great Britain when once engaged in the contest. This at least was the opinion he entertained during the short administration of Lord Fitzwilliam; and in this opinion he remained, until he found that the continuation of hostilities threatened the empire with ruin, either from the incapacity of those by whom it was conducted, or the murmurs which it occasioned. In Ireland, indeed, discontent had been spreading with incalculable velocity, and deepening as it spread. The pertinacity and insolence with which administration had rejected the petitions of the catholics, and the rapidity and inconsistency with which they granted the prayer of those petitions, at the first suggestion of the British cabinet; the obstinacy with which they refused ever to hear of reform, the advocates of which were blackened with abuse, and calumniated as traitors; the enormous encrease of court-influence, by the shameless and wanton increase of sinecure offices, the lavish profusion of titles, and above all, the trick which it was supposed the British cabinet had played off on Ireland, by sending Lord Fitzwilliam with concessions which were revoked when the supply

was

was voted; all these causes had already generated a degree of discontent in the country, of which no instance had been known in former times. The celebrated Society of United Irishmen, who associated (whatever their real principles might have been) under the pretext of reform, derived from these discontents new vigour: they had disseminated their principles through the island, and they were already embraced, by a great portion of the population of the country.

Mr. G. perceiving the danger in which the state was involved by this system of ministers, constantly resisted it with all his power. He was seconded by a small, but active and able opposition, which left no exertion untried to reconcile the court and the country, by advising measures which would have ranged every moderate and good man on the side of parliament and the throne, and thus have weakened the republican and French factions which had now become so powerful. These efforts were, unfortunately, not successful. Instead of conciliating, administration continued to exasperate; and scorning to resort to lenitives, applied the most powerful caustics: for every measure of moderation, or concession, which was proposed by Mr. G. and his party, one of severity and coercion was substituted, until the cabinet ultimately arrived at military law, and free quarters! At that critical moment, Mr. G. who could no longer hope, by his presence in the senate, to serve his country, seceded; and at the close of the parliament published a very eloquent and spirited address to his former constituents, accounting for his past conduct, and formally declining to accept of a seat in the legislature.

Such are the leading facts which have marked the life of one who, whatever may be thought of him by his opponents, while the fever of politics continues to agitate the human mind, will have his merits and defects examined

amined fairly by posterity, and, in all probability, be acknowledged by them as a great man.

Of his private life there is little generally known, because little has occurred in it to interest attention. It has passed on in a smooth manner, marked equally by the practice of every conjugal and domestic virtue. If there be any of his good qualities which verge on the confines of vice, it is his economy, of which it has been asserted that it approaches towards penuriousness, if it does not reach that point. It has been often said, that though he received in early life, from the liberality of his country, a very handsome addition to his patrimony, he never displayed, either in private or public, a munificent disposition. But it should be remembered, that the fortune which Mr. G. obtained then, constituted nearly the whole of his acquisitions: he practised in no profession, he accepted no place, and he soon saw a young family rising around him, for which the whole was not a very ample provision: for he has four children; the eldest a son of fifteen years of age.

In private life, Mr. G. displays manners that are in a high degree pleasing. Wit he seems not to possess, and he has a cast of mind too lofty for humour; but if he does not " set the table in a roar," or dazzle with the radiance of fancy, he diffuses over the convivial hour the mild charms of good-humour, and softens society with unassuming gentleness.

In conversation he appears to great advantage; for, with a mind well stored with useful learning, and conversant on every topic which occurs, he has a felicity of expression, which communicates his meaning in the most concise and impressive manner: he is not argumentative, but when an argument is instituted, his opinions are urged with great modesty, but with great strength, and
when

when victor in the contest, he generally relinquishes the field to the vanquished.

Of Mr. G's political opinions, the complexion may be known from the measures which he has supported, and the tenor of his parliamentary conduct. As they have struck the mind of the writer, they appear to be strongly *monarchical*, and *aristocratical* only so far as our constitution requires them to be; at the same time leaning towards a perpetuity of union between the two countries, and yet decidedly adverse to the existence of any British influence in Ireland distinct from that which the union of the two crowns on the head of a British prince renders indispensable. That he should, therefore, be connected with a society of men whose aim was separation from England, and the establishment of an Irish Republic, seems in the highest degree, improbable. The lustre of his name, however, has suffered a temporary eclipse; and so short-lived is municipal gratitude, that it has actually been expunged from a city which he has rendered flourishing*. At the very same time it was struck from the list of privy-counsellors.

As a public speaker, Mr. G. ranks in the highest class. In his speeches there is a grandeur which marks a mind of a superior order, and enforces at once, reverence and admiration. On every subject which he treats, he throws a radiance that enlightens without dazzling; and while it assists the judgment, delights the imagination. His style is always peculiar, for it varies its character with the occasion. At one time close and energetic, it concentrates the force of his argument, and compels conviction; at another, diffuse, lofty and magnificent, it ap-

---

* " *Cork, Sept.* 29.—By order of the Mayor, Sheriffs, and Common-Council of the city of Cork, the public are desired to take notice, that the street hitherto named *Grattan-street*, is, in future, to be called *Duncan-street*.

plies itself to every faculty of the mind, charms our fancy, influences our will, and convinces our understanding. At all times his manner is animated with a pleasing warmth, which renders it impossible to hear him without interest; but, on some occasions, he exerts a power which is irresistible. Prostitution, under its influence, forgets for a moment the voice of the minister, and place, pension, and peerage, have but a feeble hold even of the most degenerate.

To the excellence of his style he does not add the graces of action; it is forcible indeed, and sometimes expressive, but it is seldom elegant, and never pleasing. To invective, in which Mr. G. has sometimes deigned to have recourse, his manner is better adapted than to the sedateness of cool disquisition; and yet invective is not that in which he principally excels: he is more fitted by nature, and happily the situation he has filled has more frequently called him, to defend the rights of nations, and to pourtray the hopes, the fears, the expectations of magnanimous people, than to descend to a wordy contest with individuals; though, when that contest has been instituted, the weapons of Mr. G. have been found sharp, not polished, and capable of inflicting wounds which refuse to be healed.

SIR

SIR WILLIAM SYDNEY SMYTH.

THE great Admiral Howard, who lived in the reign of King Henry the eighth, was wont to say, that "a certain portion of madness was necessary to enter into the composition of an English seaman." We know not whether this assertion ought to be admitted in its full extent; yet the fact is, that some of our most celebrated naval characters have obtained renown for deeds which appear to cold-blooded men to savour of desperation, as well as of valour.

It is not our intention to detract from any man's merits, who has been, or is now, engaged in the service of his country, either by sea or land; but we are forced to say, that our admiration is not so much excited by those dazzling exploits which please the populace, as by the more steady and extensive operations of such magnanimous, but prudent commanders, who are rather bent upon general good, than romantic adventures. Each, however, has his portion of merit; and he who hazards his person with alacrity, in behalf of the country for which he fights, must always claim our respect.

Sir William Sydney Smyth was born in the metropolis, A. D. 1764. His* father was a captain in the army, and his mother the daughter of Mr. Wilkinson, a merchant of great eminence in the city. This match was so hostile to Mr. Wilkinson's sentiments, that he not only discarded Mrs. Smith in his life-time, but at his death left his whole fortune, which was very considerable, to his other daughter, the present Lady Camelford.

The

---

* Captain Smith was *aid-de-camp* to Lord George Germaine, at the battle of Minden, and was examined as an evidence on his trial. His testimony on that occasion is said to have saved the life of his protector.

Having encountered some obloquy, in consequence of his zeal, the Duke of Dorset, who was greatly attached to his younger son, Lord George, very properly

The subject of the present notice was educated under Dr. Knox, at Tunbridge-school; and at an early age was put on board a man-of-war, which profession he had adopted for himself. He rose rapidly, and at the age of sixteen was fifth lieutenant of the Alcide of seventy-four guns. He was made post-captain in 1783, at which time the restoration of peace prevented him from exercising his active spirit in the service of his country.

When the war broke out between Russia and Sweden in the year 1788, Captain Smith obtained permission from the English government to enter into the navy of the latter power, by which he was honoured with a distinguished command.

During this contest, he gave such satisfaction to the court of Sweden by his important services, that the honour of knighthood was conferred upon him; which, however, has not been confirmed by his own sovereign.

On the termination of that war, he returned to his native country, and soon after set out on his travels through various parts of Europe.

When hostilities broke out between England and France he was in Italy; and on Lord Hood's getting possession of Toulon, Captain Smith went thither and volunteered on board the British fleet. In the subsequent evacuation of that place, he was entrusted with the dangerous but important, service, of setting fire to the ships, dock-yards, and arsenal, which he performed with such astonishing skill, boldness, and success, as to call forth the warmest encomiums from Lord Hood in his account of that transaction to the admiralty.

perly took captain S. into favour; and among other gifts, presented him with a grant of land at the foot of Dover-castle, on which he has built a whimsical house. Some adjoining apartments are excavated from the rock, and the kitchen, &c. are roofed with boats. There is a tower, called " Sir Sydney's look-out;" and the writer of this has been informed, that his father, who is a staunch methodist, has lately erected a chapel there.

On

On his return to England, he had the command of the Diamond frigate bestowed on him, with which he greatly annoyed the enemy on their own coast, and made several important and valuable captures. He had afterwards some other frigates put under his direction, as commodore; with which squadron he performed some essential services, particularly in attacking a French convoy at Herqui, where he landed and demolished the fortifications. At one time Sir Sydney went with his single frigate into Brest harbour, and having reconnoitred the state of the enemy's ships, came out to sea without suspicion. He was enabled to do this, by the very fluent manner with which he speaks the French language.

At length, however, his enterprizing spirit, unfortunately, brought him into a very disagreeable situation. Being off Havre-de-Grace, April 18, 1796, he captured an armed vessel in the outer harbour; but the tide making strong up the Seine, she was driven by the force of the current near the forts. When night came on, Sir Sydney, who was determined not to lose his prize, manned and armed his small craft, and went with them to bring her off. He succeeded in boarding her, and was towing her down the river, when an alarm was given, and several gun-boats proceeded to cut the vessel off. After an obstinate resistance, Sir Sydney was at length taken, together with sixteen of his crew, and three of his officers.

The French were happy at having gained possession of one who had been so great an eye-sore to them, and conveyed him to the capital, where he was kept in close confinement, without ever being suffered to be at large upon his parole. The English government, desirous of his releafe, sent over Captain Bergeret, commander of *La Virginie*, in July following, to be exchanged for him; but the Directory refusing to accede to the terms, the French

captain

captain returned, saying, "he preferred death to dishonour." It was actually one time in contemplation to try Sir Sydney as a spy and incendiary, to which the Directory were led in consequence of his conduct at Toulon!

After a long and most rigid confinement, he at length effected his escape, April 24, 1798, from Paris, and arrived in London May 6th following. The manner in which this occurred, was represented in the papers as most extraordinary, and little short of miraculous. It was stated, that as the officers were conveying him from one prison to another, a crowd in the street occasioned the carriage to stop, on which some one opened the door, and drew Sir Sydney out, who passed unmolested through the people, and got into the suburbs; whence, by a circuitous course, with an emigrant gentleman, he arrived on the sea-coast, where they took to an open boat; and after being at sea for some considerable time, were taken up by a British frigate, which landed him and his companion in Old England. It is not unlikely that the French government took this curious method of releasing him; for it is hardly within the line of probability that such a man should have escaped from his keepers in one of the public streets of Paris, and that too in open day, without the connivance of persons in power.

His being taken at first was the effect of his own imprudence, for certainly there were officers in his ship competent enough to the service of boarding and bringing away a paltry privateer, without the necessity of the captain's going in person. Sir Sydney has since been appointed to the command of *Le Tigre*, a ship of 80 guns, taken from the French; and in which he has just sailed to the Mediterranean.

THE REV. THOMAS HAWEIS, LL.D. and M.D.

THIS gentleman is entitled to a place in our collection, as well on account of his respectability as a man of letters, as his being now at the head of that numerous and highly distinguished class of Christians, commonly called the Calvinistical Methodists.

Dr. Haweis is a native of Truro in Cornwall, and was educated at the free grammar-school in that town, where he had for his contemporary the celebrated Samuel Foote, commonly called the English Aristophanes. After receiving a good classical education, he was put apprentice to an eminent surgeon and appothecary in his native place, and served his time with great credit, on account of his fidelity and application.

Mr. Samuel Walker was at that time curate of Truro, and young Mr. Haweis was so affected with the preaching and character of that exemplary man, that his whole mind became impressed with the love of religion, and the desire of being a minister of the gospel. His friends were not willing to cross his inclinations, and he was therefore permitted to go to the University of Oxford, where he was entered of Magdalen-Hall, and in due course took his degree of LL.B.

Soon after his being admitted to holy orders, he became distinguished as a popular preacher, particularly at Oxford, where he delivered a set of discourses, which in 1760 he published, under the title of " Evangelical Sermons." Not long after he became assistant to Mr. Madan, at the chapel of the Lock-hospital, and about the same time was appointed chaplain to the Countess of Huntingdon.

While he officiated at the Lock chapel, a circumstance occurred which made a considerable noise at the time, and brought upon our divine, as well as his friends, much unmerited

unmerited odium. A gentleman who usually attended that place of worship, informed Mr. Madan, that he had a living in his gift, which he wished to bestow upon some minister of evangelical sentiments. Mr. Madan recommended Mr. Haweis, who was surprized at this generosity in a stranger. Some time after his being inducted to the living of Aldwinkle, in Northamptonshire, and which he now holds, the patron thought proper to make a demand upon him for the presentation. The matter got into print, much was published on both sides, and those who were prejudiced against the body of Christians to whom Mr. H. belonged, exclaimed vehemently against him for his conduct, as well as that of his colleague, Mr. Madan. Time, however has destroyed this prejudice, and we believe there is no person so uncandid, at present, as to admit a thought to his disadvantage, in consequence of this business.

About that period, he published a very useful and judicious commentary upon the scriptures, entitled, " The Evangelical Expositor," in 3 vols. folio.

Mr. H. continued to have the chief management of Lady Huntingdon's extensive concerns until her death, when he found himself by her will one of the principal trustees of her various chapels in town and country. In 1795 the missionary society commenced, formed upon a plan and scale certainly more adequate to the object, more promising in its appearance, and, as far as it has yet gone, more prosperous in its operation, than any other that can be mentioned. This institution equally admits churchmen and dissenters. It is marked, indeed, only by what are called the evangelical sentiments: it pays no regard to differences of opinion on the inferior questions of church government, or the manner of public worship; but it admits no missionaries except such as are firmly grounded on the essential doctrines of christianity,

anity, particularly the divinity of Christ, and the atonement by his death.

At the first public meeting of this society, held at Spafields chapel, Mr. H. preached a very affecting and masterly sermon on the occasion; and at a subsequent one, he read a memorial, in which he examined the subject with the greatest precision and accuracy, and recommended strongly that the first mission should be to the Friendly Islands, in the South-Sea, which measure was adopted. This sermon and memorial were printed in the collection of the society's papers.

In the same year he obtained, from one of the Scotch universities, the degree of doctor of physic; and lest his motives for so doing should be misunderstood, it may be proper to say, that he is one of the principal persons concerned in the Samaritan society, the object of which is to visit poor sick people at their own habitations. Now, as he was originally brought up to the practice of medicine, there was a propriety in his taking a doctor's degree in that faculty, to render him competent to give his advice, and to attend consultations, in the way of benevolence.

In 1797, the doctor published the life of that eminent and popular divine, Mr. Romaine. This performance does great credit to his talents as a biographer.

The missionary concerns seem to engross his principal attention: and, without doubt, that large and highly honourable society could not have a more able, indefatigable, or faithful person at its head than Dr. H. The accounts received from the missionaries at the Sandwich-Islands are very flattering to those who have formed strong expectations respecting this new attempt to propagate christianity in heathen lands. We understand that the society is so opulent, in respect to finances, that it is about to enlarge its sphere of operation; and that endeavours

vours will be made by it, to carry civilization and religion into other dark and uncultivated regions.

Dr. H. is still an eloquent and powerful preacher. His style is perspicuous and elegant. He never descends to that coarse method of illustration made use of by some popular preachers, nor does he entertain his auditory with quaint witticisms and ridiculous anecdotes. He has a clear method of reasoning, and seldom launches into the wildness of declamation. As a writer, he possesses great merit, on account of an elegant style, which is at once pious and fervid.

We cannot close this article, however, without expressing our astonishment and concern, that a man of Dr. H.'s judgment should be so far imposed upon, as to countenance raw youths, * who, without education, or any other qualification than mere boldness, and a certain forward conceit of their abilities, ascend the pulpit, and deliver a strange kind of jargon to their hearers. Is it because the doctor wishes to be considered as the bishop of his sect, that he commissions, as it were, these unfledged theologians to go out and preach the gospel of Christ? As a divine, and a respectable one too, of the church of England, we wish he would well consider the evil which must accrue, not merely to the ecclesiastical establishment, but to the interests of the christian church at large, by the presumption of boys and illiterate mechanics, in thus encroaching upon the ministerial office. It is this which encreases the number of infidels, and gives them cause to ridicule religion. The mistakes of an ignorant zealot are more pernicious to the interests of christianity, than the most daring attacks of avowed sceptics.

* The extreme youth of some of the missionaries has given rise to a ridiculous story, about each of them having been presented with three beautiful young women, as concubines, on their arrival at the place of their destination, &c. &c.

THE

THE RIGHT HON. HENRY DUNDAS,

SECRETARY OF STATE FOR THE WAR DEPARTMENT, &c. &c.

HENRY DUNDAS is descended from a younger branch of a * family, long eminent among the petty Barons of Lothian. During the greater part of the last century his immediate ancestors were distinguished as the most able advocates at the Scottish bar, and rose to the highest offices and richest emoluments which the law can bestow.

His father, even at an early period of his career, was pronounced by President Dalrymple, to have outshone all the competitors of his own day, in the lists of juridical contest. His eldest brother, the late Lord President Dundas, after shining as the first lawyer at the bar, was exalted to the bench, amidst the shouts of general approbation; and it is still remembered, with what august dignity, what a force and clearness of argument, he administered justice for a long series of years, at the head of the supreme civil court of Scotland.

Henry, being a younger son, by a second marriage, was destined to seek his fortune in some professional pursuit, and he very naturally chose that in which his family had been so successful. At an early period of life, he was called to the Scottish bar, and quickly attained some distinction among the junior advocates. In compliance with the custom of the young Scottish lawyers, he attempted to distinguish himself, by adopting the popular eloquence of the general assembly of the church of Scotland, of which he became a member. With very flattering success, he declaimed on the subject of patronage; disputed about forms and precedents; and strove sometimes to allay, sometimes to excite, those storms to which even that venerable body is now and then subject. A for-

* The Dundas's of Arniston.

A fortunate marriage with the heirefs of Melville, foon made him a confiderable landholder, and his fuccefs at the bar augmented daily. If his pleadings were deficient in grace, elegance and correctnefs, and his fpeeches unadorned by thofe happy allufions which polite literature can alone furnifh; they were, at leaft, rich in that moft valuable ingredient common fenfe, enlivened with wit, pregnant with found juridical difcrimination, and accompanied with apparent fincerity and much honeft franknefs of manner.

In the intercourfe of private life, he was amiable, convivial, no foe to diffipation, but of a fpirit incapable of defcending to any of the mean and ungenerous vices. In good company he would drink deep; and in affairs of gallantry, he is reported to have occafionally indulged, even to excefs. The domeftic misfortune that enfued is known to all the world, and it might appear indelicate here to dwell upon the fubject.

One of the firft admirers of Mr. Dundas's talents in early life, was the late *Lord Kaimes*, who dedicated to him his excellent work, entitled " Principles of Equity;" and on that occafion anticipated his future fuccefs.

Neither the gaieties of diffipation, nor the chagrin attendant on a family misfortune, could divert Mr. Dundas from vigoroufly purfuing that career of profeffional fuccefs which had opened before him. He rapidly attained the rank of one of the firft lawyers at the Scottifh bar; and his own merits, added to the influence of his family, foon recommended him to the notice of the crown: in fine, he became, in a fhort time, Lord Advocate for Scotland; and neither his talents nor his juridical fkill were deemed unworthy of the office.

It had been ufual with his predeceffors, to procure a feat in the Britifh Houfe of Commons; and Mr. Dundas alfo contrived to get a niche at the back of the treafury-bench.

fury-bench. His pronunciation and phrafeology were
fo replete with the peculiarities of the northern dialect,
which has not yet ceafed to prevail at the Scottifh bar,
as to excite a degree of ridicule againft his fpeeches in
the fenate, which would have proved unfavourable to
the fuccefs of almoft any other perfon. But Mr. Dundas was not to be daunted by common obftacles. He
had enough of the lawyer about him to qualify him for
legiflative bufinefs, without his mind being narrowed
by pedantry, or his eloquence too finically caft after that
model which is peculiarly fitted to the bar, but becomes
tedious, and even ridiculous, amidft national deliberations. He was quickly able to make himfelf mafter of
all the *forms* of public bufinefs, a fpecies of knowledge fo dry, fo difficult, fo infinitely ufeful in parliament, fo utterly ufelefs every where elfe. In a fhort
time, he took an active part in every debate, and poffeffed great advantage, by utterly defpifing that primnefs, precifenefs, and rigour of morality, which teaches man to embrace *the right*, in oppofition to *the expedient*.
Nor did he ever affect to afpire to that purity of patriotifm, which refufes to connect felf-intereft with duty.
He thus fpeedily obtained an almoft unrivalled pre-eminence; the artifices, the negociations, the mafterly overreachings of political intrigue, were fome of the qualifications which foon appeared to compofe the public
character of Henry Dundas: and it muft be owned, they
would not be ill fitted, in a degenerate age, to conduct
him to eminence.

The extent of dominion, the immenfe wealth, and the
great political eftablifhments of the Eaft-India Company in Afia, had about this time begun to appear too
great for a fimple commercial corporation. The amazing fortunes acquired by their fervants, had alfo provoked the moft jealous enquiries into the arts by which
fuch

such opulence could be so rapidly accumulated, and oriental influence was but too plainly discovered in the very bosom of the legislature. Mr. D. soon perceived, that a member of the House of Commons might gain much by turning his attention to the affairs of India which came before that House. In the case of Rumbold and some others, he shewed himself to be unequalled in tracing the detail of Asiatic delinquency. In the public revolutions that speedily 'ensued, he was eagerly courted by all parties; and was generally allowed to be deserving of any of the primary places in the government. His enemies have said, that, being then a needy political adventurer, he found it necessary to choose his side, from a regard to personal interest: and that the laxity of his principles rendered him sufficiently ready to change his party, on the approach of ill fortune. Now the man of North; now the man of Fox; he found himself at last the fast friend, the ministerial coadjutor, and, as they say, the convivial tutor of Mr. PITT.

Mr. Dundas's alliance with the last of these, fixed him in the rich office of Treasurer to the Navy; and during the infancy of Mr. P's administration, his counsels and parliamentary services tended not a little to ensure its stability. In short, all the measures of the British government since the year 1782, have in a great degree, been directed, or at least influenced, by him.

Since he obtained an official employment in the administration, Mr. Dundas has enjoyed one peculiar advantage, which is rather of a singular sort—that of never having attained the reputation of political integrity. Mr. Pitt, and other men who have used the ladder of patriotism in scaling the heights of ministerial power, on being obliged to abandon those popular principles which helped them to ascend, have, by their apostacy, provoked the abhorrence of the people, by whom they were

once

once adored. But this great northern commoner, having never obtained much credit with the world in this refpect, has rather rifen than fallen in the eftimation of his country, during the courfe of his adminiftration.

Of all the meafures that have lately occurred, there is perhaps, no one which will be more unfavourably viewed by the candid and benevolent in future times, than the commencement of the prefent hoftilities with France. But, whatever may be faid of the merits or demerits of thofe minifterial arts which engaged Britain in the conteft, it muft be confeffed, that in many of the meafures which the war-minifter is fuppofed to have fuggefted, fuch as that for the internal defence of the country, there appears much of that vigilance, energy, and vigour, which we have been forced to admire in the revolutionary rulers of the continent.

Mr. Dundas has alfo the good fortune to obtain the confidence of the Dukes of Buccleugh, Gordon, and Lord Hopetoun, and fo many of the other leading peers and landholders of the North, that it would not be eafy to find another minifterial director of Scottifh affairs, whofe agency would be equally acceptable to the great people of that country.

His perfonal friends, who are numerous, and doubtlefs the beft judges of his real character, are greatly attached to him. They confider him as the only practical man in the cabinet, and think that either his retreat, or his death, would be attended with the moft melancholy events on the part of the nation.

On the other hand, his enemies, who are implacable, as confidering him the author of all our prefent calamities, and the accomplice of our former ones during the American war, entertain very different fentiments. The very mildeft of them affert, that the beft wifh that can be breathed, in favour of him or his country, is, either that he may be enabled quickly to retire from the toils of his political career, or be fpeedily called, by Divine Providence, to the enjoyment of another and better world.

The few who are of no party may confider him as an honeft and refpectable private character, and as an active, zealous, and loyal ftatefman.

A. Z.

ARTHUR WOLFE,

BARON KILWARDEN,

Lord Chief Juſtice of the King's Bench in Ireland.

OF the facility with which great talents may riſe to the higheſt rank and the firſt offices in the ſtate, when properly applied, Lord Kilwarden is a ſtriking inſtance.

Born in the County of Kildare, of parents of wealth and reſpectability, he had the advantage of an early college education, in the univerſity of Dublin, and was called to the Iriſh bar in 1766. He was ſoon appointed a king's counſel, and by very laborious induſtry in his profeſſion, was making way to wealth and legal character, when, in conſequence of a high opinion of his talents, he was introduced into parliament by Lord Tyrone[*]: Yet it was ſo late as the year 1787 before he mounted the firſt ſtep of the ladder to the bench, by being appointed his Majeſty's Solicitor-general, which place he filled with great ability and integrity.

His next advancement followed cloſe on the heels of the former, being nominated Attorney-general in 1789, on the promotion of Mr. Fitzgibbon to the court of Chancery.

[*] Now Marquis of Waterford.

From a degree of candour and openness in Mr. W's manner, which intitled him to esteem and praise; he also secured many friends, even in the opposition in the House of Commons.

In June 1798 he was raised to the peerage, and to the bench, on the death of Lord Chief Justice Clonmel. As a speaker, his voice is strong and deep, it is mellow and capable of much variety. In private life, his Lordship has the highest character of being a steady friend, and an honest man.

MR. CURRAN.

OF all the opinions which have obtained a general currency, without being either founded in truth or sanctioned by experience, there are none, perhaps, which have been so widely circulated as those by which we are taught to believe, that the study of law is adverse to the operations of genius, and that a lively imagination cannot be fettered to perfonal purfuits; that to be learned, a man muft be dull, and that wit cannot be poffeffed but to the exclufion of induftry.

Among the many examples which might be adduced from antiquity, or exhibited in modern times, to prove the futility of this dangerous conceit, Mr. Curran is not the leaft ftriking. No man has acquired higher reputation for thofe powers which delight and captivate the fancy, touch the fprings of paffion, elicit tears from the foftnefs of fenfibility, or extort from gravity itfelf the roar of laughter; yet has the affiduous induftry and laborious exertions of this gentleman raifed him from the humbleft walk of life, in which his birth had placed him, to the firft rank, if not the firft place, at the Irifh bar. He has not, indeed, attained high official fituations, or rifen to thofe honours which are oftener the reward of judicious politics, than of profeffional ability; but he has acquired that which is a ftronger proof both of induftry and of talent—the unconteſted title of being the firſt advocate in his country.

Mr. Curran is about fifty years of age. He was born in the county of Cork, of parents who were undiftinguifhed by wealth or fituation; who had neither a fortune by which they could have enabled the fon to live independently, nor connections by which they could advance him to a profeffion. They were, however, capable

ble of giving him the rudiments of a liberal education, and that seems to be the only advantage which he deprived from his family. Having qualified himself for the university, he entered in the only character in which his circumstances enabled him to appear, that of a *sizer* in the college of Dublin; a situation of which the emoluments are trivial, while the marks of inferiority which distinguish it from that of the other students are of the most mortifying kind. The sizers have, indeed, their tuition free of expence; but they are obliged to keep the rolls of their tutors, and attend to the weekly distribution of the fines and punishments of the pupils. They have also their commons *gratis*, but they dine only on the fragments of the fellows' table, and are compellable to discharge, in the dining-hall, several menial services.

In this situation did Mr. C. pass his first year at the university: nor did he appear, in point of pecuniary circumstances, to stand at the head even of this humble class. It is a fact, that the man who possessed powers that could move the heart, charm the imagination, and guide the judgment of a senate or of a court, was often destitute of a whole coat!

At the usual time (two years after entrance) he obtained a scholarship; by which, and by the emoluments arising from some petty offices generally bestowed on scholars, he emerged from the distress in which he had been hitherto involved. The remainder of his college career is not marked by any peculiar circumstances; he obtained the usual honours with which the policy of the university rewards industry and talents, and is said to have made some progress in reading the laborious course which is prescribed for fellowship candidates; but whether disgusted with the drudgery, or deterred by the magnitude of the undertaking, he soon desisted from the pursuit, and turned his attention to the bar.

Previously

Previously to his becoming a student in the Inns of Court of London, Mr. Curran married a lady of his own country. This match appears to have been founded in inclination, for she did not bring him a fortune sufficient to compensate the inconveniences into which such a permanent connection must have thrown him. Of the means by which he was enabled to support himself and wife, during his studies in England, and afterwards to defray the expence of his call to the bar, nothing certain is known; it is natural to suppose, however, that with talents like his, it would not be difficult to procure a livelihood by his literary exertions. But whatever might have been the mode by which his finances were supplied, it is certain that when he came to the bar, he was in extreme poverty. He resided in Cavan-street, Dublin, a place occupied entirely by the lowest class of people, and which, in point of *gentility*, is on a level with the least reputable part of Westminster.

Mrs. Curran had now brought him a child; and being unable to indulge in the practice so common in Ireland, of sending their children to be nursed abroad, she was obliged to undergo the labour of discharging at once the duties of nurse, housewife, and cook. About this time he became a frequenter of a convivial society, originally formed by some young barristers, and called the *Monks of the Screw*. Although the members of this institution were poor, they were merry; the object of their meetings was to forget, in good fellowship, the cares of life, and relax the mind from the intenseness of legal studies. The devotion of the Monks, however, was promoted by humbler beverage than the juice of the grape, and their temple was nothing more than an upper room in a Cavan-street ale-house. Poor as such a society must have been, the circumstances of Mr. Curran were so much more humble, that they were forwarded by his connec-

even with it. As the club affected to be *select*, it became necessary at length that they should have an apartment to themselves; they therefore engaged one at a certain rent, and Mr. Curran was complimented with the use of it, for the residence of himself and his family, except only during those evenings on which the members assembled. He must have been poor, indeed, who lodged in such a mansion!"

Mr. Curran was not the only man of talents, who at that time belonged to this society, and whom a subsequent display of genius, and of learning, raised to eminence. The present Chief Baron of the Irish Exchequer, Lord Yelverton, the early intimate and friend of Curran, was one of its original members. Though more fortunate than him in his political, as well as forensic pursuits, the connection first formed and cemented between them in the poverty of their early years (for Lord Yelverton, like Curran, had to struggle with the difficulties of a narrow fortune,) has continued through every vicissitude of succeeding life, not only unbroken but in full strength.

That learning and talents are often enabled to raise themselves into notice, without the fortunate co-operation of extrinsic circumstances, is an observation which has been often exemplified in every profession; but, perhaps, more frequently in that of the law, than any other. Our young barrister, with qualities which are as likely to strike at first sight, as those possessed by any of his contemporaries, remained, however, for some time at the bar entirely unnoticed. The attention of the public was turned toward him, for the first time, in rather a singular way.

He had been engaged as agent by one of the candidates at a contested election, and in the course of the poll, it became necessary for him to make objections to a vote proffered

proffered by the adverse party, which he did in that strong and sarcastic manner for which he is so remarkable. His antagonist, a man of rude and overbearing manners, *felt* the pungency of his wit, and not immediately recognising the Barrister under a shabby coat, and a mean appearance (for nature has not been very favourable in external decorations,) he applied to him some very gross epithets. With more spirit, perhaps, than decorum, Mr. Curran leaped from his seat, seized him by the collar, and was prevented only by the interposition of the by-standers from chastising him on the spot. He, however, was not precluded from asserting his independence in that way, which could alone be tolerated in the presence of a magistrate, he therefore, in a few pithy sentences, disclosed his *mind* and his *character*; his antagonist had generosity enough to acknowledge his error, and apologized to Mr. Curran for the consequences of his mistake; nay, instead of resenting the violence with which he had repelled the insult, he granted him his friendship, and by his recommendation and patronage very essentially promoted his future interests.

From that period he began to rise rapidly. Within less than six months he quitted his gratuitous lodgings in Cavan-street, and removed nearer to the more reputable part of the town. Mrs. Curran no longer dishonoured her lord's circumstances, by appearing in the discharge of those domestic offices which are usually performed by deputy; nay, in less than a year, the rising prosperity of the family was visible in the luxury of a one-horse chair! Merit was now finding its proper level, and, in this instance at least, we no longer behold great learning and uncommon genius struggling with adversity, or sullied in the estimation of vulgar minds, by an undeserved poverty:

Within

Within two or three years more, we find Mr. Curran feated in the Houfe of Commons, and feconding, with much fportive humour, every effort of the popular party for the emancipation of the country, and the eftablifhment of its commercial freedom and political independence.

During the arduous and interefting period in which Mr. Fitzgibbon filled the office of Attorney-general, he was one of the leading men in oppofition, and of courfe came into frequent collifion with that dogmatical and haughty lawyer. The high tone of defiance on legal or conftitutional queftions with which the Attorney-general endeavoured to overbear his opponents, was more frequently ridiculed by the wit, than combated by the arguments of Mr. Curran; if, in this mode of combat, he did not always repel the blow, he at leaft evaded its force, and though he could not on every occafion boaft of victory, he at leaft efcaped defeat. On one of thefe contefts, the iffue was more ferious; it produced a duel, in which Mr. C. was the challenger, but which happily was attended with no injury to either party.

While Mr. Curran was thus fuccefsfully attentive to bufinefs, he did not fuffer opportunities of pleafure to pafs by him unenjoyed. He was naturally, indeed, a man of uncommon gaiety; poffeffing an exquifite ear for mufic, and being himfelf no ordinary performer on the *forte piano*, it was not ftrange that the Circe-like allurements of Mrs. Billington fhould have enchanted him for a time.

Although Mr. Curran has been ufually confidered a man of gallantry, he enjoys an uninterrupted claim to the character of a good father. He has one fon, who is now (1798) about to be called to the bar, and two daughters; to the education of thefe he has paid the moft affectionate attention.

It

It has been already obferved, that, in his parliamentary character, he has always been attached to the popular caufe. Indeed, from his outfet in life, he has been a *fteady* friend to the legiflative independence, to free commerce, and a reform in the reprefentation of Ireland. He has uniformly declared againft the war with France, and he has combated, with unremitted vigour, during five years, the coercive fyftem which has been purfued in Ireland. Finding the inefficacy of that oppofition, he has withdrawn, along with many of thofe with whom he had co-operated, from the Houfe of Commons, and is now known to the public only as an advocate. In this capacity he has lately defended many of his unfortunate countrymen; and is faid to be about to retire for a time, and perhaps for ever from his native country.

As a lawyer Mr. Curran has not particularly diftinguifhed himfelf, by the extent of his knowledge or the depth of his refearches: he ftands, in this refpect only, on an equality with his competitors; it is as an advocate that he outftrips them. Indeed, in this character, he has not, perhaps, his equal in the empire. With Mr. Erfkine he has been frequently compared; but in the opinion of fome who have long admired, and attentively confidered the refpective excellencies of each, the latter holds only a fecond place.

Mr. Erfkine is an acute, grave, laborious, and frequently an eloquent pleader; he turns the bright fide of his client's cafe to full view, urges its ftrong parts with the force of a mafculine underftanding, and covers its weaknefs with very ingenious fophiftry; but the jury ftill remember that Mr. Erfkine is an advocate, and are on their guard againft his arts.

Mr. Curran while he difplays as much acutenefs as Mr. E. gets nearer to the heart and paffions of his auditors; and by the ardour and animation of an eloquence

neither

neither fictitious nor forced, excludes every feeling and every thought but those which he wishes to excite. In the examination of witnesses, too, Mr. Curran is eminently powerful. In his manner he resembles Mr. Garrow, but perhaps excells even that gentleman in probing a rotten cause to the bottom, in eliciting truth from prevarication, and touching the secret strings that actuate the human heart.

Mr. Curran's parliamentary speeches seldom possess the excellence which has marked his professional defences. They display much less of the *mens divinior*; they are irregular, and desultory, and seem to be rather the play of his mind than its serious exertion. They, however, abound with admirable strokes of invective, and irony, and though they assist but little in guiding decision, on the point discussed, yet produce a good effect, by holding up political profligacy and corruption to contempt and detestation.

Of classical learning Mr. Curran seems to have early laid in a good store; his allusions to the Roman poets are frequent, and his quotations from them are prompt, and happy. It is a curious circumstance, that to study the Latin classics, and commit to memory remarkable passages formed a part of Mr. Curran's preparation for the bar; and that he continues, from his experience of its utility, to recommend his practice to the student of the municipal law.

On the score of person, Mr. Curran owes but little to nature. His stature is low, his figure meagre and ill-formed, and his whole appearance far from being prepossessing. He has, however, an eye which emits the fire of genius, and is admirably calculated to transmit either the scintillations of fancy, or that deep pathos of the heart, which he not only feels himself, but can so powerfuly excite in others. Of dress he has always been remarkably, perhaps culpably, negligent; for he has often played *Cicero* in the senate, in the garb of *Scrub!* LORD

LORD MONBODDO.

JAMES BURNET is descended from an ancient family in Aberdeenshire, and being heir to a small fortune, studied the Scotch law, and was called to the bar, or, in other words, became *an advocate* in that country.

In this situation he acquired considerable celebrity, and was employed as counsel in two causes, which engaged the attention of the public more than any brought before a Scottish tribunal in the course of a century. One of these was the great question of literary property; the other the Douglas cause. In the course of the latter he was employed to go to Paris, in order to arrange the necessary papers for the investigation of so intricate an affair.

While in that capital he procured an account of a savage girl, who had been discovered wild in the woods of Champagne, and actually went to see her; for this was a subject intimately connected with his favourite pursuit.

In 1767, Mr. Burnet was appointed one of the Lords of Session in Scotland, when, according to the custom of his country, he assumed the title of *Lord Monboddo*, from the name of his family estate. He was offered the post of one of the Commissioners of the Court of Justiciary, but declined its acceptance, on account of the unpleasant part of that office, the trying and sentencing condemned criminals!

Lord Monboddo has, however, been better known to the world as a literary man, than either as a pleader or a judge. His first publication was a "Dissertation on the Origin and Progress of Language," in six volumes, 8vo. The investigation of the origin of language, had been in vain attempted by many of the learned among the ancients, who certainly possessed materials of which we

are

are deprived. Yet the moderns have engaged in this purfuit with much ardour; and in our time Bifhop Warburton and Lord Monboddo, both men of fingular acquirements have thought deeply, and written profoundly on the fubject. After the moft extenfive refarch, they, however, have not been able to inform us how or when alphabetical writing was firft invented; but they have deferved the thanks of the curious, by *fhewing how* it might have been difcovered and introduced. The excellence of this art is fo confpicuous, that many learned men have conceived it to be an immediate communication from the Deity; and Mr. Gilbert Wakefield has written an ingenious effay on this fide of the queftion, which has been thought worthy of a place in the *Encyclopædia Britannica*; but both the judge and the bifhop have fhewn, not only the poffibility, but the probability, that we owe this grand effort of human fkill to the genius of Egypt; and this opinion has been greatly ftrengthened by the ingenious labours of Governor Pownall.

His lordfhip is alfo author of another work, in five volumes quarto, called " Ancient Metaphyfics ;" a performance remarkable for the furprizing mixture of penetration and genius, with what, in the eyes of fome, appears to be the moft abfurd whim and conceit, the attempt to prove that the *ourang o uang* is a clafs of the human foecies; and that the want of fpeech is merely accidental: this has afforded much fport, both to the wits and critics of the age. Lord Monboddo has alfo endeavoured to eftablifh the exiftence of mermaids! yet, notwithftanding thefe fingularities, the work is a truly ingenious performance, and will long enfure a place on the fhelves of the learned.

His lordfhip is, at one and the fame time, an excellent Greek fcholar, and a true chriftian philofopher. He is

ingenious

ingenious and liberal his opinions, and his conduct as a judge, never fuffers himfelf to be fwayed by either party or family connexions. At his houfe in Edinburgh, he is extremely hofpitable; and receives, with politenefs, all literary ftrangers who vifit that city. He imitates the ancients in bathing and exercife, and has attained to a very great age with out any of thofe infirmities, either of mind or body, which are the ufual attendants on extreme age. He was formerly accuftomed to retire yearly to London, and generally made the journey on horfeback; it need fcarcely be added, that in all his peregrinations, he was received with unbounded welcome by the literary men of the age.

R THE

THE HONOURABLE DAINES BARRINGTON

IS brother to the late Lord Barrington, the prefent Bifhop of Durham, and alfo to Admiral Barrington.

This gentleman was bred to the law, a profeffion in which he never made any confpicuous figure, but was fucceffively promoted to be one of the king's counfel, and a Welch judge; the latter of which ftations he refigned fome years ago, on acconnt of his growing infirmities. He has alfo poffeffed feveral fmall places under government, fuch as deputy-keeper of the wardrobe, fecretary to Greenwich-hofpital, marfhal of the admiralty, and commiffioner of ftores at Gibraltar, the laft of which only he now retains.

But if Mr. Barrington is not celebrated as a lawyer, he may juftly claim the honour of being a profound and judicious antiquary, an agreeable companion, and a truly worthy man. In 1775, he publifhed an Effay on the Probability of reaching the North Pole, 4to.; and in 1781, a volume of Mifcellanies, alfo in 4to. principally on Antiquarian fubjects.

In 1766 he prefented the world with a volume of *Obfervations upon the Statutes, from Magna Charta to the* 21 *James I.* in which he ftrongly enforces a revifal, and adds a propofal for new modelling the whole. This is a work of great merit, and a fecond edition was called for and publifhed in 1776.

To enumerate Mr. Barrington's literary labours, would be an Herculean tafk: among them we find an " Account of fome Fifh in Wales;" " Inveftigation of the Difference between the paft and prefent Temperature of the Air in Italy;" " Obfervations on Welch Caftles;" A Controverfy with Dr. Ducarel concerning " Chefnut Trees;"

Trees;" "Method of keeping Carp alive out of water;" "Two Letters on Cæfar's Invafion;" "Effay on the periodical Appearance of Birds;" "On the diftinguifhed Qualities of the Rabbit and Hare;" "Experiments on the finging of Birds;" "Correction of fome Miftakes in Ornithology;" "Account of two Welch Mufical Inftruments;" "On the Remains of the ancient Cornifh Language;" "Inquiry into the Antiquity of Clocks;" "Conjectures relative to certain Remains of vitrified Walls in Scotland;" "On Archery;" "On Mufical Inftruments;" "On Card playing."

Moft of thefe are highly entertaining, and fome of them evince the moft profound refearch.

This very ingenious man was the friend of Dr. Johnfon, and a member of the club in Effex-ftreet, inftituted by that great moralift. He ftill appertains to a fociety of *choice Spirits*, who meet at the Grecian, whither he is fupported by his man, and returns in a chair to chambers. The templars, the city beaus, and, indeed, the world in general, are much obliged to him for the improvements made in the garden facing the Thames, which exhibits more tafte and elegance, than could be expected from an antiquary.

DR. O'LEARY.

ARTHUR O'LEARY is a native of Cork, in Ireland, and a member of the moſt numerous and leaſt predominant ſect in that country.

After receiving ſome inſtruction in his native land, he was ſent to the continent, in 1747, to prepare him for the ſituation for which he was deſigned—that of a prieſt of the Roman catholic church. He accordingly reſided for ſome time at the college of St. Omer's, and became a member of the order of St. Francis.

On the completion of his ſtudies, he was appointed chaplain to a regiment in the ſervice of the prince in whoſe dominions he was educated; but not entering warmly into the meaſure of engaging the ſubjects of theſe kingdoms to enliſt in foreign battalions, he incurred the diſpleaſure of thoſe in power, and ſoon after returned to the country which had given him birth.

By the aſſiſtance of ſome friends he built a ſmall but decent chapel in his native city; and a circumſtance ſoon occurred which procured him ſome little provinci alcelebrity. A work happened, about this time, to be publiſhed in Cork, entitled, "Thoughts on Nature and Religion." It was written by a Scotch phyſician; and as no one anſwered it, Father O'Leary applied to Dr. Mann, the biſhop of the dioceſe in which he reſided, for permiſſion to enter the liſts; now the churches of England and Rome thinking alike on the matter in diſpute, he immediately granted leave. Accordingly, ſoon after this, appeared his "Defence of the Divinity of Chriſt, and the Immortality of the Soul."

When the parliament of Ireland framed a teſt oath for the Roman catholics, many perſons of tender conſciences ſcrupled to take it. On this, Mr. O'Leary publiſhed his

"Loyalty

"Loyalty afferted, or the Teft-Oath vindicated;" in which he explained the feeming difficulties that occurred, fo much to the fatisfaction of the nonjuring catholics in his neighbourhood, that they unanimoufly fubfcribed.

At that critical period, during the unfortunate war with America, when the combined fleets of France and Spain rode triumphant on the Britifh coaft, and threatened an invafion of Ireland, he addreffed his Catholic countrymen in the moft energetic language, and in fuch an effectual manner, as to merit the thanks of every good citizen.

His next publications were in reply to fome fevere charges made againft the Roman Catholics, by the late Mr. Wefley; and in thefe he refuted that odious imputation by which they are accufed of " keeping no faith with heretics."

Another valuable tract publifhed by Mr. O'Leary is called " An Effay on Toleration, and a Plea for Freedom of Confcience." In this effay the reafoning is folid and perfuafive, and the whole tenor of it tends to inculcate the principles of liberality and humanity.

Thefe fix pieces have been publifhed in a volume, under the title of " Mifcellaneous Tracts;" and it has reached a third, if not a fourth edition. It is dedicated to the " Monks of St. Patrick," a fociety of refpectable men in Ireland, who affociated for the fupport of the conftitution of their country.

In addition to the literary labours already alluded to, an excellent pamphlet publifhed in 1786, and entitled " A Review of fome interefting Periods in the Irifh Hiftory," is alfo attributed to him; and Mr. Pratt has drawn his character in a very mafterly manner, in his late novel called " Family Secrets," one volume of which is infcribed to the Doctor.

Father O'Leary, as he is familiarly called, and who is said to have received a pension from government for his public services, has lately printed a sermon on the present situation of affairs, which was originally preached at St. Patrick's chapel.

BARRY,

BARRY, LORD YELVERTON,

CHIEF BARON OF THE EXCHEQUER IN IRELAND.

LIKE many other of thofe men whofe talents and virtues have raifed them in Ireland to the higheft places in the law, Chief Baron Yelverton owes nothing to illuftrious birth, to family connections, or to wealth accumulated by his anceftors. If report be true (and it is highly honourable to him), his lordfhip's immediate progenitor was nothing more than a petty dealer in wool, in the neighbourhood of Clonmel, far from affluent in point of circumftances, and unable to do more for Barry, his fon, than to give him the rudiments of a claffical education, which enabled him to enter the univerfity of Dublin, as a fizer, a defcription of ftudents, accuftomed to receive both tuition and commons free of expence. At the ufual time he obtained a fcholarfhip, a reward given in that univerfity to diftinguifhed merit, and to which befides honourable rank, certain emoluments are annexed, in addition to board, not exceeding, however, on the whole, 20*l.* per annum.

Mr. Yelverton, before the expiration of his fcholarfhip, determined on the law as his profeffion; but to acquire knowledge in it, and afterwards to be called to the bar, requires " a portion of this world's wealth," which unluckily his finances were unable to afford.

His marriage, fhortly after, with a young lady poffeffed of three or four hundred pounds, removed this embarraffment, and enabled him, with fome literary exertions of his own, to keep his terms in London, and obtain his call to the Irifh bar in 1764. When he became a barrifter, he occupied very obfcure lodgings in Effex-ftreet, a part of the town which ftill continues to be unfafhionable. Here he remained for fome time, and proved,

proved, in his own case, that even first-rate legal talents may lie long in obscurity. The industry and ability of Mr. Yelverton, however, did at last work their way, but many years elapsed between his assumption of a wig and gown, and his becoming a character known to the public in any other way than as a professional man, labouring successfully for his client and his fee.

We do not, indeed, hear of him in a public capacity, until the occurrence of that important crisis, when the calamities of the country urged its friends to struggle with the then weakened power of Great Britain, and to obtain for Ireland an enlargement of commercial privileges, and shortly afterwards the establishment of legislative independence. Mr. Yelverton, who had now got into parliament, co-operated with the other patriots of the day in the pursuit of these objects, and was conspicuous for the energy and boldness of his exertions. When they were once attained, he not only ceased to lend his talents to the popular party, but, on the contrary, he opposed them, ranged himself on the side of the court, and resisted every attempt to attain reform in the representation by means of the volunteer associations.

In 1782, he had been raised to the important and confidential place of Atorney-general; and he acquitted himself in that situation with such unremitting zeal, in counteracting the attempts of the volunteers, and labouring for their dispersion, as effectually recommended him to the favour of government. The beneficial effects resulting from this conduct were soon apparent, for in 1784 he was raised to the bench, as Chief Baron of the Exchequer.

His elevation, though generally considered as a reward for his political services, was yet not unwelcome to the public, which could recognise, even in the unpopular senator, the learning, the talents, and the profesfional integrity of a great lawyer. Removed from the House of Commons to the bench, and yet not raised to the peerage, his opportunities of rendering political services to the administration were now greatly lessened. The consequence was, that, either relaxing in his zeal for want of occasion to exert it, or finding its fervour cooled by not being raised to a title, like his competitor Scott, who was created Baron Earlsfort in 1784, his politics appeared to be neutralised, until, in 1789, he declared himself a decided friend to the party which asserted the right of Ireland to choose her own regent, and accordingly proffered that office to the Prince of Wales. Notwithstanding this, he was created Lord Yelverton, Baron of Avonmore, in the county of Cork, June 16, 1795.

No man possesses a higher character in private life than Lord Yelverton. Simple and unassuming in his manners, with a goodness of heart which fraud and cunning but too often make the dupe of their artifices, he is beloved by all, and imposed on, even in the most trivial occurrences of life, by many. Though enjoying a strength and comprehension of intellect fitted to direct and to enlighten senates, he may be governed, misled, or baffled, by the most shallow of his domestics. Of the convivial glass no man is more fond, and yet slander has not charged him with intemperance. His lordship loves, and, without the least inconvenience to his intellects, can bear a considerable quantity of the enlivening grape.

As a public speaker, his leading characteristic is STRENGTH. His voice, full, deep, and sonorous, added to a pronunciation slow and solemn, gives great weight to what is dictated by a mind well stored with legal and general knowlege; by an understanding capable of arranging, in the most judicious manner, the excellent materials which it possesses; and by a fancy not

destitute

destitute of the powers of embellishment. His manner is animated, impressive, and almost overbearing. Of quick conception and feelings, often irritable, and apt to be roused to indignation by every appearance of oppression or of fraud, his lordship appears to display all the sensations of a good man. But on the bench, he seems, perhaps, to possess too little of that stoical apathy, which is so essential to the ascertainment of guilt or innocence; a cause is no sooner opened, than he catches, or supposes he catches, sufficient to guide his decision; and every attempt which the pleader afterwards makes to remove this first impression, his lordship strenuously resists as an unworthy endeavour to impose on his understanding, and to throw the veil of eloquence around truth and justice. This fault excepted, and to which Lord Mansfield himself was but too prone, Lord Yelverton is allowed to be an excellent judge, of inflexible integrity, and extensive legal learning.

RIGHT HONOURABLE ISAAC CORRY

CHANCELLOR OF THE EXCHEQUER IN IRELAND.

THIS gentleman is the son of a reputable, but not very wealthy, merchant of the town of Newry, in the county of Down. A considerable shew of talents, and great professions of independent and steady patriotism, rendered him in early life a favourite with the public; while easy, polished manners, added to an engaging person, procured him the friendship of his townsmen, who soon became his constituents.

Mr. Corry was bred to the law, and was actually called to the bar in the year 1779, a very remarkable period in the history of Ireland. Soon disgusted, either with the labours of the profession, or the ill success with which these labours were attended, he threw away his bag, which had never been over-charged with briefs, and became an adventurer in the field of politics.

No sooner was he seated in the House of Commons, than he became one of the most warm and animated members of the then opposition. His industry, which applied itself to every subject that emerged in the course of parliamentary business, but particularly to the calculations of revenue and finance; his fluency in debate, the correctness and animation of his language, accompanied with a very successful display of apparent modesty, rendered him not only a shewy, but an useful partisan.

For some years Mr. Corry devoted himself to the popular cause; he scrutinized every ministerial measure, railed against British influence, contended for place and pension-bills, and laboured, with much energy and effect, to obtain a similar construction of the navigation-act in both countries. But, alas! the hour was approaching, when he was no longer to grace the opposition bench, tease a lord lieutenant's secretary with patriotic motions, or embarrass the financier with the Cocker-like allusions of arithmetical eloquence!

The Marquis of Buckingham assumed the viceroyship of Ireland in 1787, and having dismissed a very considerable number of officers in the different departments for neglect and peculation, it became necessary to replace them with gentlemen possessing the public confidence. With his lordship, skill in accounts was a first-rate qualification; who, therefore, could be a better object of his favour than Mr. Corry? Mr. Corry was accordingly nominated to a post in the ordnance, of one thousand pounds per annum. The viceroy, affecting popularity, thus appointed to office a popular representative; and the popular representative, wishing to serve himself and his country, accepted the appointment.

From the days of the Marquis of Buckingham, Mr. Corry has exhibited himself, during a series of viceroys, as one of the best servants of administration, and has enjoyed a succession of very lucrative places in the ordnance, revenue, and treasury.

But although Mr. Corry, has in some degree, relinquished the love and applause of his countrymen for the smiles of a court, and the emoluments of office, it is yet but just to say, that he was not, during several years, the forward advocate of the ancient system, nor has he ever, with the shameless zeal of most proselytes, become either the slanderer or the persecutor of the party which he deserted. He has borne himself with a meekness and temperance which disarm resentment, and preserve to him the regard and esteem of those with whom he formerly acted. In many instances he has voted against the minister on questions which, in his patriotic days, he had supported; and in others, he has modestly withdrawn on a division, in order to preserve at once his place and his consistency. In the late contest between the court and the country party, he has, however, been an advocate
for

for the coercive fyftem, and acceded to all the fevere laws which were enacted previoufly to the rebellion.

Mr. Corry's perfon is manly, and his countenance expreffive of fpirit and good fenfe; thofe fcenes of gaiety and diffipation in which part of 'his juvenile days were fpent, and which contributed to give his manners that polifh which we admire, have alfo impreffed on his face fome of the indications of the *bon-vivant*. He is ftill unmarried, having hitherto fcorned the trammels of wedlock, and enjoyed the delights of love in the lefs moral way of a man of fafhion.

There is not a more influencing fpeaker in the Irifh Houfe of Commons. His voice is ftrong and mellow; his diction correct; and his ftyle fluent, copious, moderately ornamented, and always above mediocrity. On moft topics he is capable of fpeaking in a manner which always pleafes, and fometimes inftructs; but it is principally upon fubjects connected with finance, revenue or commerce, that he appears to the greateft advantage. To thefe he feems chiefly to have directed his attention, and in thefe he has acquired very extenfive and ufeful knowledge. Indeed, wherever clearnefs and ftrength can recommend a fpeaker to his auditory, Mr. Corry is calculated to command applaufe, for his underftanding is of the firft clafs. From imagination he derives little aid; his fancy is either fterile, or he repreffes its exuberance, for in his fpeeches are to be found few of thofe flowers which decorate the barren tract of inveftigation, or beautify the field of dry difquifition. His ornaments confift in extreme neatnefs of diction, fmoothnefs and fluency of periods, and well-judged arrangement of matter. Thefe, added to the correct animation of his manner, the roundfulnefs of his voice, and the effect of a good perfon, procure for his opinions a great degree of attention and refpect.

RIGHT

RIGHT HONOURABLE JOHN BERESFORD.

Mr. BERESFORD is a younger branch of that family, whose head is the Marquis of Waterford. Educated for the bar, he was called to it so early as 1761, and for some years practised with tolerable success. He was, however, at last induced to quit that laborious profession, where reward can only be obtained by the most rigid industry, for the golden prospects which opened to him in the field of political adventure. Those prospects he has abundantly realized, having raised himself to high office, and still higher influence in the state, spread his branches over the land, and struck his roots too deep in the soil to be shaken even by those dreadful storms which have lately agitated Ireland. Such is his influence, that he is reported to have procured for himself, and his various family connections, places, salaries, &c. to the amount of above 40,000l. per annum!

For many years back, Mr. Beresford has been at the head of the Irish revenue, in which situation he is said to have acquired and displayed a very profound and extensive knowledge, not only of the affairs of that department, but of the general commerce of the country. That he is a man of business, and indefatigable industry, cannot be denied; and that he possesses talents of some kind, is fully proved by the success which has crowned his endeavours.

The obtaining from parliament a sum of money, not less than half-a-million, for building, under the name of a custom-house, a palace, part of which he himself was to inhabit, establishes beyond controversy, the extent of his power, and the success of his address; while the judicious dispositions which he has made, as one of the commissioners for widening the streets of the capital, gives him

him an indisputable title to the praise of great foresight and skill.

Of a long succession of viceroys, with a single exception only, Mr. Beresford is supposed to have had the ear; they have been governed in a great measure by his councils, and they have not proved ungrateful to their adviser. The influence of a man thus circumstanced, must necessarily have become extensive; it has accordingly insinuated itself into every department of the state, and given to that family a degree of strength which enables it almost to dictate to any administration. One viceroy alone (Lord Fitzwilliam) attempted, of late, to govern without the Beresfords, and the consequence was, that he was driven from the helm. Had Lord Cornwallis presided as a civil magistrate, and thwarted their plans, he too, probably, would have felt their power.

Possessing such weight in the councils of the country, it is not to be supposed that Mr. B. ever attempts to quarrel with a measure recommended by administration. In fact, the British cabinet is said to recommend no project, which has not, in the first instance, been approved by him and a few other men of business who know the country. The celebrated commercial propositions of Mr. Orde, in 1785, however, form an exception. The alterations which were made in those propositions in England, had not Mr. B's previous concurrence; and though he at length reluctantly supported them, they miscarried, as he had very sagaciously presaged.

Although Mr. Beresford, and his family, have so much influence in the Irish administration, he does not, personally, exert himself in the House in defending or supporting the measures which he advises. He never speaks but on subjects relating to the revenue, or the business of the commissioners during the debates on wide streets. When repelling the insinuations of improper or corrupt
                                                                conduct,

conduct, with which he has been sometimes harrassed, he shews great anxiety to convince, but his declamation is unimpassioned. His voice is very clear, and sufficiently strong, but it wants variety, and has no harmony in its tones. His diction is indeed simple, but not correct, and never rises above the level of colloquial conversation.

Even his political enemies allow Mr. Beresford to possess a very amiable private character; for he must be confessed to be a good friend, father, and husband. In his person, he is tall, and though now an old man, he is yet florid, erect and handsome.

RIGHT

RIGHT HONOURABLE JOHN FOSTER,
SPEAKER OF THE IRISH HOUSE OF COMMONS.

IF the poſſeſſion of a ſtrong and correct underſtanding, much general knowledge, and a profound acquaintance with the commercial, manufacturing, and agricultural intereſts of his native country, conſtitute a juſt ground to reſpect, it is due to Mr. Foſter; for undoubtedly one more able, in point of intellect, or better informed in the very important inſtances we have mentioned, is not to be found among the public men of Ireland.

John Foſter is the ſon of the late Anthony, Lord Chief Baron Foſter. He received his education at the univerſity of Dublin, where he was contemporary with the preſent Chancellor, and Mr. Grattan. In Michaelmas term, 1766, he was called to the Iriſh bar, while his father, the Chief Baron, was yet on the bench. To Mr. Foſter, law was but a nominal profeſſion; he applied himſelf to other ſtudies, and no doubt had higher game in view, than the humble ſituation of a labouring barriſter, or even the more dignified one of a *puiſné judge*. He accordingly turned his mind towards ſtatiſtical enquiries; and in the moſt dry and difficult occupations, perhaps, in which the human mind can be employed, he made a proficiency to which he now owes his elevation to the moſt honourable office which a commoner can fill.

Shortly after his call to the bar, Mr. Foſter was returned to ſerve in parliament for the county of Louth, and ſoon became as conſpicuous for talents, as for knowledge. At that time, indeed, it was leſs difficult to become eminent in an Iriſh Houſe of Commons than at preſent, becauſe the field for exertion being narrow, much talent, comparatively speaking, was not called forth; but in any affembly of legiflators, this man was qualified to fhine; and in that of Ireland, the manly wifdom of his fyftem of corn laws, a fyftem which he began to form fhortly after his coming into parliament, will give immortality to his name. From being unable to fupply two-thirds of her people with bread, in 1770, in confequence of the operation of Mr. Fofter's plan, his country has not only become equal to feed her inhabitants without lying at the mercy of other nations, but actually to export grain to the amount of 200,000 *l.* annually.

After the agriculture of the country, the next great object of Mr. Fofter was the Linen manufacture, and this has derived, from his zeal and intelligence, nearly equal benefit with agriculture itfelf. His attention to it has been unremitted; and the regulations, from time to time, introduced by his advice, have not only greatly encreafed the quantity manufactured and exported, but fecured to Irifh linens, in foreign countries, a character which muft, for many years, operate powerfully in their favour.

During the very period in which Mr. Fofter was rendering to Ireland benefits fo important, his name was not merely odious, but even execrated among the populace, at leaft the populace of the metropolis. This is not much to the credit of popular feeling; but there are fome circumftances which may account for the fact, notwithftanding that they certainly cannot juftify it.

Although Mr. Fofter was thus laudably employed in advancing the agriculture and manufactures of the country, he was at the fame time known to be adverfe to every attempt toward eftablifhing the independence of the legiflature, and abrogating the unjuft reftrictions, by which Great Britain had fettered the commerce of Ireland. At that time, too, the manufacturers of the capital were either ftarving for
want

want of employment, or kept alive by eleemofynary contributions. Protecting duties for thefe famifhed artifans were called for, and Mr. Fofter oppofed them with all his powers. It was natural that the hungry fhould hate the man who thus declared his hoftility to meafures which it was hoped would give them bread. The remote operation of laws; however wife, the bulk of the nation could not forefee; and even if they could forefee, it would not relieve the preffure of prefent want, or enable the famifhing workmen to fatisfy the calls of nature.

Whatever Mr. Fofter's merits, therefore, might be, the populace, reafoning from what was obvious, inftead of what was remote, looked on him with deteftation; his having declared an opinion againft the utility of promoting the filk manufacture, was another caufe which raifed him a hoft of enemies. This prejudice continued for feveral years, and at one time, fuch was the general deteftation, that it was thought neceffary to give him a guard for his protection.

In 1785, Mr. Fofter was appointed Chancellor of the Exchequer; an office, for which his comprehenfive and methodical mind, added to his extenfive knowledge of the refources of the country, admirably fitted him. In 1786 he, however, refigned the Chancellorfhip, on being chofen Speaker of the Houfe of Commons, in which dignified fituation he has fince continued. At the commencement of the late parliament, the friends of Mr. W. B. Ponfonby made a powerful effort in fupport of *his* pretenfions to the chair; but they were unable to counteract the influence which the experience, talents, and information of Mr. Fofter defervedly gave him. He was accordingly chofen then by a large majority; and by the prefent Houfe of Commons, he was elected without oppofition, moft of the popular member having feceded.

The duties of this high office are discharged by him with great ability. Deeply read in the law and privileges of parliament, no incident occurs in which he is not able to guide the conduct of the house, while his punctuality, love of order, and good taste, give facility to business, and a decorous elegance to legislative arrangements.

As a politician Mr. Foster seems to have acted steadily upon one principle, that of promoting, to the utmost of his power, the interests of Ireland, so far as those interests did not interfere with any of the interests of Great Britain. Where a competition would exist, he has uniformly been swayed by the latter. There is another strong feature in his political character; he has always professed himself averse to the admission of Catholics to the privileges of the constitution. On the bill for allowing them to vote at elections, he delivered a speech against that measure, confessedly the best which was made in either house on the subject.

In private life, Mr. Foster appears rather high bred than affable; displaying more of the lofty manners of the last age, than the easy and familiar habits of the present. His style of living is magnificent, and his relish for *improving* insatiable. To these causes, perhaps, it is to be attributed, that, with an income of not less than 8000 *l. per annum*, he is still an embarrassed man. Mrs. Foster was created Baroness Oriel in 1790.

CHARLES

CHARLES BURNEY, MUS. D. F. R. S.

THIS gentleman, whose celebrity is equally great in the literary and the musical world, is a native of Shrewsbury, and was born in 1726. He received the rudiments of his education at the free grammar school of that town, and completed it at the public school of Chester. At the latter place he commenced his musical studies, under Mr. Baker, organist of the cathedral, who was a pupil of Dr. Blow.

He returned to Shrewsbury about the year 1741, and continued the study of music, under his half-brother, Mr. James Burney, who was an eminent organist and teacher of music in that town.

In 1744 he met with Dr. Arne at Chester, who perceiving his talents to be respectable, prevailed upon his friends to send him to London. He continued to profit under the instructions of that celebrated master full three years.

In 1749, he was elected organist of St. Dione's back-church, Fenchurch-street, with an annual salary of only thirty pounds; and the same year was engaged to take the organ-part at the new concert established at the King's-arms, Cornhill, instead of that which had been held at the Swan tavern, burnt down the year before. At this time he composed for Drury-lane theatre the following musical pieces, viz. Robin Hood, a comic opera by Moses Mendez; and Queen Mab, a pantomime; which last had astonishing success, being played every winter for nearly thirty years.

Being in an ill state of health, which, in the opinion of his physicians, indicated a consumption, he was prevailed upon to retire into the country. Accordingly he went to Lynn Regis, in Norfolk, where he was chosen organist,

with

with a salary of one hundred pounds a-year. Here he continued nine years, and formed the design of compiling his *General History of Music*.

In 1760, his health being established, he gladly returned once more to the metropolis, with a large and young family, and entered upon his profession with an increase of profit and reputation. His eldest daughter, who was then about eight years old, obtained great notice in the musical world by her astonishing performances on the harpsichord.

Soon after his arrival in London, he composed several much-admired concertos; and in 1766 he brought out at Drury-lane theatre a translation of Rousseau's *Devin du Village*, which he had executed during his residence at Lynn. It had, however, no great success.

In 1769, he had the honorary degree of Doctor of Music conferred upon him by the university of Oxford; on which occasion he performed an exercise in the musical school of that university. This exercise, consisting of an anthem of great length, with an overture, airs, recitatives, and choruses, was several times afterwards performed at the Oxford music meetings; and, under the direction of the famous Emanuel Bach, in St. Katherine's church, Hamburgh.

The year following he travelled through France and Italy, as well with a view to improvement in his profession, as to collect materials for his intended *History of Music*, an object which he had seldom out of his mind, from the time he first conceived the idea of such a work. In 1771, he published his "Musical Tour; or, Present State of Music in France and Italy." This work was very well received by the public, and is so good a model for travellers to keep their journals by, that Dr. Johnson professedly adopted it as his when he visited the Hebrides. Speaking of his own book, "I had," said the Doctor, "that clever dog Burney's "Musical Tour in my eye."

In

In 1772, he travelled through the Netherlands, Germany and Holland, and in the course of the next year he published an account of his journey in two volumes octavo. The same year he was also elected Fellow of the Royal Society.

In 1776, appeared the first volume in quarto of his " *General History of Music.*" The remaining volumes of this very elaborate and intelligent work were published at irregular periods; and the five, of which it now consists, were not completed till the year 1789.

In 1779, at the desire of Sir John Pringle, Dr. Burney drew up for the Philosophical Transactions " An Account of Little CROTCH, the Infant Musician, now Professor of Music in the University of Oxford." The grand musical festival in 1785, in commemoration of HANDEL, held in Westminster-abbey, was considered as deserving of a particular memoir; the historian of music was fixed upon as the most proper person to draw it up. Accordingly, the same year, a splendid volume was published by Dr. Burney, in quarto, for the benefit of the musical fund. In this work the Doctor displayed eminent talents as a biographer; and the Life of Handel is one of the few good memoirs which exist in our language.

In 1796, he published the " Life of Metastasio," in three volumes, octavo; but this performance wants that arrangement and judicious selection which characterize his former publications. Besides these productions, Dr. Burney wrote " The Cunning Man ;" " An Essay towards a History of Comets ;" " Plan of a Public Music School," &c. &c.

His musical works, in addition to those already mentioned, are; Sonatas for two Violins and a Bass, two parts. Six Cornet Pieces, with an Introduction and Fugue for the Organ. A Cantata and Songs. Six Duets for two German Flutes

Flutes. Six Concertos for Violins, &c. in eight parts. Two Sonatas for a Piano Forte, Violin, and Violoncello, two parts. Six Harpſichord Leſſons, &c. &c.

Dr. Burney has been twice married, and has had eight children, of whom ſeveral have manifeſted very ſuperior abilities.

His eldeſt daughter was celebrated for her extraordinary muſical powers.

The ſecond, Madame D'ARBLAY, is univerſally known and admired as the author of Evelina, Cecilia, and Camilla.

The eldeſt ſon, JAMES, ſailed round the world with Captain Cook, and afterwards commanded the Briſtol, of 50 guns, in the Eaſt Indies: he has publiſhed ſome judicious tracts on the beſt means of defending our iſland againſt an invading enemy.

The ſecond ſon, Charles Burney, LL.D. is maſter of a reſpectable academy at Greenwich, and well known in the learned world by his profound knowledge of the Greek language, and his maſterly claſſical criticiſms in the Monthly Review.

For many years Doctor Burney reſided in the houſe (No. 36, St. Martin's-ſtreet, Leiceſter-fields) formerly occupied by Sir Iſaac Newton; during the laſt ten he has inhabited an elegant ſuite of apartments in Chelſea college, where he enjoys a handſome independency. He ſtill ſpends ſeveral hours every day in his library, which is ſtored with a great variety of valuable and curious books, many of them collected during his travels.

D. W.

WILLIAM HERSCHEL, LL. D. F. R. S.

THIS country has the faireſt right to enrol the ſubject of the preſent article in the number of her ornaments, as his extraordinary abilities have been brought into action, ſtrengthened, and properly directed, under the auſpices of the Britiſh ſovereign.

Dr. William Herſchel is a native of Hanover, and was born November 15, 1738. He was the ſecond of four ſons, all of whom were brought up to their father's profeſſion, which was that of a muſician. In addition to theſe, Mr. Herſchel, ſenior, had two daughters; and therefore, burdened with ſo large a family, and in a poor country too, it is not at all a matter of wonder that the education which he beſtowed on his children was but ſcanty. Finding, however, in William a lively and inquiſitive genius, beyond what appeared in the other ſons, he gave him the advantage of a French maſter, under whom he made a rapid progreſs in the attainment of that language. Luckily, the tutor had a metaphyſical head, and ſo fond was he of his favourite ſtudy, as well as thoſe branches of ſcience which are connected with it, that he was deſirous of making his pupil acquainted therewith. From this worthy man young Herſchel gained a tolerable knowledge of logic, ethics, and metaphyſics; and his attainments therein excited in his mind a ſtrong and inſatiable thirſt for learning, with the commendable reſolution of exerting himſelf to the utmoſt to improve his ſtock of intellectual treaſures. Theſe, indeed, were all his inheritance, except a muſical inſtrument, and ſome manuſcript muſic. With this ſtore, unpromiſing as it was, our adventurer bade adieu to his native country while the flames

of

of war were spreading around it, and arrived in London in the year 1759. Here he was lost in the crowd of candidates for employment, and we may well suppose that his situation in a strange country, without friends, and in but indifferent circumstances, must have been both painful and irksome. Mr. Herschel had not only a steady but a virtuous mind. Hereby he was enabled not only to bear up with fortitude against disappointments, but to persevere with alacrity in improving himself in an occupation, which hardly seemed to promise him a comfortable subsistence.

Finding but little prospect of succeeding to his wish in the metropolis, he prudently resolved upon going into the country; where musical professors being few, the chance of success must be the greater. After visiting different places in the north of England, his good fortune brought him to Halifax, where an organist being wanted, his merits were tried, and he procured the appointment. Here he also taught music with approbation and profit. The love of learning still prevailed, and at this place he devoted his spare hours to the study of the languages, beginning with the Italian, on account of its intimate connection with his profession. From the Italian he proceeded to the Latin, in which he made an eminent progress. He then attempted the Greek, but, after a little application, he abandoned the study of this language, considering it as too dry and abstracted for his purpose.

In these pursuits, Mr. Herschel was entirely self-taught; and he holds out, in consequence, an excellent and pertinent example to those young persons whose education has been circumscribed within common limits, through the penury or narrow-mindedness of their friends.

A determined heart, and persevering application, we see, from this instance, will overcome obstacles that are apparently insurmountable.

But

But it was not to the dead and living languages only that Mr. Herschel bent his ardent and refolute mind. He attempted to gain a knowledge of the moft abftrufe fciences. His firft effort was to make himfelf mafter of the *theory of harmonies*; and it is obfervable, that the book which he made choice of for this purpofe, was no other than the profound and intricate treatife of the learned Dr. Smith upon that fubject. He got through this work, however, without any affiftance; and fo great was the pleafure which he derived from it, that he refolved upon ftudying the other branches of mathematical learning. He began with algebra, which he foon maftered; thence he proceeded to Euclid, and fo on to fluxions. The ground-work being thus laid, the ftudy of the other fciences became eafy.

His fituation at Halifax was favourable to his grammatical and mathematical purfuits; and it is well that he thus laid in a thorough ftock of found knowledge in what may be called his retirement. In 1766 he exchanged this place for one of a very different defcription, being elected organift to the Octagon chapel at Bath. Here he entered at once upon a great round of profeffional bufinefs, performing at the rooms, theatre, oratorios, and public and private concerts, befides having a great number of pupils. In fuch a hurry of employment, and in the immediate circle of luxury and amufement, very few men of Mr. Herfchel's profeffion and age would have found time to purfue ftudies feemingly fo unprofitable and ununinterefting as mathematics.

So far, however, from relaxing in his fcientific ftudies, he purfued them with increafing ardour, and after a day of hard labour, he commonly retired at night to his mathematical books, and fpent many hours in an unwearied attention to the moft abftrufe queftions in geometry and fluxions.

In the Ladies' Diary, for 1780, appeared an elegant and profound

profound anſwer by him to a very difficult prize queſtion, reſpecting the vibrations of a muſical chord, loaded in the middle with a ſmall weight.

About this time his ſtudies were chiefly directed to optics and aſtronomy. The pleaſure which he had experienced from viewing the heavens through a two-feet Gregorian teleſcope, which he borrowed at Bath, made him deſirous of poſſeſſing a complete ſet of aſtronomical inſtruments. His firſt object was to get a larger teleſcope; and being ignorant of the price at which ſuch inſtruments are uſually charged, he deſired a friend in London to buy one for him. This gentleman, ſurpriſed at the ſum demanded for the teleſcope, declined purchaſing it till he had informed Mr. Herſchel of the circumſtance. Our aſtronomer's aſtoniſhment was equal to that of his friend's; but inſtead of dropping his purſuit, he formed what many would have regarded as a moſt romantic reſolution, that of making a teleſcope for himſelf. He did not content himſelf with a ſpeculative idea, but from the ſcanty inſtructions he could gather out of optical treatiſes, actually ſet about this arduous undertaking. Diſappointment ſucceeded diſappointment; but all this only ſerved to act as a ſtimulus to his ardent mind, and at length his perſeverance was crowned with ſuch ſucceſs, that, in 1774, he enjoyed the exquiſite ſatisfaction of beholding the heavens through a five-feet Newtonian reflector, of his own workmanſhip. Our modern Galileo did not reſt at this attainment, great as it was, but, with a laudable ambition, ſet about making inſtruments of a greater magnitude than had hitherto been known. After conſtructing thoſe of ſeven, and even ten feet, he thought of forming one not leſs than double the latter ſize. So great was his patience, ſo determined his perſeverance, that, in perfecting the parabolical figure of a ſeven-feet teleſcope, he did not make leſs than

two

two hundred fpecula before he obtained one that would bear any power that was applied to it.

While he was thus laborioufly employed in his mathematical purfuits, he did not negleƈt the immediate duties of his profeffion. Yet fo much did his new occupation engage his mind, that he has frequently ftolen from the theatre or the concert-room, to look at the ftars, and then return again in time to bear his part among the mufical performers. This conftancy to Urania was at length moft bountifully rewarded, by the difcovery of a new planet in our fyftem, to which he gave the name of *Georgium Sidus*; but which foreign aftronomers have generally termed *Herfchel*.

This important difcovery was made in the night of the 13th of March, 1781. It was by no means a mere accidental circumftance which favoured our aftronomer with the view of this planet; but the refult of a regular, patient, and fcientific chain of obfervations. When he firft faw it, he was not quite certain that it belonged to our fyftem; but a clofer enquiry enabled him to afcertain with exaƈtnefs its planetary difk, as well as its motion.

This difcovery was communicated the fame year to the Royal Society; and in confequence of it, Mr. Herfchel was unanimoufly eleƈted a member, and had the annual gold medal beftowed upon him for his fervice to the interefts of fcience.

The year following, his Majefty took him under his immediate patronage, and conftituted him his aftronomer, with a handfome penfion. On this he quitted Bath, and his mufical inftruments, and went to live at Slough, near Windfor, at a houfe appointed for him by his royal mafter.

Here he was enabled to carry on his projeƈts with vigour, and thofe which had hitherto failed of fuccefs, were now brought to perfeƈtion. While at Bath, he had formed the bold fcheme of conftruƈting a telefcope of thirty feet, and

actually

actually made several trials to carry his object into effect. But though he failed there, since his residence at Windsor, he has far exceeded this design, and completed an instrument of no less than forty! The irregularities in the speculum, and the impossibility of rendering the parts of so enormous an instrument as this mathematically exact, have hitherto prevented his being able to make any actual observations with it. It is a vulgar error, that the discoveries of Dr. Herschel have been occasioned by the enormous magnifying power of his telescope; the fact is, that no such large power is necessary, or useful; and that all Dr. Herschel's discoveries have been made with reflectors of from ten to twenty feet, and with powers of from sixty to three hundred. His discoveries are to be ascribed to his laudable perseverance, and not to the size of his great telescope, which is rather an object of curiosity than of utility.

In 1783, he discovered a volcanic mountain in the moon, and in 1787 made further observations upon that planet, and found two others therein, which emitted fire from their summits. In prosecuting his enquiries respecting his own planet (if we may be allowed so to express ourselves), he has discovered it to be surrounded with rings, and to have six satellites.

For all these important additions to the stock of national knowledge, our astronomer had the honour of receiving from the university of Oxford the degree of a Doctor of Laws; which is the more creditable, as that learned body is very sparing of its academic honours upon persons who have not been educated within its walls.

Dr. Herschel has been a regular contributor to the Philosophical Transactions ever since his first communication in 1781, respecting his discovery of the new planet. Some of his papers are extremely curious; and he has hazarded a

few

few bold conjectures respecting the sun, and other planetary bodies, which would hardly have been received from a less accurate observer.

In his astronomical pursuits the doctor is materially assisted by his sister, Miss Caroline Herschel, who has distinguished herself greatly by her application to this sublime study, and has communicated to the Royal Society some very ingenious reports of observations made by her upon the starry orbs.

Dr. Herschel is a man of unassuming manners, a free, communicative, and pleasant companion; and enjoys that vigour of constitution which is so essential to an astronomical observer in a climate like that of England. It may be hoped, that his name will endure as long as the planetary system, to illustrate which he has devoted his life.

SIR

SIR NASH GROSE

IS a native of London, and fon of Edward Grofe, Efq. Being defigned for the bar, he was admitted of Lincoln's Inn, in Trinity term, 1756. In a fhort time he difcovered very refpectable profeffional abilities, and eftablifhed a character which foon procured him an extenfive fhare of bufinefs.

After about eight years practice as a barrifter, he was called to the degree of fergeant, and being confidered as a found lawyer, on the deceafe of that moft refpectable man, the late patriotic Sergeant Glynn, he took the lead in the court of Common Pleas. Mr. Grofe had the happinefs of uniting what very few attain, the talent of a fpecial pleader with a confiderable portion of eloquence.

In 1787, without the intervention of great friends, powerful alliances, or parliamentary intereft, he was raifed to a feat in the court of King's Bench, of which he is now the third judge: and foon after this promotion his majefty conferred the honour of knighthood upon him.

In his judicial capacity, he has conducted himfelf fo as to avoid reflection or reproach; and this, in the prefent times, evinces no fmall degree of integrity. Being entirely unconnected with political parties, he cannot reafonably hope to fucceed to the Chief Jufticefhip of either of the courts, and therefore has no other object in view but to difpenfe juftice with credit to himfelf, and advantage to the public; for he is now arrived at what to him may be looked on as the *ne plus ultra* of his profeffion.

P.

MR. KEMBLE

IS brother to the celebrated actress, Mrs. Siddons, and the eldest son of Mr. Roger Kemble, who was many years manager of an itinerant company of comedians.

When a boy, Mr. K. used to appear on his father's stage in such characters as suited his age, but was not by him designed for a theatrical life. The Kemble family are catholic, and the old gentleman placed his son John at a Roman catholic academy in Staffordshire; whence he was sent to the English college at Douay, in order to be qualified for the church.

While there, he was equally noted for the strength of his memory, and admired for his happy mode of delivery.

But being at length tired of the college trammels, he forsook his studies, and returned to England, before the age of twenty, without his father's consent. Having landed at Bristol, he walked to Gloucester, where hearing that the company was at Brecknock, he proceeded thither, but met with a cool reception; his father, indeed, actually refused to relieve him; but the actors generously assisted him with money, by way of subscription, to which his father, according to a report, which we trust is unfounded, was with difficulty persuaded to add a guinea!

On this, he returned to Gloucestershire with his pittance, and joined Chamberlin's company, with whom he made his first essay on the stage of a small town in that county. His profits from this were scanty and his distress great, which sometimes involved him in rather ludicrous situations.

Kemble's chief fault seemed to be an unaccountable negligence, but he was still looked on as a rising actor. In hopes of procuring more profit and reputation than his prefent fituation afforded him, he joined with the manager of Cheltenham theatre, in order to give a mifcellaneous entertainment. Young Kemble was to lecture, and his partner to enteitain the company with *fleight of hand tricks!* Kemble obtained great credit by his eloquence, but neither of them gained much money; and we have only to lament, that fuch men fhould have been reduced fo low by the frowns of the fickle goddefs.

After this, our theatrical hero joined a company at Worcefter, where he remained until his fifter introduced him to Mr. Younger; from which time he gradually improved, until he obtained a high degree of eminence in his profeffion.

About this period he produced " Belifarius," a tragedy, and a poem called " The Palace of Mercy."

From Younger's company he was introduced to that of Mr. Wilkinfon, at York; who being appointed manager at Edinburgh, took him along with him; there he was well received, and delivered *a lecture on oratory*, which gained him reputation as a man of letters.

Mr. Kemble played in Dublin in 1782, at Smock-alley theatre, and fucceeded admirably, particularly in Jephfon's " Count of Narbonne." His fifter foon after procured him an engagement at Drury-lane theatre.

His firft appearance in the metropolis was in Hamlet, and but few firft appearances in London have given greater fatisfaction. His folemn demeanor and ftyle of acting are admirably fuited to the character. He has often repeated it, but always in an improved ftate; and his Hamlet is now, perhaps, as finifhed a portrait as any on the ftage. Since that period he has performed a great variety of tragic characters, always refpectably, and fometimes with acknowledged excellence.

His person, action, and deportment, joined to a distinct and classical utterance, fit him particularly for a tragedian. The pathetic complaints of Jaffier are, however, delivered with torpor, nor is his voice equal to the bursts of rage in Richard, or Macbeth. In the lover he is also defective; but in the despair of Beverly, the jealousy of Othello, and the inquietude of royal John, he is peculiarly successful. His great fault is the always aiming at being original, in which he frequently fails; but yet in those attempts he sometimes strikes out new beauties. On the whole, he is one of the first performers of the present day.

Mr. Kemble has produced a farce called the " Projects," and has altered Bickerstaff's comedy of " 'Tis well it's no " Worse," into a farce called the " Pannel," as well as Louvet's " Lodoiska;" he has also fitted the old play of " Love in many Masks," for the modern stage.

On Mr. King's quitting the management of Drury-lane, Mr. Kemble was appointed his successor; but it is certain the house under his controul was not very successful: this, however, may be attributed partly to want of taste in the town, and partly to want of countenance in a certain quarter; for he assuredly possesses the talents requisite to judge of new pieces, and a sufficient knowledge of the stage to get up such as are old in the best manner.

Mr. Kemble married the widow of the late Mr. Brereton. It is said that the daughter of a deceased minister of state was strongly attached to him, which coming to the father's ears, he prudently offered a fortune of 3000 *l.* on condition he would marry, immediately, any lady he liked. He accordingly cast his eyes on Mrs. Brereton, and thus secured to himself a considerable accession of fortune, and a most excellent wife.

MISS SEWARD.

THIS lady, so well known, and so much respected in the literary world, is the only daughter of the reverend Mr. Seward, rector of Eyam, in Derbyshire; prebendary and canon-residentiary of Litchfield.

Being an author himself, he was fond of giving his daughter a taste for letters, particularly poetry; and at the early age of three years she could repeat the L'Allegro of Milton: at nine she could recite the first three books of Paradise Lost with spirit and propriety. About the same age she converted several of the psalms into English verse.

But her mother not approving this turn for poetry, persuaded her to relinquish her literary pursuits; she still, however, indulged now and then in her beloved occupation, and sacrificed by stealth to the muses.

A friend of the family happening to doubt whether the poems shewn as her's had not received some paternal assistance, he called one evening when he knew her father was absent, and requested the young lady to favour him with a few lines on any subject, adding " Let me write a stanza, " and you finish it; he accordingly indited one, and left her: on the succeeding morning she presented him with some verses, which convinced him of her merit and his own injustice.

On the death of an only and beloved sister, which happened a few years after, she wrote an Elegy as she was sitting in the garden. Other poems flowed rapidly from her pen; and becoming acquainted with the late Lady Miller, of Bath-Easton, she was a frequent and successful candidate for the prize bestowed at that villa.

Her

Her firſt regular publication was a beautiful Elegy on the death of Captain Cook, which, with an " Ode to the " Sun, (a Bath-Eaſton prize poem,) were publiſhed in quarto (1780.) In the courſe of the next year, ſhe compoſed a " Monody," on her friend Major André. Theſe two productions induced Dr. Darwin to ſay, that ſhe was the inventreſs of " epic elegy." Since that period, ſhe has written " A Poem to the Memory of Lady Miller;"— " Louiſa," a poetical novel; an Ode on " General Elliot's return from Gibraltar;" and " Llangollen Vale."

Miſs Seward has alſo diſtinguiſhed herſelf as a tranſlator, for ſhe has clothed one of the moſt elegant of the Latin poets in an Engliſh dreſs, having preſented the public with a new verſion of ſeveral of the Odes of Horace. They have been thought ſomewhat too diffuſe, but are allowed to exhibit proofs of a claſſical taſte and fine imagination.

EARL

EARL OF CLARE,

LORD HIGH CHANCELLOR OF IRELAND.

WHETHER we confider the importance refulting from official fituation, or that which great activity, confiderable talents, and indefatigable zeal, always attach to their poffeffor, this nobleman is certainly the firft man in the Irifh adminiftration. Whatever may be the fate of that unhappy country, fo far as that fate is influenced by the prefent conteft, it may be fairly attributed to his wifdom or to his weaknefs, to his firmnefs or to his folly.

Lord Clare, although now occupying the higheft law-office in Ireland, and poffeffing almoft unlimited influence in its councils, cannot boaft a long line of noble anceftors.

He is removed but two degrees from a man in the humbleft walk of fociety—a *catholic* peafant—whofe life was diftinguifhed only by a gradual tranfition from extreme poverty to an honourable competency, and that too acquired by ufeful induftry.

With the change produced in the circumftances of the family, a change feems to have alfo taken place in its creed, for while yet a very young man, we find the late Mr. Fitzgibbon, his lordfhip's father, a ftaunch and zealous proteftant. It is faid, however, that he was originally deftined to officiate at a popifh altar, and that he had actually received the education which was confidered neceffary to fit him for that ftation. If this account be true, it is at leaft certain that either the maturity of his judgment, or a change in his views, foon made him *recant his errors*; for he was yet in early life, when he was called to the Irifh bar, to which catholics were then inadmiffible, and at which he afterwards became a highly efteemed and fuccefsful pleader.

During

During that period, the bufinefs of the courts was monopolized by a few eminent barrifters; but the talents and the induftry of Mr. Fitzgibbon forced him forward in fpite of envy, and in a few years he himfelf became one of thofe who, in fome refpects, claimed all the honours and the emoluments of the profeffion. So fuccefsful indeed was he, that in the courfe of a life not uncommonly long, he is faid to have realifed a fortune of nearly 8000l. per annum.

Of this gentleman, Lord Clare was the only fon. A profeffion in which the father had been fo fuccefsful was naturally chofen by him for a favourite child, who was to fupport the future fortunes and honours of the family. He was accordingly entered at an early age a ftudent of the univerfity of Dublin, where he was contemporary with fome of the moft celebrated men who have diftinguifhed themfelves in all the recent and important tranfactions that have occurred in Ireland; fuch as the late Mr. Flood, Mr. Grattan, Mr. Fofter, the prefent fpeaker of the Irifh Commons, &c. He is yet remembered by fome of the old members of that feminary, on account of the ability and induftry which even then marked his character.

Having completed his courfe of collegiate ftudies, and kept his terms at the Temple, he was at length called to the Irifh bar, with advantages poffeffed by few at the outfet of life, and thefe were fupported by a high character, and a fortune which, even independent of any encreafe from the fuccefs of forenfic labours, fecured to him fomething infinitely beyond a competence. Affluence, however, did not produce in Mr. Fitzgibbon what is too commonly its effect on the youthful mind—an indolent apathy. His affiduity in profeffional purfuits was not exceeded by any of his rivals at the bar; and though there was no man who drank more deeply of the cup of pleafure, yet few toiled through more bufinefs, or in the difcharge of it difplayed more of that accuracy of knowledge which is the refult only of attentive induftry.

It was by the obfervance of a rule of life which none but ftrong minds have ever prefcribed to themfelves, namely, " to fuffer no portion of time to pafs without filling it either with bufinefs or with pleafure," that Mr. F. was enabled to unite thofe generally incompatible purfuits. With fuch application, and with talents certainly above the common level, though perhaps far below that at which his friends would place them, he foon rofe to eminence.

In the Houfe of Commons, of which he became a member fhortly after his call to the bar, by the operation of this principle, aided by a kind of eloquence, which, though it was neither very brilliant nor very perfuafive, yet being accompanied by a certain air of confident fuperiority, a confiderable effect was produced; and he was foon efteemed one of the moft efficient fupporters of the party he efpoufed.

Without affecting popularity at any time, he launched into political life, uninvited and unbought, the partifan of the court, and the profeffed contemner of the *profanum vulgus:* in this fentiment he has been wonderfully confiftent.—From his firft entrance he has not, in one fingle inftance, ftarted from the track before him. His conduct has been marked by an unvaried and uniform fupport of the Britifh cabinet, and an avowed, perhaps a revolting contempt, for the principles, motives, and objects, of what has been called the popular party.

He had not been long in parliament, before the calamities brought upon Ireland by the continuance of the American conteft, rendered it neceffary to feek, in an enlargement of her commerce, for fome remedy againft a general bankruptcy. The Commons urged by the cries of a famifhing people, called for what was then denominated " a free trade," and Mr. F. much to his honour, *did not oppofe* the application.—

The

The defencelefs ftate in which the kingdom had been left, by drawing off the troops to ferve on a diftant continent, fuggefted to the community the neceffity of arming for felf-defence. Mr. F. appeared in the ranks as a private; but it would be unjuft to charge him with participating in thofe high-flown fentiments of national pride, and love of freedom, which foon began to actuate the volunteer army, and which no doubt gave *fome* ftrength to the fubfequent declaration of legiflative independence by the Irifh parliament. He rather feemed to be carried forward by the irrefiftible impulfe of national fentiment, than to have advanced with it toward the goal. Accordingly, when an occafion occurred of retiring without difhonour from a caufe fo little congenial to his principles, he feparated from the vulgar herd. The moment chofen by him was during the difcuffion of the long-agitated queftion, relative to the SIMPLE REPEAL of the fixth of Geo. III. From that time to the prefent he has continued the zealous advocate for a ftrong and energetic government, and the powerful opponent of every man who attempted to reform, or innovate on prefent eftablifhments.

When Mr. Scott was appointed Chief Juftice of the King's Bench in Ireland, Mr. Fitzgibbon fucceeded him as Attorney General. No man was ever better fitted for the office. His firmnefs, his confidence in his own powers, and the bold tone with which he hurled defiance at his parliamentary opponents, on every queftion connected with legal or conftitutional knowledge, often appalled the minor members of oppofition, and fometimes kept even their chiefs at bay. Thefe qualities, however, did not always conftitute a fure defence. The repulfe which on one memorable evening of debate, he experienced on the part of the late LORD, then Mr. O'Neil, of Shane's Caftle, whofe manly and honeft mind caught fire at the haughty and dictatorial language

with

with which the Attorney General had dared to addrefs him, is remembered by thofe who were then converfant in the politics of the day, and probably will not foon be forgotten.

But though this daring, and, as it is often called, overbearing fpirit, did fometimes mifcarry, in general it infured him fuccefs. A remarkable inftance of its efficacy occurred at a time when the minds of the people were extremely agitated by the rejecting of their petitions for reform, and for protecting duties. At a moment when the ferment feemed to have arifen to a very dangerous height, an aggregate meeting of *all the inhabitants* of the metropolis was, on a requifition of feveral refpectable perfons, convened by the high fheriffs of Dublin. The Attorney General was then the moft unpopular man in the country; and the mob had for fome time been in the habits of offering perfonal infult to thofe whom they fufpected of being adverfe to their wifhes. Unawed, however, by thefe circumftances, Mr. F. attended only by one or two friends, made his way through the crowd, reached the huftings, interrupted a popular orator in the midft of his harangue, told the fheriffs that they had acted illegally in calling the meeting, commanded them to leave the chair, and threatened them with an information *ex officio* * if they prefumed to continue in it. He then left the aftonifhed affembly, amidft the hiffes of the mob; and the fheriffs inftantly diffolved the meeting.

Hitherto Mr. F. had acted with an adminiftration which poffeffed both the power and the will to reward his exertions. When the event of the king's illnefs, in 1789, unhinged the Irifh government, he ftood in different circumftances. On that occafion, a majority of the parliament, among whom were many of the oldeft fervants of the crown, declared for

the

---

* A profecution without the intervention of a Grand Jury, received by him.

the right of Ireland, as an independent country, to choofe its own regent. The Britifh cabinet controverted that right, and infifted that the regent chofen by the Britifh Parliament fhould be the regent for both countries. Mr. F. though no longer fupported by a majority, remained firm to his Englifh friends, and refifted with his wonted boldnefs, not only the voice of the people, but what was of more immediate concern, a vaft parliamentary majority. The unexpected recovery of his Majefty, to Mr. F. certainly an happy event, rewarded his fuperior wifdom, or his greater forefight; for on Lord Lifford's death, he was created a baron, and appointed Chancellor: it is alfo not a little memorable, that he is the firft Irifhman who has filled that important office!

So far as refpects juftice, the country has had no reafon to lament his appointment, for his activity and difpatch have made chancery fuits almoft ceafe to be an inheritance. He has banifhed chicane and unneceffary delay from his court; and though his decrees may fometimes be blamed as premature, the paucity of appeals feems to augur, that all complaint on this fcore is groundlefs.

Since his elevation to the bench and the peerage, he has had repeated opportunities of difplaying his former fpirit, and expreffing, with even more effect than before, his deteftation of popular claims, and particularly that of reform. He has fhewn an equal abhorrence of the catholic pretenfions to fhare in the privileges of the conftitution. Of their claim to the reprefentative franchife, it is known that he was the decided enemy; and though by the paternal regard of his majefty, and the prudence of the Britifh cabinet, the conceffion of that privilege was recommended to the Irifh legiflature, and adopted in confequence of that recommendation, yet *his* opinion remained unchanged. With refpect to fubfequent claims, the Britifh miniftry have paid more attention to his advice.

His Lordſhip was lately in London, and was reported to have left the ſeals in commiſſion, in order to complete a plan which at one time would have been viewed with diſlike by both countries. But ſuch is now the miſerable ſtate of his native land, that any change muſt be for the better ; and if an UNION is attended with nothing elſe than a ceſſation of carnage, every good man muſt rejoice at the proſpect of it.

W.

RICHARD

RICHARD CUMBERLAND, Esq.

IS the son of Dr. Denison Cumberland, late Bishop of Clonfert and Killaloe, in Ireland, and great grandson of the learned English divine, Dr. Richard Cumberland, Bishop of Peterborough, author of a treatise on the Law of Nature, *Origines Gentium*, &c. By the mother's side he is grandson of the celebrated critic, Dr. Richard Bentley.

Mr. Cumberland was educated at Trinity College, Cambridge, where he took the degree of B. A. By the friendship of the late Lord Sackville, better known by the title of Lord George Germaine, he was introduced to the office of Trade and Plantations, where he succeeded the late Mr. Pownall as secretary, in which post he continued until the suppression of that appointment by Mr. Burke's bill, when he retired on a pension.

Mr. Cumberland, while a very young man, wrote some verses on the birth of the Prince of Wales. His first publication was the " Banishment of Cicero," which was refused by Mr. Garrick, but appeared in print in 1761. This should have been rather called a dramatic poem than a tragedy.

The " Summer's Tale," and the " Brothers," two comedies, were his next productions; but neither of them have added much to his reputation.

In 1771, he was reconciled to Garrick, with whom he had been on bad terms ever since the refusal of his tragedy, and that gentleman brought out his " West Indian" in a capital style. This piece has stamped Mr. Cumberland's character as an excellent dramatic writer, and it is certainly one of the most sterling comedies on the English stage.

He now began to be esteemed one of the best dramatic writers of the age, and also one of the most prolific; for

next

next year he produced the " Fashionable Lover," which was well received; as was likewise, in 1774, his lively farce called the " Fate of Pandora, or a Trip to Newmarket." His " Choleric Man, which came forth in 1775, is said to have some affinity to Sir Richard Steele's " Tender Husband:" his " Battle of Hastings," a tragedy, was rather badly received. In 1776, he published a thin quarto volume of Odes.

About the year 1780, he was sent on national business, to Madrid, but did not appear there in a public character. On his return, he published, in 1782, " Anecdotes of eminent Painters in Spain, during the Sixteenth and Seventeenth Centuries," two volumes, 12mo. Next year he brought out a tragedy on the stage, called the " Mysterious Husband," and addressed a Letter to the Bishop of Landaff respecting ecclesiastical grievances. It contained some wit, and was ably answered by an anonymous writer.

In 1785, he had much business on his hands; for he produced " The Carmelite," allowed to be the best tragedy he has written; and also a comedy, called the " Natural Son."* In the course of the same year, he published a character of his deceased friend, Lord Viscount Sackville, and the first edition of the Observer. Next year a second edition appeared; and the subsequent additions have now swelled the work to five volumes. These essays abound with pleasing and instructive information, and discover extensive reading.

In 1787, Mr. Cumberland presented the world with " An accurate descriptive Catalogue of the Paintings in the King of Spain's Palace at Madrid;" soon after this the comedy of the " Impostors," and a novel in two volumes, called

---

* Miss Plumptre has lately presented to the public another " *Natural Son*," being a faithful and elegant translation of KOTZEBUE's famous play of that title, and which has been so much admired on the British stage, under the altered title of *Lovers' Vows*.

called " Arundel," made their appearance. In the latter he is accufed, but on very flight foundation, as feeming to palliate adultery and duelling.

After this, his talents feem to have lain fallow for fome years, as he did not produce any thing until 1792, when he publifhed his poem called " Calvary, or the Death of Chrift." Next feafon he wrote the fongs and chorufes in the comic opera of the " Armourer." In 1794, he produced the " Box-lobby Challenge," a comedy ; and alfo his defervedly-efteemed comedy of the " Jew," a play written with the laudable intention of removing the ftigma which accompanies that unhappy and much-perfecuted people. His attempt of the next year confifted of the " Wheel of Fortune ;" he alfo prefented the town with another comedy, called " Firft Love," and another novel, in four volumes, called " Henry."

His mufe, which muft be allowed to be a fpirited one, feems to know no repofe ; for in 1796 he produced " Days of Yore," a drama in three acts; and the next year " The Laft of the Family." His laft piece is the comedy of " Falfe Impreffions."

When we confider the number, the merit, and the exquifitenefs of his writings, Mr. Cumberland muft be allowed to rank high as a dramatic writer.

SIR ARCHIBALD MACDONALD.

Sir Archibald Macdonald is the third son[*] of Macdonald of Slate, in the isles; his mother was of the house of Eglinton.

Mr. Macdonald was bred to the English bar, but had never any great practice. His business consisted chiefly in Scotch appeals. Yet if not highly successful in his professional career, he was at least deserving of success; and his good fortune having at length introduced him to the acquaintance of the daughter of a noble Marquis, who consented to their marriage, Mr. Macdonald in consequence of this connexion beheld the highest honours of the law lie open to his view.

By the interest of his noble father-in-law, he was accordingly appointed, in 1780, a king's counsel and a Welch judge; he had been before brought into parliament for Hendon, and at the general election which occurred during the year he put on his silk gown, he was returned for Newcastle-under-line, a borough under the influence of Marquis, then Lord, Stafford.

In parliament, he of course followed the line of politics pursued by the family into which he was adopted, that is, he supported Lord North, until he began to totter. As a parliamentary speaker, Mr. Macdonald was easy, fluent, intelligible, and concise.

Lord Stafford, on joining Mr. Pitt, procured for his son-in-law the place of Solicitor-general (1784), and in 1788, on the promotion of Sir Peter Arden to the Master of the Rolls, he was knighted, and appointed Attorney-general in his room. It is no less remarkable than true, that the possession

---

[*] He was a posthumous child.

feſſion of theſe two high offices in the law did not bring Sir Archibald any conſiderable addition of practice as a counſel. The number of his proſecutions were thought to have greatly affected the liberty of the preſs.

However, after a few years longer ſtay at the bar, he was promoted to be Chief Baron of the Exchequer, having previouſly been called to the degree of Sergeant at Law.

In conſequence of his marriage with Lady Louiſa Gower he has ſeveral children.

P.

MRS. SIDDONS.

WHEN woman paſſes through that thorny path of pleaſure the ſtage, without being drawn aſtray by the temptations which perpetually aſſail the traveller, our eſteem and veneration ought ever to await her. In this age, degenerate as it is, we have had the pleaſure of ſeeing many females ſupporting unſullied charaƈters in theatrical life, and among them this lady certainly claims pre-eminence from her ſplendid powers, joined to an unſpotted fame.

Miſs Kemble (for this was her maiden name) was the eldeſt daughter of the manager of an itinerant company of comedians, and made her firſt eſſay as a ſinger, but ſoon abandoned that line and attempted tragedy. Early in life ſhe conceived a paſſion for Mr. Siddons, in which not being indulged by her parents, ſhe quitted the ſtage, and hired herſelf as lady's maid in the family of Mrs. Greathead, of Guy's-cliff, near Warwick, where ſhe remained about a year; and then reſolving to unite herſelf with the man of her affeƈtions, ſhe was married to Mr. Siddons, and ſoon after joined a ſtrolling company of no great reputation. Both ſhe and her huſband had, however, the good fortune to be engaged by Mr. Younger to perform at Liverpool, Birmingham, &c. With him ſhe remained a few years, and acquired both profit and reputation, which latter procured her an engagement at Drury-lane houſe, where ſhe performed ſuch parts as Mrs. Strickland, Mrs. Epicene, and the Queen in Richard the Third. She was, however, conſidered merely as a ſecond-rate aƈtreſs; and being unfortunately placed in an after-piece written by the editor of a newſpaper, which had the ill luck to be damned, the

ſcurrilous

scurrilous author left no opportunity of injuring her reputation, and she quitted the London boards for a time, to return to them afterwards with increased lustre.

At Bath, whither she repaired, she was observed to improve rapidly, and is said to have been usefully assisted by the lessons of Mr. Pratt, then a bookseller in that city. There she attracted the notice of the audience, and had the good fortune to be patronised by the Duchess of Devonshire, who procured her another engagement at Drury-lane. Before she quitted Bath, she spoke a farewell address, which she herself had written, and which she delivered with her usual excellence.

She made her second appearance at Drury-lane, on the 10th October 1792, in the character of " Isabella," and astonished the house with such a display of powers, as they had seldom witnessed before. Her fame was soon spread abroad, and the theatre overflowed every night ; the taste for tragedy returned ; and the manager, whose " Critic" seems to have been expressly written to drive Melpomene from the stage, received " golden favours" from her votaries. Far from proving ungrateful, he generously gave Mrs. Siddons an extra-benefit, and increased her salary. Her good success was the means of introducing her sister, Miss F. Kemble, on the same stage ; and she performed " Jane Shore," while her near relative played " Alicia," on her first appearance. The latter, however, not altogether fulfilling the expectations of the public, honourably withdrew, in consequence of a marriage with Mr. Twiss, a literary gentleman, and a well-known traveller.

Mrs. Siddons's *extra*-benefit was given her before Christmas ; she then appeared in " Belvidera," and gained fresh laurels, and an enormous receipt. The two counsellors Pigot and Fielding were so highly delighted, that they collected a subscription among the gentlemen of the bar, of one hundred guineas,

guineas, and prefented them to her, accompanied with a polite letter, as a token of their efteem. This was an honour which, we believe, has not been conferred on any actor or actrefs fince the time when Booth gave fuch general fatisfaction in the character of "Cato."

In the fummer, this great and amiable actrefs went to Dublin, the inhabitants of which were equally aftonifhed at her powers. On her return for the winter (1783-4), fhe performed, for the firft time, " by command of their Majefties." During the fucceeding fummer, fhe took a fecond trip to Ireland, and alfo vifited Edinburgh, in both of which places, fhe not only received great falaries, but very confiderable prefents from unknown hands, particularly a filver urn which was fent after her to London, on which were engraved thefe words, *" A reward to merit."*

Envy and malice, as ufual, purfued merit; and to thefe alone we can attribute the attack made on her in a newfpaper, refpecting her treatment of an unhappy fifter, &c. Thefe reports had, however, fuch an effect on the town, that on her firft appearance on the ftage in 1784, fhe was faluted with the cry of " *off! off!*" Her friends at length obtained her a hearing; and her hufband and brother, by means of uncommon exertions, fucceeded in refuting the calumnies to which fhe had been expofed. She was accordingly reftored to public favour. Although fhe had conducted herfelf during this conteft with great compofure, yet it made fuch an impreffion on her mind, that fhe determined to retire to Wales with the few thoufands fhe had then faved; but the perfuafions of her friends, and a confideration of the welfare of her family, made her alter this refolution.

Their Majefties about this time paid her much attention. Her talent in reciting dramatic works had been highly fpoken of, which reaching the ears of the royal family, fhe was

frequently

frequently invited to Buckingham-houfe, and Windfor, where fhe and her brother often recited plays.

As fome relaxation, on account of her health, had now become neceffary, fhe quitted Drury-lane for a time, and performed at Weymouth, Plymouth, Liverpool, &c. with additional reputation. She alfo vifited feveral of her noble patrons, among whom Lord and Lady Harcourt ftood confpicuous. By means of thefe friends and accomplifhments fhe has acquired a very good fortune, has a confiderable fhare or at leaft a mortgage on Drury-lane theatre, and is bleffed with a family that promifes to be her comfort in old age.

We lament exceedingly, the recent death of her beautiful and accomplifhed daughter, and moft fincerely condole with a mother, whofe exquifite fenfibility muft have been agonized by fo unhappy an event.

Nature has beftowed on Mrs. Siddons a majeftic perfon, a ftriking countenance, and a fine voice; the judgment with which fhe modulates the laft of thefe, has never been excelled, perhaps never rivalled, by any other actrefs. The flexibility of her features, the expreffion of her eyes, and the grace of her deportment, have feldom been equalled. She poffeffes the whole art of fpeaking, for which the late Mrs. Yates was fo juftly famed, combined with the impaffioned ftyle of playing, of Mrs. Crawford, while in her meridian.

She has lately had an engagement with the Drury-lane managers, at a certain fum for each night's performance, by which means fhe avoids injuring her health by the conftant repetition of theatrical exertions.

Mrs. Siddons refides in Great Marlborough-ftreet, and is upwards of fifty years of age. In private life fhe is regarded as an economift, but as a truly amiable and exemplary wife and mother. P.

DOCTOR

DOCTOR JOHN DOUGLAS,

BISHOP OF SALISBURY.

THIS prelate, who is a native of Scotland, has been long celebrated both in the clerical and literary world. He was educated at Chrift-church, Oxford, of which college he was a ftudent in 1738, and having taken orders, fettled in Shropfhire. During his refidence there, he publifhed " Milton vindicated" (1748); a work in which, with uncommon acutenefs, he detected the grofs forgery of Lauder, who with equal impudence and ingenuity had reprefented Milton as a plagiarift.

He next entered the lifts with George Pfalmanazar, and Archibald Bower; the former of whom pretended to be a native of Formofa, and the latter a commiffioner of the holy inquifition at Macerata.

Thefe fucceffive exertions of critical abilities introduced him to public notice, and procured him many friends; he afterwards publifhed, in the year 1754, " Criterion," an anfwer to David Hume on miracles. His firft work had recommended him to the learned, the laft to the religious world; and about the year 1760, he began to reap the benefit they entitled him to, for he was then appointed one of the King's chaplains; in 1762 he was nominated one of the Canons of Windfor, and foon after prefented to the united livings of St. Auftin and St. Faith, in London.

Among the many friends Dr. Douglas had made, was the late Lord Bath, who bequeathed him his library. But General Pulteney being unwilling to part with it out of the family, paid him the full value, and on his death, about three years after, left it once more to him. From Windfor,

our

our divine was, in 1776, removed to be a canon of St. Paul's; and after poffeffing that canonry about twelve years, he was, in 1788, advanced to the Deanry of Windfor.

In thefe fituations, the Doctor not only enlarged his circle of friends among the great, but was introduced to the notice of the king and queen, and acquired a confiderable degree of royal favour. He was next raifed to the epifcopal bench, on the death of Dr. Law, Bifhop of Carlifle, and on the tranflation of Dr. Barrington to Durham, in 1791, he was tranflated to Salifbury; by the poffeffion of which fee, he has become chancellor of the order of the garter.

The epifcopal character of Dr. Douglas is a fubject of univerfal admiration, while benevolence and candour diftinguifh him in private life. Regular in the difcharge of the duties of his high ftation, he commands the love and refpect of his diocefe. In fhort, as a dignified clergyman and fcholar, a gentleman and a chriftian, he is equally refpected and admired.

When the fhips fent out on difcovery under Captain Cook returned, Dr. Douglas was appointed to infpect and arrange the journals; and the admirable introduction prefixed to that work is the offspring of his pen.

The doctor was a member of the Literary Club in Effex-ftreet, inftituted by Dr. Johnfon, Murphy, &c.

Z.

SIR JOHN SCOTT,

HIS MAJESTY'S ATTORNEY-GENERAL.

IT has been remarked, of late years, that in confequence of the mode now in vogue, of beftowing the favours of government, the bar is the only line in which a man can rife by merit alone to the firft honours of his profeffion; but we believe even here fome grains of allowance muft be made; for the fubject of our prefent enquiries, although poffeffed of great merit, would never have reached the ftation he now occupies, without powerful patronage.

Sir John Scott is the fon of a * tradefman of no great opulence, at Newcaftle upon Tyne. His elder brother, Sir William Scott, who was bred to the practice of the civil law, was formerly advocate-general, and is now judge of the Admiralty court. John was admitted a ftudent of the Middle Temple, in Hilary term, 1772, and after paying the moft affiduous attention to his ftudies, was called to the bar at the ufual period.

Our young barrifter was troubled with what few gentlemen of the profeffion have occafion to complain of—a certain timidity of character, which made him fhun the courts as a pleader for a confiderable time, and employ himfelf chiefly in the bufinefs of a draughtfman in chancery, in which he was allowed to be able, and had great practice. He found, however, that this branch of the profeffion was equally injurious to his health and advancement in life, and he at length determined to roufe himfelf from that fpecies of torpor to which he was naturally inclined.

---

* His father was what is there termed a *coal-fitter*.

He

He accordingly betook himself to a more public and active line; and in a short time evinced that he was apt and ingenious at reply.

Sir John was not long at the bar, before he attracted the notice of the late chancellor*; and as he always avoided opposition to the bench, received great countenance in his practice: it is even said that the chancellor one day took him aside after the business of the court was over, complimented him on his merit, and offered him the place of one of the masters in chancery then vacant. This he politely declined; and he had the satisfaction to find that he had acted right, as his business continued to encrease rapidly.

About the year 1783, he obtained a patent of precedency, which entitled him to all the honours of a king's counsel, and freed him from certain disadvantages attendant on that station. He had just before been introduced into parliament through the interest of his friend, Lord Thurlow, with Lord Weymouth, who seated him for the Borough of Weobly. Mr. Scott was said to have struck a bargain with his right honourable patron, when he accepted this situation, which, if true, was much to his honour; viz. " that he " should be at liberty to vote as he pleased." He might, however, have spared himself this trouble, for as soon as he got into the house, he acted decidedly with the Pitt party, and in the debate on Mr. Fox's India bill, placed himself in opposition to the late Mr. Lee, then attorney-general. Although in this attempt he did not acquire much importance as a parliamentary speaker, yet he gained every thing he could wish for, by his connexion with those whose cause he espoused; for they took the first opportunity to promote him. Accordingly, in 1788, he was advanced to be Solicitor-general, in the room of Sir Archibald, then Mr. Macdonald, promoted to be attorney-general. When these two were presented to the king, the attorney-general received the

---

* Lord Thurlow.

honour of knighthood. The officer in waiting was then ordered to bring up Mr. Scott, when the latter begged leave to decline; but the king, *who knows the real value* of these things better than any other man, perhaps, in his dominions, replied, " pho, pho, nonsense! I will serve them both alike." Thus Mr. Scott gained honours unasked, and even against his will.

In the business of the regency, Sir John was said to be the man whose legal talents formed the basis of the minister's plan of conduct

In 1793 he was made Attorney-general; and while in this post, he has prosecuted, perhaps, more men for libels, than ever fell to the lot of any two of his predecessors!

The part he took during the state trials at the Old Bailey will never be forgotten; for after a wonderful display of candour, he laboured through a speech of nine hours to convict a man of a crime of which the length of his own oration alone was a strong presumptive proof of innocence.

He now stands as the most likely candidate for the seals; and should any thing happen to remove the present Chancellor, during Mr. Pitt's continuance in power, he will, in all probability, succeed him.

DUKE

DUKE OF NORFOLK.

CHARLES HOWARD, Efq. of Grayftock, in Cumberland, a collateral branch of that noble family, fucceeded to the title of Norfolk in 1777, on the death of Edward, the ninth duke; and his fon, the prefent duke, then affumed the appellation of Earl of Surrey.

In 1767, while Mr. Howard, he married a Mifs Mary Ann Coppinger, of Ballyvolane, in Ireland, who died foon after, in childbed, and, in 1771, he received the hand of Mifs Frances Scudamore, daughter of C. F. Scudamore, Efq. of Home Lacey, in Herefordfhire, by the repudiated Duchefs of Beaufort, with whom he got a large fortune; but by neither of them has he any children. This laft lady, indeed, has been in a very melancholy ftate of mind for many years, and lives retired at one of his Grace's feats. The Duchefs is celebrated for the fmart repulfe fhe is faid to have given the amorous Duke of Queenfbury a few years fince.

Some time previoufly to his acquifition of the title, Lord Surrey had renounced the errors of the Romifh church, in which he had been bred, and was of courfe eligible to fit in either houfe of parliament. Accordingly, at the general election in 1780, he was returned for Carlifle, in oppofition to the intereft of Sir James Lowther. As foon as his Lordfhip took his feat, he joined the party of oppofition, and with it laboured to ftem the torrent arifing from the encreafing influence of the crown, until the complete defeat of the minifter, in 1782. It is well known that the North adminiftration having clung faft to their places, Lord Surrey gave notice in the Houfe of Commons of a motion which

would

would effectually remove them; but the premier anticipated the difgrace, by declaring " that he was no longer minifter."

In the change which foon after took place, his lordfhip was appointed Lord-lieutenant of the weft riding of the county of York, and under the coalition miniftry he was nominated a lord of the treafury.

When the Shelburne miniftry came in, Lord Surrey oppofed them, and joined the coalition; and when that party was driven from power, he ftill efpoufed their caufe.

He now became a member of the fociety for conftitutional information, took an active part in the bufinefs of parliamentary reform, and attended public meetings when that queftion was brought forward; on this account he has been charged with inconfiftency, as he is known to be as deeply concerned in the *traffic in boroughs* as any nobleman of this age; but he has always folemnly affured his friends, that he is ready to facrifice every fpecies of influence of that kind, and fupport a meliorated fyftem, which he holds to be effentially neceffary for the prefervation of the conftitution.

On the death of his father he fucceeded to his title and feat in the Houfe of Lords, and there, as before, has uniformly fupported the popular caufe.

His friendfhip for Mr. Fox has ever been fteady and invariable, and to this alone may be attributed his late difmiffion. At a late annual meeting, to commemorate the return of his friend for the city of Weftminfter, the Duke is faid to have given the old whig toaft of " Our Sovereign, the " Majefty of the People." In the memory of fome of the youngeft men now living, this has been repeatedly drank without offence; and why any exception fhould at prefent

be

be taken at it, remains to be explained. The fact, however, is, that the Duke of Norfolk was difmiffed from his lord lieutenancy, and from the command of a regiment which he had trained with the utmoft care, while he had alfo generoufly refigned the emoluments derived from it, to increafe the comforts of his favourite *corps*.

Report has whifpered that his grace was greatly affected by thefe marks of royal difpleafure ; but he furely could not be hurt by the lofs of nominal influence or diftinction, although, it may readily be fuppofed, that to be torn from a fet of men with whom he had lived in the habits of friendfhip for many years, would undoubtedly give him pain. But, if any thing could tend to produce additional chagrin, it muft be to fee a man with whom he had been in the habits of acting with cordiality for fo many years, pluming himfelf in his fpoils, and ftooping to a minifter whofe conduct he had reprobated.

The Duke, as a *bon vivant*, is furrounded by thofe who are capable of keeping " the table in a roar," and his hofpitalities at Home-Lacey are in the firft ftyle of magnificence.

As an orator, he poffeffes an eafy delivery, and evinces a mafculine underftanding ; but he never attempts any of thofe rhetorical flourifhes which captivate the ear, without laying hold of the underftanding.

His grace has been known to perform many generous actions. He kept the place of fecretary to the Earl Marfhal, vacant for a confiderable time after the death of poor Brooks, until, as he faid, he could find fome one worthy to fill it, although earneftly folicited by many for the appointment. Mr. Dallaway having publifhed his ingenious book on the fcience of heraldry, the Duke directly beftowed the office on him, unafked.

His

His father had about him when he died a great number of perfons of the catholic perfuafion, who, on the lofs of their patron, concluded they would be difmiffed by his proteftant fucceffor; but he generoufly directed that their ftipends and allowances fhould be paid them, as in the lifetime of his predeceffor.

JOSEPH

JOSEPH TOWERS, LL. D.

THIS gentleman has diftinguifhed himfelf in the annals of patriotifm, in the republic of letters, and in the pulpit of the diffenters: he was not, however, intended for a divine; Dr. Towers, like his great precurfor and friend, Dr. Franklin, having been originally bred a printer.

At a very early period of his life, from a fincere conviction, obtained by *reading*—that great bane of all tyranny, civil and ecclefiaftical!—he became firmly attached to the principles of liberty, both in refpect to church and ftate; and no man has been more zealous in behalf of the freedom of his country, and of mankind. This favourite idea has, indeed, been warmly cherifhed by the fectaries in general, and they muft be allowed to have fanned the facred flame, and kept it alive in the nation, during the moft alarming and critical periods.

After his call to the miniftry, Dr. T. was chofen paftor of the congregation of proteftant diffenters at Highgate; this occurred in 1774, and in 1778 he was nominated morning-preacher to the diffenters at Newington-green. In the latter of thefe offices he fucceeded the worthy, pious, and amiable Dr. Price, who had been appointed to the congregation at Hackney. He continued, however, to officiate at Newington-green, in the afternoon, for fome years; and his colleague and himfelf feemed perfectly agreed relative to the leading points in politics and religion.

On the 4th of November, 1788, being the completion of a century from the Revolution, that event was celebrated with great folemnity; and the doctor, at the requeft of a committee, delivered what may be termed a *civic fermon* on the occafion, which was liftened to with great attention, and printed afterwards at the requeft of the ftewards.

While

While the Society for Conſtitutional Information flouriſhed, the name of Dr. Joſeph Towers ſtood conſpicuous among the moſt active of its members. He had been ballotted for in 1782, and continued to act with it until 1794, when the books and papers were ſeized by order of government, and the ſecretaay taken into cuſtody. On the 13th of June, of the ſame year, the doctor received an order to attend the Privy Council on the day following, which he accordingly obeyed; and was examined relative to the proceedings of a club which boaſted of the Duke of Norfolk, the Duke of Richmond, the Earls of Effingham, and Derby, Sir William Jones, Mr. Sheridan, Drs. Price, Kippis, John Jebb, Mr. Erſkine, &c. &c. among its aſſociates. On this occaſion, Dr. T. although viſibly depreſſed by the yellow-jaundice, evinced great firmneſs, and was diſmiſſed without being obliged to give bail, at the voluntary interceſſion of a dignified clergyman then ſitting as a member of the board, and who is ſuppoſed to have been the preſent Archbiſhop of Canterbury.

On the eſtabliſhment of the ſociety called " The Friends of the People," he was alſo voted a member.[*]

The

---

[*] This ſociety was founded in the year 1792, under the name of " The Society of the Friends of the People, aſſociated for the purpoſe of obtaining a Parliamentary Reform."

This inſtitution is ſuppoſed to have excited conſiderable alarm in the adminiſtration; for, in the advertiſement notifying its exiſtence, a liſt was publiſhed of the firſt hundred aſſociators, among which were no leſs than forty members of Parliament, viz. the Earl of Lauderdale, Mr. Grey, Mr. Whitbread, Mr. Francis, Mr. Tierney, Mr. Erſkine, Mr. Sheridan, &c. &c.

This ſociety publiſhed a very accurate account of the ſtate of the repreſentation of England and Wales, the ſubſtance of which was afterwards formed into a petition, and preſented to the Houſe of Commons by Mr. Grey, on the 6th of May, 1793. In this petition it was aſſerted, with what truth we pretend not to determine, that eighty-four individuals did, by their own immediate authority, ſend one hundred and fifty-ſeven members to Parliament; and that, beſides theſe, one hundred and fifty more, making

in

The life of this gentleman prefents few other memorable events, his literary labours excepted, which evince a feries of ftudy and toil, feldom to be met with, even in thofe who have dedicated their whole time to letters alone.

His principal works are the following:

1. In 1763, "A Review of the genuine Doctrines of Chriftianity, &c. 8vo. with the name annexed.

2. In 1764, an anonymous "Enquiry into the Queftion, Whether Juries are, or are not, Judges of Law as well as Fact; with a particular reference to the Cafe of Libels." In this, Dr. Towers took the conftitutional and affirmative fide of the queftion, not only in refpect to libels, *but in all cafes whatever*; this doctrine was ably fupported by the late Lord Camden fo far as concerns the former, and has alfo received the fanction of the legiflature in a bill, but too little attended to by either judges or juries.

3. He is the author of the firft feven volumes of " Britifh Biography;" the firft volume of which was publifhed in 1786.

4. Between fifty and fixty articles of the new edition of the Biogr. Britann. with the letter T. annexed.

5. In 1773, " An Examination into Sir J. Dalrymple's fcandalous Attack on the memory of Sydney and Ruffel."

6. In 1774, " A Letter to Dr. Johnfon, occafioned by his recent political Publications." See Bofwell's life of Johnfon, vol. II. p. 200, 201, and 202.

7. In 1786, " An Effay on the Life and Writings of Dr. Johnfon."

8. In 1788, Memoirs of the Life and Reign of Frederick III. King of Pruffia. (A fecond edition has been fince publifhed.)

9. " Obfervations on Mr. Hume's Hiftory of England."

And 10. An Oration delivered at the London Tavern, on the 4th of November, 1788, on occafion of the commemoration of the Revolution, and the completion of a century from that great event:—

After remarking, that great and interefting events, involving in the whole three hundred and feven, were returned to that Houfe, not by the collective voice of thofe whom they appeared to reprefent, but by the recommendation of feventy powerful individuals: fo that the total number of patrons were one hundred and fixty-four, who returned a decided majority. Thefe ftatements, the fociety obferved in their petition, which was entered on the journals, they were ready to prove at the bar.

volving the happiness of nations, have always been celebrated by mankind, he recurs to the important epoch, which placed William III. on the throne of the Stewarts:

"Of this nature, and of this tendency," says he, "is the event which we are this day assembled to commemorate. It is an event, which must ever be regarded as one of the most important recorded in the British annals. It is an event, which, at the period when it happened, justly excited the attention of surrounding nations. It is an event which will ever reflect honour upon our ancestors, and the remembrance of which should at all times, excite in their descendants an ardent zeal for the liberties of their country, and for the rights of human nature.

"That when all the efforts of regal tyranny were employed to overturn the liberties of England, they should have been still more fully established at the REVOLUTION; that, in consequence of that most important event, this country should now have enjoyed an high degree of liberty, civil and religious, for an entire CENTURY;—is a just subject of national exultation, and of gratitude to the supreme Ruler of the Universe, from whose providential dispensations Great Britain has derived such signal and such invaluable blessings.

"It is among the highest honours of this country, that its inhabitants have been distinguished, in almost every period of their history, by their firm, manly, and intrepid opposition to the encroachments of tyranny. On a variety of occasions have our ancestors nobly asserted their rights as men, and as citizens. In the senate, and in the field, they have repelled the attacks of tyrants, and maintained the honour, the dignity, and the liberties of their country. Many efforts have been made by the possessors of power to overturn these liberties; and, at the period previous to the Revolution, such was the despotism of the measures adopted by the then reigning prince, that, if they had been tamely submitted to by the people, the liberties of England would have had no longer an existence."

It is thus that he mentions the wrongs that led to, and the patriots who distinguished themselves during that and a former period.

"To enter into a particular enumeration of the facts that preceded, and that attended the Revolution, would take up more time than would be suitable to the nature of such a meeting as

the

the prefent. I fhall, therefore, here only obferve, that when the illegal, the unconftitutional, and the tyrannical adminiftration of king James the Second, had rendered it neceffary that all who had any attachment to the liberties of their country, or to the Proteftant religion, fhould make a firm and united ftand againft him; when he affumed a power of fufpending the laws, and of trampling on the conftitution;—an illuftrious band of patriots arofe, who projected the REVOLUTION, and who adopted thofe meafures that at length brought it to a glorious completion. Among the principal promoters of the Revolution, we may particularly enumerate the earls of Devonfhire, Shrewfbury, and Danby, Lord Delamer (1.), Lord Lumley, Admiral Herbert, Admiral Ruffel, Henry Compton, Bifhop of London, and Henry Sydney, brother to the illuftrious Algernon.

" Of characters of this kind our country has happily produced too many to be now diftinctly enumerated: but it cannot be improper on this occafion to mention the names of JOHN HAMPDEN, who oppofed the unjuft claims of regal tyranny in the famous cafe of Ship-money, and who nobly fell in the caufe of his country in Chalgrove-field; of the virtuous, the amiable, the patriotic Lord RUSSEL; of the high-fpirited and illuftrious ALGERNON SYDNEY, whofe admirable writings in the caufe of freedom brought him to the fcaffold; and of JOHN LOCKE, who has explained the true nature of civil government, and eftablifhed the rights of men on the moft unqueftionable principles. And among the diftinguifhed votaries of liberty in this country, our great and illuftrious bard, the fublime MILTON, fhould not be forgotten. Even the fplendour of his genius has not fecured him from the moft virulent attacks from the partizans and advocates of defpotic power; and his zeal in fupport of the great rights of mankind, fhould, therefore, the more endear his memory to thofe who are actuated by the fame generous principles. He is juftly entitled to our veneration for the ardour of his patriotifm, as well as for that elevation of genius, which enabled him to reflect fo much honour on his country by his immortal writings.

(1) Henry Booth, Lord Delamer, afterwards created Earl of Warrington, was a nobleman of amiable and irreproachable character, who is faid to have been one of the original projectors of the Revolution, and who was one of the firft that appeared in arms in its fupport, after the landing of the prince of Orange. But he was not perfectly fatisfied with the manner in which fome points were adjufted at the Revolution.

The various publications of Dr. Towers, the boldnefs of his principles, his unabated zeal, and the fide he had taken during the American conteft, all tended to render him confpicuous. The Doctor was admitted, in 1779, to the academical honours of the univerfity of Edinburgh, having received the degree of LL. D.

Several of Dr. Towers's tracts, &c. have been lately re-publifhed in three vols, 8vo. with an admirable portrait of the author prefixed, an outline fketch of which is given in our frontifpiece.

He is a widower, and has a fon, who is librarian of Dr. Williams's library, in Red Crofs-ftreet.

He appears to have wifhed for more retrenchments of the regal prerogative, and to have thought, that the liberty of the fubject was not fufficiently fecured and afcertained even under the new fettlement. Mr. Granger fays of him, in his Biographical Hiftory of England, that " he was a man " of a generous and noble nature, which difdained, upon any terms, to " fubmit to fervitude; and whofe paffions feemed to centre in the love of " civil and religious liberty." In Lord Delamer's " Advice to his Children," printed in his works, he fays, " There never yet was any good man, who " had not an ardent zeal for his country."

LORD THURLOW.

OF all the *learned professions*, as they are usually called, that of the law is the most propitious, in this country at least, to such as possess talents, but are destitute of fortune. It affords a greater variety of opportunities for a young man to bring both his natural and acquired parts into a conspicuous point of view, and consequently to turn them to an advantageous account, than any other; and where sterling abilities are united with industry and application, the chance of success is highly flattering. In support of this assertion, one might refer with great confidence to the catalogue of eminent persons, who have filled the first legal departments of this kingdom for centuries past: the court calendar, and the peerage of the present day, will furnish proofs still more decisive.

Edward, Lord Thurlow, was born, A. D. 1735, at Ashfield, an obscure village in the county of Suffolk, of which his father, the * reverend Thomas Thurlow (who died in 1762), was vicar, and whence he himself derives his barony. The family, like most others who bear the same name with a great man of former times, is said to be descended from the celebrated Thurloe, the secretary of Oliver Cromwell; but if so, the heralds have omitted the circumstance, for it is not mentioned in the peerage. †

The

---

* He married Elizabeth Smith, of Ashfield, by whom he had issue,
1. The present Lord.
2. Thomas, who died Bishop of Durham, May 27, 1791, aged 56; and,
3. John, a manufacturer at Norwich, who died March 4, 1782.

† A story formerly circulated, if true, does great honour to his lordship, as it evinces a total abnegation of that silly vanity which sometimes accompanies even great characters.

The subject of the present sketch, after receiving a tolerable education from his father, who is said, perhaps unjustly, to have attended to the learning *only* of his children, he was removed to Cambrige, where he was entered of Caius college, under the tuition of Dr. Smith, the present master. While there, his conduct was so irregular, and his spirit so haughty, as often to provoke academic censure. The frequency with which this was administered, had no other effect upon a mind naturally untractable, than to produce occasions for stricter discipline. At length it was hinted to him pretty plainly, that a voluntary departure from Cambridge would be a prudent step on his part, to prevent the highest punishment that an university can inflict. He accordingly quitted his college without taking any degree, and repaired to the metropolis, where, after spending some considerable time, and exhausting his finances, in a manner, we may suppose, not very different from that which had distinguished him elsewhere, he engaged, at the entreaty of his friends, in the study of the law, and accordingly entered himself of the Inner Temple. How he conducted himself in this new situation is little known; but those who remember him say, that there was nothing either in his application or his conversation, that warranted any expectation of his subsequent celebrity. Even long after his being called to the bar, he continued unknown and unnoticed, and consequently unemployed. At length a fortunate circumstance occurred, which gave him an opportunity of shewing to the world that he was possessed of powers of the first order.

On being asked by a flatterer, while Lord High Chancellor, " if he was " not descended from the great secretary Thurloe?" he is said to have replied as follows: " There were two of that name in my county, Sir; the one " Thurloe the statesman, the other Thurlow the carrier.—I am descended " from the latter."

der. By some means or other, with which we are not acquainted,* he was employed to arrange and state the case of Mr. Archibald Douglas, in the great legal contest with the Duke of Hamilton; and this task, which was a very complex and important one, he executed in a most masterly manner.

About this time he also acquired the favour and patronage of Lord Weymouth; and from that moment the path to honours and emoluments lay smooth before him; for not long after he was made one of the king's counsel, then (in 1770) appointed Solicitor-general, and in a few months more he succeeded Sir William de Grey, as Attorney-general. It is very remarkable, however, that the university of Cambridge never named him, according to usual custom, one of its standing counsel. Whether this neglect proceeded from a recollection of his former conduct, or from his having left college without taking a degree, is uncertain. But though unmindful of him, it redounds to his honour, that on his advancement to the Chancellorship he remembered his old tutor, as well as his college associates, and conferred favours upon them which they never could have expected, more especially from one who had met with a treatment bordering on severity at their hands. Many anecdotes of his generosity might be related; but one shall suffice.

While at college, he was often too licentious with his tongue, and entering once into a dispute with an elective and temporary officer, he was asked " whether he knew " that he was talking to the *dean?*—" Yes, Mr. *Dean*," replied Mr. Thurlow; and never afterwards saw him without reiterating " *Mr. Dean! Mr. Dean!*" which set

them

---

* He had signalized himself before this, in a cause, in which the late earl of Winchelsea and Mr. Luke Robinson were concerned; and it is not at all unlikely, that it led to his being retained in the great Scotch contest, about to be mentioned.

them at variance. When he became Attorney-general, they met by accident; and he addressed his old friend, *unwittingly*, " How do you do, Mr. *Dean?*" which so hurt the old *cantab*, that he left the room without making him any reply. On his obtaining the office of Lord Chancellor, he took an opportunity of meeting once more with his quondam acquaintance, and again addressed him with " How do you " do, Mr. *Dean?*" " My Lord," replied the other sullenly, " I am not now a dean, and therefore do not deserve the " title." " But you are a dean," said his lordship; " and " to satisfy you that it is so, read this paper, by which " you will find that you are Dean of ——: and I am so " convinced that you will do honour to the appointment, " that I am sorry any part of my conduct should have given " offence to so good a man."

He was twice elected member of parliament (if his *nomination* may be so termed) for the borough of Tamworth, in Staffordshire; and during the time he sat in the House of Commons he was greatly respected by both sides for the candour, integrity, and talents, which he uniformly displayed. There he became a firm and undaunted supporter of the measures of the existing administration, and certainly no man was ever called upon to defend a more unpopular one. Lord North found his eloquence, promptitude, and resolution, of such vast service to him against his numerous and powerful adversaries, that in return he gave him the great seal, in June, 1778; at which time he was created a peer.

On entering upon this high office he shewed a firmness, and an integrity, rarely equalled. It had been usual with former chancellors to make considerable alterations, on their advancement, in the officers of their court, with a view to serve their dependants, or oblige their ministerial friends: and in particular, the commissioners of bankrupts were commonly changed. On the present occasion, however, hardly

any

any alterations were made; and only one perfon was difmiffed, which he owed to his own imprudence, in foliciting the influence of his lordſhip's miſtreſs.

The fituation of the chancellor in the Houfe of Lords, as fpeaker, is not only of great importance, but of peculiar delicacy, and requires much addrefs. The hereditary members of the conftitution are generally fraught with lofty fentiments, and feel but little inclination to bend to the authority of a man raifed from among the herd of practitioners in the inferior courts. Although the powers vefted in the fpeaker be very great, yet they had feldom been exercifed over a debate in reftraining the exuberances of the noble orators; the confequence of which was, that they frequently wandered wide of the queftion, befides committing other irregularities inconfiftent with the dignity of fo auguft an affembly. Lord Thurlow determined to exert himfelf in reforming thefe abufes, and ſhewing that a chancellor ought to be looked up to with deference, inftead of fitting, as had been too often the cafe, a mere cypher. His interference in the debate, to preferve order, and to confine the members immediately to the point, excited no fmall furprize and diffatisfaction; at laft the Duke of Grafton, feeling himfelf hurt at a check which he had experienced, remonftrated againſt it with great fharpnefs. For this he received a correction on the inftant, in terms that were pointedly fevere, yet fpiritedly decorous; and from that moment Lord T's character and authority rofe to the proper level in that houfe.

During the remainder of the North adminiftration, he continued an uniform and able defender of the meafures of government. Indeed, a ftronger proof of the univerfal efteem in which he was held by all parties could not be adduced, than in his retaining the feals at the exprefs requeft of the new miniftry. He never, however, cordially united with Lord Shelburne, when that nobleman was at the head of affairs, though he held the chancellorship during the whole of his short-lived administration.

On the entrance of the coalition junto into power, his Lordship resigned his station with becoming dignity; but resumed it again when that strange monster was driven out by the united voice of the people.

Few men in that post have gained such a degree of popularity as Lord Thurlow; and it ought to be observed, that the times in which he has lived have been extremely critical, and that he has had to encounter many events of a very difficult nature.

The most remarkable period in his life, and that upon which his future biographer will have to dwell with the greatest complacency, is the epoch of the king's illness. No situation could be more trying; and certainly no man ever conducted himself in a trying situation with greater fortitude or wisdom. His integrity on that occasion was, indeed, conspicuous; and he had the rare satisfaction of receiving for his reward, the grateful acknowledgments of both prince and people at the same time. His speeches on the Regency question, will ever remain upon record as the most precious memorials of unshaken rectitude; and that declaration which in a manner may be said to have electrified the House of Peers, " When I forsake my king in the hour of his dis-" tress, may my God forsake me!" ought to be engraven upon his monument.

After having acted with Mr. Pitt, in perfect unison, ever since that gentleman came into office, till the present eventful war, a marked difference of opinion in the cabinet at length rendered the resignation of one or other of these statesmen unavoidable. Accordingly Lord Thurlow delivered up the great seal, in a manner, and in terms that affected his royal master very forcibly. Doubtless his Majesty could not but recollect, at that moment, the service, which the ex-
chancellor

chancellor had rendered him in that awful season when he was, as it were, shut out from society, and oppressed with the most severe of human maladies!

From that time, Lord T. has contented himself with enjoying the *otium cum dignitate*, in his retirement at Dulwich. But though he has withdrawn himself from the present ministry, he has not petulantly joined the phalanx of opposition. His mind is superior to party connexion, which, at the best, is but a mean kind of bondage. While in office, he preserved an independent spirit, and was always ready to express his dissatisfaction at the measures of his colleagues in power; and now that he has no share in the government, he is equally free in reproving or commending either ministers or their opponents.

His great characteristics are steadiness, uniformity, and inflexibility, which often proceed to a length that, in others, would be termed obstinacy. No man can shake him from his purpose, when his opinion is once fixed. With this spirit of determination, is, however, united a powerful principle of integrity. In all the situations which he has filled, he has conducted himself in such a manner that no enemy can find an occasion to fasten any suspicion upon him. Though a stranger to gentleness of voice or manner, he possesses a large and very liberal mind. In the disposal of preferments, his chief regard ever was to merit; and he has been often known to resist the influence of his ministerial associates, in order to bring in those whom he supposed to be better qualified for the vacant offices.

As a public speaker, he possesses great powers; and though devoid of the more winning graces which steal their way to the heart, he carries home conviction to it, by a select arrangement of words, a dignity of utterance, a close and logical mode of argument, and a singular expressiveness of countenance.

With

With such qualifications, and such virtues, not to possess some failings would be more than falls to the lot of humanity. Those of his lordship arise entirely from a defect in his early education, and from a peculiar cast of his mind. Juvenile habits and indiscretions are rarely so altered in more advanced life, as not to leave some tincture of their influence, unless in very flexible dispositions alone.

Lord Thurlow's character is replete with integrity and liberality; and therefore a few imperfections may the more reasonably be excused. * Coarse language, at times, is said

---

* One of the most learned men of the present day, perhaps, dipped his pen in the *gall* of party prejudice, when he drew the following character of his lordship under the name of Novius:

"Minas possumus contemnere vocémque fulmineam Thrasonici istius Oratoris τῦ τὰς ὀφρῦς κυανέας ἐπηρκότος, cujus vulticulum, uti Noviorum istius minoris, ferre posse se negat Quadruplatorum genus omne et Subscriptorum. Quid enim? truculentus semper incedit, tetérque, et terribilis aspectu. De supercilio autem isto quid dicendum est? annon reipublicæ illud quasi pignus quoddam videtur? annon senatus illo, tanquam Atlante cœlum, innititur?

"Ferunt profectò Novium in 'summa feritate esse versutissimum, promtúmque ingenio ultra Barbarum.' Quod si demseris illi aut σφοδρότητα quanta in Bruto fuit, aut πικρότητα verè Menippeam, aut προσώπυ σκυθρότητα propriam et suam, facilè eidem juris nodos legúmque ænigmata ad solvendum permiseris.

"Fervido quodam et petulanti genere dicendi utitur, eodèmque, nec valdè nitenti, nec planè horrido. Solutos irridentium cachinnos ita commovet, ut lepores ejus, scurriles et prorsús veteratorios diceres. Omnia loquitur verborum sanè bonorum cursu quodam incitato, itémque voce, qua ne subsellia quidem ipsa desiderant pleniorem et grandiorem. In adversariis autem lacerandis ita causidicorum figuras jaculatur, ita callida et malitiosa juris interpretatione utitur, ita furere et bacchari solet, ut sæpè mirere tam alias res agere optimates, ut sit penè insano inter disertos locus.

"Fuit ei, perinde atque aliis, fortuna pro virtutibus. Didicit autem à Muciano, satis clarum esse apud timentem, quisquis timeatur. Corpore ipse ingens, animi immodicus, verbis magnificus, et specie inanium magis quám sapientia validus, studia ad se Optimatium illexit, eámque adeptus est auctoritatem, quæ homini novo pro facundia esse posset. Scilicet, quæ bonis Titio, Seioque turpissima forent, Novium nostrum maximè decent, siquidem
è subsellis

said to escape him; and some facetious barristers have pretended to observe an oath *quivering* on his lips, while sitting at Lincoln's Inn; but the unmannerly stranger has never been allowed to escape, though his unwilling retention was, doubtless, a painful emotion.

His lordship was never married, but he has several natural children.

Although he rents a house, and maintains a regular establishment, in St. James's-square, yet he never sleeps in town; but retires instantly from the House of Peers to his residence, near Dulwich, in Surrey.

è subsellis elapsus de Tribunali nunci pronuntiet, et ex Præcone aionum factus sit institor eloquentiæ senatoriæ. Quam igitur in civitate gratiam dicendi facultate Q. Varius confecutus est, vastus homo atque fœdus, eandem Novius intelligit, illa ipsa facultate, quamcunque habet, se esse in Senatu consecutum——

————" Ellum, *confidens, catus* :
Cùm faciem videas, videtur esse quantivis pretii :
Tristis severitas inest in voltu, atque in verbis fides."

" Of that orator, who carries menace and terror in his brow, we think the eloquence Thrasonic, and despise its loudest thunders; whose aspect, like the younger Novius, repels all underlings and petitioners," &c.

W.

THE MARQUIS CORNWALLIS.

THE fubject of this memoir has acted with fuccefs in the character of a ftatefman as well as a foldier. Like the Roman confuls of old, he has received and difpatched ambaffadors; he has declared war, and granted peace. He fought for the prefervation of an empire in America; he retained and enlarged the Britifh dominions in Afia; and, in Europe, he has humbled the enemies of his country, and, by his energy and humane policy, has crufhed a civil war in the bud.

Marquis Cornwallis, whofe family is very ancient and honourable, was born December 31ft, 1738, and feems to have been intended from his cradle for the army. He accordingly entered into the fervice at a very early age, and we find him in 1758, when only twenty years old, and at a period when promotions were lefs rapid than at prefent, a Captain in Colonel Craufurd's light infantry, under the title of *Lord Broome*. Three years after this, he accompanied the Marquis of Granby to the continent, in the honourable and confidential capacity of one of his *Aids-de Camp*, and was of courfe attendant on the perfon of that gallant nobleman during the campaign. It was thus, in the fields of Germany, and under the moft fkilful and celebrated generals of the day, that Lord Broome acquired the rudiments of the art of war, and prepared himfelf to command others, by firft learning to obey.

In 1761, he was promoted to the rank of lieutenant-colonel of the twelfth regiment of foot; and we then find him difcharging his civil as well as military duties, by fitting as a reprefentative in Parliament for the Borough of Rye.

On

On the death of his father, who was the fifth peer of his family, in 1762, he, of courfe, vacated his feat in the Houfe of Commons, and appeared in the Houfe of Peers, under the title of Lord Cornwallis. In 1765, he was nominated one of the lords of the bed-chamber; and about the fame time, was honoured with the appointment of *Aid-de-camp* to his prefent Majefty, which was tantamount to a promotion in the army.

His fpirit, however, was manly and independent. The favours of the crown did not make him forget the duties of the peerage; for he voted frequently againft the minifter, and fometimes adopted what is called the *popular fide* of the queftion; in particular, when the memorable bill for fecuring the legiflative power of Great Britain over the American colonies was introduced into the upper houfe, Lord Cornwallis was one of the five who refufed their confent. This feeble, but refpectable oppofition, was headed by the venerable Earl Camden.* He alfo, on another remarkable occafion, entered his proteft againft the queftion to vote away privilege in matters of libel.

Luckily for the nation, his political did not interfere with his military career; for, in 1766, he was promoted to the command of the thirty-third regiment of foot, which he ftill holds; and two years afterwards, married Mifs Jemima Tulikens Jones, daughter of James Jones, Efq. whofe fingular fucceffion to a large fortune is related at large in the memoirs of the facetious Tate Wilkinfon. With this lady, who brought him two children (a fon and a daughter), he enjoyed every felicity the connubial ftate is capable of yielding, until he was called on to embark with his regiment for America.

* Lord Mansfield rallied his Lordfhip on this occafion, on account of the youth of his affociates. " Poor Camden!" faid the Chief Juftice, " Could " you only get four boys to fupport you?"

America. On this occasion, Lady Cornwallis, inconsolable at the idea of parting from him, after urging every plea that affection could suggest, applied to his uncle, then Archbishop of Canterbury, who, at her request, procured the King's leave of absence. But, notwithstanding all the fondness of the husband, duty prevailed over affection, and a nice sense of honour urged her dearly-beloved lord to forsake her. The separation was, however, too much for her weak nerves to bear; she literally fell a prey to love, sunk beneath the weight of her grief, and died; thus affording a most singular and romantic instance of conjugal affection!

Shortly after his arrival in America, we find his lordship serving under Sir William Howe, with the rank of Major-general, and acting as an able and indefatigable partisan.— Having landed, in November, 1786, on the Jersey shore, at the head of a detached corps, and found Fort Lee evacuated, he instantly penetrated into the country, and took possession of the province. At the end of the campaign, he repaired to New York, with a view to embark for Great Britain; but having received advice of the disastrous affair of Trentown, with the unpremeditated gallantry of a soldier, he deferred his voyage, and returned to the Jerseys.

His Lordship's first enterprize in 1777, was an attempt to surprise an American post in his neighbourhood, in which he in part succeeded. Soon after this, he received orders from General Howe to abandon the Jerseys, and in July he embarked with the English commander-in-chief in the expedition to the Chesapeak.

This was not a contest in which large armies contended with each other, and in which the fate of a battle was to decide the lot of an empire. On the contrary, it was what the French term a *petite guerre*; a war of posts and of skirmishes, of night marches and surprises, in which the climate and the sword cut off thousands, without putting a period to
hostilities.

hoftilities. It is in vain, therefore, to expect any very fplendid achievements on fo narrow a field of enterprize, when it is recollected that both armies would have fcarcely conftituted an advanced guard to a continental general, in the conflicts we have fo recently witneffed.

In feveral. of the fubfequent events, his lordfhip took a very active part. He commanded a confiderable body of troops at the paffage of the Brandy-wine, and after driving the enemy before him, entered and took poffeffion of Philadelphia, on the 24th of September, 1777. This was then confidered a very important acquifition; but it was foon difcovered, that a country might be over-run without being fubjugated, and that the poffeffion even of a province, does not always depend on fecuring the capital.

From that period until 1779, when he embarked as a Lieutenant General with Sir Henry Clinton for the fiege of Charleftown, he feems to have had few opportunities of fignalizing himfelf. On the furrender of the place, the command of South Carolina, with about 4000 troops, devolved upon him. On hearing this, General Gates, who had rendered himfelf fo famous by the capture of Burgoyne and his army at Saratoga, took poft near Camden, where he had collected about 3,600 men. Lord Cornwallis, inftead of being daunted at this event, advanced with an inferior force; and on the morning of the 16th of October, a fevere action took place, which was foon decided by the fpirit of the Britifh troops, who, after a fmart fire, had recourfe to their bayonets; and the Americans having at length given way, were purfued nearly twenty miles. Seven pieces of cannon, the greater part of the baggage, and a thoufand prifoners, conftituted the trophies of this day.

Early in 1781, General Arnold, who had now relinquifhed both the caufe and the fervice of his native country,

Y   had

had landed in the Chefapeak, where he did confiderable mifchief to his former affociates. Lord Cornwallis, on hearing of this, determined to effect a junction with him, in order to overwhelm the Marquis La Fayette, fince fo much celebrated for his patriotifm and fufferings during the French revolution, as commander-in-chief of the national guards.

Accordingly, having difpatched the gallant Colonel (now the patriot General) Tarleton with the cavalry, and Colonel Simcoe having been fent forward by Arnold, with the Queen's rangers, they took poffeffion of the fords on the Nottoway and the Meherrin, the only rivers that intervened; and a junction accordingly took place between the two armies at Peterfburgh, on the 20th of May. Immediately after this, the Britifh army croffed James-river, at Weftover, in purfuit of the French commander, who by this time had decamped from the neighbourhood of Richmond, and retired towards the back country with fuch celerity, that it was impoffible to overtake him.

In the mean while, Sir Henry Clinton, who was apprehenfive for the fafety of New York, blamed Lord Cornwallis for penetrating fo far; and a coolnefs from this moment feems to have taken place, which ended in a fubfequent difpute and appeal to the public. No fooner were the difpatches received, however, than his lordfhip, knowing that obedience is one of the firft duties of a foldier, abandoned Portfmouth, and concentrated his forces at York and Gloucefter.

General Wafhington, on learning this, was defirous to ftrike a blow, that might poffibly put a period to the war, and he had actually formed the daring project of capturing the brave Earl and all his forces. Rochambeau, the French commander, entered with great fpirit into the fcheme; and it unluckily proved but too fuccefsful. The combined armies

of

of France and America accordingly paffed through Philadelphia, and at length arrived, on the 28th of September, in fight of York-town, at which the Britifh troops ftill remained pofted, in confequence of difpatches from the commander-in-chief, promifing immediate relief. Lord Cornwallis on this withdrew his forces within the place, in full confidence of holding out, until the arrival of the promifed fuccours. The works thus abandoned by him, were occupied next day by the confederates, and the town regularly invefted.

The Englifh commander being now reduced to the alternative of either furrendering or attempting to efcape, of courfe preferred the latter, and actually conceived the idea of croffing the river, furprifing Brigadier Choife, who was pofted on the other fide, mounting his own infantry on the cavalry of the vanquifhed, and thus effecting a retreat, which would have been infinitely more glorious than any victory.

In purfuance of this defign, the light infantry, &c. were actually embarked in boats, and tranfported to the Gloucefter fhores, in the courfe of the night; but a violent ftorm having arifen, the troops were driven much lower than was intended, and prevented, during a confiderable time, from returning. In this diftrefsful fituation, and deftitute even of ammunition, his lordfhip, unwilling to expofe the remains of his gallant army to an affault, confented, on the 17th of October, to capitulate; and the terms were, on the whole, not unfavourable.

Lord Cornwallis now returned to his native country, in order to repofe himfelf after the fatigues of an unfortunate war, and enjoy all the happinefs that can poffibly enfue from the fweets of private friendfhip and public efteem.

During the political contests that took place in 1782, and 1783, his lordship was for a time deprived of his place as Lieutenant of the Tower of London, which he had obtained several years before ; but in the year 1784, it was restored to him. The calm that ensued after the peace, prevented his talents from being called into action for some years ; but the affairs of India no sooner began to assume a critical aspect, than a man was looked for, who united in his own person the esteem and confidence of the king, the ministry, and the people. Cornwallis was accordingly pitched upon, and immediately appointed to the high, honourable, and important situation of governor-general of Bengal.

No sooner did he arrive there, than a war took place with Tippoo Sultaun, son of the famous Hyder, who, from humble beginnings, attained great power, acquired extensive territories, and organized an immense army. The conduct of hostilities was at first intrusted to the Madras government; but little or no progress being made, the governor-general left Calcutta, and proceeded to the scene of action, where he arrived on the 12th of December, 1790. Having instantly assumed the command of the grand army, he proceeded to Vellore, and seemed to meditate an attack on the Mysore country, by the Baramahal Valley. The Sultaun, unacquainted with European tactics, was deceived by this motion ; for the English soon after made a rapid march to the Muglu Pass, through which they penetrated with little or no opposition.

Within a few miles of Bangalore, Tippoo's army at length displayed itself on the heights, in excellent order ; and it soon appeared that his subjects, as if in love with despotism, were attached both to his person and government. Notwithstanding this, Bangalore was immediately invested,

and

and the *pettah*, or town, stormed and taken on the very next day. The reduction of the fort itself followed soon after.

The army having been joined by the Nizam, and a reinforcement of 5000 men, under Colonel Oldham, Lord Cornwallis determined to march against Seringapatam, the capital of Tippoo; and on the 13th of May, the army arrived within sight of a place, the capture of which was expected to put a period to its toils, and reward all its labours. As the Sultaun had posted thither a few days before, and occupied an advantageous camp, it was determined to carry it, if possible, by surprise; but this scheme proved abortive, from the vigilance of the enemy, who were, nevertheless, obliged to abandon their position.

It was impossible, however, at this period, to attempt the siege of so formidable a place as Seringapatam; for, in addition to a variety of other causes, there was an absolute deficiency in the article of provisions.

Having therefore sent notice to General Abercrombie, who was marching to his assistance, to return, the Commander-in-chief destroyed his battering train, and retreated to Bangalore, being joined on his march thither by 30,000 Mahrattas.

Early, however, in the ensuing spring, the British army retraced its steps, and appeared once more before the metropolis of the Mysore, where it found Tippoo again strongly entrenched. He was, however, attacked, and obliged, as before, to retreat. The Bombay army forming a junction soon after, regular approaches were made, redoubts were raised, and had it not been for some unlucky events, in respect to which his lordship was entirely blameless, the sultaun, after being stripped of his capital, and bereaved of his power would have lain prostrate at his feet.

He,

He, however, was obliged to accept of such terms as the English commander chose to dictate. He consented to cede part of his dominions, paid a large sum of money, undertook to furnish a still more considerable portion of treasure, within a limited period, &c. and entrusted two of his sons to the care of Lord Cornwallis, with whom they were to remain as hostages for the due performance of the treaty; and here it is but justice to a prince, whom we are accustomed to style a *barbarian*, to observe, that he fulfilled every article with the most scrupulous punctuality.

This important war being now ended, highly to the honour of the British arms, Lord Cornwallis returned to England, without being enriched by a post, in which avarice and rapacity could easily have realized a princely fortune—but he neither exacted a *jaghire* from the conquered sovereign, nor increased his own income, by venality or extortion.

Honours and employments, both so well earned, awaited him at home. He had before been invested with the insignia of the Garter; he was now (1792) created a Marquis, admitted a member of the Privy Council, and in addition to his other appointments, was nominated to the lucrative office of Master-general of the Ordnance.

Returning once more to the bosom of domestic happiness, the marquis seemed to promise to himself a life of ease and quiet in his native country. Such, however, was not his destiny. Ireland was disorganized, and the English power there shook to its very centre. It was even doubtful how long it would appertain to Great Britain; for it was menaced by insurrection within, and invasion from without. One of these events had actually taken place, and the other soon followed.

In this critical state of affairs, the eyes of the cabinet, and the nation, were once more turned towards him, and he was invested with the Viceregal powers, amidst the acclamations of both kingdoms. His adminiſtration has been ſhort; but it has been ſuccefsful. The infurgents have been beaten, the difaffected have been difarmed, and an invading enemy has been taken captive. But his adminiſtration has been accompanied by merits, of another, and of a better kind; for military defpotifm has ceafed, the fyſtem of plunder and free quarters has been checked, and the torture, the rack, the whip, the ſcourge, and the halter, aboliſhed, as inſtruments not within the pale of legitimate government !

D_R.

Dr. JOSEPH PRIESTLEY, F.R.S. &c.

THE names of Galileo and of Prieſtley, excite a multitude of melancholy ideas!—Late poſterity will, however, do them juſtice; and although too late to be heard by the injured individuals, will rectify the miſtaken opinions of their contemporaries. It will be ſcarcely believed, indeed, that within a few years of the commencement of the 19th century, an illuſtrious philoſopher ſhould have been driven from his native country on account of his ſuppoſed political opinions; and that a brutal mob ſhould have been allowed, in the name of " Church and King," to have deſtroyed his dwelling, threatened his perſon, and rendered his life unſafe, in the land which gave him birth!

Dr. Joſeph Prieſtley was born March 13th, 1733, at Birſtell-field-head, near Leeds, in Yorkſhire. This part of the country, for a long ſeries of years, has been celebrated for its manufactures, and the Prieſtleys were one of the firſt families engaged in the broad-cloth trade. The Doctor, while only ſeven years of age, was taken into the houſe of an aunt, Mrs. Keighley, and was brought up by her huſband, who having no child of his own, adopted, and appears to have transferred that affection to him, which nature had intended for his own offspring.

Mr. Joſeph Keighley, after whom young Prieſtley was, moſt probably, named, was a remarkable character. He had been once, like St. Paul, a great perſecutor, and like him too became a convert. So violent was he againſt the diſſenters, that he was accuſtomed to find out their meetings, which, during the times of perſecution, began about eleven o'clock at night, and ended at two o'clock in the morning.

Happening

Happening once to difcover their place of worfhip, he determined to fecrete himfelf in a convenient place, in order to develope their heterodoxical tenets, expofe their herefies, detect their plots, and deliver them over to the vengeance of the civil magiftrate. The event, however, was far different from what might have been expected from a man feemingly led aftray by blind prejudices; for after attending to their rites, inftead of delivering the minifter up to punifhment, he took him home to his houfe, and fupported him there, until liberty was opened to the fect.

Under this fingular perfon, Jofeph Prieftley was brought up, and foon difcovered an amazing attachment to learning. At the age of eleven, he furprifed all who faw him, in confequence of his early proficiency. At that time, he read, or rather devoured, Bunyan's works; and it was then thought that he would become one of the firft Calviniftical teachers of his day. But as the Prieftleys were then in a flourifhing ftate, and acquired a certain degree of opulence and confideration by trade, they were inclined to bring him up to bufinefs. He, however, was at laft fent to the academy at Daventry, under the care of Dr. Afhworth, with an intention of being bred to the diffenting miniftry, and his uncle dying, his aunt paid the expences of his education.

But while the zealots for Calvinifm were looking forward with complacency to the time when their apoftle was to commence his pious labours, a change took place, from conviction in his religious tenets; for at this period he became acquainted with fome Arian and Baxterian minifters, whofe arguments appeared to be ftronger than thofe with whom he had heretofore been accuftomed to affociate.

When about twenty years of age, he fettled, for a little time, with a congregation at Needham in Suffolk; but as the opinions of the teacher did not correfpond with thofe of his flock, and he was too honeft to conceal his fentiments, he

was

was soon deserted. In this situation, he accepted of an invitation to Namptwich in Cheshire; although those who wished for his moral and spiritual assistance, were not able to promise him more than 30*l. per annum.* In order to eke out this scanty income, he acted as a schoolmaster; and happening to attract the notice of men capable of appreciating his worth, he soon acquired celebrity.

At this time, there existed a college at Warrington, in which the sons of many respectable dissenters were brought up, and where also a great number of young men were qualified for the ministry. Thither Mr. Priestley was invited, and taught the *belles lettres* in that institution, then in the zenith of its reputation.

As it was now a proper time for him to settle in life, and the means of maintaining a family presented itself, he determined to marry; and was accordingly united to Miss Wilkinson, daughter of Mr. Wilkinson, of Bristol.

But the period had now arrived, however, when a great revolution was to take place in this once celebrated and flourishing seminary. The principal supporters of the academy, and those who had been most liberal in their subscriptions, being cut off in the course of nature, and not being succeeded by men equally warm in their zeal, a speedy dissolution was threatened.

At this time, the Doctor received an invitation to preside over a flourishing and opulent congregation at Leeds, and was advised by his friends to remove thither.

After some years residence there, Lord Shelburne, now Marquis of Lansdowne, engaged him to superintend the education of his eldest son, Lord Wycomb, and he continued in that capacity during seven years. At the end of that period, he retired with an annuity of 150*l. per annum:* had he remained ten years, the sum would have amounted to 250l. and fourteen years attendance, would have raised it to 300l. according to previous agreement.

Soon

Soon after this, he had an invitation to Birmingham, where he continued until his place of refidence, and the meeting-houfe in which he officiated, were both burnt to the ground!

A little fubfequent to this cataftrophe, Dr. Prieftley fucceeded his old friend, Dr. Price, in the diffenting meeting at Hackney; but his fituation being rendered particularly unpleafant, and even unfafe, on account of the times, he purchafed an eftate in America, and removed thither in 1794.

Since his arrival in America, he has experienced many diftinguifhed acts of favour and civility, but thefe have been counterbalanced by fevere afflictions, for he has buried a wife and a fon.

The publications of Dr. Prieftley are fo numerous, that a bare analyfis of them would fill a volume of itfelf. Hiftory, Divinity, Education, Politics, Philofophy, Metaphyfics—all thefe, at different times, have been the fubjects of his lucubrations. But it is as an experimental philofopher, that his name and his works will be handed down to pofterity. His chemical labours do honour to the nation that produced and exiled him. It is to him we are indebted for a knowledge of the element in which we exift; and, alas! at the very moment he had extended the empire of fcience, and analyfed the properties of air, he was, in a manner, interdicted that of his native country, and forced to breathe the atmofphere of another hemifphere!

MISS HANNAH MORE.

THE controversy respecting the intellectual talents of women, as compared with those of men, is nearly brought to an issue, and greatly to the credit of the fair sex. The present age has produced a most brilliant constellation of female worthies, who have not only displayed eminent powers in works of fancy, but have greatly distinguished themselves in the higher branches of literary composition. Our own country has the honour of enrolling among its literary ornaments many females, to whom the interests of poetry, morality, and sciences, are greatly indebted. Among illustrious living ladies may, with justice, be mentioned the names of Barbauld, Robinson, Cowley, Smith, Radcliffe, Piozzi, Seward, Lee, Hays, Inchbald, Cappe, Plumptre,* Trimmer, Yearsley, Williams, D'Arblay, Bennet, Linwood, Cosway, Kauffman, and Siddons. The female who is the subject of the present notice is well known to the literary world, by several elegant, ingenious and useful publications. A few particulars respecting her, therefore, will not only be amusing to those who have read her works, but will also be instructive to young persons in the way of example.

Miss Hannah More is the eldest of three maiden sisters, who were the daughters of a poor but very worthy peasant at Hanham, a village near Bristol.

Hannah, notwithstanding the domestic drudgery which necessarily fell to her lot, improved her mind during the few leisure hours she could spare in reading. It may be well supposed that her stock of books was but small. The
first

---

* The able translator of Kotzebue's " Natural Son," and Count of Burgundy, &c.

first which fell in her way was the *Pamela* of Richardson, the humble source of an innumerable offspring: happy it would have been for the interests of virtue and literature, had the progeny been but as innocent as the parent.

The literary attainments, sobriety, modesty, and industry of *Hannah More*, were spoken of with general respect in her native place, and at length raised her, through the patronage of some respectable persons there, to the useful and comparatively important station of the village school-mistress. Her genius struggled above all the obstacles of that lowly condition, and she acquired such a degree of knowledge, as to enable her, with her sisters, to enlarge the school, and to undertake the education of young persons above the situation of those to whose improvement their attention had hitherto been directed. So great, at length, was their reputation, that several ladies of fortune and discernment prevailed upon them to remove to Bristol, about the year 1765, where they opened a boarding-school in Park-street. This seminary, in a short time, became the most respectable of its kind in the West of England; and many females of rank received their education in it.

Among others, who had the advantage of profiting by the instruction of Miss More and her sisters, was the celebrated Mrs. *Robinson*, well known for her various elegant publications in prose and verse.

Miss *More* had the good fortune of having for a next-door neighbour the Reverend Dr. *Stonehouse*; who perceiving her merits, distinguished her by his friendship, which he manifested by his instructions and his recommendation. Both of these were of the most essential service to her interests in the line of her profession; and also in the cultivation of her literary taste. The doctor was a man of extensive acquaintance, general knowledge, and elegant manners. He condescended to examine the occasional effusions of her

pen,

pen, and also to correct them, and through his hands all her early efforts passed to the press. The first of these was entitled " The Search after Happiness, a Poem," which was printed at Bristol, under the doctor's eye; and on its publication in London was so favourably received, as to encourage the author to further exertions of her powers. She next published " Sir Eldred of the Bower, and the Bleeding Rock, a legendary Tale;" which style of writing was become fashionable, through the success of Dr. Goldsmith's sweet story of Edwin and Angelina.

Miss *More* now turned her attention to dramatic poetry, and produced a tragedy entitled FATAL FALSEHOOD; which was tolerably well received; but not so much as her PERCY, a tragedy, which met with universal applause. She also wrote another tragedy, called the INFLEXIBLE CAPTIVE; which fell short of the merit of her other dramatic pieces. The success she met with in this way, was owing, in a great measure, to the immediate and commanding patronage of Garrick, who entered warmly into her interests, through the recommendation of Dr. Stonehouse, with whom he was very intimate.*

She

* The doctor was one of the most correct and elegant preachers in the kingdom. When he entered into holy orders, he took occasion to profit by his acquaintance with Garrick, to procure from him some valuable instructions in elocution. Being once engaged to read prayers, and to preach at a church in the city, he prevailed upon Garrick to go with him. After the service, the British Roscius asked the doctor what particular business he had to do when the duty was over: " None," said the other: " I thought " you had, (said Garrick), on seeing you enter the reading-desk in such a " hurry."—" Nothing (added he) can be more indecent, than to see a " clergyman set about sacred business as if he were a tradesman, and to go " into church as if he wanted to get out of it as soon as possible."

He next asked the doctor " What books he had in the desk before him?" —" *Only* the Bible and Prayer-book."—" *Only* the Bible and Prayer-book,"
replied

She afterwards printed a small volume of " Essays for Young Ladies," in which she has recommended to them a variety of ingenious and excellent observations upon the most important subjects, expressed in elegant language. In 1782, she published a work, perhaps the most popular of all her pieces, entitled " Sacred Dramas ; to which is added, Sensibility, a poetical Epistle." In this volume, she has dramatized, in a very natural and feeling manner, some of the most affecting and instructive narratives in the sacred history. Many of these had been previously performed by her pupils; and had given so much satisfaction to those who had seen the performances, or read the pieces, as to occasion numerous solicitations that they might be printed. The voice of the public accorded with the sentiments of private friendship, and these dramas have not only gone through several large editions, but, we believe, they have been, and are now frequently performed in respectable boarding-schools.

Her next production was in a different style of composition ; it was entitled " Bas Bleu, with the Tale of Florio," 1785. This poem is somewhat in the manner of Fontaine, and hits off the prevailing follies with great smartness and taste. The foundation of it was the *Blue Stocking* club, instituted by Mrs. Montague.

In 1788, appeared a small volume, called " Thoughts on the Manners of the Great ;" which attracted an uncommon degree of curiosity. As it was anonymous, some conjectured it to be the performance of one person, and some of another. The present Bishop of London, Mr. Wilberforce, and many others, were reputed to be its authors; but at length it was
discovered

replied the player; " why you tossed them backwards and forwards, and " turned the leaves as carelessly as if they were those of a day-book and " ledger."

The doctor was wise enough to see the force of these observations, and in future he avoided the faults they were designed to reprove.

discovered to have issued from the pen of Miss More. In this work she attacked, with great spirit, the encreased licentiousness of high life.

In the period between these two publications Miss More and her sisters had resigned their school, in favour of Miss Mills, and retired to a neat cottage, which they had purchased with the fruits of their joint industry, at the foot of the Mendip hills.

Here they instituted a Sunday-school, which has greatly encreased, and been abundantly blessed under their pious and judicious management.

In 1791, our author published, without her name, a useful and popular little volume, entitled " An Estimate of the Religion of the Fashionable World." This well-timed performance exposes strongly that lifeless profession of Christianity which is the general characteristic of the higher orders of society. She has herein the honour of having preceded Mr. Wilberforce, and some other eminent persons, in pleading for the necessity of a sound religious faith, in order to an acceptable course of moral practice.

About this time a society was formed, whose object was the instruction of the poor in morality and religion. The plan adopted was, to print striking, amusing, and instructive tracts, adapted to the capacities of common persons, and coming easily within their ability to purchase. On this ground the Cheap Repository was established, by which many thousands of most useful pieces have been circulated in the manufacturing towns and villages of this kingdom. In this benevolent design Miss More was one of the first concerned, and towards the success of it she has been particularly assisting by her excellent contributions. Among other useful tracts of her writing we shall only mention " *The Shepherd of Salisbury Plain,*" a little performance which persons

persons of a refined taste may read with pleasure and profit. She also endeavoured to counteract the progress of those political principles which the French Revolution had made so fashionable; and printed some small tracts, particularly one entitled " Village Politics," in the way of dialogue, which obtained a wide extent of circulation.

Miss More has the credit of having drawn Mrs. Yearsley, the celebrated poetical milk-woman, from her obscurity into public notice and favour. When she had discovered this remarkable phenomenon, she immediately began to exert her benevolence, and by her unwearied assiduity procured a liberal subscription to the poems of this child of nature. She also drew up an interesting account of the milk-woman in a letter to Mrs. Montague; which letter, in order to enlarge the subscription, was published in the newspapers and magazines of the day. By the attentions of Miss More, a sum was raised sufficient to place the object of them in a situation more suitable to her genius. But we are sorry to add, that a disagreement almost immediately followed the publication of the poems in question, between the author and her patroness; which is said to have been occasioned by the latter's taking the management of the subscription-money into the hands of herself and some select friends. The motive with which this was done is greatly to the credit of Miss More and her friends, as it was no other than a desire to provide permanently for Mrs. Yearsley and her young family. She, however, had a different opinion, and thought it was unjust in them to withhold from her the management of her own property. She went further, and endeavoured to represent her best friend as actuated by unworthier sentiments, the worst of which was, that of *envy*. Some attacks were, in consequence, made upon Miss More in different publications; but, conscious of the purity of her own views, she passed over those invidious attempts to prejudice the public mind against her in silence.

Another remarkable phenomenon in that neighbourhood also attracted Miss More's curiosity and benevolence about that time. A strange female, of elegant figure and manners, had been seen, for some considerable time, hovering about the fields near French-hay, and Hanham, of whom no particulars could be known. She thankfully received any humble food that was presented to her by the peasants; but always took up her night's lodging under a hay-stack. Various attempts were made to gain from her the place of her birth, but in vain. It was evident that she was a foreigner, and strange surmises were naturally formed, respecting her country and connexions. Miss More's humanity was roused upon this interesting occasion; and chiefly by her means the fair stranger found a comfortable asylum in the house of Mr. Henderson, at the Fishponds, father of the celebrated, but eccentric, John Henderson, of Pembroke college, Oxford.

Our benevolent author wrote an account of the " Maid of the Hay-stack," which was printed in most of the publications of the period.

Miss More has long been honoured with the particular friendship of some of the most distinguished personages in the kingdom. She spends some months in the year at the Duke of Beaufort's seat in Gloucestershire. She is also greatly esteemed by the Bishop of London, Mr. Wilberforce, and other persons eminent for literature and piety.

In the village where she resides, with her sisters, a great and pleasing reformation has been accomplished by their means. Every Sunday evening the children of the Sunday-schools, under their immediate patronage, are assembled in the school-room, together with the farmers' servants, and

such

such other grown persons as chuse to attend. In this little congregation prayers are offered up, a plain discourse read, and hymns sung. Pertinent questions are proposed to the adult part of the auditory, on the plain truths of Christianity; and the whole of this pleasing service is concluded with a cheerful hymn of praise to the God of all these mercies.

N. S.

MR. ALDERMAN BOYDELL,

In a volume containing the biography of the eminent artists of this country, claims a peculiar and pre-eminent distinction; for though the productions of his own *burin* cannot be classed with those of men who have devoted their lives to the practical part of their profession, he has rendered more real service to the English school than the whole mass of our English nobility, and may very fairly be denominated the father of the arts in Great Britain.

He was born on the 19th of January, 1719, at Dorrington, in Shropshire, of which place his grand-father was vicar.* His father, who was a land-surveyor, intended his son for his own profession; and had it not been for one of those little accidents which determine *the path that men are destined to walk,* he had wasted that life, which has been so honourable to himself, and beneficial to his country, in measuring and valuing the acres of Shropshire squires, and the manors of Welsh baronets. Fortunately for himself, and the arts, a trifling incident gave a different direction to his mind, and led him to aim at the delineation of scenes more picturesque than the ground-plans of houses, boundaries of fields, or windings of obscure roads.

While he was yet very young, chance threw in his way " Baddeley's Views of different Country Seats;" amongst them was one of Hawarden Castle, Flintshire, which being the seat of Sir John Glynn, by whom he was then employed in his professional capacity, and in the parish of which his father was an inhabitant, naturally attracted his attention.

---
* He was afterwards vicar of Ashbourne, and rector of Mapleton, both in Derbyshire.

tion. An exact delineation of a building he had fo often contemplated, afforded him pleafure, and excited an aftonifhment eafier to conceive than defcribe. Confidering it as an engraving, and naturally reflecting that from the fame copper might be taken an almoft indefinite number of impreffions, he determined to quit the pen and take up the graver, as an inftrument which would enable him to diffeminate whatever work he could produce, in fo much wider a circle. This refolution was no fooner made, than it was put in execution; for with that fpirit and perfeverance which he has manifefted in every fucceeding fcene of his life, he, at twenty-one years of age, walked up to the metropolis, and at the age of TWENTY-ONE bound himfelf apprentice for feven years to Mr. Toms, the engraver of the print which had fo forcibly attracted his attention.

Thefe, and accidents equally trifling, fometimes attract men of ftrong minds into the path *that leads direct to fame*, and have been generally confidered as proving that they were born with fome peculiar genius for fome peculiar ftudy; though after all, genius is, perhaps, little more than what a great moralift has defined it—" *A mind with ftrong powers, accidentally directed to fome particular object*; for it is not eafy to conceive that a man who can run a given diftance in a fhort time with his face to the eaft, could not do the fame thing if he turned his face to the weft." Be this as it may:—It is recorded of Cowley, that by reading Spenfer's Faerie Queen, he became a poet. Pope fays of himfelf, that while yet a boy he acquired his firft tafte for poefy by the perufal of Sandys's Ovid and Ogilby's Virgil; Sir Jofhua Reynolds had the firft fondnefs for his art excited by the perufal of Richardfon's treatife on Painting; and, as we have before obferved, Mr. Alderman Boydell was induced to learn the art of engraving by the coarfe print of a coarfe artift, reprefenting a mifhapen Gothic caftle.

His

His conduct, during his apprenticeship, was eminently aſſiduous; eager to attain all poſſible knowledge of an art on which his mind was bent, and of every thing that would be uſeful to him, and impelled by an induſtry that ſeems inherent in his nature,*whenever he could, he attended the academy in St. Martin's-lane to perfect himſelf in drawing; his leiſure hours in the evening were devoted to the ſtudy of perſpective, and learning French without the aid of a maſter;— to improve himſelf in the pronunciation of the language he had thus acquired, he regularly attended at the French chapel. After very ſteadily purſuing his buſineſs for ſix years, finding himſelf a better artiſt than his teacher, he bought from Mr. Toms the laſt year of his apprenticeſhip, and became his own maſter; and the firſt uſe he made of his freedom was to return into his own country, where he married a very deſerving young perſon to whom he had an early attachment, and with whom he lived many years in great felicity. During his ſtay he made many drawings, in Derbyſhire and Wales,‡ which he afterwards engraved: but his firſt publication made its appearance in 1745, immediately after he was out of his time, and was entitled *the Bridgebook*; it conſiſted of ſix ſmall-ſized landſcapes, deſigned and engraved by himſelf, and ſold at a ſhilling. With this the public were pleaſed, and the ſale of it encouraged and enabled him to proceed with vigour in his future works. The paper and printing would now coſt more than the ſum the book was at that time ſold for.

The

---

* How ſtriking a contraſt does his conduct form to that of Chatelaine, who was at the ſame period employed by Mr. Toms, and in the ſame workſhop etched and engraved at one ſhilling an hour; but who, with all his taſte and talents, and he had much of both, was ſo diſſipated and idle, that at the expiration of the firſt half-hour he frequently demanded his ſixpence, and retired to a neighbouring ale-houſe to expend it.

‡ Among theſe were a view of the ſtraits in Dovedale, Matlock baths, Cromford, Beeſton caſtle, Cheſter caſtle, Conway caſtle, and Denbigh caſtle.

The arts were then at a very low ebb; inferior prints, from poor originals, were almoſt the only works which our Engliſh artiſts were *thought* capable of performing, nor were they (with the exception of the inimitable Hogarth, and two or three more,) in general, qualified for much better things. The few people who had a taſte for higher art, gratified themſelves by the purchaſe of Flemiſh and Italian pictures, or French prints; for which, even at that period, the empire was drained of very large ſums of money. This, to a young man, who felt that his own intereſt was hurt, and the nation diſhonoured, and who was conſcious that, with proper encouragement, better things might be done, muſt have been a mortifying proſpect. But though he might lament that the courſe of the ſtream ran ſo much againſt his own and his country's intereſt, his powers did not then enable him to turn the current; he, therefore, for the preſent, followed it, and deſigned and engraved many views of places in and about London; which were generally publiſhed at the low price of one ſhilling each. Beſides theſe, he copied many prints from Vandevelde, Brooking, Berghem, Oſtade, Caſtiglione, Salvator Roſa, &c.*

The facility with which he drew, etched, and managed the dry needle, enabled him to complete a great number of prints; and with a view of ſhewing the improvement of the art ſince the time of their publication, the alderman lately collected the whole into one port folio, and publiſhed it at five guineas.† In his introduction to this work, he fairly remarks:

" That

---

* Even at this period, he was ſo much alive to fame, that after having paſſed ſeveral months in copying an hiſtorical picture of Coriolanus, by Sebaſtian Concha, he ſo much diſliked his own engraving, that he cut the plate to pieces.

† The number of theſe prints, which were drawn and engraved at a time when the artiſt had much other buſineſs to attend to, diſplayed uncommon induſtry;

"That to the lovers of the fine arts it may be an object of some curiosity, as it was from the profits of these prints that the engraver of them was first enabled to hold out encouragement to young artists in this line, and thereby, he flatters himself, has somewhat contributed to bring the art of engraving in England to such a state of superiority. It may likewise be added, that *this is the first book that ever made a Lord Mayor of London.*

Few men have had the happiness of seeing, in a single life-time, such a rapid improvement; and the publisher will be gratified, if in the future history of the art, his very extensive undertakings shall be thought to have contributed to it. When the smallness of this work is compared with what has followed, he hopes it will impress all young artists with the truth of what he has already held out to them—that *industry, patience, and perseverance, united to talents, are certain to surmount all difficulties.*"

To return from the alderman's precepts, to his publications. Finding that the taste for prints encreased, and that sums larger and larger were annually drawn out of this country by French artists, he sought for an English engraver who could equal, if not excel them—and in Woollet he found one. The temple of Apollo from Claude, and two premium pictures by the Smiths of Chichester, were among the first that he engraved; but the Niobe, and the Phaeton, from Wilson, which were published by subscription at 5s. each, were the two great pillars on which Woollet's well-earned

industry; and the manner in which many of them are executed, evince talents, that practice, and his constitutional perseverance, would have rendered highly respectable. The man who could engrave such a print as the Medea and Jason, from Salvator Rosa—if he had not become the first in his profession—must have been *in the very first line*. The pen and ink drawing of Wrexham-church, several views in Derbyshire, &c. and a very correct and spirited copy from Hogarth's enraged musician, are now in the possession of Mrs. Nicol, of Pall-mall.

earned reputation was built. For the first of them, the alderman agreed to give the engraver fifty guineas;* and, when it was completed he paid him a hundred. The second, the artist agreed to paint for fifty guineas, and the alderman paid him one hundred and twenty. *Proof prints* were not, at that time, considered as having any particular value; the few that were taken off to examine the progress of the plate, were delivered to such subscribers as wished to have them, at the same price as the common impressions. Several of these have been since bought in public auctions, at ten pounds each. At Mr. Hilliard's sale, one of them sold for eleven guineas.

The number of fine—of inimitably fine prints which have been since that time engraved in this country, have, indisputably, fixed the English school above every other in Europe; and been a very important article in the commerce of this nation, by altering the balance immensely in our favour.

The alderman has not confined himself to prints; he has also done more towards establishing an English school of historical painting than any other man: it is hardly necessary to say, we allude to the Shakspeare gallery; an undertaking of a magnitude that was never before attempted, and conducted in a manner that must astonish every nation in Europe. With that enthusiastic ardour which he feels for the promotion of the arts, he has presented to the corporation of the city of London several very valuable pictures; which are placed in the council chamber, at Guildhall. Some of them are calculated to commemorate the actions of those heroes who

* The immense difference between the prices paid to artists *now* and *then*, is almost incredible:—the Messrs. Boydells, in their advertisement to the print of Major Pearson, assert, that painting the picture, engraving the print, and every incidental expence, cost them the immense sum of five thousand pounds.

who have done honour to the British name;* and others, to imprefs on the minds of the rifing generation the fentiments of virtue, induftry, and prudence, in feveral very well-imagined allegorical reprefentations, painted by Mr. Rigaud, Smirke, Weftall, &c. Such is the flight memorial of his conduct, as an artift and protector of the arts. On his conduct as a citizen, it is not neceffary for this page to record any eulogium. In the different offices of alderman, fheriff, and firft magiftrate of the city of London, he has acted in a manner that will be remembered, and by many remembered gratefully;—for though inflexibly juft, he was ever merciful; and when hufbands came before him, with complaints of their wives; mafters, of their fervants or apprentices; fathers, of their children; he invariably, and often fuccefsfully, tried to reconcile them to each other, and accommodate their differences.

To the duties of his office he has ever been peculiarly attentive; and very often, when it was not in his rotation, fupplied the place of a brother alderman. This, confidering the great attention neceffary to his own bufinefs, is no flight trouble; but he has been enabled to do it from having generally arranged his bufinefs, fo as to be beforehand with the duties of the occafion. In this, his character is diametrically oppofite to that of the late duke of Newcaftle; of whom George II. once faid, that *he loft an hour* every morning, and was *running after it* all the reft of the day.

Of the alderman's fimplicity of manners, integrity of mind, and private worth, much might be faid—but he *lives* —and may his life and health be prolonged, and continue to be honourable to himfelf and ufeful to his fellow-citizens!

* The half length of Lord Heathfield, is, perhaps, the fineft portrait that Sir Jofhua Reynolds ever painted.

MR. GEORGE DYER.

THE subject of this memoir is descended from reputable parents; very early in life, he, himself, was sent to Christ's hospital, a most excellent institution, which has furnished the universities with admirable scholars, the church with many learned divines, the navy with able officers; and what, in a commercial nation like this, is no small praise, the exchange, with enterprising and successful merchants.

The youthful student discovered an astonishing attachment to books; and what, in such an institution, is no trifling distinction, actually got to the top of the school sooner than ever was known before his time.* This rare instance of assiduity, was accompanied by a passion, which but seldom attends on industry—a strong propensity for poetry. Pope, speaking of himself, says:

> " As yet a child, nor yet a fool to fame,
> " I lisp'd in numbers, for the numbers came."

This seems to have been also the case of George Dyer, with only this difference, that while the one wooed the muses in his vernacular tongue only, the other had likewise recourse to a foreign idiom, and addressed the daughters of Jupiter and Mnemosyne, in what is supposed to have been their native language. This classical taste, particularly his ardent attachment to the Greek and Latin authors, at length procured him a patron in the person of Dr. Askew, a physician of great fortune, and considerable influence; distinguished for his knowledge of Greek literature, and his valuable collection of

---

* It may not be amiss here to observe, that his masters were the Rev. Peter Wholley and Rev. James Penn, both known to the world, as literary men.

of books and MSS. in the fame language. Pleafed with the early proficiency, and congenial difpofition of the young man, he took an intereft in his ftudies, and purfuits; and prefaging that he would diftinguifh himfelf at fome future period, promifed that he fhould fee him amply provided for. But, alas! fuch is the uncertainty of human life, that this worthy man was cut off foon after; and that, too, at a time, when his pupil only beheld the *bloffoms*, and had not yet realized the *fruits* of expectation.

Notwithftanding this fevere lofs, he repaired to Cambridge; and, in confequence of the connexion above alluded to, chofe Emanuel college, where his friend had been educated.

It may not be improper here to obferve, that a confiderable time previous to this epoch, Mr. Dyer acquired fomewhat of a gloomy caft of mind, and connected himfelf with many of the fectaries. In confequence of this, the claffics were no longer fuch favourites as before; *modern* religionifts were recurred to, in preference to *heathen poets*; and even the ruling paffion was fufpended: for the mufes and methodifm do not affort well together!

During the greater part of his ftay at Emanuel college, George led a retired life; frequenting only the company of fome few men who happened to think like himfelf. His religious propenfities do not feem, however, to have altogether relaxed his ardour for ftudy, as his application was ftill confpicuous; though his mind revolted at the trammels of collegiate difcipline. This is not at all to be wondered at, when his *favourite purfuits* are recollected; for men of fervid imaginations are unwilling to fubject themfelves to the rigors of the Alexandrian fchool; and although Ptolemy, king of Egypt, difdained not to become the pupil of Euclid, yet but few poets or religionifts have evinced a turn for mathematics. Indeed, fuch an averfion is not difficult to be accounted for: this fublime fcience is founded on *demonftration*, and it

is

is not on such a basis, that either the fancy of the one, or the superstition of the other, can possibly be erected.

Mr. D's studies were accordingly confined to Metaphysics, Theology, and the Classics. Some time before he had taken his degree, his mind began to range abroad, and to speculate freely, relative to systematic christianity, and abstract enquiries concerning first truths. If this propensity be not unfortunate, it is, at least, *unprofitable*; more especially to a young man like the present, all of whose hopes in life originated either from his college or the church. The consequence was, that after a fit of melancholy, the stern dictates of principle got the better of all interested views, and the theologian (for such he had now become) determined to overstep the threshold of the church.

All golden dreams of preferment being thus blasted in the very outset, by the breath of conscientious scruples, Mr. D. naturally turned his mind towards a situation, for which he seems to have been admirably adapted, both by the excellence of his education, and the placidness of his manners. Instructed himself, he, accordingly, determined to instruct others, and for some time assisted the Rev. Dr. Grimwood, who then kept a very respectable academy at Dedham, in Essex, from which he has lately retired.

But he at length determined to return to Cambridge, where he made an open avowal of his dissent from the established church. While at the university, he had become acquainted with a very extraordinary man, the Rev. Robert Robinson, the apostle of the Baptists, with whom he for some time resided; at this period, he preached occasionally in his meeting-house, which almost faced Emanuel college; he also appeared frequently in the pulpits of others of the dissenting clergy, both at Cambridge, Oxford, &c.

After signalising himself in this manner for some time, without any particular adherence to creeds or systems, Mr. D. at length determined to put a period to his mission.

Having

Having repaired to Cambridge, he was encouraged to undertake a work on the subscription to the XXXIX articles of the church of England. Many of the dissenters countenanced the plan; and there were not wanting several even within the walls of the university who encouraged it, such as the Rev. Mr. Tyrwhitt, who actually introduced a grace for the removal of what he conceived to be an intolerable burden, Mr. Hammond, fellow of Queen's, and Mr. Friend, fellow of Jesus'.

Having now acquired a certain degree of reputation from his "Inquiry into the Nature of Subscriptions," &c. he determined to try his fortune in London. His first occupation in the capital required great memory, and some talents; these he possessed, but it was attended with a degree of drudgery that proved intolerable. He accordingly soon discovered, that the office of reporter of the debates in the House of Commons was unsuitable to his disposition; he therefore quickly relinquished it, and published a second edition of his book on subscription, greatly enlarged and improved. It is a miscellaneous composition, and abounds with politics, theology, metaphysics, criticisms on the scriptural text, an examination of the fathers, &c. About the same time he printed a volume of poems.

Mr. D. now formed an extensive acquaintance among men of letters, and engaged in the business of professional criticism, being at that time employed in writing for the Reviews; he also assisted gentlemen in acquiring, or regaining their knowledge of the classics.

It should be observed here, that on his arrival in the metropolis he threw off his black coat, and assumed, in all respects a *secular appearance,* except in respect to his hair, which still favoured of the ecclesiastical tonsure: he, however, has lived long enough in the world to see even this become fashionable; for, after having been confined for

some

fome centuries to the clergy, it has been recently adopted by the *beau monde*.

On his coming to town, he found party difputes and opinions running very high; but although he himfelf had been an orator in the pulpit, and was accuftomed at times to fpeak *extempore*, yet he never delivered his fentiments in any fociety of the reformers; for he feems to have confidered himfelf in his *political noviciate*, and to have preferved the referve, fo rigoroufly enjoined to the difciples of the Samian fage. But although filent himfelf, he may have been faid to have, literally, *opened the mouths of others*; as he wrote feveral fongs for political clubs, calculated to promote feftivity, and relax the brow of care from the fatigues and difappointments of life.

Soon after the much-dreaded " Rights of Man," which had nearly effected a revolution in the political world, made its appearance, Mr. Dyer publifhed the firft edition of " The Complaints of the Poor People of England," with the motto of " fiat juftitia." This muft be confeffed, even at that time, to have been a bold pamphlet; now it would be *intolerable*, and might fubject publifher, author, and, perhaps, printer, to the unfriendly greetings of his Majefty's Attorney-general!

His next work was a treatife on the " Theory and Practice of Benevolence," intended as an appendix to the former; it contains fome facts relative to the ftate-prifoners.

After this followed his " Memoirs of the Life and Writings of Robert Robinfon, late Minifter of the Diffenting Congregation, in St. Andrew's Parifh, Cambridge."

The next performance, of any fize, by Mr. Dyer, appears to be " The Poet's Fate," produced in 1797, in which he traces in fome very good lines, the fufferings and diftreffes of the votaries of the mufes not only in modern, but alfo

―――" In ancient times, long ere poor Butler figh'd,
" Or dinnerlefs the polifh'd Lovelace died."

This is to be followed by " Poetic Sympathies."

He has publifhed, befides thofe already enumerated, a Satirical Prologue to the celebrated Latin comedy of Ignoramus, in which he does not fpare even *lawn fleeves*, when a proper occafion offers; and he has lately undertaken to print his poetical works, for which there is the promife of a handfome fubfcription.

On the whole, George Dyer muft be allowed to be a fingular character. In order to furnifh his mind with facts, and gratify his eye with a pleafing romantic fcenery, he undertook, and actually accomplifhed, a tour, principally, if not wholly, *on foot*, through the moft interefting parts of England, Scotland, and Wales. No man in this country is more converfant with what may be termed the cradle and the grave of genius—the free-fchools and the prifons of the ifland, moft of which he has vifited in perfon. The prefent ftate of his mind, in refpect to religion, we are wholly unacquainted with; of all the ancient fects, however, he feems moft to refemble the Peripatetics, who placed the *fummum bonum*, " not in the pleafures of paffive fenfation, but in the due exercife of the moral and intellectual faculties." Like them too, he has been accuftomed to imbibe or retail inftruction while he walked; and as this country has not, like Athens of old, a *Peripaton*, he frequently indulges in the ftreet, or the public road.

There is another peculiarity obfervable in this gentleman: this confifts in the rejection of all titles from his works; for which, he fays, he has hiftory, philofophy, and even Chriftianity on his fide. He alfo obferves very fhrewdly in one of his publications, " that thofe artificial diftinc-
" tions which originated in tyranny, and are perpetuated by
" cuftom, lie at the bottom of many ferious evils that exift
" in fociety."

A.

Mr. D'ISRAELI.

THIS gentleman is the only son of a respectable Italian merchant, who has long resided in this country, and who is well known and esteemed upon 'Change.

The early part of his youth was passed at the country residence of his father at Enfield, where he was sent to a neighbouring school. Here he learnt nothing but a little imperfect Latin; enough, however, to perceive that there were beauties in Virgil and Horace, which his pedagogue could not assist him in discerning and appreciating. After a residence of several years, the affectionate care of his parents assisted him with a variety of masters; but as he revolted against the discipline of elementary knowledge, it was resolved that he should be sent to a private seminary in the city of Amsterdam. A year had scarcely passed under his new tutor, when he became the master of his master. If he had made no progress in classical literature, he had now, however, acquired a considerable knowledge of all the modern languages; he declaimed passages from the plays of the Spanish Calderon, the Luciad of the Portuguese Camoens, the Jerusalem of Tasso, and particularly from the Henriade of Voltaire. He formed a passionate attachment to the higher class of French writers; he felt with all the energy of taste, the rich imagination and seductive periods of Rousseau, the pointed and brilliant diction of Voltaire, and the concifeness and delicacy of Montesquieu.

On returning to his native country, he again retired to the country-house of his father. He now indulged more extensively in an uninterrupted perusal of authors of taste.

He faw, with pleafure, that he was neither adapted by nature, nor defigned by his friends for a commercial life. Having made a tour through France and Italy, he returned with a valuable collection of books, particularly in the French language. He now had a confirmed tafte for the literature of that refined and volatile people; and, as he has obferved, among them he not only found works of tafte, not elfewhere to be met with, but a vaft refource for the *Materia Literaria,* which exifts in no other nation.

The earlieft performance avowedly by Mr. D'Ifraeli is " A Poetical Epiftle on the Abufe of Satire," which was written, we underftand, to gratify a certain man of letters, who was his neighbour, and who fmarted under the fcourge of Peter Pindar. As a firft production, it exhibits his poetical talents to confiderable advantage. This effufion afterwards procured him the friendfhip of Dr. Wolcot, who has not only encouraged his poetical efforts, by unequivocal marks of his approbation, but conferred on him ftill more ufeful fervices, by many proofs of his friendfhip.

In 1790, Mr. D'Ifraeli made a more formal appearance in public, by addreffing a poem, entitled " A Defence of Poetry," to the prefent laureat. The whole edition, excepting the few copies fold, was burnt by the author; undefervedly, it feems, for the Monthly Review of March, 1791, gives it the following character:—

" Mr. D'Ifraeli is among the few modern poets who have at-
" tained their favour (the mufes); they appear, from the tefti-
" mony before us, to have diftinguifhed him from the crowd, and
" to have allowed him a plenteous draught from their fountain of
" infpiration. He is not without a knowledge of the requifites of
" genuine poetry: his verfification is elegant, flowing, and har-
" monious; nor can we read this fpecimen of his abilities, without
" perceiving that he has devoted his days and his nights to our im-
" mortal Pope."

In 1791, from these elevations of poetry, our author descended into the humble, but, with him, the agreeable and entertaining path of compilation. The first volume of his " Curiosities of Literature" was published anonymously; but the fascination of public favour induced him to prefix his name to the second. These compilations soon became popular, and have been a source of numerous imitations. The volumes form a rich repository of literary anecdote, and contain many original and well-written criticisms. The rapid sale of three large editions is the best proof of the public opinion.

As an original writer, he soon afterwards produced his " Dissertation on Anecdotes," of which work the Critical Review for January, 1794, observes, that

" This is an eccentric, an ingenious, and philosophical per-
" formance. The author, in a very masterly way, vindicates the
" detailer of anecdotes from the charge of being a literary trifler,
" and his remarks are extremely sensible and entertaining; they
" are given in a lively strain of reasoning, and form a very judi-
" cious and curious speculation."

This was followed by his " Essay on the Literary Character." The merits of this ingenious and original performance are too generally known to require any eulogium in this place.

In 1796, he produced a volume of Miscellanies; it is not so original as his two former productions; but the diction, as usual, is highly polished, and the anecdotes are uncommon and curious.

His last performance was a philosophical novel, in two volumes, under the title of " Vaurien." The chief object of this work was to satirize certain literary eccentricities and *monstrosities* which have lately been obtruded upon the public. Some of the game was doubtless fair; a few characters were, however, too much overstrained and caricatured to imprefs every reader with the juftice of the attack. To exaggerate is the common failing of all fatyrifts and caricaturifts, and Mr. D'Ifraeli may not, perhaps, have exceeded the ufual licence.

He is at this time engaged upon a work, which, from a publifhed fpecimen,* promifes confiderably to exalt his reputation as a fine writer. It is to confift of feveral romances, embellifhed with original poetry.

Mr. D'Ifraeli is unmarried, and at this time about thirty years of age. His habits and connexions are as ftrictly literary as thofe of any refident of the metropolis. Few perfons read and write more; fcarcely any compofe with equal rapidity; and, if clofe application do not injure his health, the execution of fome of his literary defigns promife confiderable future gratification to the public.

A. D.

* Vide Monthly Magazine, page 368, May, 1798.

THE REV. DAVID WILLIAMS.

THE life of this gentleman is not barren of incident, for unlike that of moſt men of letters, his has been active and enterprizing; and very few of his movements have been unaccompanied with a correſpondent effect.

Mr. Williams was born in Wales. His father's circumſtances having become ſomewhat embarraſſed, in conſequence of ſome unſucceſsful ſpeculations in mines, he ſought for refuge from the reflections incident to the ſtate into which he had involved himſelf, and numerous family, by flying to the comforts of religion.

He at this time reſided in Glamorganſhire, where his ſon David was born; who, with his other children, were ſent to a neighbouring ſchool for education. Old Mr. Williams, by aſſociating with the methodiſts, had imbibed their principles and enthuſiaſm; and reſolved to train up his ſon to the church, probably intending him for a teacher among his ſect, and, no doubt, expecting him to become one of its ſaints!

David diſcovered lively and promiſing abilities; but ſuch as by no means qualified him for the ſtation allotted him, to which, indeed, he had an inſuperable repugnance. Yet a parent's dying injunction controlled his reſolution, and he went reluctantly through the preparatory forms of education, neceſſary to fit him for the diſſenting miniſtry.

His firſt appearance, in the character of a preacher, was at Froome, in Somerſetſhire; where, although he could not conceal the diſlike he entertained to the primneſs and preciſeneſs of the diſſenters; yet he ſoon made himſelf beloved and admired by his congregation. His reputation for abilities, spread so rapidly, that at the age of twenty-two, he was invited to Exeter, as the successor of two celebrated pastors; and he underwent the requisite formalities of ordination, in order to qualify him for the ministry in the Arian congregation there.

Soon after this, he embarked in a plan which originated at Liverpool, to introduce a Socinian liturgy among the dissenters. A society, for this purpose, had been founded at the Octagon chapel there, by the persons who had conceived the design; and Mr. Williams soon persuaded his congregation to adopt it; this affords no common instance of their attachment to him! In that city, he might have lived an easy and agreeable life; but he at length became disgusted at some hypocritical schemes, discovered by him, and actually determined to quit the West of England.

On his arrival in London, he received some distinguished civilities from the dissenters, and did duty at one of their congregations at Highgate, until he had prepared a plan of education which he meant to carry into practice.

While at Highgate, he preached a course of "Sermons, on Religious Hypocrisy," which he published in two volumes, 8vo. In 1770, he wrote a poignant "Letter to Mr. Garrick, on his conduct and talents as manager and performer;" this was followed by a work called "the Philosopher," consisting of three polemical conversations; with dedications to Lord Mansfield, and the bishop of Gloucester.

When a respectable body of clergy, chiefly dissenters, met at the Feathers tavern, to petition for relief in the subscription to the thirty-nine articles, Mr. Williams was applied to, and at their solicitation, drew up some "Essays on public Worship, Patriotism, and Projects of Reformation;" which were printed and published, but are said to contain sentiments approximating more towards deism than

than his employers wifhed. An appendix was added afterwards, which is peculiarly fevere on the conduct of the diffenters, with whom he afterwards broke off all connexion.

About the year 1773, he brought forward his plan of education, founded on the outline given by Commenius, when he was invited here, to reform the Englifh fchools; and whofe defign was fruftrated by the civil wars. Mr. Williams diftinguifhed himfelf, on this occafion, in fuch a manner, that although he was a ftranger in the neighbourhood, and his religious tenets lay under fome imputation among the orthodox, yet he met with great encouragement. The *honorarium* of his pupils, was high; but, notwithftanding this, their number was confiderable. He was now in a fair way of making his fortune, and of introducing a more rational and eafy mode of education; when, at this critical period, he loft his wife, a lofs, which, notwithftanding all his philofophical fortitude, he was unable to fupport: he accordingly fled both from his habitation and inftitution, to take fhelter in the remote part of Derbyfhire, where, for fome time, he indulged his melancholy.

While at Chelfea, he publifhed a Treatife on Education, in a duodecimo volume; which contains fome uncommonly acute and judicious remarks on that fubject, and difclofes his fentiments with refpect to revealed religion.

During his refidence there, the celebrated Dr. Franklin, with whom he was intimate, took refuge in his houfe, from the ftorm he apprehended would follow Mr. Wedderburne's unwarranted attack on him at the council-board; an event which is faid to have had more effect towards the crifis which foon followed, than can be eafily imagined. And here, we are affured it was that the philofopher of Penfylvania, concerted with his friend the plan of a deiftical and philofophical

philofophical lecture. This fcheme was, at length, carried into practice; for on his return to London, Mr. Williams opened a chapel in Margaret-ftreet, Cavendifh-fquare, in which he was fupported by feveral perfons of confequence and fortune, &c. &c. The complexion of his difcourfes, was, however, neither relifhed by churchmen nor diffenters; accordingly, although many went to hear him, few enrolled their names as members.

While officiating in this capacity, he publifhed the Inauguration Sermon, two volumes of Lectures on the Univerfal Principles of Religion and Morality; and a Liturgy for the Chapel. Notwithftanding a variety of obftacles, he continued his labours, during a period of nearly four years; but as the fubfcribers did not increafe, he removed to a private room, where he delivered his opinions before thofe who fupported the inftitution. His fociety was, indeed, fmall; but it was as refpectable as any in England.

Mr. Williams's other publications confift of a pamphlet on "The Nature and Extent of Intellectual Liberty;" "A Plan of Affociation, on Conftitutional Principles," a tract written at the time of the riots in London; "Letters on Political Liberty;" occafioned by the county meetings and affociations, in 1782; "Lectures on Political Principles," and "Lectures on Education;" and, a "Hiftory of Monmouthfhire," in one volume, 4to.

Several anonymous works have been attributed to Mr. Williams, fuch as "Royal Recollections;" but it is fo infinitely beneath his abilities, that no one of his friends can allow it to be his. The "Leffons to a Young Prince," and "An Apology for profeffing the Religion of Nature in the eighteenth Century," may poffibly have come from his pen, and they are not unworthy of it. Some of the above works, which muft be allowed to poffefs a large fhare of intrinfic intrinsic merit, shew that Mr. W. had early turned his thoughts to political enquiries; and this important branch of knowledge is said to have been first suggested to his mind, in consequence of his assistance having been called for, in some parliamentary transactions.

His religious and political opinions at length connected him intimately with the popular party in this country, and his celebrity recommended him to the notice of the *Girondists* in France, who invited him over to assist him in the formation of the constitution. He was intimately acquainted with Brissot * while in England; and this journey, which introduced him to the friendship of all the great political leaders of the day, was not unaccompanied with some personal danger: for, as he recommended mercy to the king, the Jacobins branded him with the title of royalist, and he was actually denounced as such in their club. Mr. Williams saw so clearly the designs of this faction, and was so certain of the result, that he foretold to their opponents, when he parted with them, that, if they did not destroy the Jacobins, the Jacobins would soon destroy them †!

Soon

---

* Brissot first became acquainted with Mr. Williams in consequence of the writings of the latter. On his return to his native country, amidst the turmoils of one of the most wonderful revolutions that ever agitated mankind, he consulted Mr. W. as his oracle, and was forewarned by him of his danger. Had he followed his advice, the present situation of France, and, indeed, of Europe, might have been more auspicious!

† The celebrated Madame Roland speaks highly of the political talents of Mr. Williams, in many parts of her very animated work.

" Paine," says she, " is better calculated to produce a revolution, than to
" assist in the formation of a constitution. He seizes, he establishes, those
" grand principles, the exposition of which strikes every one at first sight,
" ravishes a club, and produces enthusiasm at a tavern; but for the cool
" discussion of a committee, for the connected labours of the legislator, I
" consider

DAVID WILLIAMS

" as infinitely more proper.

" Williams,

Soon after his return, a very extraordinary inftance of the offence he had given to a certain quarter occurred. He had been engaged by Mr. Bowyer, of Pall Mall, to write the Hiftory of England, from the Revolution to the prefent time; this was defigned as a continuation of Hume, and was to be ornamented with fuperb plates. The firft artifts in the kingdom were employed on the occafion, and Mr. Williams's name was announced in the profpectus, evidently written by himfelf. But this engagement with the public was broken, after the intended author had made every neceffary arrangement incident to fo grand an undertaking. In fhort, he was informed by Mr. Bowyer, that his fervices *muft* be difpenfed with, in confequence of certain intimations of the difpleafure of a great perfonage! Mr. Bowyer, however, found that a compromife was neceffary to protect him from a fuit in chancery.

We have now detailed fome of the events, by which the life of this extraordinary man has been marked. What his employment may be at prefent, is not generally known, but he ftill continues to diftinguifh himfelf by his laudable exertions in fupport of a moft ufeful inftitution, " The Literary Fund," of which he is faid to be the founder; and is fuppofed to be occupied during the feffion, by parliamentary ftudents.

Againft fo bold, fo manly, and fo able an advocate in behalf of civil and religious liberty, much malignity has occafionally

---

" Williams, although, like him, created a French citizen, was not nomi-
" nated to the convention, where he would have proved infinitely more
" ufeful. But the government invited him to Paris, where he paffed fome
" months, and converfed often with the principal deputies.

" A fage thinker, a real friend to mankind, he appeared to me to com-
" bine their modes of happinefs, as well as Paine defcribed thofe evils that
" conftituted their mifery."

fionally been difplayed; to deprecate fuch malignity, or defend him from the attacks of the enemies of fuch principles, would be fuperfluous; becaufe it would be unneceffary. We leave the friend of Franklin, and Roland, to defend himfelf, whenever an affailant fhall appear worthy of fuch a conteft.

GILBERT

GILBERT WAKEFIELD, B. A.

THIS gentleman boafts a name well known in the annals of claffical literature; and it is alfo intimately connected with the queftions that have lately agitated the minds of the THINKING part of the community, on the fubject of religion; nor has it been without celebrity in the field of political controverfy. Refpecting fuch a perfon, the opinions of his fellow citizens will be as various, perhaps, as their principles. Our judgment, too often, *Cameleon-like*, borrows its decifions from the hue of party; and, unfortunately, we are never lefs candid, than when political and religious enmities warp around, and pervert the mind from its natural bias towards juftice.

An outline of Mr. Wakefield's life has already been laid before the public by himfelf[*], and from it we learn, " that he was introduced into this planet on February 22d, 1756, in the parfonage-houfe of St. Nicholas, in Nottingham, of which church his father was then rector." It appears that his paternal grandmother claimed her defcent both from the Ruffell family, the illuftrious head of which, in the reign of the fecond Charles, bled for the caufe of freedom; and that great lawyer, Sir Edward Coke, the latter part of whofe life was devoted to the liberties of his country. With fuch progenitors, added to a fpirit of liberal enquiry, it is but little wonder that he fhould dare to think for himfelf, and become a ftickler for the popular caufe!

On

---

[*] " Memoirs of the Life of Gilbert Wakefield, B.A." 1 vol. 8vo. 1792.

On his origin, however, Mr. W. does not seem to plume himself:

"Malo pater tibi fit Therſites, dummodò tu fis
"Æacidæ fimilis, Vulcaniaque arma capeſſas;
"Therſitæ fimilem quàm te producat Achilles."

"Give me Therſites' ſon, who bravely wields
"Vulcanian armour in embattled fields,
"Before Therſites of Achilles' line;
"Degenerate offspring of a ſire divine!"

From his earlieſt infancy, the ſubject of theſe memoirs appears to have evinced a diſpoſition of mind uncommonly grave and ſerious. In addition to this, he diſplayed an ardent thirſt for knowledge, ſeldom equalled, perhaps never ſurpaſſed in any human boſom; and what is truly wonderful, it has always continued unimpaired to this hour. At the age of three years and three months, when he went to the ſchool of an ancient female, ſtill in exiſtence, he could ſpell the longeſt words, repeat his catechiſm without heſitation, and read the goſpels with fluency;—for this early proficiency, he was indebted to the attention of a kind mother. During the following Whitſuntide holidays, and at Chriſtmas in the ſame year, he diſplayed a memory equally precocious.

When he had attained his ſeventh year, he was initiated in the Latin language, at the free-ſchool of Nottingham, under the Rev. Dr. Samuel Beardmore, afterwards maſter of the Charter-houſe; but to this reſpectable ſcholar and gentleman, whom he characteriſes "as an acrimonious divine," he diſavows any obligations whatever, and, after a lapſe of thirty years, he ſtill recollects his threats.

At the age of nine he was removed to Wilford, near Nottingham, then under the direction of a preceptor, of different character, a man of unparalleled ſimplicity of manners; he erred, however, in being "righteous overmuch,"

for

for he subjected the pupils to a rigorous confinement, of no less than thirteen hours daily: with the intermission of only one hundred and twenty minutes, for breakfast and dinner. This practice is unfavourable to health, and militates against the salutary maxim of the Roman poet:

" Et puer es; nec te quicquam, nisi ludere, oportet;
" Lude; decent annos mollia regna tuos."

On the elder Mr. Wakefield's promotion to the vicarage of Kingston he was removed from restraints too irksome, even for a boy of his application, and placed under his father's curate. There, again, he was unfortunate, for his new preceptor proved to be one of those " pedagogical Jehu's," satirised by a great English* divine; and, indeed, it is not a little remarkable, when the importance of the subject is considered, how few are qualified for the task of instruction, and how careless parents in general are, respecting the choice of those who are to form the infant minds of their offspring.

At the age of thirteen, Mr. Wakefield, at length, found in the person of the Rev. Richard Wooddeson, father of the present Vinerian professor, a preceptor better suited to his taste, at least so far as discipline was concerned. His academy seemed a kind of *hot-bed* for seedling authors; Messrs. Steevens, Keate, Gibbon, Hayley, and Baron Maseres, being all nurtured there; yet he himself, hardly ever published any thing, and his store of latinity does not appear to have been great; but he possessed a benignant temper, and although armed with a *ferula* to the *full* as awful as the sceptre of a despot, his was a gentle reign.

After tasting the streams of Greek and Roman literature at their fountain head, his parents began to think of sending him

---

* See the discourse on " Education," (in his printed sermons, 6 vol. 8vo.) by Dr. Robert South, public orator of the university of Oxford, prebendary of Westminster, &c. &c. an able man, and a great time-server, but who could not get a bishoprick!

him to the univerfity, on which a ftudentcy in Chrift-church, Oxford, was offered him; this he *luckily* efcaped, in confequence of his father's predilection for his own college; and it ftill feems to afford a fubject of exultation to the fon, even in his riper years; as " orthodox theology, high church politics, and paffive obedience to the powers that be, fit enthroned," according to him, in a feminary, once " nutrix heroum," the venerable nurfe of Somers, Hales, Selden, Chillingworth, and Locke.

At length he obtained a fcholarfhip in Jefus College, Cambridge; and it fo happened, that he exactly fuited the intention of the founder, who preferred " the fon of a living clergyman, born at Nottingham," both of which conditions, as may have been obferved, happened to be united in him.

As foon as he was fettled at the univerfity, Mr. W. refumed his claffical ftudies, which had fuffered a long fufpenfion, in confequence of a putrid fore throat and fever, followed by a vacation of feveral months. The college lectures in algebra and logic, were, however, particularly odious to him. So enamoured was he of claffic ground, that it was long before he could prevail upon himfelf to approach the lefs inviting regions of fcience and philofophy. At laft, however, he overcame his prejudices, and actually opened Euclid, " The old Carpenter," as he was jocularly termed by a young man, who, like himfelf, had become a mathematician by compulfion.

During a five years continuance at Cambridge, he rofe by five o'clock in the morning, during both winter and fummer; but notwithftanding this, which implies a fevere attention to ftudy, he was fond of fociety at his meals.

In the third year of his refidence, he became a candidate for Dr. Browne's three medals, and accordingly produced a couple of odes in Greek and Latin, and alfo a pair of epigrams; the firft and laft exercifes, according to his own
opinion,

opinion, were unworthy of the reward, but he thought he was hardly ufed refpecting the Horatian ode; and had not the fon of Dr. Cooke, then provoft of King's, been a claimant at the fame time, it is highly probable, that he would have fuccceded.

His academical ftudies had hitherto refufed leifure for theological enquiries; a branch of learning, which his native ferioufnefs of difpofition, and his fpirit of enquiry rendered peculiarly appofite. At laft, during the long vacation of 1775, he began to cultivate Hebrew, without the aid of which, he deemed an acquaintance with the text of the new teftament impoffible.

On January 16th, 1776, he took his degree of B. A. with feventy-four other candidates for academical honours; and, on this occafion, he was nominated to the fecond poft. Soon after this, (April 16th,) he was elected fellow; and, in the courfe of the fame year, he printed at the univerfity-prefs, a fmall collection of latin poems, with a few notes on Horace, by way of appendix.

In 1777, he obtained the fecond of the four yearly prizes, prefented by the members for the univerfity. In 1778, he finifhed an exercife, at inns, &c. during a journey, which he had begun at college; this he trufted to the fidelity of a crofs-country waggoner, and firft learned his fuccefs through the medium of a London newfpaper! He thus appears to have been *fecond* wrangler, *fecond* medallift, and the *fecond* in the bachelor's prize for both years.

On the 22d of March, 1778, he was ordained a deacon by Dr. Hinchliffe, bifhop of Peterborough, in the chapel of Trinity college, at the age of twenty-two years and one month. It would appear, that previoufly to this period, the ftudent had enquired into the nature and tendency of fubfcription, having fince regarded his acquiefcence, in this point, as the moft difingenuous action of his whole life;

and

and ftigmatifed fome of the articles, as " unfufferably ftupid, " beyond the fottifhnefs of even Hottentot divinity."

On April 14th, Mr. W. left the univerfity for the curacy of Stockport, in Chefhire.

He did not, however, remain long here, for we find him, foon after, with his brother at Richmond, decidedly averfe to the renewal of fubfcription, and embarraffed at the idea of ecclefiaftical functions.

It is not a little remarkable, that Mr. W. feems, on this occafion, to have been nearly in the fame dilemma, in which a member of the very fame univerfity, and affuredly the greateft genius of his age, found himfelf about a century and a half before; for Milton thus expreffes himfelf, without any fcruple on the occafion, to a correfpondent who wifhed him to take orders, " to which," fays he, " by the intention of my parents and my friends, I was deftined of a child, and in mine own refolutions, till coming to fome maturity of years, and perceiving what tyranny had invaded the church, that he who would take orders, muft fubfcribe flave, and take an oath withall, which, unlefs he took, with a confcience that would retch, he muft either ftrait perjure or fplit his faith; I thought it better to prefer a blamelefs filence before the office of fpeaking bought and begun with fervitude and forfwearing."*

Every confcientious refolution, more efpecially when in evident oppofition to felf-intereft, favours of magnanimity; and fuch was actually the cafe in both inftances. Shut out from church preferment by principle, Mr. W. bethought himfelf of a lefs lucrative fituation, and accordingly applied for Breewood-fchool, in Staffordfhire, which he moft probably would have *obtained*, had it not been, that, even in

---

* " Reafon of Church Government, B. II. p. 41. edit. 1641, in 4to." See alfo the Hollis' edition of Milton's profe works, page 6.

this inftitution, fubfcription was actually neceffary, as if education were indiffolubly connected with the eftablifhed faith!

Soon after this difappointment, he accepted a curacy at Liverpool; and having here probed the creed of his forefathers to the quick, his refolution of detaching himfelf altogether from the church, became daily ftrengthened: notwithftanding this, he continued to preach a little longer, and his difcourfes feem to have had fuch an effect, even in that place, that one merchant (wonderful to tell!) was actually perfuaded at the interceffion of his wife, to fell his fhare in a privateer. Would to God, that he could have prevailed on the people of this fecond Nineveh to have relinquifhed their traffic in human blood!

On March 23d, 1779, he vacated his fellowfhip by marriage.

About the fame time, he exchanged the curacy of St. Peter's for that of St. Paul's, where he had more leifure for his ftudies; from an humble attempt to eftablifh a day-fchool, he was diverted by an offer of the tutorfhip of the claffical department at Warrington academy, in Lancafhire, whither he removed in Auguft, 1779. In this feminary, where he feems to have lived in great cordiality with his colleagues, he commenced his theological career, as an author, by a new tranflation of " the firft Epiftle of Paul to the Theffalonians," which appeared in 1781. A few months after, he publifhed his " Effay on Infpiration," on which fubject, he feems to agree with Dr. Geddes, the tranflator of the Bible; then his treatife on " Baptifm," begun and completed in nine days. Next year, his " New Tranflation of St. Matthew," with notes, &c. made its appearance; and this was finifhed within the compafs of a few weeks.

- In

In addition to these labours, he cultivated his acquaintance with the original Hebrew text of the old Testament, learned the Syriac and the Chaldee, acquired the Samaritan character, read the Pentateuch therein, and the Syro-Chaldaic version of it; to these were added the Æthiopic, Arabic, and Persic; lastly, he obtained a facility in the Coptic version of the New Testament, and made some improvements in the lexicon and grammar of that language. When to all this are added the daily avocations of a teacher, he must be allowed to have achieved more than Herculean labours!

On the dissolution of the Warrington academy, a removal took place in the autumn of 1783, to Bramcote, within four miles of Nottingham, where Mr. W. endeavoured, but in vain, to procure a few respectable pupils. In this rural retreat, he published the first volume of "An Enquiry into the Opinions of the Christian Writers of the three first Centuries, concerning the Person of Jesus Christ;" but notwithstanding the commendation of many excellent judges, he was not encouraged by the sale, to proceed with the continuation.

In May, 1784, we find him a second time fixed at Richmond, advertising for pupils, and renewing his applications to his friends. At Michaelmas, we again hear of him in his native town of Nottingham, and there he had three or four pupils under his care for several years, on very handsome terms; and about this time, he was elected an honorary member of the Philosophical Society of Manchester, in consequence of his "Essay on the Origin of Alphabetical Characters."

In 1786, he was seized with a pain in his left shoulder, and remained ill for two years, during which period he seems to have soothed his mind by "Remarks" on Mr. Gray's poems, and a new edition of the Georgics of Virgil, accompanied with criticisms. In the beginning of 1788, he attacked

attacked Dr. Horsley, whom he designates as " not the least conceited and audacious controversialist of ancient or modern days;" and in the autumn of the same year, he let off a fly cracker against the church, under the title of " Four Marks of Antichrist, or a Supplement to the Warburtonian Lecture."

The year 1789 ushered in his " Remarks on the Internal Evidence of the Christian Religion;" and also the first part of " Silva Critica;" the latter, which is from the Cambridge press, was published with a view to unite theological with classical learning, and to illustrate the scriptures by light borrowed from the philology of Greece and Rome.

On the establishment of the new college at Hackney, Mr. W. was deemed a proper person to fill the office of classical instructor; and he was at length appointed to this station, in July, 1790. His connexion, however, with the institution, was dissolved at the end of eleven months, having retired in June, 1791: the seminary did not long survive the loss.

Towards the latter end of the same year, appeared his " New Translation of the Teament, with Notes," in three volumes, 8vo. in a few weeks after, he published his pamphlet on " Religious Worship;" and in March, 1792, he favoured the world with " Memoirs of his own Life."

After a pretty considerable interval, in 1794, appeared " The Spirit of Christianity compared with the Spirit of the Times in Great Britain;" this is a politico-religious pamphlet, in which the author, with a manly freedom, enquires how far the public measures of the government, in the origin and continuance of the present war, are congenial to the precepts and the spirit of the gospel. Much about the same time, appeared the first volume of a new edition of " The Works of Alexander Pope, Esq. with Remarks and Illustrations." On this occasion, notwithstanding

ſtanding his taſte for the poets of antiquity, he allows that Pope ſometimes tranſcends even the original, particularly in he following four lines in his tranſlation of Homer, deſcribing the buckler of Achilles!

> "Thus the broad ſhield complete the artiſt crown'd
> "With his laſt hand, and pour'd the ocean round:
> "In living ſilver ſeem'd the waves to roll,
> "And beat the buckler's verge, and bound the whole."

"This is truly poetry to the life," added he:

> "Thoughts that breathe, and words that burn."

The ſame year alſo beheld "An Examination of the Age of Reaſon," in which, although Mr. W. boldly and ably defended chriſtianity, yet by conceding ſuch parts of the ſyſtem as were unſupportable by ſound reaſon, and more eſpecially by conſidering *national churches* not only "as hay and ſtraw, which might be removed without any difficulty, or confuſion, from the fabric of religion," but as an "incruſtation which has enveloped, by gradual concretion, the diamond of chriſtianity," he gave offence rather than ſatisfaction to the eſtabliſhed clergy, who did not chooſe that even their faith ſhould be defended at the expence of their tythes. This was ſoon followed by "Remarks on the general Orders of the Duke of York," in which, although the author ſtill contends againſt the juſtice of the war, he is yet candid enough to allow the conduct of his Royal Highneſs, on this occaſion, to have been great and magnanimous.

In 1795, appeared a ſmall volume of "Poetical tranſlations from the Ancients," and alſo "A Reply to Thomas Paine's ſecond Part of the Age of Reaſon," in which the beſt friends of Mr. W. while they allowed his talents, lamented that he did not defend chriſtianity with more of its

genuine

genuine spirit. The author himself dissented from the dissenters—and why could he not allow another man to dissent from him?

Persevering with unabated ardor in his career, in 1796, came forth his " Reply to the Letter of Edmund Burke, " Esq. to a noble Lord ;" in which he once more exhibited himself as a dauntless champion in the field of liberty, against a man whose rapturous eloquence had formerly excited his warmest panegyrics. He also published an 8vo. volume of " Observations on Pope," in the course of the same year.

" A Letter to Jacob Bryant, Esq. concerning his Dissertation on the War of Troy," at length appeared; however heterodox the author might be in matters of faith, he was a zealous oppugner of all heresies from the received classico-orthodoxical opinions. Another letter, on a very different subject, addressed to Mr. Wilberforce, respecting his " Practical View of the prevailing religious System of professed Christianity, &c." was published in 1797. In this, he exhibits the flagrant falling off in point of " vital christianity!" between the religionist and the politician, the favourer of war, and the opposer of the slave trade. In a former publication,* he had most forcibly characterised the same gentleman, " as a politico-theological satyr, with one breath cooling the burning anguish of the African, and with another in the same instant blasting the spring from the year, by giving his vote to an abandoned minister, for the extirpation of half the youth of Europe by the sword !"

Early in 1798, appeared " A Reply to some parts of the Bishop of Landaff's Address to the People of Great Britain." This pamphlet, which exhibits much personal respect to Dr. Watson, has become a Pandora's box, and produced an infinite variety of evils; it has been even thought to commit

the

---

* " A Reply to the Letter of Edmund Burke, Esq. to a noble Lord."

the safety of the state. Two convictions have already taken place, on the part of two booksellers, neither of whom were the original publishers; and it is not a little memorable, that it appeared, on the oath of an unobjectionable witness, that one of these (a man of unimpeachable morals, and most respectable character), was ignorant of the introduction of the pamphlet in question, into his shop, which happened to be brought thither on the suggestion of a servant, and was actually removed by the master, on hearing that it had been deemed libellous.*

It is but justice, however, to observe, that Mr. Wakefield came forward, on the prosecution of the original publisher :† and manfully offered to immolate himself to the resentment of the law officers of the crown :

" ——————— in me convertite ferrum,
" O! Rutuli! mea fraus omnis :—nihil iste nec ausus,
" Nec potuit ——————————.''

This *boon* being denied, he soon after addressed " A Letter to Sir John Scott, on the subject of a late trial in Guildhall." On that occasion, either not finding a bookseller, who would endanger his liberty, or not wishing to bring any person but himself into jeopardy, the pamphlet was advertised to be sold at his *own house*. In this publication he complains, in language which has given great offence, that the attorney-general had wielded " the sword of the law," with stern severity ; and in reply to an extra-judicial opinion from the bench, he sets the saying of an Athenian lawgiver, in opposition to the opinion of a British judge.

Undaunted

---

* The writer of this memoir was present in court, and lamented greatly, that Mr. Erskine did not make his chief stand on the grand distinction between the agency of a servant, *civiliter and criminaliter*, as the principal is implicated only in the first, and not in the second instance, which includes *libels*.

† Mr. Cuthell.

Undaunted by the threats of profecution* uttered in open court, and before his own face, by Sir John Scott, Mr. Wakefield, fince this epoch, has been employed in a controverfy with a Dr. Glaffe, refpecting the prifon in Cold Bath-fields. Certainly the fpirit of our laws difclaims every idea of torture, in refpect to all perfons, and clofe imprifonment in regard to political offenders in particular. Indeed, the latter, during the reign of Charles I. became the fubject of enquiry and complaint, and was at length redreffed. In other days, the rumours that have gone forth, concerning this newly-invented mode of durefs, would long, ere this, have become a fubject of parliamentary inveftigation; and it is to be hoped, that even the prefent age is not fo degenerate, if a real grievance fhould be found to exift, as to permit our mild, humane, and excellent code to be perverted with impunity.

Mr. Wakefield at prefent refides at Hackney, with his amiable family, confifting of a wife, formerly Mifs Watfon (niece to his quondam rector), four fons and two daughters. In perfon, he is about the middle fize; and there is an air of primitive fimplicity in his countenance and fomewhat of an *apoftolic* caft about his face; arifing, perhaps, in fome degree, from his high and polifhed forehead, and the baldnefs of his front and temples.

In converfation he is remarkably mild and gentle, and his manners are pleafing. His memory is fo uncommonly tenacious, that it can retain minute facts, and even dates, after a confiderable lapfe of time. No man is more beloved and refpected by a very extenfive circle of acquaintance. His perfonal activity is equal to that of his mind and pen. His habits are ftrictly domeftic and literary. He is a pattern of abftemioufnefs, and fhares in its happy refults, never partaking

---

* He has fince been ferved with an information *ex officio*.

taking of ſtrong liquors; and from a laudable principle of humanity, totally abſtaining from the uſe of animal food.— Mr. W. muſt, even by his enemies if they know him perſonally, be pronounced to be a man whoſe conduct is ſolely actuated by principle, and an inflexible love of virtue. He may err, but his faults are not the depravity of his heart— they can only reſult from too ardent an imagination, or from the miſtakes of his judgment.

A. S.

MR. OPIE.

NEITHER the parents, nor the education, nor the fortune of this eminent artift, would have conferred on him any diftinction in fociety, and, like the Englifh painters of the laft century, he might have worked at fo much by the *fquare yard*, had not nature conferred on him a portion of genius that foon diftinguifhed him from the vulgar herd.

Seemingly doomed, by inevitable circumftances, to work at the bottom of a faw-pit, or on the roof of a houfe, juft as the avocations of a country carpenter required, he yet found means to emerge from that fituation, and to move in a refpectable fphere in life. The late George Anderfon, A. M. and accountant-general to the Board of Control, contrived by chalking a few mathematical figures on the door of his brother's barn, in which he threfhed, to engage the attention of a benevolent patron, and to extricate himfelf from his mental bondage.

A fimilar accident difcovered the bent of John Opie's mind, and a painted board effected for him what a chalked gate had done for his acquaintance, as Dr. Wolcott, who had himfelf a tafte for drawing, and lived in the neighbourhood, happened to fee, and was pleafed with the labours of the felf-taught boy, of whom he, perhaps, exclaimed:

" NON SINE DIIS ANIMOSUS PUER!"

He accordingly took him under his protection, cultivated his talents, pointed his efforts, and taught him to afpire to

fame

fame and fortune. The master, with an aptitude bordering on the romantic, had transformed himself from a surgeon to a clergyman, and he now, with almost unexampled goodness, metamorphosed the apprentice of a carpenter into an historical painter.*

After some previous instruction, the pupil repaired to Exeter, where he began to earn a livelihood by his pencil. He then changed his place of abode, from a provincial city to the capital, and successively removed from a little court in the neighbourhood of Leicester fields, first to Great Queen-street, and then to the politer air, and more fashionable situation, of Berners-street. He had been four or five years in the metropolis, however, before he began to exhibit, as it was not until 1786, that any of his pictures appeared at Somerset-house.

From that moment wealth and reputation seemed to attend his efforts; he first was nominated an academician elect, then a member of the Royal Academy, and what was infinitely more profitable, became a " fashionable painter." For the Shakspeare gallery he executed several pictures, and is generally allowed to excel in historical compositions.

His beggars, old men, old women, and assassins, are admirable. The portrait of Mrs. Wolstoncraft, painted by him, excelled in verisimilitude; but his characteristical excellence consists in strength; and Reynolds himself, although he is praised for having transferred the soul into the countenance,

---

* It has been improperly suggested by the writer of the account of Dr. Wolcott, while mentioning the unfortunate coolness that took place, some censure was due to Mr. Opie; but we learn that no such thing was meant, either to be insinuated, or asserted; and if it had been, that it was quite undeserved.

nance, could never give, perhaps, fo bold and fpirited a likenefs of the male head, as Opie.

This artift has been twice married. His firft match was unpropitious, and did not add much to his felicity; his fecond wife (late Mifs Alderfon, of Norwich) is a moft accomplifhed, and no lefs beautiful woman; and we truft that the union of painting and literature will contribute to the mutual happinefs of the parties.

LORD ROKEBY.

(With a Prefatory Dissertation on Beards.)

THE *human beard,* at present deemed an unseemly excrescence, was considered by all the nations of antiquity as one of the greatest ornaments of the person; and gods, as well as mortals, were supposed to be decorated with this emblem of wisdom and virility. That of Aaron is described as flowing to his girdle, and the ambassadors of David, after having received the nearly indelible affront of being *shaved,* were advised to remain at a distance from the capital, until their beards had grown to the proper length. In many of the eastern countries this is still considered as a necessary, and even a beautiful appendage; and while the Turks carefully cover with their turbans, the hair that grows on their heads, they preserve, comb, perfume, and ostentatiously display, that which springs from the chin.

The northern nations seem also to have evinced a great veneration for their beards, and it is not yet much above a century since these have fallen into obloquy and disuse even in this country: they are, however, still retained by the *serfs* in Russia and Poland, and by the *boors* in Norway.

In our own island, the upper lips and chins of the northern barons in the train of the Conqueror, exhibited a small portion of beard, and the Saxo-Britons, who opposed them, had theirs still better ornamented. After the introduction of linen, which was but little known in this country before the conquest, beards seem to have disappeared by degrees, as if comporting only with the frowzy covering of a flannel shirt. We still, however, find vestiges of them even in more modern periods. That of James I. appears to have been broad and bushy. During the civil wars, Charles I. is both painted and described as wearing a narrow-pointed beard appended to the lower part of his chin, and *mustachios* on the upper lip; the great Algernon Sydney appears in the plate engraved by Basire, from a drawing of Cipriani, prefixed to the Hollis' edition of his works, to have worn *mustachios** only; but most of the republicans of that day seem to have nursed their beards in proportion as they polled their heads.

Both the French and Austrians appear of late to have considered whiskers as an appendage to the military dress, and from the inroads they have lately made in this country, on the human face, it bids fair to be soon nearly as much shaded by them as it was formerly by the beards.

These preliminary remarks will not appear totally misplaced, perhaps, to such as are acquainted with the person of the noble lord whose memoirs are here offered to the public, as his beard forms one of the most conspicuous *traits* of his person; and he is the only peer, and, perhaps, the only gentleman of either Great Britain or Ireland, who is thus distinguished.

MATTHEW ROBINSON, Baron Rokeby, of the kingdom of Ireland, and also a baronet, is descended from a very old and respectable family, being a branch of the Robinsons of Struan, in Scotland, whence his ancestors emigrated about one hundred and fifty years since, and settled in Kent; they soon after acquired some lands in the north riding

---

* The celebrated Sir William Temple, who flourished at a later period, is painted by Sir Peter Lely with *whiskers*.

riding of Yorkshire, which came to them by an intermarriage with the heiress of Robert Walters, of Cundall, in the latter end of the last century.

Sir Septimus Robinson, Knt. father of the present peer, was gentleman-usher to George II. He gave his son, Matthew, a most excellent education; but it was, perhaps, never suspected by the old courtier that he would become one of the most sturdy patriots of his age, a " Whig," according to the real meaning of the word, and as such, an assertor of the true principles of English liberty, which called in William III. and placed the present illustrious family on the throne. After a good foundation of classical learning, he sent him to Cambridge, where he remained for several years; and he appears to have made considerable progress in his studies; for he procured a fellowship there, which he retains to this day.

In 1754, he succeeded, on the death of his father, to his estate in East Kent, and appears to have lived at his mansion there, with all the easy affluence, hospitality, and splendor, that characterised the English gentry of that day, when a land-tax at about two shillings in the pound, and a trifling malt-tax, constituted their only burdens. During the winter, part of his time was spent in the capital, and in the summer season, he was accustomed to pass away a month or two at Sandgate castle, where he enjoyed a charming prospect of the coast of France; while sea-bathing, to which he was much addicted, was to be had there in great perfection.

In consequence of his vicinity to Canterbury, and a family connexion with that place,* he had many opportunities of cultivating an intimacy with the principal inhabitants.

Being

---

* This, until of late, was carefully kept up; his brother, Charles, who had been originally bred to the sea, but afterwards became a lawyer, having been successively Recorder, and one of the members for that city.

Being a man of engaging manners, shrewd sense, and independent fortune, they determined to nominate him their representative on the first vacancy. He was accordingly brought into parliament by them, and he faithfully discharged all the important duties annexed to that situation for a long series of years.

We find Mr. Robinson, during the whole of the American war, one of the most strenuous oppugners of a measure pregnant with gigantic mischief, and which by the enormous encrease of our national debt, generated oppressive taxes, and became the parent of incalculable misfortunes to ourselves and our posterity. Not content with opposing Lord North with his voice in the senate, he entered the lists against him with his pen, and published a pamphlet pregnant with sound sense, manly argument, and liberal sentiment. In fine, it was then looked upon as one of the most able productions of that day; and it struck the author of this narrative, who borrowed it some years since from one of his relatives, as a kind of *political-prophecy*, of the calamities which actually arose out of a system of taxation without representation, and coercion without power.

He lived long enough to see all his predictions verified. Our legions either withered away in a distant country, or, if victorious, they only retained in subjection such portions of territory as were covered with soldiery, or immediately adjoined the spot on which they encamped;—all else was hostile. Conquest itself became precarious, and defeat was inevitably attended with the endless variety of evils incident to disaster in an enemy's country. At length Burgoyne was captured at Saratoga; France declared herself in favour of the insurgent colonies; Holland and Spain became our enemies; Cornwallis, who has since fought under better auspices in India and Ireland, laid down his arms to Rochambeau and Washington; and a bleeding and exhausted empire was

was obliged to accede to the humiliating, but neceſſary, preliminary of American independence.

The eſcape of all the authors of that difaſtrous conflict from puniſhment, and the ſpeedy reſtoration of one* of them to power, difguſted many good men of that day; and it required, indeed, but little foreſight to preſage the many evils with which *impunity* was connected. Mr. Robinſon appears to have entertained theſe, or ſimilar ſentiments, and to have retired from the ſcene with a degree of virtuous indignation highly appropriate and becoming.

What contributed to this, perhaps, was his bodily infirmities. From his youth he had been ſubject to many ſevere fits of illneſs, and, in addition to theſe, his hearing and his ſight were confiderably affected. In this ſtate of body and mind, he deemed it highly improper for him any longer to occupy a ſeat in parliament, as he could not either diſcharge his duties with fidelity to his conſtituents, or ſatisfaction to himſelf. Impreſſed with this ſentiment, he addreſſed a letter to the inhabitants of Canterbury, in which he took an affectionate leave of them, and is ſaid to have mentioned to one of the principal citizens (perhaps the late Alderman Barham), " that they ought to chooſe a younger, and more
" vigorous man, as a ſucceſſor;—one who had eyes to ſee,
" ears to hear, and lungs to oppoſe, the *tricks* of future
" miniſters!"

From this period his hiſtory becomes that of a private gentleman. He refided conſtantly at Mountmorris, and lived equally without oſtentation, and without meanneſs. He planted, improved, and embelliſhed. His houſe was open to all reſpectable ſtrangers, and he was much viſited, on account of the ſingularity of his manners, and the ſhrewdneſs of his remarks. A great friend to agriculture,

C c   his

---

* Lord North, in conſequence of the memorable coalition!

his tenants in him experienced a most excellent landlord. As for himself, he seems to have banished the deer from his park, as an unprofitable luxury, and to have supplied their place with black cattle and sheep, of which great numbers are always to be seen there.

It was most probably about this time that Mr. Robinson first permitted his beard to grow; for it must have taken many years to attain the *patriarchal* length which it at present assumes. He also addicted himself to many other seeming singularities; and imagining, perhaps, that sea-bathing was good for the disorder * he was chiefly afflicted with, he built a little hut on the beach near Hythe, about three miles from his own house, in order to enjoy the advantages resulting from it. It is most likely, however, that he indulged to excess in this *medicine,* for he frequently remained in the water, until he fainted.

Finding the distance too great, perhaps, for him to walk,† he constructed a bath, so contrived as to be rendered tepid by means of the rays of the sun only; it is immediately adjoining his house, and he has found prodigious benefit from ablutions, or rather immersions therein.‡

On

---

* A disease of the intestines.

† He was generally accompanied in these excursions by a carriage, and a favourite servant, who got up behind when he was tired. Mr. Robinson, with his hat under his arm, proceeded slowly forward, on foot, towards Hythe, realising, as it were, the picture of Gray, in which he paints the venerable figure of one of the Welch poets:

—— " Loose his beard and hoary hair,
" Stream'd like a meteor to the troubled air."

If it happened to rain, he would make his attendants get into the post-chaise, observing, " that they were gaudily dressed, and not inured to wet, therefore might spoil their clothes, and get ill."

‡ The writer of this sketch, happening to be in the neighbourhood, towards the latter end of the summer of 1796, determined to see Mr. Robinson, who had then acceded to the title of Lord Rokeby. On his way to

Mountmorris,

On October 10th, 1794, he succeeded, by the death of his uncle, Richard Robinson, Bishop of Armagh, primate of Ireland, and Baron Rokeby of the same kingdom, to his honours as an Irish peer. The patent of creation was granted to that dignitary, February 26th, 1777, and by it the remainder is to vest in the present lord; but, as Mr. Robinson was either angry that his nephew, Matthew Robinson, who sat in the last parliament for Boroughbridge, in Yorkshire, should

Mountmorris, at the summit of the hill above Hythe, which affords a most delightful prospect, he perceived a fountain of pure water over-running a bason which had been erected for it by his lordship. He was informed that there were many such on the same road, and that Lord R. was accustomed to bestow a few half-crown pieces, plenty of which were always kept by him loose in a side-pocket, on any *water-drinkers*, he might happen to espy, partaking of his favourite beverage, which he was sure to recommend with peculiar force and persuasion.

On my approach to the house, I stopped during some time, in order to examine it. It is a good plain gentleman's seat; the grounds were abundantly stocked with black cattle, and I could perceive a horse or two, on the steps of the principal entrance.

After the proper enquiries, I was carried by a servant to a little grove, to the right of the avenue, which being entered at a small swing-gate, a building with a glass covering, dipping obliquely towards the south-west, presented itself, which at first sight appeared to be a green-house. The man who accompanied me opened a little wicket, and, on looking in I perceived a bath, immediately under the glass, with a current of water, supplied from a pond behind. On approaching a door, two handsome spaniels, with long ears, and apparently of King Charles's breed, approached, and like faithful guardians denied us access, until soothed into security by the well-known accents of the domestic. We then proceeded, and gently passing along a wooden floor, saw his lordship stretched on his face at the further end. He had just come out of the water, and was dressed in an old blue woollen coat, and pantaloons of the same colour. The upper part of his head was bald, but the hair on his chin, which could not be concealed, even by the posture he had assumed, made its appearance between his arms on each side.

I immediately retired, and waited at a little distance until he awoke; when arising, he opened the door, darted through the thicket, accompanied by his dogs, and made directly for the house, while some workmen employed in cutting timber, and whose tongues only I had heard before, now made the woods resound again with their axes.

should have been so poorly left, after the splendid hopes held out to him, or really entertained objections to titles of all kinds; certain it is, that he declined the honorary appellation, and is said to have declared, that he could not on any account have accepted an English peerage, meaning thereby, perhaps, that he considered the former as merely *titular*.

Lord Rokeby is nearly eighty years of age; the upper part of his body, by assuming a *curvature*, makes him appear shorter than he would otherwise be. There are certain oddities discoverable in his dress, which is always plain, and even mean; his forehead is bald, but in return for this, the under part of his face is well furnished with hair, which, however, gives somewhat of a squalid appearance to his whole person.* His food principally consists of beef-tea, which is always ready for him on a side-board; and he is very abstemious in respect to drink, water being esteemed by him as superior to all other liquids whatever. He abhors fires, and delights much in the enjoyment of the air, without any other canopy than the heavens; even in winter his windows are generally open. He was much attached to the fair sex in his youth, and even now is a great admirer of female beauty.

In respect to politics, his conduct through life, and to this very hour, has been eminently consistent; it is to principles, not men, that he looks up; and he seems to consider a Stewart, or a Guelph, entitled to our praise or our hatred, not on account of their names (for these have no magic with him!) but the difference of their respective modes of government.

At the last general election, he crossed the country to Lenham, and at the *Chequers* inn, at which he halted, was

surrounded

---

* There is a pretty good likeness to be met with of Lord Rokeby in the stationers' shops at Canterbury. It consists of a half-length coloured print.

surrounded by the country people from all the adjoining parts, who took him for a Turk! Thence he proceeded to the poll-booth, and gave his vote for his old friend Filmer Honeywood.

Many ridiculous stories are fabricated respecting his lordship, and among others, that he will not permit any of his tenants to sow barley, because barley may be converted into malt, and malt would pay a tax towards carrying on the war, which he conceives to be an unjust one, &c. &c.

The family of Lord Rokeby has long possessed a literary turn, and he himself may be justly considered as a man of letters. It was a relative of his who wrote the celebrated treatise on *gavel-kind*. His eldest sister, Mrs. Montagu, has triumphantly defended the memory and genius of Shakspeare, against the criticisms, perhaps, of the* greatest man of the day. His other sister, Mrs. Scott, who died in 1795, wrote several novels, some of which have attained considerable reputation; his nephew, and successor, Morris Robinson, has a taste for poetry; and Matthew Montague, the brother of the latter, and heir to the celebrated lady of the same name, is author of a pamphlet on Mr. Pitt's administration.

As for his lordship himself, he published the valuable, and now very *scarce* tract, alluded to before, and at an age when most old men think only of themselves, he has not been inattentive to what he considers the dearest interests of his country; having, in 1797, published an excellent pamphlet, entitled, " An Address to the County of Kent, on their Petition to the King for removing from the Councils of his Majesty his present Ministers, and for adopting proper means to procure a speedy and a happy Peace; together with a Postscript concerning the Treaty between the Emperor of Germany

* Voltaire.

Germany and France, and concerning our Domestic Situation in time to come."

In short, his lordship, *even independent of his beard*, which alone attracts the gaze of the multitude, may be considered as a very singular man.

He lives a considerable portion of his life in water, tempered by the rays of the sun.

He travels on foot at a time of life when men of his rank and fortune *always* indulge in a carriage.

He is abstemious, both in respect to eating and drinking, amidst a luxurious age, wallowing in the excesses of both.

He has attained to great longevity, without having recourse to the aid of pharmacy, and, indeed, with an utter contempt of the venders and practitioners of physic,* whose presence he is reported to have interdicted.

He has written a sensible pamphlet, at an age when every other man (Cornaro, perhaps, only excepted) has relinquished his pen.

By temperance, exercise, and perhaps, also, in consequence of frequent bathing, his body is so braced, as to enable him to sit in winter without a fire. He has also combated, during a long life, a very infirm constitution, and a disease generally considered as fatal.

And lastly, what is, perhaps, more singular than all the rest, he has been *wonderfully* consistent; for he has never once, in the whole course of his life, been found to swerve from

---

* I have heard that when *a paroxysm* was expected to come on, his lordship has told his nephew, that if he staid he was welcome; but that if he called in medical assistance, out of a false humanity, and it should accidentally happen, that he (Lord R.) was not *killed by the doctor*, he hoped he should have sufficient use of his hands and senses left, to make a new will, and disinherit him.

from his principles; in fine, he will carry to his grave the character of being virtuous and independent in a country becoming famous for its servility, venality, and corruption.

May the day that is to put an end to his existence be far off, and may his mind be cheered, at the last awful moment, with the recollection of his benevolence and his patriotism!

S.

LORD NELSON.

REAR-ADMIRAL, now Lord, Nelſon, to whom his country is ſo much indebted for his brilliant ſervices, is the fourth ſon of the Rev. Mr. Nelſon, late rector of Burnham-Thorpe, in the county of Norfolk, in the parſonage-houſe of which pariſh his lordſhip was born, September 29th, 1758. His father's family came originally from Hilborough in the ſame county; where they poſſeſſed a ſmall patrimony, and the patronage of the living. His mother was Miſs Suckling, daughter of the Rev. Dr. Suckling, of Suffolk; granddaughter of the late Sir Charles Turner, of Warham, of this county, by his lady, the ſiſter of Sir Robert Walpole. Captain Suckling, his maternal uncle, was his lordſhip's early and very valuable friend in life. He was an officer in the ſea-ſervice; in which he firſt commanded the Raiſonable of ſixty-four guns; then the Triumph; and laſtly died comptroller of the navy. This gentleman married a ſiſter of the preſent Lord Walpole, and was, of courſe, much in Norfolk. He took young Nelſon, at twelve years of age, from North Walſham-ſchool, in the ſame county, and entered him as Midſhipman on board the Raiſonable. Here the nephew ſerved ſome time, with the valuable officer who now commands that ſhip off the Mauritius; and with Captain Charles Boyles, his friend, and neighbour in the country, then alſo a midſhipman: and from this ſhip they both removed with Captain Suckling into the Triumph, when he obtained the command of her.

On April the 10th, 1777, Mr. Nelſon was made a lieutenant, and ſent out by his uncle to Sir Peter Parker, in Jamaica, who then commanded upon that ſtation. He was by Sir Peter ſhortly afterwards made maſter and commander.

On

On the 11th of June, 1779, he was appointed poſt captain, and at the concluſion of the American war, returned home. Capt. Nelſon was next ſent out in the Boreas frigate, to the leeward iſland ſtation; and had under him, his Royal Highneſs the Duke of Clarence, who commanded the Pegaſus. Here the captain is ſaid to have rendered a ſignal ſervice to his Royal Highneſs, for which he afterwards honoured him with his friendſhip.

It was upon this ſtation, and we believe about this period, that his lordſhip formed a matrimonial alliance with his preſent lady, Mrs. Neſbit, of Nevis, widow of Dr. Neſbit, phyſician, and niece to the governor of the iſland: and, when the marriage ceremony was performed, the Duke of Clarence, it is ſaid, gave away the bride. And here it would be unjuſt not to mention a report, which does credit to the captain's integrity, and nice ſenſe of honour: Mr. Herbert, governor of the iſland, was extremely rich, and had an only child, a daughter, who was to have inherited her father's fortune. By marrying without his conſent, ſhe had forfeited his eſteem, and was upon the point of being diſinherited in favour of his niece; when the admiral generouſly interfered—and had the pleaſure, before his marriage, of reſtoring the daughter to her parents' affection, and the fortune to its natural channel.

While his lordſhip continued upon this ſtation, he had under him a ſmall ſquadron of frigates; and was particularly active in ſuppreſſing ſmuggling, a practice but too prevalent in thoſe ſeas. This vigilance was acceptable to all parties, except the ſmugglers, and their friends; who threatened, and would actually have involved him in expenſive litigations, had not the Admiralty interpoſed to reſcue him from their malice.

Upon quitting the ſtation, he returned to his native country, and, as there was no immediate call for his ſervices,

services, retired with Mrs. Nelson to the parsonage house at Burnham; which his father gave up to him, preferring a residence in the neighbourhood. In this retreat, his lordship led a quiet, domestic life for some years; like Gil Blas, at Llyrias, inclined to write over the door of his cottage:

> "Inveni portum. Spes & Fortuna valete;
> "Sat me lusistis: ludite nunc alios."

and, like him, inclined to return into the world, when more active scenes demanded his attendance.

By his lady, the admiral has no family; but there is a son of Lady Nelson, by her first marriage, (Mr. Nesbit,) who is a post-captain, and has served under his lordship during the whole period of the present war. Besides his wife, and her son, Lord Nelson has now living of his near relations, first, his father, who resides near Ipswich; next, his eldest brother, Maurice, a clerk in the navy; two brothers, clergymen, William, Rector of Hilborough, Suckling, Rector of Burnham-Thorpe; and two sisters, both married.

Upon the breaking out of the present war, his lordship was early appointed to the command of the Agamemnon, of sixty-four guns. Of this ship's company, a considerable part was raised in the counties of Norfolk and Suffolk; and not a few in his own neighbourhood. The general opinion of his conduct and abilities, as an officer, was such, that several gentlemen were desirous to place their sons under his command; and some of considerable respectability solicited, and obtained this favour: in particular, the Rev. Mr. Bolton, his lordship's relation, and the Rev. Mr. Hoste and Wetherhead, his friends, entered their sons as midshipmen on board the Agamemnon; and, it must be owned, that if they wished to give them a just knowledge of their profession, founded on a valuable body of experience, they could not

have

have selected a better master. Poor Wetherhead fell nobly at Santa Cruz, the others still continue with his lordship, and have merited his esteem and affection.

From the commencement of the war, to the present moment, the public are in possession of the general out-lines of his lordship's life. During a considerable part of the time that he commanded the Agamemnon in the Mediterranean, scarcely a gazette appeared, but it contained an account of some service performed, or of some enterprise undertaken. If a merchantman was to be cut out of harbour, a battery to be dismounted, a town to be attacked, the commodore generally placed himself in the " hottest battle," and exposed his person to the same danger as the meanest seaman. Such voluntary contempt of danger, although it is not always prudent in the commander, is certainly generous, and often leads to success. Men will do more, and with greater pleasure, when they find that nothing is required on one hand, but what is submitted to on the other: and great examples will justify great expectations.

In a profession like the sea-service, calculated to raise heroes, by inuring the mind to difficulty and enterprise, it would be unjust to extol one character at the expence of others; yet in the triumph of that glorious day, when lord St. Vincent, with a far inferior force, beat the Spanish fleet off cape St. Vincent, and captured four of their large ships, no inconsiderable share belongs to Nelson. The San Joseph, and the San Nicholas, both vessels of superior force, struck to him. The sword of the Spanish Admiral, which he received upon quarter-deck, and which the Spaniard refused to deliver to any but his lordship, he presented to the corporation of Norwich; as he has done lately that of the French Admiral Blanquet, to the corporation of London.

Upon

Upon the occasion of the action off Cape St. Vincent, his lordship was created knight of the Bath; and, about the same time, Rear Admiral of the Blue.

In estimating Lord Nelson's services, it is not an individual atchievement we have to admire, in which, perhaps, good fortune had at least as much share as good conduct; but it is a series of successes, for the most part planned with judgment, and executed with spirit. " Some men," says Lord Bacon, " follow Fortune, others *lead* her." The admiral appears to be of the last description. The glorious battle of the Nile, for which he has recently been rewarded with a peerage, has engaged so much attention, and has already been so minutely described, that it is unnecessary to enlarge here on the subject. It will stand upon record, as one proof, among many, of what British sailors, commanded by able officers, can effect in her arduous enterprizes. The celebrity of Lord Nelson's name, has added another laurel to the honours of a county, already distinguished for the eminent characters it has produced.* We learn from the history of Norfolk, that at the little village of Cockthorpe, not far from Burnham, three seamen of great celebrity were born; namely, Sir John Narborough, Sir Cloudesley Shovel, and Sir Christopher Minns.

When men have raised themselves by their abilities to any unexpected elevation in the ranks of society, their habits in private life become objects of curious enquiry. Though the *great* man may shine in the bustle of the world, it has well been observed, that the *man* can only be seen in private.

Piety, or a just sense of the superintending providence of God—the virtue, without which all others are but as " dust and

* While the politician regards the late battle with an eye that includes *all Europe*, the rustics of Burnham observe, that it was fought on " Burnham fair-day;" and consider this as not the least valuable circumstance attached to the event.

and afhes"—has confiderable influence on Lord Nelfon's mind, as is known to his more intimate acquaintance; and as may be collected from the proëmium of his difpatches to Earl St. Vincent, after the battle of the Nile: " My Lord, ——— ". ALMIGHTY GOD has bleffed his Majefty's arms by a great victory," &c. Parental piety, which the Romans efteemed fo highly, as well as conjugal tendernefs and affection for relations, which are the foundations of our focial fyftem, are alfo confpicuous in his character. His attention to his father was always remarkable; the old gentleman had a practice, when the weather permitted, of walking for an hour before dinner: the admiral, however occupied, fcarcely ever failed to accompany him in thefe walks. When, after the unfuccefsful attempt at Santa-Cruz, his lordfhip lay ill, in confequence of the amputation of his right arm,* and it was uncertain what might be the event, it is faid that his principal anxiety was for his relations, rather than himfelf; and that he wrote to the Admiralty, with his left hand, recommending Mr. Nefbit to their notice, in cafe he fhould die.

His attachment, however, to relations is not ftronger than is his regard for ftrangers in diftrefs. He entertains a juft fenfe of the duties of benevolence: † inftances of which might eafily be adduced, did the limits of this memoir permit. And fo ftrong are his feelings of private friendfhip, that, when returned from a diftant climate, he has been known to fhed tears upon meeting an old friend unexpectedly. To fome, thefe circumftances may appear trivial, and light; but

---

* When Lord Nelfon received the wound that fhattered his right-arm, he was in a boat, and held a fword that had been given him by his uncle, Captain Suckling, which he prized highly. Upon this occafion, he had the good fortune to fave it from falling into the water, by catching it with his left hand. This circumftance is faid to have given him peculiar pleafure.

† The noble Admiral, laft winter, fent down a large collection of blankets to his native village, to be diftributed among the poor.

but to others, no less discerning, they will appear interesting; because they display feelings inseparable from magnanimity, and afford the best insight into his real character.

When we compare Lord Nelson's present with his former fortune, and consider the early period of success and elevation in life, we may, perhaps, *inadvertently* conclude, that he has been exuberantly rewarded. When, however, on the other hand, we call to mind the loss of an eye, and an arm, in the service of his country; a wound received in the head; a position carried, which the French, the best engineers in the world, deemed impregnable; an expedition frustrated that alarmed all Europe;—we must readily retract such conclusions. That he has risen to his present eminence without the co-operation of powerful friends, is perfectly unnecessary to remark. In a state of society, men are formed for each other, and exist by mutual support; but whatever favours of this kind Lord Nelson may have received, he has amply deserved by the merit of his conduct. How different this, from those cases, in which some men, without any personal abilities, are raised to the first ranks in society, by the mere *force* of *patronage*; and, like the stone of Sisyphus, are always likely to recoil on the heads of those that raised them!

In respect to person, Lord Nelson is about the middle height; thin, and somewhat inelegantly formed. He is a man of few words, and plain manners; but possesses great sincerity, and a sound understanding. He is evidently a man of genius; since no one but a master in the profession could have discovered the *only* point in which the French line was vulnerable, and have availed himself of it so dexterously. Although the attack at Aboukir was successful, it was not made without considerable hazard, since the Culloden, which should have led into action, under the command of an able officer, actually ran aground. During the last war, Admiral Barrington, in the West-Indies, took nearly a simi-

lar

lar pofition to that of Aboukir; which was confidered as impregnable; and, in fact, when the French made their attack upon him, fuch it proved.

In every point of view, we are warranted in concluding, that Lord Nelfon has rendered a moſt important ſervice to humanity by his late decifive and fplendid victory. If the hoftile cabinets of Europe fhould prudently avail themfelves of its impreffion upon the enemy, and of the proud and commanding fituation in which it has placed their forces, an honourable and glorious peace may be the happy refult. The profpect of a general and lafting amnefty is, indeed, the only point of view in which the defolations of war can be, in any degree, tolerable to a feeling mind; the dreadful price of one victory, well improved, tends to prevent further effufions of blood. An enemy grows more reafonable as he becomes lefs powerful; and thus partial evil is productive of univerfal good. A. N. S.

LORD VISCOUNT HOOD,

ADMIRAL OF THE BLUE.

THE spirit of the christian religion is manifestly averse to war, but notwithstanding this, certain it is, no class of the community has produced a greater number of naval and military officers than the clergy of Great Britain.

The subject of this article was born in Somersetshire, and his father was first vicar of Butleigh, in that county, and then rector of Thornecombe, in Devonshire. His place of residence and education, after he had grown up, being in a maritime situation, gave him a taste for a seafaring life; and his propensity to that calling being irresistible, he was stationed on the quarter deck of a man-of-war, and entered on the books as a midshipman. Happening to serve under Admiral Smith, who sat as president of the famous court-martial on the unfortunate Byng, he attained the rank of lieutenant, by his patronage, and distinguished himself, on various occasions, by his personal intrepidity: in consequence of one act of gallantry in particular, he received a wound in the hand, but happily effected his purpose, which was the most desperate an officer can be employed in—that of cutting out and capturing a vessel belonging to the enemy, by means of an armed boat.

In the beginning of the memorable contest, denominated from the period of its duration *the seven years war*, he was promoted to the rank of post-captain, and soon after obtained the Vestal, a frigate of thirty-two guns. Having left Portsmouth, on the 13th of February, 1759, under Admiral Holmes, and happening to be to windward, he descried the Bellona, a French vessel of equal force, commanded

manded by Count Beauhanoir; on this, Captain Hood instantly made sail *a-head*, came to close quarters, and commenced and continued an action of nearly four hours duration, which ended in the capture of his antagonist.

On this occasion, he certainly had the advantage over the enemy, in what is emphatically termed *a clear ship*, just out of port, while the count's had been distant many months from Europe, and was then on her return from Martinico, which had been attacked by an English squadron, and soon after surrendered to his Majesty's arms. This, however, was considered as so gallant an action, that the famous circumnavigator, Lord Anson, then at the head of the admiralty, presented the young captain to George II. who had the command of the Africa of sixty-four guns immediately conferred upon him, as a reward for his conduct.

On the peace of Paris, Captain Hood, with a crowd of other brave sea-officers, as well as the vessels they had commanded, were *laid up in ordinary*. He, however, had the good fortune to be moored in a very prosperous birth; for knowing that interest in times of tranquillity was to the full as good as merit during hostilities, and induced, no doubt, also by the still more powerful seductions of love and attachment, he had contrived, in 1753, to form a matrimonial alliance with Miss Susanna Lindzee, daughter of the Mayor of Plymouth, a gentleman who possessed great interest in the corporation. By this lady, he had a son, born in the course of the succeeding year, who is now the Honourable Captain Hood, an officer not inferior to his father in point of bravery and enterprize, and who has distinguished himself very eminently in the course of the present war, by the seaman-like conduct he displayed in escaping from the batteries of Toulon, the port of which he had entered under the idea of its being still in the possession of the English.

When the unfortunate conteft took place with America, the fubject of thefe memoirs accepted a command, and it is not a little memorable, that but one* military, and no one naval officer feemed to think it either unconftitutional or unjuft. In November, 1768, we find him on the Bofton ftation, and it is much to his honour that while General Gage, and fome other officers, were deceiving the nation and the miniftry, about the quiet and peaceable difpofition of the inhabitants in general, and anticipating the fpeedy punifhment of Wafhington, Adams, Hancock, &c. then denominated " rebels" but now recognized by recent treaties among " our good and faithful allies," he boldly and manfully told the truth, and defcribed the colonies as in a ftate of ferment and diffatisfaction, not eafily to be quieted.

In a fhort time, France, governed by the ufual policy of ftates, and deeming this a fair opportunity, by difmembering the colonies, to leffen the ftrength and diminifh the refources of Great Britain, determined to exert herfelf in behalf of America; and foon after the capture of General Burgoyne, Louis XVI. entered into a commercial treaty with that power, now afpiring to attain the independence which it had meditated and proclaimed. On this, the king of England withdrew his ambaffador from Verfailles, and declared war.

The dominions of France being fuppofed moft vulnerable in the extremities, it was determined to fend a powerful fleet to the Weft-Indies. Sir Samuel Hood, now an admiral,† and a baronet, went thither, and foon diftinguifhed himfelf by his intrepidity and fkill, particularly in the Baffe-Terre Road, February, 1782; when, with an inferior fleet, he foiled the Count de Graffe. That officer, who began to be celebrated, in confequence of his exploits in America,

* Lord Effingham, afterwards governor of Jamaica.
† He received his flag in 1780.

America, intended to make a defcent on Barbadoes, the oldeft of our fettlements in the Weft-Indies; but being driven to leeward by the currents, he determined to attack St. Kitts, at which place he had arrived with twenty-nine two-deckers; but the Englifh fquadron, confifting of only twenty-two large fhips, formed a line of battle, and manœuvred in fuch a manner as to entice the French admiral to quit the anchorage, which was inftantly occupied by his more dexterous antagonift. Next morning, Sir Samuel was attacked by the whole French fleet, but he gave them fo warm a reception, that they were foon obliged to fheer off.* Notwithftanding this fervice, and the prediction of the Englifh commander refpecting the defence of the Brimftone hill, St. Kitts foon after furrendered to General Bouille, then a moft enterprifing commander, and now an emigrant in this country.

In the important victory of the 12th of April, of the fame year, which would have been ftill more memorable in the annals of Great Britain, had it not been eclipfed by the brilliant achievements of a recent period, we find Admiral Hood acting as fecond in command; and it is thus that Sir George Brydges Rodney, Bart. commander in chief, fpeaks of his fervices in his difpatches, dated Formidable, April 14th, 1782.

" It has pleafed God, out of his divine providence, to grant
" to his majefty's arms a moft complete victory over the fleets of
" his enemies, commanded by Count de Graffe, who is himfelf
" captured, with the Ville de Paris, and four other fhips, befides
" one funk in the action.

" Both fleets have greatly fuffered; but it is with the higheft
" fatisfaction I can affure their lordfhips, that though the mafts,
" fails, rigging, and hulls of the Britifh fleet are damaged, yet the
" lofs

* " Many of the French fhips muft have fuffered very confiderably, and
" the Ville de Paris was upon the heel all the next day, covering her fhot-
" holes. By information from the fhore, the French fhips have fent to
" St. Euftatius upwards of 100 wounded men."

Letter from Sir S. Wood, Bart. to Mr. Stephens of the Admiralty.

"loss of men has been small, considering the length of the
"battle, and the close action they so long sustained, and in which
"both fleets looked upon the honour of their king and country
"to be most essentially concerned. The great supply of naval
"stores lately arrived in the West-Indies, will, I flatter myself,
"soon repair all the damages his majesty's fleet has sustained.

"*The gallant behaviour of the officers and men of the fleet I have
"the honour to command, has been such as must for ever endear them
"to all the lovers of their king and country. The noble behaviour
"of my second in command,* SIR SAMUEL HOOD, *Bart.* who in
"both actions most conspicuously exerted himself, demands my warm-
"est encomiums. My third in command, Rear Admiral Drake, who
"with his division led the battle on the 12th, deserves the highest
"praise,* &c.

Immediately after the engagement, Admiral Samuel Hood, to whom the French admiral had struck his colours, was dispatched by Sir George to the Mona Passage, in order to intercept such of the enemy's squadron as might endeavour to escape in that direction. In consequence of this, he captured two line-of-battle ships and two frigates, on the 9th of April, 1782, with the loss of only six killed and fourteen wounded, and on the commander in chief's repairing to Port-Royal harbour, in Jamaica, with the enemy's ships, and such of his own squadron as were crippled, he left his second, with all the men-of-war capable of keeping the sea, amounting to about twenty-five sail of the line, off Cape François, in St. Domingo, with a view to watch the enemy's motions, and prevent any further hostile movements on their part.

The peace, that soon after ensued, once more interrupted the professional exertions of Admiral Hood; he was now decorated,

---

* Sir Samuel on this occasion led the van division, consisting of the Royal Oak, Alfred, Montague, Yarmouth, Valiant, Barfleur, Monarch, Warrior, Belliqueux, Centaur, Magnificent, and William. He himself was stationed on board the Barfleur of 90 guns; his own captain was Knight; the other captains were Burnett, who led the whole on the starboard tack, and Bayne, Bowen, Parry, Goodall, Reynolds, Wallace (Sir James,) Sutherland, Inglefield, Linzee, and Wilson.

corated, however, with Irish honours, and launched by the ministry on the ocean of politics. Sir George Rodney having been created an English baron, a vacancy for Westminster ensued, and it was fondly hoped that the tide of popularity would set in so strong in that city, which is the usual residence of royalty, that he would be returned without difficulty; this, however, proved fallacious, and his son experienced the mortification of being obliged to withdraw his father's name.*

At the dissolution of parliament, in 1784, the conduct of the coalition ministry had so thoroughly disgusted the nation, that his lordship once more started, and that too under more fortunate auspices; for we find that during the memorable struggle, in which Sir Cecil Wray and Mr. Fox were rival candidates, the name of the gallant admiral stood at the head of the poll.

In the preceding parliament he also represented the same constituents; but they were so disappointed in respect to his exertions, and so thoroughly disgusted with his attachment to the ministry, in opposition to their declared sentiments, that at the last general election he deemed it prudent to accept of a peerage, instead of an elective seat in parliament; and administration having thus secured him an honourable retreat, they immediately put another of their naval adherents into nomination, who, after a celebrated contest, proved finally successful.

No sooner had a contest with France taken place, than the eyes of the people and the cabinet were directed towards the most able commanders in the naval service, and fixed in particular on Lord Hood. That nobleman was accordingly placed at the head of a powerful fleet, and sent to the Mediterranean. France, at this moment, was distracted by civil broils, and a grand effort was now made by the English ministry, in conjunction with the royalists of the south,

to

* Lord John Townsend was the successful candidate.

to dismember the empire, or at least to destroy one of her grand naval arsenals. We accordingly find Admiral Lord Hood taking possession of Toulon, and holding it for several months. It was destined, however, that a sudden change of fortune should restore the second sea-port to the republic. Accordingly that place being invested, General O'Hara, the governor, who had made a *sortie,* was unfortunately wounded, and taken prisoner; and Lord Hood's dispatch from on board the Victory, announcing this event, was blamed for being less delicate than the occasion required. Soon after this the troops under General Dugommier stormed and took the heights, and such was the resolution of the besieging army, and the conduct of Ricard, Freron, Barras, and Robespierre, jun. joined to the skill of young Buonaparte, then acting as an engineer, that the town soon ceased to be tenable.

In consequence of this event, it was at length determined to evacuate the place; and as it would have been cruel to have left such of the natives as had preferred the dominion of England to that of their own country, the men-of-war were crowded with the wretched inhabitants; and on board the ROBUST alone, although she is but a third rate, about 2,300 of them were brought off.

On this occasion, ten sail of the line in the harbour, and three sail of the line on the stocks, were destroyed, under the directions of Sir Sidney Smith, then acting as a volunteer, and three sail of the line and four frigates were brought off*. Immediately

---

* Here follows a summary of the particulars of that celebrated event:

Burnt	15
Escaped the flames	8
Brought off by Lord Hood	3
Burnt at Leghorn (Le Scipio)	1
Sent to Brest with refractory seamen	4
Total	31

N. B. The French assert that several men-of-war, supposed to have been burnt by the English, have since been equipped and sent to sea.

Immediately after thefe memorable exploits, Lord Hood quitted the outer bay of Toulon, and rendezvoufed with his fleet at the Hieres, where they were lucky enough to fhelter themfelves during a very heavy gale of wind.

But it was not to the capture of this great arfenal, that the admiral confined his exploits. Early in the fame year, he had blockaded the port of Genoa, which was loudly exclaimed againft at that period, as an infringement of the laws of nations, and a grofs violation of the neutrality of that petty, but *then* independent, ftate. Our fleet in the Mediterranean alfo bridled the grand Duke of Tufcany, and forced him into compliances which, had it not been for his powerful family alliances, might have ended in the annihilation of his petty fovereignty.

In February, his lordfhip had alfo made an unfuccefsful attack on the ifland of Corfica; from which he was obliged to defift in confequence of a violent gale of wind, which drove him to fea; and on the 29th of the fame month he anchored at Porto Ferraro. The next attempt on Corfica proved infinitely more fortunate; for that little ftate, which Genoa affected to denominate a kingdom, and which conferred " a barren crown" on the head of Theodore, was annexed, for a fhort time, to the dominions of Great Britain; but after fwallowing up immenfe wealth, it was *happily* for the nation wrefted from us by the enemy.

After performing thefe fervices, Lord Hood retired to his native land; and notwithftanding he is now in the vale of years, he is equally ready, as before, to hoift his blue jack, and command the fquadrons of his country.

His majefty at all times has been ready to reward his merits. He was created a baronet when the king vifited the fleet at Portfmouth, in 1783, at which time he was portadmiral there, in the room of Admiral Pye, then lately deceafed; in September, 1783, he became a baron of Ireland :

land; and on May 28th, 1796, a viscount of Great Britain. His lady was created a peeress of Great Britain, March 27th, 1795, and his brother, Alexander-Arthur, Admiral of the White, Vice-Admiral of Great Britain, a Knight of the Bath, and Baron of Great Britain, May 28th, 1796.

The heralds, in allusion to the element on which he has distinguished himself, have given him a *brace* of mermaids for supporters; and the motto

"VENTIS SECUNDIS,"

must be allowed to be peculiarly appropriate.

F. I N I S.

www.ingramcontent.com/pod-product-compliance
Lightning Source LLC
Chambersburg PA
CBHW022105290426
44112CB00008B/557